Criminal Abuse of Women and Children

An International Perspective

Criminal Abuse of Women and Children

An International Perspective

Edited by
Obi N.I. Ebbe and Dilip K. Das

CRC Press
Taylor & Francis Group
Boca Raton London New York

CRC Press is an imprint of the
Taylor & Francis Group, an **informa** business

CRC Press
Taylor & Francis Group
6000 Broken Sound Parkway NW, Suite 300
Boca Raton, FL 33487-2742

First issued in paperback 2019

ISBN-13: 978-1-4200-8803-8 (hbk)
ISBN-13: 978-0-367-86432-3 (pbk)

Library of Congress Cataloging-in-Publication Data

Criminal abuse of women and children : an international perspective / editors, Obi N.I. Ebbe and Dilip K. Das.
p. cm.
Includes bibliographical references and index.
ISBN 978-1-4200-8803-8 (alk. paper)
1. Women--Crimes against. 2. Women--Abuse of. 3. Children--Crimes against. 4. Child abuse. 5. Women--Crimes against--Case studies. 6. Children--Crimes against--Case studies. I. Ebbe, Obi N. Ignatius. II. Das, Dilip K., 1941- III. Title.

HV6250.4.W65C757 2009
364.15'55--dc22 2008054782

Visit the Taylor & Francis Web site at
http://www.taylorandfrancis.com

and the CRC Press Web site at
http://www.crcpress.com

Contents

Foreword

As is vividly illustrated throughout the pages of this book, abuse of women and children is not a problem unique to certain parts of the world. The exploitation of people, particularly women and children, does not stop at country or even regional borders. It transcends geographical boundaries, as well as economic, cultural, religious, political, and social divisions. It happens in developing countries and in developed countries. It occurs where there is economic destitution and where there is economic prosperity. This grievous reality highlights that so, too, must boundaries be transcended by measures targeted to prevent abuse, prosecute its perpetrators, and protect and assist its victims.

Responses targeted to end abuse of women and children and the impunity of those who abuse them begin with strong commitment from states. Essential to that commitment is the ratification of the United Nations Convention against Transnational Organized Crime and its supplementary protocols, including the Protocol to Prevent, Suppress, and Punish Trafficking in Persons, Especially Women and Children, and the Protocol against the Smuggling of Migrants by Land, Air, and Sea. Central to the spirit of these instruments and essential to their meaningful implementation is strong cooperation between states as parties in the protection and assistance of victims of criminal abuse.

These considerations guide the work of the United Nations Office on Drugs and Crime (UNODC), which in this context is proud to introduce *Criminal Abuse of Women and Children: An International Perspective*, the work of more than 20 academics and practitioners from around the world. From the different perspectives and experiences of these contributors, we are taken through the historical context of criminal abuse of women and children. We are reminded that abuse is not only physical but also deeply emotional and psychological. We are shown the diverse socioeconomical, cultural, religious, political, and familial contexts in which people are victimized. We are reminded of the particular vulnerability of children to exploitation and abuse and the role that poverty plays in fueling that vulnerability. Power relationships between men and women, between the empowered and the disempowered, between employers and employees are explored. The relationship between increased consumerism and the commodification of people is flagged. We learn about the role that culture and religion can play in victimizing women and children and, conversely, the role that they can play in preventing abuse and protecting vulnerable people. Revictimization is presented not only as the repeated abuse of a victim but also as the continued abuse through the trauma of stigmatization and ostracization.

We are also presented with key lessons in collectively responding to these issues. We learn the power of informal mechanisms to operate alongside criminal justice systems and of the need for multiagency responses to harness strong international partnerships. We learn of the essentiality of community-based policing built on trust between law enforcers and those they are committed to protect. We are reminded that legislative responses alone are inadequate when they are not substantiated with strong education of both potential victims and potential abusers, of men and women, of employers and employees, of adults and children, of law enforcers, prosecutors, and the judiciary.

Although UNODC may not unequivocally agree with all of the views expressed in this book, it strongly supports the valuable discourse that is generated as a result of their expression. Beyond this, UNODC hopes that such multidisciplinary and cross-cultural dialog on abuse of women and children may contribute to multidisciplinary and cross-cultural action against it.

Anti–Human Trafficking and Migrant Smuggling Unit
United Nations Office on Drugs and Crime
Vienna, Austria

Acknowledgments

We are profoundly indebted to the practitioners and scholars of the 14 countries of the world who have contributed to this book. They are as follows: Maximilian Edelbacher (Austrian Federal Police); Robert Harnischmacher (police consultant, Germany); William Hughes (police, United Kingdom); Gabriele Ndolo (police, Kenya); Antoine Azonhoume (police, Benin); Vicky Karimi (social work, Kenya); Lindiwe Mtimkulu (police, South African Police Service [SAPS] and the SAPS team); Agbonkhese Moses; Olufunke Justina Aruna, and Michael Folami (academics, Nigeria); Victor Luga (police, the Philippines); Yateendra Singh Jafa (police, India); Wang Su-Huan and Chang Ching-Li (Police University, Taiwan); Elena Azaola (researcher, Mexico); John Murray (police, Canberra, Australia); John Paul and Michael Birzer (academics, United States); and, finally, the anonymous author from Bahrain in the Arabian Gulf. It is perhaps rare to find a volume on the abuses of women and children with contributions from such a diverse group of practitioners as well as researchers. C. M. Jessica Li of the City University of Hong Kong and Michael Berlin of Coppin State University (Baltimore, MD) deserve thanks for their contribution to the Introduction and the Conclusion of this book.

The Royal Canadian Mounted Police, British Columbia Institute of Justice, Office of the Solicitor General of British Columbia, Vancouver, and Abbotsford Police Departments (British Columbia), and, last but not least, University of the Fraser Valley (British Columbia) made it possible to gather all these experts under the auspices of the International Police Executive Symposium (IPES) at its 12th Annual Meeting in Canada (http://www.ipes.info). We convey our heartfelt gratitude to all of them for their generous hospitality and excellent arrangements for the meeting.

We are grateful to the United Nations Office on Drugs and Crime (UNODC) for the Foreword to this book, in which "it strongly supports the valuable discourse" and "hopes that such multidisciplinary and cross-cultural dialog on abuse of women and children may contribute to multidisciplinary and cross-cultural action against it." We thank the Anti-Human Trafficking and Migrant Smuggling Unit of UNODC for this most valuable contribution. We are particularly grateful to Dr. Slawomir Redo of the Justice and Integrity Unit at the Governance, Security, and the Rule of Law Section at UNODC for his cooperation and support.

We are very much obliged to April Matthews of the Human Resources Office of the University of Tennessee at Chattanooga whose professional typing skills helped in the completion of this manuscript. Our thanks to Marva McGee, secretary of the Department of Sociology, Anthropology, and Geography at the University of Tennessee at Chattanooga for providing some secretarial help to this work.

Ana Mijovic-Das, MD, traveled to Canada to help with the 12th Annual Meeting of the IPES, which generated the chapters for this book. We acknowledge her worthy contribution with a deep sense of appreciation.

Carolyn Spence has been more than just an editor to us. She has been an inspiration because she most enthusiastically and selflessly went beyond her call of duty to render all forms of assistance, solicited as well as unsolicited, to make it possible to bring this project to fruition. We thank her from the bottom of our hearts.

Contributors

Olufunke J. Aruna
Department of Sociology
Adekunle Ajasin University
Akungba Akoko, Nigeria

Elena Azaola
Center for Advanced Studies and Research in Social Anthropology
Mexico City, Mexico

Antoine Azonhoume
Benin Police Headquarters
Cotonou, Benin

Michael L. Birzer
School of Community Affairs
Wichita State University
Wichita, Kansas

Chang Ching-Li
Central Police University
Taoyuan County, Taiwan

Dilip K. Das
International Police Executive Symposium
Guilderland, New York

Obi N. I. Ebbe
Department of Sociology, Anthropology, and Geography
University of Tennessee at Chattanooga
Chattanooga, Tennessee

Maximilian Edelbacher
Major Crime Bureau
Federal Police of Austria
Vienna, Austria

Michael Folami
Adekunle Ajasin University
Adekunle Ajasin University
Akungba Akoko, Nigeria

Robert F. J. Harnischmacher
International Security and Media Consulting
Lippstadt, Germany

William Hughes
Serious Organised Crime Agency
London, United Kingdom

Yateendra Singh Jafa
Indian Police Service
New Delhi, India

Vicky Karimi
Urgent Action Fund–Africa
Nairobi, Kenya

Victor Luga
Philippine National Police
Manila, The Philippines

Agbonkhese S. Moses
Department of Sociology
Ambrose Alli University
Ekpoma, Nigeria

Lindiwe Mtimkulu
Cape Town Police
Cape Town, South Africa

John Murray
Ancra Consulting
Melbourne, Australia

Gabriel O. Ndolo
Office of the President
Kenyan Provincial Police
Embu, Kenya

John Paul
Department of Sociology
Washburn University
Topeka, Kansas

Wang Su-Huan
Criminal Investigation Bureau
National Police Administration
Taipei, Taiwan

Introduction

DILIP K. DAS AND C. M. JESSICA LI

An Overview

This book, *Criminal Abuse of Women and Children: An International Perspective*, presents the extent and causes of criminal abuse of women and children as well as how cases of abuse are handled in different parts of the world, particularly in Europe, Africa, Asia, the Middle East, and the Americas. The chapters from Australia (Chapter 18) and the United States of America (Chapter 19) do not directly address the primary concerns of the book, but they deal with some important issues connected with its theme. In 19 chapters, more than 20 academics and practitioners, through reviews, surveys, observations, interviews, and reviews of the literature, provide comprehensive analyses on forms of abuse and offer critical comments on the existing control measures for this phenomenon.

Readers will come across interesting cross-cultural, international perspectives on the topics discussed in the book, including the following:

(1) Criminal abuse of women and children has been a disturbing phenomenon since ancient times; presently, it prevails in almost every corner of the world.
(2) Each society has its unique causes for the criminal abuse of women and children; eastern and western societies appear to have totally different underlying forces for the same phenomenon.
(3) The majority of the governments in the world have initiated prevention and control measures, but most of them are far from effective.

To tackle criminal abuse of women and children, numerous attempts have been made at cross-national or national levels. Human trafficking,[1] which involves a disproportionate number of female and child victims, has primarily focused on the criminal abuse of women and children. In response to this situation, the United Nations Office of Drugs and Crime (UNODC) formally launched in March 2007 a global initiative to fight human trafficking through raising the awareness of and fostering commitment to counter trafficking in persons, facilitating partnerships with governments and other related parties

[1] According to the United Nations, human trafficking is the acquisition of people by improper means such as force, fraud, or deception with the aim of exploiting them.

to mobilize resources to support action, and implementing correspondent projects on local, regional, and international levels (United Nations Office on Drugs and Crime, 2008).

Although the abuse of women and children is prohibited in legal terms in almost every country in the world, it prevails everywhere. Every government has put forth some effort to combat this offense through prosecution, relief work for victims, offering training to the staff serving in the criminal justice system, education for vulnerable groups, and the like. Unfortunately, all these interventions are far from adequate to tackle this problem effectively. Its root causes, namely poverty and inequality of power, have not been sufficiently addressed. Furthermore, the phenomenon of "globalization" has indeed intensified this problem. For instance, the increase of immigration from the east to the west in Europe has resulted in prostitution businesses breeding rapidly. Consequently, more and more women and children who are sexually exploited and abused have been victims of human trafficking. In most African countries, inequality of power among the two genders forces women to remain at a disadvantageous position in society. Their dignity and other human rights are not guaranteed, and so they are at great risk of being physically and sexually abused. In some Asian regions, the concept of "shame" brings the victims other harms: being stigmatized and excluded by the society. What is missing when formulating prevention against and treatment for the criminal abuse of women and children is "social integration" and "alleviation of poverty," which are regarded as prerequisites.

The book is organized into five parts, each containing several chapters. The first part provides an overview of the criminal abuse of women and children. The second part takes the perspective from Europe. The third part contains the perspective from Africa, and the fourth part adopts perspectives from Asia, the Middle East, and the Americas. The fifth part presents applied perspectives.

Theoretical Considerations

Obi N. I. Ebbe presents a general picture of the criminal abuse of women and children in the first four chapters of this book.

Chapter 1 provides definitions and historical antecedents of criminal abuse of women and children. Criminal abuse can be physical, emotional/psychological, and sexual, and it is defined differently in different societies. Through an overview and historical survey, Ebbe shows that this kind of abuse and exploitation is related to the subordinate social status of women and children. In both ancient times and the Middle Ages, women were treated as second-class citizens.

Chapter 2 offers explanations in regard to the abuse of women and children by relating it to political power, religion, personalities of abusers, family violence, and socioeconomic conditions of the victims of human trafficking. Recent social phenomena, such as poverty and social gaps, have intensified this particular type of offense.

Chapter 3 provides a detailed account of criminal abuse of children. In western societies, family disorganization and alcoholism in families are regarded as contributing factors to this problem. Conversely, people's maladjustment to social and economic conditions in both developed and developing countries, such as when alcoholism and drunkenness of adults become more frequent, makes exploitation of children inevitable.

Chapter 4 is a comprehensive introduction to control and prevention of criminal abuse of women and children. It refers to informal control mechanisms (for example, close kinship residential patterns allow relations and family members to immediately intervene when an adult is physically battering his wife, sister, son, or daughter), religious intervention, and the criminal justice system. Still, there are obstacles to effective control of this offense. For example, many third-world countries do not strictly enforce the laws because of corruption, and legalized brothels exist in some countries. As indicated above, these chapters are intended to present a theoretical overview of the phenomenon of abuse of women and children.

Country Perspectives

This book covers the various facets of abuse of women and children and the control measures in 14 different countries. The chapters about the United States and Australia do not directly address the issues relating to abuse of women and children but dwell more on police strategies that can be conducive to investigation and control of this sensitive phenomenon. The chapter on Bahrain, unlike the chapters from the 13 other countries, contains only good news. This small country in the Arabian Gulf claims to be free from the abuse phenomenon prevalent in the other countries.

In Chapter 5, Maximilian Edelbacher gives an overview of the criminal abuse of women and children in European countries, including Austria, Bulgaria, Finland, Germany, Greece, Hungary, Luxembourg, Macedonia, Moldova, the Netherlands, Norway, Romania, Croatia, and the United Kingdom. Inequality in power relationships between men and women, prostitution, gambling, illegal immigration, trafficking in women from Eastern Europe, and child pornography all accelerate the criminal abuse of women and children. The Council of Europe also admits that sexual exploitation is still at a high level in European countries. There are more than 600 brothels in Austria, and more than 90 percent of the women come from foreign countries, especially from the former dependencies of the Soviet Union. Among the countermeasures based on policy, legislation, and criminal procedures adopted in Austria, the victim–witness protection programs are worthy of attention.

In Chapter 6, Robert F. J. Harnischmacher provides an alarming picture of child sexual abuse in Germany. In 2004, 20,000 children were recorded in police statistics as the victims of sexual exploitation and violence. Meanwhile, rape of women is prevalent in this country. Nevertheless, the author reminds us of the high "dark figure" of unreported crimes attached to this offense. Harnischmacher also makes a connection between this type of sexual abuse and the nightlife; women and children are traded to the "red-light scene." In fact, with the extension of the European Union and the growing population of Europe, Germany has become a paradise for Eastern European criminal activities. The police experts estimate that, since 2004, more than 140,000 prostitutes from Eastern Europe are illegally in Germany. Regarding child sexual abuse, the author points out the clues evident in a child victim, such as physical, behavioral, and emotional signs. In response to this problem, the Federal Ministry of Justice has reviewed the existing range of punishment. More stringent penal assessment of cases of sexual abuse has been suggested.

In Chapter 7, William Hughes looks at the trafficking of women and children that mostly results in assault and rape in the United Kingdom. The precipitating factors that facilitate trafficking, such as cheap travel among European states, poverty, poor education, technological advances, lack of international cooperation, and so on, are mentioned. To crack down on trafficking, some strategies are advised: a strong legislative approach, support to victims, a multiagency operational response, preventive and reduction strategies, as well as overseas partnerships. However, some obstacles are anticipated; one of the most important ones is noncooperation of victims with law enforcement agencies. The traffickers can use various means to threaten the victims, such as reprisal against their families back home or exposing their illegal residence status. A proactive prevention approach, the National Intelligence Model, is supported by the author.

In Chapter 8, Gabriel O. Ndolo states that criminal exploitation of women and children is rampant in Kenya. The author looks at the nature and extent of criminal exploitation of these two most vulnerable segments of the population in this country, offers reasons that contribute to this phenomenon, and also examines the existing strategies to deal with it. The author believes that the more economic and status power one has, the greater is the likelihood of one exploiting others. Unless social and economic inequality between genders and the problems of poverty are substantially eliminated, the hardship that women and children bear can hardly be lessened. To keep property in their hands is the most effective solution.

In Chapter 9, Antoine Azonhoume investigates criminal abuse of women and children in Benin, a small West African country with a high illiteracy rate of 35 percent. According to Azonhoume, the Benin people, as a result of cultural and poverty factors, violate the most elementary human rights every day. For example, according to the custom of "levirate," a widow is forced to take as a spouse a member of the family of her departed husband, and she is required to sleep near the dead body of her departed husband before the burial to show her honor. Also, different kinds of child trafficking have been taking place in this country. In addition to making improvements in the citizens' economic condition and educational opportunities, it may be beneficial to restrict the number of children per family.

In Kenya, in Chapter 10, Vicky Karimi uncovers criminal abuse of domestic female and child workers in that country. As a result of poverty and lack of education, engaging in domestic work is probably the only way for children and women to earn a living. Power inequality between employers and employees contributes to physical and sexual abuse. In some cases, children go unpaid. The author calls for a correction of the misconception of traditional sexual division of labor, a forum for victims to express their suffering, abolishing child labor at the national level, education for employees and their employers, and a comprehensive study to assess the current status of this problem.

As discussed in Chapter 11 by Lindiwe Mtimkulu and a South Africa Police Service team, criminal exploitation of women and children in South Africa is rampant. The authors found from the previous research studies that women are more likely to be abused by their parents, spouses, and relatives than by strangers. Similar to the situations of other countries, poverty and unemployment are believed to be the facilitating factors. In addition, a consumerist lifestyle that promotes the importance of possessions can lead to gender-based violence. Even worse, the myth that the rape of a child or elderly woman can cure HIV/AIDS intensifies the extent of the problem. Substance abuse by parents also plays a part in this problem. The chapter ends with some responsive measures, including the empowerment of victims and better integration of the government departments in charge of justice, safety and security (police), correctional services, social development, home affairs, foreign affairs, and the national defense force.

As described in Chapter 12 by Agbonkhese S. Moses, Olufunke Justina Aruna, and Michael Folami, trafficking in women and children in Nigeria is a new form of slavery. In fact, according to a 2001 United Nations International Children's Emergency Fund report, 80 percent of young women engaged in prostitution in Italy are Nigerians; around two million women and children are trafficked each year. The authors state that the low recorded arrest rates and inadequate successful prosecutions of traffickers are related to the low social status of women and children victims in Nigeria. This makes Nigerians ignore the criminality of human trafficking. To tackle this problem, poverty alleviation is of urgent need.

In Chapter 13, according to chief superintendent Victor Luga, the nature and extent of criminal exploitation of women and children are wide in the Philippines. Some children who are sexually abused at home eventually end up as sex workers. Luga describes clear categorizations of the girls engaged in different prostitution activities, for example, street sex workers, casa girls, bikini bar girls, karaoke bar girls, high-class prostitutes and international prostitutes, prostitutes in schools, prostitutes through the Internet, and the like. To tackle this problem, the Philippine National Police has undertaken some measures, such as giving information, promoting gender sensitization, and providing training programs for police officers on the protection of women and children. The empowerment of victims and their families is regarded by the author as essential.

In Chapter 14, Yateendra Singh Jafa presents a frightening picture of the criminal exploitation of women and children in this largest democracy in the world. According to Indian police statistics, in 2001, every hour one woman was sexually harassed, four were molested, six suffered cruelty by husbands and their relatives, and two were raped. Meanwhile, considerable segments of the children in India are neglected and victimized. For instance, 50 percent of the children between the ages of 6 and 15 are out of school as a result of poverty and a lack of access to educational facilities. Furthermore, there were cases of abuse of women and children by police and civil servants. Although the Supreme Court of India and the National Human Rights Commission have initiated several measures, problems still exist. Responsive administrations, police support, effective justice delivery system, and prompt as well as adequate actions against the guilty government officials are perceived by Jafa as essential prerequisites to counter this evil.

In Chapter 15, Wang Su-Huan and Chang Ching-Li discuss multidisciplinary criminal case processing for sexual abuse cases. The authors point out that more than 95 percent of all victims of sexual abuse in the Taiwan area are women, and more than 90 percent of the suspects are males; the average number of this type of case is between 13,000 and 19,000 each year. They identify three major characteristics of sexual violence that happens in Taiwan, namely, (1) low report rate, (2) low conviction rate, and (3) high repeated offense rate. Most of the workers serving the criminal justice system attribute the low report rate to victims' worry about "the damage to personal reputation." In fact, according to traditional Chinese belief, female purity is completely damaged after sexual abuse. Victims suffer from impaired relationships with their social networks. In summarizing the features of "reducing repeat interrogation for victims of sexual assault," the authors emphasize that "people" are the biggest asset to gear up the prevention efforts for this offense.

In Chapter 17, Elena Azaola describes and explains the phenomenon of commercial sexual exploitation of children in Mexico based on a study using qualitative and quantitative data collection methods. This chapter outlines the characteristics of the exploited children, who are predominantly girls between the ages of 13 and 18, and the exploiters, who are mainly Mexican men and some foreigners. Their clients are, as noted, primarily Mexican men from all sectors, ages, and social conditions. Such factors as poverty, previous sexual abuse by a family member, and substance abuse are discussed. One point the author makes is that "deterioration in sociability" weakens the intergenerational cohesion that is likely to make children less resistant to sexual exploitation. She also says that restoration of social cohesion is of great importance.

In Chapter 18, John Murray advocates that, if the philosophy of community policing is abolished or diminished in Australia, an adverse effect on investigations into the criminal exploitation of women and children will become unavoidable. According to Murray, successful prosecutions depend on information; a community–police relationship that is based on mutual trust is more likely to uncover matters that are helpful in identifying sexual exploitation. Meanwhile, in terms of prevention, only community policing can allow the community to focus on the importance of notifying early warning signs of sexual exploitation.

In Chapter 19, John Paul and Michael Birzer point out the shortfalls brought by the rise of the "getting tough on crime" message in the United States, adding that it would probably reduce the sense of safety in the community. Therefore, they propose reengineering the paramilitary police culture. It can be done through (1) implementing community policing as a mechanism for trust-building initiatives, (2) ending the over-reliance on technology by the police, and (3) removing the aggressive and military-style crime-fighting image.

Different from other contributors, the author (anonymous) of Chapter 16 indicates that criminal exploitation of women and children in the Kingdom of Bahrain is not prevalent. Official statistics reveal that the majority of Bahraini children (92 percent) are registered at government and private schools. Most of the women engaged in prostitution are non-Bahrainis. In addition to legal protection, education and social care mechanisms and some protective factors are worth mentioning, such as a small population (only 700,000 citizens total), Islamic values and Arab customs dictating caring for females and children, the Bahraini women's adherence to tradition that keeps them away from being involved in undesirable deeds, strong family ties that encourage parents to monitor their kids closely, and the fact that the country is free from undesirable influences of international prostitution networks.

In brief, this book will enable the readers to understand that abuse of women and children is a universal phenomenon. As such, it calls for concerted global action as a whole as well as action at every level: national, regional, and local.

References

Anonymous. 2009. "Criminal Exploitation of Women and Children in the Kingdom of Bahrain." In *Criminal Abuse of Women and Children: An International Perspective*, edited by O. N. I. Ebbe and D. K. Das. Boca Raton, FL: CRC Press/Taylor & Francis Group, pp. 275–288.

Azaola, E. 2009. "Commercial Sexual Exploitation of Children in Mexico." In *Criminal Abuse of Women and Children: An International Perspective*, edited by O. N. I. Ebbe and D. K. Das. Boca Raton, FL: CRC Press/Taylor & Francis Group, pp. 289–308.

Azonhoume, A. 2009. "Criminal Abuse of Women and Children in Benin." In *Criminal Abuse of Women and Children: An International Perspective*, edited by O. N. I. Ebbe and D. K. Das. Boca Raton, FL: CRC Press/Taylor & Francis Group, pp. 137–148.

Ebbe, O. N. I. 2009a. "Causes of Criminal and Noncriminal Abuses of Women." In *Criminal Abuse of Women and Children: An International Perspective*, edited by O. N. I. Ebbe and D. K. Das. Boca Raton, FL: CRC Press/Taylor & Francis Group, pp. 23–46.

Ebbe, O. N. I. 2009b. "Control and Prevention of Criminal Abuse of Women and Children: Domestic and International Approaches." In *Criminal Abuse of Women and Children: An International Perspective*, edited by O. N. I. Ebbe and D. K. Das. Boca Raton, FL: CRC Press/Taylor & Francis Group, pp. 63–72.

Ebbe, O. N. I. 2009c. "Definition and Historical Antecedents of Criminal Abuse of Women and Children." In *Criminal Abuse of Women and Children: An International Perspective*, edited by O. N. I. Ebbe and D. K. Das. Boca Raton, FL: CRC Press/Taylor & Francis Group, pp. 3–22.

Ebbe, O. N. I. 2009d. "The Scope and Causes of Criminal Abuse of Children." In *Criminal Abuse of Women and Children: An International Perspective*, edited by O. N. I. Ebbe and D. K. Das. Boca Raton, FL: CRC Press/Taylor & Francis Group, pp. 47–62.

Edelbacher, M. 2009. "Criminal Exploitation of Women and Children: An Austrian Perspective." In *Criminal Abuse of Women and Children: An International Perspective*, edited by O. N. I. Ebbe and D. K. Das. Boca Raton, FL: CRC Press/Taylor & Francis Group, pp. 75–98.

Harnischmacher, R. F. J. 2009. "Criminal Exploitation of Women and Children in Germany." In *Criminal Abuse of Women and Children: An International Perspective*, edited by O. N. I. Ebbe and D. K. Das. Boca Raton, FL: CRC Press/Taylor & Francis Group, pp. 99–112.

Hughes, W. 2009. "The Nature and Extent of Trafficking in Women and Children in the United Kingdom." In *Criminal Abuse of Women and Children: An International Perspective*, edited by O. N. I. Ebbe and D. K. Das. Boca Raton, FL: CRC Press/Taylor & Francis Group, pp. 113–122.

Jafa, Y. S. 2009. "Criminal Exploitation of Women and Children in India: Its Control." In *Criminal Abuse of Women and Children: An International Perspective*, edited by O. N. I. Ebbe and D. K. Das. Boca Raton, FL: CRC Press/Taylor & Francis Group, pp. 219–238.

Karimi, V. 2009. "Criminal Exploitation of Women and Children: Domestic Workers in Kenya." In *Criminal Abuse of Women and Children: An International Perspective*, edited by O. N. I. Ebbe and D. K. Das. Boca Raton, FL: CRC Press/Taylor & Francis Group, pp. 149–160.

Luga, V. 2009. "Criminal Exploitation of Women and Children in the Philippines." In *Criminal Abuse of Women and Children: An International Perspective*, edited by O. N. I. Ebbe and D. K. Das. Boca Raton, FL: CRC Press/Taylor & Francis Group, pp. 199–218.

Mtimkulu, L. 2009. "Criminal Exploitation of Women and Children: A South African Perspective." In *Criminal Abuse of Women and Children: An International Perspective*, edited by O. N. I. Ebbe and D. K. Das. Boca Raton, FL: CRC Press/Taylor & Francis Group, pp. 161–184.

Moses, A. S., Aruna, O. J., and Folami, M. 2009. "Trafficking of Women and Children in Nigeria: Slavery in the Modern Era." In *Criminal Abuse of Women and Children: An International Perspective*, edited by O. N. I. Ebbe and D. K. Das. Boca Raton, FL: CRC Press/Taylor & Francis Group, pp. 185–196.

Murray, J. 2009. "Criminal Exploitation of Women and Children: The Role of Community Policing." In *Criminal Abuse of Women and Children: An International Perspective*, edited by O. N. I. Ebbe and D. K. Das. Boca Raton, FL: CRC Press/Taylor & Francis Group, pp. 311–322.

Ndolo, G. O. 2009. "Criminal Exploitation of Women and Children: The Kenyan Experience." In *Criminal Abuse of Women and Children: An International Perspective*, edited by O. N. I. Ebbe and D. K. Das. Boca Raton, FL: CRC Press/Taylor & Francis Group, pp. 125–136.

Paul, J., and Birzer, M. L. 2009. "The Militarization of the American Police Force and Its Impact on the Victimization of Women and Children: A Critical Assessment." In *Criminal Abuse of Women and Children: An International Perspective*, edited by O. N. I. Ebbe and D. K. Das. Boca Raton, FL: CRC Press/Taylor & Francis Group, pp. 323–338.

Su-Huan, W., and Ching-Li, C. 2009. "Sexual Abuse in Taiwan: Multidisciplinary Criminal Case Processing." In *Criminal Abuse of Women and Children: An International Perspective*, edited by O. N. I. Ebbe and D. K. Das. Boca Raton, FL: CRC Press/Taylor & Francis Group, pp. 239–274.

United Nations Office on Drugs and Crime. 2008. *UNODC and Human Trafficking*. http://www.unodc.org/unodc/en/human-trafficking/index.html (accessed September 23, 2008).

Introduction

I

1 Definition and Historical Antecedents of Criminal Abuse of Women and Children

OBI N. I. EBBE

In all of the centuries of ancient, medieval, and modern times, a significant number of normal men and women, sadists, necrophiles, and pedophiles have penetrated sacred parts of women, girls, and boys against their will, the innocence of the girls and boys notwithstanding. In their ruthless, mindboggling acts, these societies' pathological men and women have made virgins bleed in pain and anguish, and boys and girls vomit in disgust.

What a society sees as abnormal behaviors, unfortunately, some of its members see as pleasurable activities. Some behaviors are condemned by tradition and custom, whereas some are proscribed by law. In either case, there are human beings who see violation of conduct norms and national legislation as a way of balancing the contradictions of the social system. For some human beings, disorder must challenge the social order, and order and disorder must exist in symbiosis.

Unmistakably, criminal minds look for laws to violate, and we have some men and women in society who see aberrant behaviors as normal behaviors because a society creates both behaviors and defines one as good and the other as bad. For some people, there is no difference between them, but some of those who see a difference between good and bad take delight in bad behaviors as their own identity.

Undeniably, some people are biologically or psychologically sick persons. Their biological and chemical makeup or their psychological development renders them incapable of engaging in normal behaviors, but they are not insane. Additionally, there are others who are not emotionally or psychologically sick, but their criminal behaviors are beyond insanity. They never demonstrated any signs of psychosis before their horrendous criminal acts: Jeffrey Dahmer, who confessed to killing and dismembering 15–17 young men and boys, putting their body parts in his refrigerator; visionary serial killers who claim that they killed in response to spiritual voices that commanded them to murder (Holmes and Holmes 1994; Albanese 1999); and "angels of death," nurses who kill babies, such as Beverly Attill and Genene Jones.

We could assume that persons such as Jeffrey Dahmer, Ted Bundy, John Wayne Gacy, and visionary serial killers were possessed by the devil, because there are no empirical explanations for their behaviors. If satanic possession cannot explain these outrageous acts, then what made them commit such heinous crimes? Science has no explanation in those cases.

In this study of criminal abuse of women and children, we are going to see women and children abusers who had minds like those of Jeffrey Dahmer, Beverly Attill, Genene Jones, John Wayne Gacy, and Andrei Chikatilo. In the analysis and definition of abuse of women and children, we are going to see signs of legitimation crisis within the minds of some individuals as rationale behind prohibition of certain behaviors, especially in the areas of parents and their children, husband and wife, master and servant, and employer and employee.

Problem of Definition

There is no consensus among social scientists about what constitutes an abuse of a child when the child is under the care of a parent or parents or a guardian. However, societal norms set a line of demarcation between the boundaries of acceptable corrections of a child and physical, emotional, psychological, and mental injury to the child. In traditional societies or non-industrialized societies of Asia, Africa, South America, and the Middle East, customs and traditions set the boundaries of conduct norms. In some of these traditional societies that were colonized by Europeans, the colonial law did not effectively nullify the conduct norms and the traditional methods of treating women and children.

In more advanced industrialized countries, such as the United States, Russia, the United Kingdom, Germany, France, Italy, and the Netherlands, the nature of economic organization created alienation and consequent breakdown in family cohesion. The breakdown in family cohesion brought high divorce rates and the consequent abandonment of children. The disorganized family structure brought stress, frustration, and aggressive behavior within the family. In these advanced economies, laws instead of conduct norms had to be used to define and control behaviors and attitudes. Therefore, the definition of abuse of women and children is not the same in all countries.

Unmistakably, what is child abuse in the United States may be a normal parental or teacher's expected minimum correction of the child. Similarly, a man's severe admonition of his wife with a push that lands her on the couch may be construed as wife abuse in the United States but not in many societies in Africa, the Middle East, and South America. Furthermore, the women may not see that she is being abused. She may see it as a customary response from her husband for what she has done wrong.

Definition

Abuse of women and children can take three forms: physical, emotional/psychological, and sexual. Abuse of a woman or a child is any act or failure to act that is based on violence that is very likely to lead to physical, emotional, psychological, or sexual harm or injury. Also, it includes any extortionary threats of imminent harm, comprising coercion to unwanted acts, denial of financial support, constant threats of divorce or abandonment, and deprivation of peace of mind.

Deductively, physical abuse of women may include pushing, pulling hair in anger, kicking, punching, choking, head bumping, stabbing, twisting the ear, mutilation, biting, aggravated assault, and murder. Sexual abuse of a woman may include nonconsentual kissing, rape, unwanted squeezing of the breasts, forced prostitution, forced pornography, forced undesirable sexual acts, forced oral and anal sexual intercourse, forced sex with a dog, forced group sex, or forced participation in a drunken orgy.

Emotionally and psychologically, a woman is abused when a man poses an extortionary threat to harm her or her children if she fails to meet his demands. This threat is very traumatizing when such a threat is repeated frequently and from a husband or a long-time boyfriend, including verbal condemnation of the worth of the woman, belittling the woman in a public place, refusing to allow the woman to leave the house alone for shopping or to meet other women (forced isolation from others, including the woman's parents), setting the woman against her children, telling lies against the woman (his wife or girlfriend), refusing to communicate with the woman (physically and verbally), destroying the woman's precious personal property, such as clothes, jewelry, and wares, prohibiting the woman from certain expenditures and buying clothes for herself, warning the woman about the dangers of divorcing him, and stalking.

In the area of abuse of children, corporal punishment is illegal in most western societies. The societies "spare the rod and spoil the children." In third-world countries and semitertiary economies, corporal punishment is allowed in schools and in family homes. This is because, in these third-world countries and semitertiary societies, alcoholism and drug addiction among parents and school teachers are virtually nonexistent. In effect, there is little or no chance of abusing the child through corporal punishment. In advanced economies, alcoholism and drug abuse play a significant role in some parents and school teachers physically abusing the kids. In effect, corporal punishment had to be abolished both at home and in schools. Therefore, what constitutes child abuse in America may not be child abuse in Ghana, Kenya, Mexico, or Nigeria. For instance, there are 12 behaviors that are defined as status offenses in the United States: "Truancy from school, sexual misconduct, using profanity, using tobacco, using alcohol, disobeying school officials, curfew violation, idleness, running away, disobeying parents, having delinquent friends, and immoral conduct" (Siegel and Senna 1981). Under the *parens patriae* philosophy of the juvenile justice system in the United States, "status offenders are put in the hands of the juvenile court, when it is determined that the parents are unable or unwilling to care for or control them, and their behavior will eventually hurt themselves and society" (Siegel and Senna 1981). In contrast, of the offenses listed above as status offenses in the United States, only two of them (sexual misconduct and curfew violation) can bring a juvenile to the attention of the police and the juvenile court in Nigeria (Ebbe 1988, 1992). An adult can also be arrested and prosecuted for sexual misconduct and for curfew violation, thereby making them nonstatus offenses in Nigeria. It is important to note that juvenile use of tobacco and alcohol is not deviant behavior in Nigeria; therefore, such use is by no means a delinquent act. Although the other six status offenses (truancy from school, using profanity, disobeying school officials, idleness, running away, disobeying parents, having delinquent friends, and immoral conduct) constitute deviant behavior, they are not legal violations in Nigeria and, consequently, are not reported to the police. Parents, the juvenile's peers, the school headmaster or principal, and the community or village members act as informal control agencies for such behaviors (Ebbe 1988, 1992).

Of all the 12 status offenses in the United States, 10 can be handled by a parent, headmaster, class teacher, or school principal in Nigeria. Any punishment given to the child will not be labeled child abuse, and no child or any other person will "call 911" or emergency services.

Unmistakably, a school headmaster or principal taking a severe disciplinary action commensurate with the gravity of the offense against a child or juvenile, anywhere in the world, should not be construed as child abuse. Therefore, physical abuse of a child should be defined as any battery or corporal punishment meted out to a child that goes beyond the use of reason and minimum standards of discipline.

A child may be abused through neglect. When a parent or guardian deliberately refuses to provide a child, under his or her care, the necessary basic needs and care when that parent or guardian is capable of providing those needs or care, then that becomes the child neglect form of abuse. For instance, in the heartrending book *A Child Called "It": One Child's Courage to Survive*, authored by the victim Dave Pelzer (1995), when his mother routinely refused to feed him while his siblings were fed, that is the neglect form of child abuse.

Emotional, psychological, or mental abuse of a child is often perpetrated verbally. When a threat of future harm or punishment is made routinely against a child for very insignificant errors and the threat is sometimes carried out and sometimes not, the child is continuously mentally tormented. Nagging, scolding, warning, defining the child, qualifying the child, comparing the child with bad kids, lying against the child, and blaming the child on a regular basis will emotionally and mentally drain the child, especially when all of the above come from a parent or guardian. It is even more traumatizing to the child if the sight or presence of the child provokes the parent or guardian. This prompts the parent or guardian to instantly rebuke the child for no reasonable cause, just like in the case of Dave Pelzer. What happens in such a situation is that the child's heart drops into his stomach at the sight of his hateful parent or guardian. It becomes a living hell for the child. Dave Pelzer, whose mother fed him ammonia, gave him a used diaper of his younger sibling to eat, and made him eat what she forced him to vomit, "prayed for the world to end" (Pelzer 1995, 62–69). The end of the world would prevent him from meeting his mother that afternoon. It is mental torture for a boy to live like this under his mother's roof with a father whose absence is better than his presence.

At ages of 10 and 13, I lived a life almost like that of Dave Pelzer but not in the hands of my dear mom. Instead, it was in the hands of my elder half-brother, Sam. He was an elementary school teacher. He was single, and I was his house boy. I had to do everything a village wife had to do in the way of cooking meals, fetching water from a stream three miles away, fetching firewood, sweeping the rooms and compound, and washing my master's clothes. And I was only ten years old. However, all of the above were not abuses to a 10 year old in my culture. The abuse was in Sam never appreciating what I did. Everything I did was verbally condemned. In most cases, I was flogged for irrelevant mistakes; I cooked while in tears because I had been flogged for arranging the chairs in the living room in a manner that he did not like or I walked into the living room from the kitchen and unexpectedly saw him making love on a cushion chair with one of his girlfriends in broad daylight. Although I was the person cooking and preparing the meals, I was starved. Every food I cooked was measured. He knew the amount that I was to bring to him. If the amount I brought to him was less than he expected, he would come to the kitchen and take some of the small portion that I had left for myself. On many occasions, what was, in fact, left for me to eat only provoked my appetite and hunger. I had already been warned not to eat my food until he had eaten. This is because sometimes he would return in the evening in the company of one of his girlfriends; he would take all the food for dinner for himself and his girlfriend and left virtually nothing for me. Each time I visited my hometown, usually on foot, which was 15 miles away, my mother would notice that I was not eating well. She commented on that, but I never acknowledged it for fear that Sam would flog me.

The worst of the emotional and mental torture that I experienced at the hands of my half-brother/master was when he told me to make soup with a type of coco-yam that only a very poor woman would use to make soup among the Igbos. It is called *ede-eko*. After this type of coco-yam is pounded and put in a soup to thicken the soup, it leaves some small balls of coco-yam in the soup. There are some housewives who could handle *ede-eko* very well in making soup, but I was 10 years old and did not know how I could prevent the small balls of coco-yam from being left in the soup. So after I made the soup and some small balls of coco-yam remained, Sam grabbed a kitchen broom and hit me with it all over my body, head, back, legs, and hands while I writhed in pain on the kitchen floor. My whole body had blisters from the broom. Two of the school teachers living next door at the "teachers quarter" ran to my rescue, but it was too late. Before they could force the entrance door open and get to the kitchen area, Sam had exhausted his physical energy and walked to his bedroom. The two teachers picked me up and told me to go and clean myself. When the teachers left, Sam went to the kitchen and scooped out small balls of coco-yam in the soup and put them on a plate as I stood by watching him. He ordered me to eat the small balls of coco-yam and said, "That will be your dinner." I was very hungry. I had never eaten something like that before. Because I had no choice, I ate it. I did not tell my mother and father about this and the other abuses before this one. My mother was going to learn about all of these physical and emotional abuses three years later.

The academic year was coming to an end, which usually ended in December in Nigeria in the late 1950s to 1960s, and Sam was to enter a teacher training college for the next two years. I heaved a sigh of relief.

For the next two years, I went to a school in my hometown, St. John's Catholic School, and lived with my mom and dad in a peaceful polygamous family of five wives and 19 children in 11 separate brick houses, including my father's private customary court. During this period, I actually had time to play soccer with some other kids, a luxury I did not have while living with Sam.

I was 13 when Sam completed his teacher training courses, and I had to live with him again according to my father's orders. He was posted at a Catholic school about 18 miles away from my hometown. The town where the school was located was in a different county (Okigwe district) from my own county. Schools in my home county (Orlu district) were not charging tuition fees at the elementary school level, but schools in the Okigwe district were charging tuition fees. My father, who was 80 years old and a flag bearer of Western education in my town, had declared that he was old and that all the money he had saved was going to be for his burial ceremonies. Sam was expected to pay my school fees, because I was living with him and serving him and he was still single. However, Sam refused to do so. My mother, a hard-working businesswoman and farmer, took it on herself to pay my school fees although I was a servant to a son of her co-wife in another district/county. Sam had a younger brother, Malachy, who was four years my junior living with us, and he was paying his school fees. Despite the fact that my mother was paying my school fees and giving us some food stuff each time I visited home, Sam treated me like a cur in the household. Everything I did was held in disdain, and I was an eyesore to him. Everything his young brother did was treated as excellent, although Malachy often cursed him and talked back to him, which I would not dare.

My only happiness throughout this second time of living with Sam was my brilliant performance at school. I was in Standard Four (America's sixth grade), and I was at the top of my class in three key subjects: Mathematics, English, and General Knowledge. However, Sam's scolding, nagging, flogging, threatening, and refusal to buy my textbooks, exercise books, pens, and pencils frustrated my mother. She began to question me as to why I should continue to live with Sam. I refused to give any response. It was two months before mid-year. The deadline to transfer back to my home county's school, Saint John's Catholic School, Umuobom, had passed. Another option was returning to live with my parents; I hoped that my dad would see the injustice of my being a house servant to my elder half-brother while my mother paid my school fees and bought my textbooks and stationary. That prospect was looming when my school was preparing for the Saint Michael's annual sports competition among all the schools in the large Urualla Parrish. I was allowed to compete at my school. In the three-legged race, my partner and I beat every competitor at the school.

The Saint Michael's sports events always lasted for two days. The first day is the heat, and the second day is Saint Michael's Day, the final competition. My half-brother Sam was jealous of my successful performance in three-legged race, so he stopped me from participating so that I would not receive any accolades. He was the school games master, so his decision was final. He told me to stay home and not to participate in the Saint Michael's sports competition. He left for the Saint Michael's events in the company of his younger brother, who had no event in which to compete. My training partner had to enter the competition with another boy who we never trained with at our school. They were able to win the heat. On the final day, they came in second place. When he returned, he came to me and said, "Obi, if you and I had paired up at the St. Michael's three-legged race, we would have taken first place." "Really?" I asked. "We would have given the second pair many yards behind us," he added on the verge of tears. Instantly, it rang like a bell in my mind that my elder half-brother, whom I loved so much, did not love me. It was not long before I gained my final freedom.

The straw that broke the camel's back came when my school levied one shilling on every student from Standard One through Standard Five for the preparation of the coming of the Catholic bishop to administer the sacrament of Confirmation. My stingy half-brother/master ordered me to go to my mother to get the one shilling. In the early 1950s, one shilling was a lot of money. At that time, one shilling could buy you pants. When I reluctantly and inevitably told my mother that my school wanted us to contribute one shilling for the coming of the bishop, she raised her face and eyebrow in anger and indignation as if I had stabbed her, but the anger was not toward me. "What did Samuel say about it?" she yelled. "He told me to come and tell you," I replied. "So, Samuel cannot pay one shilling contribution for you. Now, you must come back here and live with me. There are many things you can do for me in this house, so that I can see the benefit of my paying your school fees and all school expenses. You can walk 18 miles to school from here or drop out of school until the end of the year," she declared. My mother gave me the one shilling and I went back to school and paid it. Four days after I paid the one shilling, it was Friday. Before going to school in the morning, I put all of my life's belongings in my school bag. After school, I headed to my hometown without telling Sam. I left him with his younger brother Malachy. I walked 18 miles to school for one week before one of my classmates informed me that he told his mother about me, and she said that she knew my mother and that I could live in her house and attend school from there. I was pleased, and my mother and I went with my boarding cooking ware and food to thank my friend's mother.

My elder half-brother Sam never confronted me at school to ask me why I left, and he never came to my mother's house to ask why she withdrew me from serving him.

Throughout the period that I was living with Sam, I was under mental torture and emotional distress. It has to be understood that physical abuse may leave invisible scars and be forgotten, but emotional abuse lasts a lifetime. Each time an abused child remembers it, even as an adult, the pain returns.

Shown above is what may constitute physical, emotional/psychological, and mental abuse of children, demonstrating that the problem of defining abuse is real. As crime is relative to time and place, so, too, is what constitutes abuse of women and children, and is not of modern origin. Therefore, let us look at the phenomenon in the history of human society.

Historical Antecedents

From the ancient times to the medieval epoch, patriarchy reigned supreme. The adult married male was the indisputable head of his household. His wife and children lived at his mercy and disposal. Throughout the cultures of the world in ancient times, traditional norms did not protect women from men's aggression as we have them today. The nullification of female authority and equal status at home and in the community in the ancient period was kept alive by custom and tradition. This custom was kept alive even up to the Roman times of the medieval period. For the Romans, a woman was to be seen but not heard. She was kept at home for the pleasure of her lord, her husband.

In the Dark Ages or medieval times, it was a taboo to give formal school education to a woman. In fact, medieval universities, including the University of Timbuktu (Mali) near the River Niger in Africa, the University of Paris (France), the University of Bologna (Italy), and Oxford University (England), had no female students at all. Oxford University, which was started by monks in 1092, did not admit women until the late 19th century. In both ancient times and the Middle Ages, women were treated as second-class citizens in most societies of the world, a derogatory classification that survived into modern times in some societies in the Middle East, Africa, and Asia, and in western societies until the 20th century.

Women were the subjects of sacrifices to gods of ancient, medieval, and early modern societies of the pre-Christian period. Next to women in human sacrifices were girls and boys. In a modern account, *Things Fall Apart* by Chinua Achebe (1959), when a woman from a certain town was brutally assassinated by a man from a neighboring town and the offender was known, the whole town was seen as the offender. The victimized town started to prepare to wage a war against the offending town. To ward off the calamities of war, the people of the offending town met with the victimized town to peacefully settle the matter. The solution agreed on was for the offending town to give a young woman to replace the murdered woman to the victim's husband and give a boy, named Ikemefuna, to the victimized town to offer as a sacrifice to appease the earth-god who was desecrated. Okonkwo was appointed guardian of Ikemefuna. On one ill-fated day, Okonkwo and some elders took Ikemefuna on a short trip, but the boy Ikemefuna did not know that the trip was going to be his last one with Okonkwo, a man he called "Daddy." On that day, Ikemefuna was slaughtered for the earth-god of Umuofia town (Achebe 1959). The sacrifice of women, boys, and girls was common in all primitive societies.

Sexual Atrocities in the Castles and Corridors of Power in Medieval Times (500–1453 AD)

Ancient religious practice was fraught with paganism, and paganism often used human beings as sacrifices to the gods. Such sacrifices mainly involved children. Undeniably, the Middle Ages (the Dark Ages or medieval times, 500–1453) inherited some of the pagan practices of ancient times.

The Christian doctrines of the medieval times condemned the pagan practices of the ancient period. Unfortunately, the Christian doctrines about sexual norms were very rigid and very hard for some Christians to adhere to comfortably. The previous pagan rules were very open about sexuality. The pagan methods were unmistakably demonism or satanism but were very attractive to follow with regard to sexual practices. Consequently, some

Christians dropped Christianity and followed satanism (Klaits 1985; Purkiss 1996; Russell 1972; Summers 1992). Some fallen priests (renegade priests) joined the satanic cults and offered human sacrifices as a means of solving the various problems of the cult members (Wedeck 1961).

Throughout the Middle Ages, pervasive desires to fall in love or to get a man in love were very strong and prevalent. Consequently, philters and love potions emerged in satanic cult masses. Men and women sought the love of each other by diabolical and irrational means. To achieve one's aim, he or she had to resort to diviners, witches, or sorcerers, who prepared philters and love potions to get the love of the man or woman desired. These philters and love potions were prepared, in the main, with the blood and pubic hair of virgins, the blood of children, and the genital parts of boys, girls, and children (Taylor 1815; Wedeck 1961; Masters and Lea 1963; Rohdes 1925).

During the Dark Ages, there grew up a young boy with a great fortune, who became a hero as well as a French nightmare. He was Gilles de Rais (1404–1440). It is necessary to tell his story for one to see the picture of satanic religion in medieval society and the criminal use of women and children in that era.

Gilles de Rais was born in 1404, and at the age of 11 he inherited a great fortune and increased it by marrying a very rich woman, Catherine de Thouars, at the age of 16 (Masters and Lea 1963; Trevor-Roper 1969). Rais was a devout Christian, handsome, and very skilled in military stratagy. He was so brave that, at the age of 20, he fought and rode by the side of Joan of Arc (1412–1441). In fact, he was the chief lieutenant of Joan of Arc. His youthful meritorious bravery earned him the love and admiration of King Charles VII (1403–1431), who awarded him the title of Marshal of France (Masters and Lea 1963; Cavendish 1985).

In the affairs of men and women, for every bright surface, there must be a darker speck. That is the epitome of the greatness of Gilles de Rais. Rais entered into a love affair despite his wealthy wife. Satan always strikes where there is peace. Rais was engulfed in this ill-fated love affair. He "became the platonic lover of Joan of Arc," a woman "whose 'voices' dictated that she save France" (Masters and Lea 1963). Rais was the guardian and protector of Joan of Arc.

As an Englishman would put it, "if wishes were horses, beggars would ride." Things fell apart when Joan of Arc was captured and burned at the stake. Gilles de Rais felt that all of his spiritual devotion to God was in vain. He felt that the Maid of Orleans, Joan of Arc, was betrayed by the Catholic Church. Consequently, he turned himself into a satanic fiend unrivaled in the narratives of heinous perverse crimes against humanity. Rais resorted to acts contrary to the worship of God. He felt that satanic services to achieve one's goal quickly were better than God's way.

With the loss of Joan of Arc, a woman Rais had seen as with God, indomitable and invincible, yet who failed to protect her, called Satan to be his guard. He swore never to have sexual intercourse with another woman for the rest of his life. He abandoned his wife and their only child and hid himself in his castle at Tiffauges. His welcomed companions became dissolutes, sycophants, and wastrels. His wealth of gold was spent in "several rounds of lavish orgies." When his wealth disappeared, he resorted to alchemy. His castle became a concentration of alchemy laboratories.

Rais was not getting what he wanted from the alchemy laboratories. All of the attempts by Rais with the alchemists and magicians did not yield any gold. At one hopeless point, an Italian renegade priest, an alchemist and sorcerer, Antonio Francisco Prelati, told him that "a mortal cannot hope to achieve the transmutation of base metals into gold without the help of Satan" (Masters and Lea 1963; Klaits 1985). The former priest Prelati also told him that, to get the help of Satan, Rais must commit and dedicate the most abominable and horrendous crimes in his name. Without hesitation, Rais lured hundreds of boys to his castle. With the help of the renegade priest, he killed the boys in his chamber and used their blood to write evocations and formulas. Satan did not respond; no ordinary metals were changed into gold. However, in the process of seeking gold by satanic means, he found "sadistic satisfaction and pleasure" in the torture and killing of innocent children whom he lured into his castle. Before he was caught, he killed over 800 children (Masters and Lea 1963; Trevor-Roper 1969).

Satan always gets the blood of his man. Gilles de Rais was Satan's man, and Rais had no place to hide. After the many missing boys and children were traced to his castle, he was arrested on September 13, 1440, at the order of Jean, the Bishop of Nantes. The great Baron Gilles de Rais was brought to trial. He was charged, among other criminal violations, with "the killing, strangling, and massacring of innocent children." Also added to the charges were "evoking demons, making pacts with them, and sacrificing children to them" (Masters and Lea 1963; Rhodes 1965). To avoid torture, Rais confessed his crimes before the French tribunal. Given his high position in the French royalty, he was granted the mercy of being strangled and burned. His family was allowed to pick up his corpse and subsequently buried him in a Catholic ceremony in a Carmelite churchyard. Those who helped Rais kill the innocent children, including Antonio Francisco Prelati, were given months of imprisonment. The ecclesiastical and civil authorities seized a fabulous amount of wealth left by Gilles de Rais.

When satanic sacrifices were going on in the castles and corridors of power, obviously not all of them were detected. Additionally, small towns and villages had their individual satanic diviners who used boys and girls to try to solve the problems of their consultants. Many of those satanic diviners were never caught or reported. They slipped into the category of hidden crimes. So the number of children slaughtered in the Middle Ages for satanic sacrifices is inestimable. The abuse was like a normative behavior in the minds of the satanic sadists.

Now we are going to investigate the centuries following the Middle Ages. The early modern times were not much different from the medieval times when it comes to Christianity and Satanism.

Sexual Atrocities in the Castles, Kingdoms, and Corridors of Power of the 16th to 18th Centuries

Modern times, especially from the 1500s to the 1700s, inherited the atrocities of the medieval era. In the kingdoms of modern kings and queens, unspeakable atrocities were committed against women and children. In those kingdoms, abuse of women was not only a prerogative of men. Many women in history slaughtered their fellow women and children. Sex-driven monsters pervade the pages of history. Countess Elizabeth Bathony of Hungary and Catherine La Voisin of France are the most notorious erotic criminals in history (Masters and Lea 1963). Sadistic sexual perversion drove their thirst for the blood of young women and girls.

Countess Elizabeth Bathony was a sadistic sexual monster. In a very short time, she murdered more than 600 children after sexually molesting them and then used their blood as body lotion. It was an assigned duty of one of her maids and a former lesbian lover, Barsovny and Otros, to procure and kidnap girls for the countess. These individuals attracted the girls and unsuspecting young women with promises of jobs in the castle. In some cases, they lured the girls to a secret location near the Castle Csejthe and drugged them until they were incoherent or beat them into insensibility (Masters and Lea 1963). These girls were then locked in a room. At the order of the countess, a group of the girls were brought before her, and she and her lesbian lover and the kidnapped girls engaged in sexual orgies. In a predesigned method, the girls were killed one after the other. To rejuvenate herself, or so she believed, she bathed herself in the blood of the dead girl. No one suspected her of such monstrous evil because she was very beautiful and of royal blood. Besides, she was a widow of Hungary's great "Black Hero" and cousin to the Prime Minister of Hungary, Gyorgy Thurzo. "Kings and Cardinals, bishops and judges, sheriffs and governors bore proudly the name Bathony...The great Sigismund Bathony, Prince of Transylvania, was her kinsman" (Masters and Lea 1963). It was not easy to accuse her of any murderous acts when it became evident in the peasant town that many girls and children were missing. Undeniably, the odoriferous deaths, torture, and unfathomable lesbian orgies engulfed the countess in an ominous aura.

Unmistakably, Countess Elizabeth Bathony could not escape the law of commensurate desserts, because she was surrounded by her witch nurse, Ilona Joo, and other witches, magicians, and sorcerers who convinced her that human sacrifices and her bathing in blood would make her look younger and more beautiful (Masters and Lea 1963). In their sacrifices, they used the skulls and bones of small children. In a short time, Elizabeth and everyone involved in her schemes started to derive profound erotic pleasure from sadistic orgies of torture and the killing of young girls.

These young girls were not murdered instantly. If it had been so, it would have been more merciful. Instead, their blood was drawn piecemeal as the need arose. It could take a week before a young girl died. The girls' hands and legs were slit with knives and blood was drawn for rituals and baths. The torture chamber was a pool of blood (Masters and Lea 1963).

Unmistakably, there is a time in the life of a professional criminal when reason will disappear and being caught becomes inevitable. Eventually, the frequency of girls and children going missing set off a cloud of fear and suspicion. Nobody knew which direction to focus the suspicion. Rumormongers were at work in every nook and corner of the towns and villages. Any mention of Countess Elizabeth Bathony having some girls who visited the castle but never returned was quickly discarded. This is because it was inconceivable for a widow of the great "Black Hero," a lady of royal ancestry, surrounded by the elite of Hungary as kin, to besmear her hands and royalty with heinous acts of such a bloodthirsty nature.

Countess Elizabeth and her maids and guards never had a second thought about being caught and the consequences of their sadism. She was in ecstasy, but she did not know that the dark clouds of rumors were gathering. Rumors of the happenings at the Castle Csejthe reached every village, and servants in the corridor of power at King Matthias of Hungary told the king of the rumors. However, the prime minister was not willing to investigate the allegation against Countess Elizabeth Bathony. When the village priests headed the campaign against the happenings in the castle and alleged that the castle was a home of vampires, the prime minister had to direct the investigation himself.

Given the great status of Countess Elizabeth Bathony, the prime minister, the governor, the priest, soldiers, and policemen invaded the castle on New Year's Eve, when the countess and her co-sexual vampires would least expect any outside disruption. As the team of invaders quietly and carefully approached the castle, they found the entrance gate unguarded. Near the threshold of the door of the great hall "lay the pale, lifeless body of a young girl, the blood completely drained from her body" (Masters and Lea 1963, 20). At a short distance from the door, they saw another girl who was still alive. They noticed that her body had been repeatedly slit and a large amount of blood drawn. Farther on, they saw some bodies of murdered girls chained to a pillar. Their blood had been drained from their bodies. In the dungeons of the castle, the invaders "found several dozen children, girls, and women many of whom had been bled repeatedly by the Countess and her household." Others had not yet been molested and were "fat and in excellent health, for all the world like animals ready to be shipped off to the slaughter house" (Masters and Lea 1963, 21). The team of invaders caught the countess and her sadistic party unawares. The invaders saw them "in the midst of a drunken and depraved orgy," a scene too awful to describe.

The members of the countess's household were all arrested immediately and taken to the nearest penitentiary. Countess Elizabeth Bathony herself was confined to the castle and heavily guarded. They were all tried at the Royal Supreme Court. Some members of the countess's household testified against her. There were up to 21 judges at the trial. The evidence against the countess and her royal attendants overwhelmed the Royal Supreme Court.

All of the accused were in the court except the principal defendant, Countess Elizabeth Bathony. She was permitted to remain in her apartment in the castle. She was convicted in absentia. She and her murderous party of "witches and sorcerers, diabolists and alchemists," were found guilty of the murder of at least 80 located dead bodies. All of the countess's attendants were sentenced to death, some by execution and others by torture according to the modus operandi of their perpetration of the crimes in the castle.

Countess Elizabeth received what amounted to life imprisonment in her apartment in the castle. Her incarceration was tantamount to a death penalty because she was not allowed to come out of the apartment. All the doors and windows of the apartment were sealed. The authorities only left an aperture in one of the windows through which food could be passed to her. Four years after the sentencing, Countess Elizabeth Bathony died on August 21, 1614, when it was observed that food passed to her through the window had not been taken for days. She was 54 years old.

The Witch Catherine La Voisin and Children

The early centuries following the Middle Ages saw an advanced stage of satanism. Witchcraft and sorcery became the order of the era. French society during the reign of King Louis XIV (1638–1715 AD) fell into decadence. Whereas Christian religion continued to place rigid rules on human sexuality, satanism went underground as the church and state were considered as one and in control of moral rules and church doctrine.

The members of French aristocracy fulfilled sexual fantasies by having the body of a naked woman placed on an alter around which participants cavorted in the nude. The witchcraft rituals that emerged suited their sexual perversion. Although many witches were executed during the Inquisition in the earlier centuries, the reign of French King Louis XIV was a low-principled period, with unrestricted immorality. Lords and ladies sought Satan to grant them high offices and wealth (Williams and Williams 1978).

During this decadent French regime was born Catherine Monvoisin, known as "Catherine La Voisin." She married a poor jeweler but was promiscuous throughout her marriage. She was a fortuneteller in the street and became very popular when her predictions came true. A promiscuous woman usually knows many people and gets into many activities, and Catherine was no exception. By the time she was 20, she had become a midwife, a beautician, and a herbalist. Among her stock-in-trade were palmistry, prophecy, astrology, and face reading. Men and women seeking wives or husbands and those who wanted to get rid of their spouses or get new ones flooded her chamber.

Eventually, Catherine discovered that she could make more money through Satan's wages than the small money she was making through midwifery and other petty services. When the established Catholic Church wanted her to dismantle her practices, she convinced them that her activities were supportive of church teachings and acceptable to the church. They let her continue her services, and many wealthy men and aristocrats became her clients. La Voisin's chamber or temple was a dark room.

The modus operandi of Catherine La Voisin was invoking Satan by staging satanic or black masses. She was the priestess and was assisted by many renegade priests. There was no satanic mass without sacrificing a baby or a child to achieve the ends of a client. La Voisin's most trusted renegade priest was Abbe Guilborg. Abbe Guilborg was a gifted alchemist, and La Voisin desperately needed him for the many female lovers he kept in Paris (Masters and Lea 1963; Williams and Williams 1978). Guilborg had many illegitimate children, and he sold them to Catherine La Voisin for use as satanic sacrifices during her masses.

It was very costly to get babies for her sacrifices, so, as a result, La Voisin built a home for unwed mothers. She took care of them throughout their pregnancies, and when the babies were delivered, she used them in her sacrifices at no additional cost. With the sexual laxity of the period, there were too many unwed mothers in her home and she had an abundance of sacrificial infants. She provided for girls who had no financial means at no charge, but her charges to the women of the aristocracy covered her seemingly humanitarian service. However, some of the girls she pretended to be caring for never saw their 16th birthdays.

Great Parisian ladies of means attended the satanic temple of La Voisin, including the following: Olympe Mancini, Contesse de Soissons, who wanted the death King Louis XIV's mistress Louise de La Valliere; Francoise-Athenais, Marquise de Montespan, another amorous mistress of King Louis XIV; and the Contesse de Gramont ("La belle Hamilton"). In fact, Madame de Montespan, as a great mistress of Louis XIV of France, wanted to retain the king's dying love, and, to accomplish her goal, she sought the services of Catherine La Voisin and practiced occult and satanic rites and engaged in amatory masses, concoction of philters, and child sacrifices at La Voisin's temple (Wedeck 1961).

In amatory satanic masses, the priest, usually Abbe Guilborg, placed a chalice on the belly of the female supplicants, kissed their bodies, and read from the satanic prayer book, bound in human skin. Urine was the holy water. The host, replacing the bread in a traditional Catholic mass, was a toad and turnip. During the amatory mass, love powder was also produced. Among the ingredients of the powder were the bones of toads, the teeth of moles, Spanish flies, iron filings, human infant blood, and mummy or the dust of infant human remains (Masters and Lea 1963; Cavendish 1968; Williams and Williams 1978). After completion of the rituals of the amatory mass, the priest received an infant from the acolyte in black robes. The priest "raised the child aloft and deftly slashed its throat" (http://www.unexplainedstuff.com). Holding the sacrificial infant, the priest invoked satanic agents "Astaroth and Asmodeus to accept the sacrifice of the child," so that the supplicants at the satanic mass might receive their hearts' desires (Cavendish 1985).

When Catherine La Voisin was at the peak of her wealth and satanic glory, her end was in sight. One of the great French police detectives, Desgrez, was monitoring La Voisin's Black Sabbats. One day, one of Desgrez's men recognized the crest on one of the coaches waiting by the outside walls of La Voisin's temple of doom (Black Sabbat) as belonging to Madame de Montespan, the mistress of King Louis XIV. It was reported to Desgrez that the royal mistress Madame de Montespan had served as the naked, living altar at one of Catherine La Voisin's satanic masses. Desgrez and his boss, La Reynie, director of the Chamber Ardente, the king's strongly supported chamber, developed a list of notable French men and women who were attendants to La Voisin's satanic masses. The list included Madame de Montespan and other mistresses of the king. To avoid the exposure of the decadence of the French court to French enemies, the king surreptitiously allowed favorites of the French court to be deleted from the list and let them leave the country on an extended vacation.

After the favorites of the French court had left the country, the short list of La Voisin's satanic mass participants was released. Evidence against the king's mistresses and other favorites was suppressed. The number one person on the list was Catherine La Voisin. She was arrested along with her accomplices. Catherine La Voisin faced the grand inquisitors, where she confessed her sins and crimes before holy priests, confessions that were used against her. Catherine La Voisin was convicted after she confessed to having sacrificed more than 2,500 children. She was tortured for 24 intermittent hours before she was sent to the stake on February 23, 1680. On the stake, before she was burned, she cursed the day she was born.

In the same period as Catherine La Voisin, in 1686, Appolonia Mayr was a female servant who was in love with a man she hoped would marry her. She was pregnant. When it looked as if the young man might not marry her, she murdered her unborn baby, because according to her, "the Devil had promised that if she killed her child, her lover would marry her" (King 1987). But the Devil's promise was in vain, and her life thereafter was devoid of peace.

The next account epitomizes the satanic mind as portrayed by a queen.

Queen Zingua of Angola and Women and Boys

In the 1600s, there was a man who killed his brother and his son to take over their throne and made himself the King of Angola. In 1632, his sister, Zingua, murdered him and ascended to the throne and became the Queen of Angola in South-West Africa.

The moment Zingua ascended the throne, she promulgated a law that laid down "the vulgivaguability of women: one which, that is to say, made their cunts as universally free to be fucked as the air is to be breathed" (Masters and Lea 1963, 10). She kept a large number of young adolescent males and girls as husbands and wives. The duty of these young boys and girls was "to try to satisfy or attempt to satisfy her insatiable sex needs," and all her male and female lovers were summarily murdered postcoitus (Masters and Lea 1963, 157).

Queen Zingua was a nymphomaniac. There was little duration between the end of one sexual act with one unfortunate boy or girl and the beginning of the next sexual encounter with another. The boys and girls were not allowed to escape. They were murdered before her eyes, and she sucked their blood and ate their bodies. The painful cry of children when she sexually molested them turned her on. It is recorded that her "cruelty, cannibalism, nymphomania, and general viciousness" is beyond controversy. Her voracious appetite for human flesh was as ravenous as her appetite for sex. On one occasion, Zingua slaughtered 113 children in two days (Masters and Lea 1963, 158). The number of mass butcheries is inestimable. Unfortunately, she was profoundly feared by the Portuguese colonizers because she was ready to kill and eat them.

Queen Zingua gave the kiss of death, because every man or woman that made love with her was executed. She was very beautiful and was compared with "Cleopatra, Pantasilea, Semiramis, the famous Judith, and Artemis" (Masters and Lea 1963). Some young men admired her, but Zingua had a trick to get the young men. She would arrange for very strong warriors to fight each other until one killed the other; she enjoyed the bloodshed. Whoever was victorious in the battle would have to make love with her. After the lovemaking, she killed the man. Ironically, it was a man's honor and reward to please her three times: once by slaying his opponent in combat, once on the royal couch, and, at last, by affording her the pleasure of witnessing his own painful death (Masters and Lea 1963; Williams and Williams 1978).

Zingua was so bloodthirsty that anybody who disobeyed any one of her many decrees was put to death and grounded in a mortar. It was noted on one occasion that Zingua passed an edict throughout her kingdom that "every pregnant girl and woman under thirty years of age be ground or pounded to death" (Masters and Lea 1963, 11). She took delight in hearing the cries and seeing the pain and bleeding of virgins as she tried to deflower them. Even after she became a Christian in her later years, she surrounded herself with virgins, and the penalty for any other person deflowering them was death (Masters and Lea 1963). Unlike Countess Bathony, Rais, and La Voisin, Queen Zingua was not executed because she was the head of state and beyond incrimination (Ebbe 1990). Zingua died at the age of 80. She was one of the most notorious modern nymphomaniacs.

In the next chapter, we are going to look at the causes of criminal and noncriminal abuse of women in the contemporary world.

References

Achebe, C. 1959. *Things Fall Apart*. New York: McDowell Obolensky.

Albanese, J. S. 1999. *Criminal Justice*. Boston: Allyn and Bacon.

Cavendish, R. 1985. *Werewolf—Man, Myth, and Magic: The Illustrated Encyclopedia of Mythology, Religion, and the Unknown*. Toronto: Marshall Cavendish.

Ebbe, O. N. I. 1988. "Juvenile Justice System in Southern Nigeria." *International Journal of Comparative and Applied Criminal Justice* 12(2):191–204.

Ebbe, O. N. I. 1990. "Heads of State: The Vice Kings and Narcotic Barons." *International Journal of Comparative and Applied Criminal Justice* 14(2):280–287.

Ebbe, O. N. I. 1992. "Juvenile Delinquency in Nigeria: the Problem of Application of Western Theories." *International Journal of Comparative and Applied Criminal Justice* 16(2):353–370.

Encyclopedia of the Unusual and Unexplained. http://www.unexplainedstuff.com, accessed February 21, 2008.

Holmes, R. M., and Holmes, S. T. 1994. *Murder in America*. Englewood, CA: Sage.

King, F. X. 1987. *Witchcraft and Demonology*. Middlesex, UK: Hamlyn Publishing Group.

Klaits, J. 1985. *Servants of Satan: The Age of the Witch Hunts*. Bloomington: Indiana University Press.

Masters, R. E. L., and Lea, E. 1963. *Sex Crimes in History: Evolving Concepts of Sadism, Lust-Murder, and Necrophilia—from Ancient to Modern Times*. New York: Julian Press.

Pelzer, D. 1995. *A Child Called "It": One Child's Courage to Survive*. Deerfield Beach, FL: Health Communications, Inc.

Pelzer, D. 1997. *The Lost Boy: A Foster Child's Search for the "Love" of a Family*. Deerfield Beach, FL: Health Communications, Inc.

Purkiss, D. 1996. *The Witch Is History: Early Modern and Twentieth-Century Representations*. New York: Routledge.

Russell, J. B. 1972. *Witchcraft in the Middle Ages*. Ithaca, NY: Cornell University Press.

Rohdes, E. 1925. *Psyche: The Cult of Souls and Belief in Immortality Among the Greeks.* London.

Siegel, L. J., and Senna, J. J. 1981. *Juvenile Delinquency: Theory, Practice, and Law.* St. Paul, MN: West.

Summers, M. 1992. *The History of Witchcraft and Demonology.* Secaucus, NJ: Castle Books.

Taylor, J. 1815. *Apparitions; or the Mystery of Ghosts, Hobgoblins and Haunted Houses, Developed,* 2nd ed. London: Lackington, Allen, and Co.

Trevor-Roper, H.R. 1969. *The European Witch-Craze of the Sixteenth and Seventh Centuries.* New York: Penguin.

Wedeck, H. E. 1961. *A Treasury of Witchcraft: A Sourcebook of the Magic Arts.* Avenel, NJ: Gramercy Books.

Williams, S. R., and Williams, P. J. 1978. *Riding Nightmare: Women and Witchcraft.* West Hanover, MA: McClelland & Stewart.

Causes of Criminal and Noncriminal Abuses of Women and Children

2

OBI N. I. EBBE

This chapter investigates and discusses the causes of criminal and noncriminal abuses of women separate from those of children. Although women and children have certain things in common, there are some variations in the nature of their positions in society and the nature of their abuses. Woman and children vary in age, role expectations, and knowledge of the social system, and a child could be a woman's dependant. Comparatively, women and children can be abandoned by the head of the household (husband/father).

In contrast, children can be moved from place to place with little or no resistance from them. Also, children can easily be deceived and made to believe that a certain behavior is normal when it is not, especially when an adult, with ties of consanguinity with the child, wants to exploit the child's sexuality. Children are innocents, and they have not reached the use of reason. In effect, they are prey to incestuous relatives and sexual predators.

Abuse and the "Nature" of Women

Women, by their nature, are physically weaker than men. In all cultures, women are socialized to be submissive and made to let men do most physical activities. It is not the choice of women to be submissive. The culture in which they are raised nurtured and groomed them to be obedient to men and made them not engage in common physical or sports activities with men. Also, the history of God's creation of human beings sets the order of a man's relationship with a woman.

God created Adam, bible history tells us, and took a rib of Adam to create Eve. Eve, being weak minded, was easily deceived by Lucifer, and she in turn deceived her only man, Adam. Henceforth, God made Eve subservient to Adam. Throughout the whole world, in all cultures, women are made subservient to men by custom, religion, and creation. Unmistakably, the socialization process, in all cultures, helped to propagate the subservience and subordinate status of women in every society. Even in matriarchal societies, men still guide the female head of household. There is no female monarch (queen) in world history that surrounded herself with female servants at all levels and protected her monarchy with female soldiers. Men have always run the show in all societies, from ancient times through the Middle Ages to modern times. Men have always treated women as followers and not as leaders.

When a woman tries to lead a country, some men treat her as being a deviant, even in modern civilizations. After many centuries of British politics, it was only in 1979 that Great Britain elected its first female prime minister, Margaret Thatcher. The United States, after more than 200 years of independence, has never had a female president. Hillary Rodham Clinton's attempt to be the first female American president in 2009 failed. She was defeated in the Democratic primary elections by an African-American male contender who went on to become the first African-American president.

Many women throughout the world do not want to challenge men. If women in America united behind Hillary Clinton, the American presidency would have been hers in 2009. Unfortunately, most women see themselves as followers. Even when a woman volunteers or is pushed by men to lead, she will still rely on men. Thus, men see women as the weaker sex.

As a result of the weak nature of women and their subservient socialization, it is very easy for men, as well as women in positions of power, to abuse women.

Cross-Cultural Variations

The way women are treated varies from culture to culture. There are very few matriarchal societies in the world. Some of them include the Ashanti of Ghana, the Nagovisi of New Guinea and Northern Australia, the Garo in Meghalya State in North-Eastern India, and the Mechinguenga of Peru. In such societies, a mother is the head of the household and not her husband. Inheritance in such a society is traced through the mother instead of through the father. Still, in matriarchal societies, the woman's authority is limited by physical requirements of the social system. The same woman who is the head of the household can be battered by her husband, which often happens among the Ashanti, without any societal condemnation or negative sanction. In a matriarchal society, the mother/woman being the head of the household does not protect her from being abused by her husband.

Some cultures require adult female circumcision. This is a very painful abuse of a woman. There are some cultures in Africa, Asia, and Oceanic Islands where females are not circumcised until they reach adult age; otherwise, they will not be allowed to marry. The circumcision is performed without local or general anesthesia, because custom and tradition of the tribe does not countenance any anesthetic intervention. Most societies in Africa allow circumcision to be performed from the first day a baby is born to the eighth day. Circumcising a woman is torture and physical abuse.

Marriage customs can be a source of abuse of a woman. In many societies in Africa, Asia, and among the Aborigines of Australia, bride wealth or dowry is required before a man can take a woman to his house as his wife. In some cultures, this dowry or bride wealth can be costly. Sometimes, the dowry can be paid in the national currency. However, in some societies, it is a marriage feast that may last three or four days, and the cost is paid by the bridegroom. After all of the costly ceremonies and dowry are paid and the man (bridegroom) finds his wife to be disobedient or lazy, it becomes a reason for the man to beat his wife mercilessly.

There are some tribes in the Punjab of northwest India that require the parents of the bride provide some wealth to the bridegroom for the bridegroom to look after their daughter. If parents do not provide enough money or wealth to the bridegroom, many Indian men beat their wives mercilessly, and in some cases, kill them. Unmistakably, some Indian women have committed suicide because of incessant harassment and abuse by their husbands.

Another cultural factor that leads to abuse of women is barrenness. In all societies, the main purpose of marriage is for procreation. When a woman fails to conceive after one to two years of marriage, it becomes a concern to men in most cultures, especially men in Asia, Africa, the Middle East, and Central and South America. The man's love for his wife begins to fade when there is no conception shortly after marriage. Physical abuse of the woman begins and makes it very uncomfortable for the woman to remain in the marriage. Unfortunately, in some cultures, divorce is not an option. The woman lives in misery.

The situation gets worse for the barren woman if she lives in a polygamous society, which 80 percent of world cultures practice. In a polygamous society, the barren woman's abuse is intensified and her misery heightened when her husband, in an attempt to get a son, marries another woman, usually a younger woman. When the second wife of the man conceives and bears a male child for the man, it becomes a social indictment of the first wife. At this point, some people in the society treat the barren woman with sympathy, but, in some circles within the same society, she is treated like an outcast. When the abuse from her husband becomes unbearable, especially when her husband uses her barrenness to insult her at home and in public, the woman leaves her husband and marries another man. Some of the barren women have conceived and gotten children from their new husbands. In most polygamous societies, there is no court marriage or court divorce. Once a man's wife chooses to leave her husband, the marriage is over. The dowry will not be repaid until the woman remarries.

The abuse of a barren wife can be emotional and psychological. There are sexual and barrenness innuendoes from her husband, brothers-in-law, and sisters-in-law that can keep the barren women in mental anguish, sometimes causing a severe loss of appetite. Unmistakably, she is also sexually starved, especially when the barrenness has lasted for five to six years since the beginning of the marriage. This occurs when her husband marries a second, younger woman and he concentrates his sexual activity on his new bride. Very often this barren, first wife, sits alone in her house, crying and lonely.

Political Power and Abuse of Women

From the Roman emperors to the monarchies and democratic heads of states of modern times, some women have been criminally abused to further political interests or to demonstrate political and economic power. Queen Elizabeth I of England surreptitiously jailed Mary Queen of Scots, moved her from castle to castle, and, finally, falsely accused her of treason and beheaded her. The type of treatment meted out to Mary Queen of Scots pervaded many monarchies of the 19th and 20th centuries all over Europe, Africa, and Asia.

In the contemporary era of democratic governments, absolute monarchies, and dictatorships, some women have been murdered, assassinated, jailed, or made to commit suicide by some heads of state and corrupt politicians. Undeniably, it has been alleged that some heads of state and their wives have been involved in narcotics smuggling. In most cases, they used women to execute their criminal enterprise. However, when the woman is caught, the head of state and his cronies get the woman assassinated before she can divulge the identity of her accomplices to the police, and they kill any journalist who attempts to uncover the illegal scheme (*West Africa Magazine* 1987a,b; Ebbe 1999, 2003).

Many politicians, all over the world, think that being a politician at the national level means "cheat on your wife and chase all beautiful women who are less than half of your age." Other politicians resort to patronizing street prostitutes and call girls. When it appears that their extramarital sexual activities are going to ruin their political careers, they get the woman murdered or criminally induced to commit suicide before she could reveal her clients.

There were two suspicious suicides in the United States between 2006 and May 7, 2008. The headline read, "D.C. Madam Commits Suicide in Florida" (*Chattanooga Times Free Press* 2008). Deborah Jeane Palfrey was indicted by a federal grand jury for "running a high-end Washington, D.C., prostitution ring." The federal jury convicted Palfrey on April 15, 2008 of running prostitution services that catered to members of the political elite of Washington. Palfrey denied that her escort services engaged in prostitution. The trial concluded without revealing details about the services and who the clients of the sexual enterprise were. "Senator David Vitter, a Louisiana Republican, was the only fall guy, but did not take the witness stand" (*Chattanooga Times Free*

Press 2008). Deborah Jeane Palfrey was scheduled to be sentenced on July 24, 2008, for what the U.S. Attorney's Office said would be about five or six years in prison. Instead, two weeks after her conviction, Palfrey was found dead by her mother. It was ruled suicide.

Furthermore, Brandy Britton, one of the escort service employees, formerly a professor at the University of Maryland, Baltimore County, was arrested in 2006 on prostitution charges. She committed suicide in January 2007 before she was scheduled to go to trial (*Chattanooga Times Free Press* 2008). Given what I have observed in the criminology of power and from similar situations in Asia, Africa, and Central and South America, such "suicides" are a power play by those who fear that, if the convicted woman goes to prison, she would reveal the identity of her clients, her clients being the political and business elite. The fall of the governor of New York in 2008, Eliot Spitzer, is another example of politicians having extramarital sex. Many women have lost their lives when lured by men's money and political power. A woman having a sexual affair with a politician is playing with a double-edged sword.

Money is power, and some politicians have the money. With money, they make some women engage in sexual practices that poverty and greed drives them into agreeing to perform. Some women who left the life of prostitution have revealed their ugly and sadomasochistic practices with politicians and rich businessmen. Some heads of states and other politicians have impregnated their hired help, provided them a decent home, and paid them very well not to reveal who impregnated them so as to save their marriages and political positions. The future of the woman is ruined, and the child born out of wedlock is labeled a bastard.

The surreptitious sexual life of some politicians can be seen in the life of former U.S. Senator Strom Thurmond (1902–2003) from South Carolina, a white man, who was in the Senate from 1954 to 2003. He fathered an African-American child but kept his paternity a secret, although he financially supported the black mother and daughter. The incident did not come to light until 2003, when the child born from the secret love affair was already in her 50s. Thurmond acknowledged that he was her father just a few months before he died on June 26, 2003. It appears that the sexual affair that produced Thurmond's black daughter occurred when he was the governor of South Carolina, from 1947 to 1951. The position of power is the key to sexual exploitation of women. As one eminent American politician put it on the Larry King Live show, "I did what I have done because I could." That also can explain a politician's sexual relationship with a page or an intern.

At the time this book was written, there were two high-profile court cases in the United States filed by former housemaids/nursemaids for sexual molestation and abuse by their employers: a husband and wife. Some housemaids refuse to go public with their sexual abuses and molestations for fear that nobody would believe them, or because of shame, or the danger of losing a boyfriend, or being blamed by their parents.

Some men have lost their self-respect, and, incapable of controlling their sex drives, they succumb to the amorous glances of their babysitters. A case example is a senior bank official of the African Continental Bank in Enugu, Nigeria. This middle-aged man married a beautiful woman in her early forties, who was an accountant in a different bank. This woman brought her younger sister, who dropped out of high school to be her housemaid. By middle 1970, the housemaid was in the second trimester of her pregnancy.

When the man's wife suspected that her younger sister, and maid, was pregnant, she confronted her one evening about it. The housemaid acknowledged that she was pregnant. Her sister yelled, "Why and who is responsible for this?" "It is your husband," the housemaid replied. "What!?" the man's wife exclaimed and rushed into their bedroom to confront her husband. I was living on the third floor of a building right opposite their bungalow on the same street. The woman verbally set their house ablaze that night. For the man, it was his longest night. They sent the young housemaid to their village to live about 140 miles away. In my culture, for a woman to be pregnant and have a baby without a husband, it is like a death sentence. In the 1970s, among the Igbos of Nigeria, it was unthinkable for such a woman to find a man who would marry her. The Igbos practice hereditary patrilineal stratification. In effect, a child born out of wedlock has no lineage. In Igbo culture, a boy born out of wedlock is a curse to himself.

In western societies, when a single woman has a child, the government takes care of the child and her mother. In third-world countries, such as Nigeria, Ghana, Mexico, and Sri Lanka, the woman is marooned. She is on her own. In third-world societies, not only are the woman and her child economically abandoned, but the woman becomes a social outcast. The man who impregnated her will not come near her again, and the governments have no mechanism or laws to make such men pay child support. In some of these societies, some single mothers succumb to marrying old, poor farmers, who use the women as slaves in farm labor.

Religious Factors

Religious doctrines have been used to abuse women in many parts of the world. It is mindboggling why some Islamic doctrines in Nigeria would require a wife to remain indoors all day long for some days (*poda*) and not be allowed to come out during the daytime. At night, she may be allowed to go somewhere nearby in the company of a maid and come back to the house shortly. The Muslims say that such a woman is in *poda*. At the same time, her husband can go anywhere he wants, day or night. Muslim women are not allowed in the mosque to pray with the men. Why? Are women not children of Allah (God)? Islamic religion prescribes stoning, flogging, or a death sentence for a woman who commits adultery and flogging for a woman caught in fornication, but the man who fornicated with the woman or committed adultery with the women is let free.

Every year, many women are trafficked to Lebanon from Africa, Asia, and South America and deployed in underground brothels. Some of these foreign women have been flogged and shamed in public for fornication, but nothing was done to the Muslim males who fornicated with them (Ebbe 2007). Catholic doctrine, in agreement with the scripture, holds that fornication is a sin and adultery a mortal sin, but some Catholic priests have molested, raped, and sexually abused many girls and women. The faith of these girls and women are totally destroyed. Before the sexual encounter with the priest, these girls and women were dedicated Catholics and believed in the sanctity of the Catholic doctrines. What the priest has done to her contradicts what she had learned about God and the Christian teachings. Those girls and women who were abused by Catholic priests are emotionally and psychologically destroyed. The Catholic church in America has paid over $12 billion in settling lawsuits against their priests for sexual abuses.

Christian protestant pastors are even worse. Some pastors run away with a member's wife, leaving the parish in disarray. Some pastors father children of unwed mothers without taking care of them. In some cases, they take care of them without coercion, but, in others, the courts have to force them to pay child support. In either case, the single mother's life is ruined. Very often, the female members walk away because of fear of the pastor's backlash, that members may blame her as being responsible for the pastor's infidelity, or that telling anybody about the incident would come to nothing. In fact, reporting sexual molestation by a Catholic priest is more likely than reporting a rape by a protestant pastor, because accusation of a Catholic priest will bring more money to the victim than that of a protestant pastor.

Among the protestant denominations, there are those in western society who proscribe polygamy deeming such marriages as bigamous and punishable by three to seven years imprisonment. The problem with polygamous marriages in societies where they are legal has been stated above, but, in western societies, women who are engaged in them, in the main, did so by coercion. Sexual starvation is one of the weapons a polygamous husband uses to control his wives. In these totalitarian religions in America, female members are physically disciplined whenever they disobey their husbands. These women are shielded from the world outside their enclosed ranch. The United States has had Jim Jones' Peoples Temple, the Branch Davidian sect in Waco, and now the "Yearn for Zion" Ranch in El Dorado, Texas, where minor female residents are conditioned to expect and acquiesce in sexual relationships with adult males at the ranch after being spiritually married to the men (*Chattanooga Times Free Press* 2008).

Criminal abuse of women by some religious organizations is noted worldwide. In the 1960s, a Catholic priest in Nigeria impregnated a young woman. When the rumor gradually spread, the priest got his younger brother to marry the woman. Shortly after the marriage, the priest's brother killed the woman. The murderer did not serve more than one year in prison. When it comes to abuse of women by Christian priests, like rape, only a small percentage of the incidents are reported.

Satanic and Wealth Cults

Satanism is another form of religion. Satan makes promises to its members through its intermediaries. The main life wire of Satan is to get people killed in either cold blood or through illnesses. This is because "the dead cannot praise God," the scripture tells us. Satan, through its intermediaries of human and nonhuman elements, can tell its members to sacrifice a human being to it to get a desired favor. In effect, the adherents of satanism often have to sacrifice human beings to it.

Satanism created different types of cults all over the world. Both the ancient and medieval times had satanic religious services like those of Countess Elizabeth Bathony and Gilles de Rais mentioned in Chapter 1. In ancient and medieval times, it was in the form of paganism. Under satanism are paganism, witchcraft, sorcery, and clandestine, underground wealth and protection cults. All of them use human beings as sacrifices, as happened in the Dark Ages. All members believe Satan will respond to what is requested faster than praying to the Almighty God. The problem that satanists disregard is when Satan wants a human being sacrificed to it and the member fails, the member loses his or her life. Throughout the world, there are wealth-producing satanic cults. Members are carefully and secretly recruited. Once invited to the cult, the neophyte is given conditions of membership. What he is going to sacrifice depends on what he wants Satan to do for him. According to *Living in Bondage* (a Nigerian movie based on facts), those who choose to be wealthy are usually asked to sacrifice the person they love most in their family. The choice is almost always the man's wife, his mother, or his son or daughter.

The problem with satanic sacrifices is that, most of the time, the human being sacrificed is a girl or a woman. The story of satanic wealth cults in West Africa was often told in my elementary school days in the late 1950s and 1960s. When *Living in Bondage* came out in the 1980s, I was not surprised, but I was shocked about what I saw and how it happened.

Satan tempted Jesus Christ (Matthew 4:1–10). Therefore, there is nobody that cannot be tempted by Satan. Paganism, which survived up to the 20th century, created some shrines in African societies in which the keepers of the shrine had to kill a stranger for the shrine. Some of the shrines required the blood of a woman or a virgin. The *Ikoro* shrine of Aro-Ndizuogu, which was receiving human blood and skulls every year, survived stringent colonial control of paganism up to the 1950s. It is believed that *Ikoro* keepers today only kill a cow for the shrine.

Shrines that required the blood of a stranger very often received the blood of women and children, because it was easier to kidnap women and children than to kidnap adult males.

Modern laws of nations prohibit human sacrifices, but satanic cults still find ways to sacrifice human beings (women and children) without being caught. In some cases, cults have resorted to using body parts of human beings to substitute for a whole human being (Ebbe 1999, 2003). Every year in the United States, there are missing adults and children. When you stop by the entrance of a Wal-Mart Super Center, you can see photos of many missing persons on the wall. Most of them are women and children. Where are they? Some of them have been killed for various satanic sacrifices, but some of them are still alive and enslaved in labor or sexual bondage. There will be more on this when we go to causes of criminal abuse of children.

Abnormal Male Personalities

There are many abnormal personalities in history who were not insane but murdered so many women and children. Here we present men who criminally abused women to death. Later we will discuss those who abused children.

The abnormal male personalities are the serial killers who targeted women. The first recorded abuser of women and sex killer was "Jack the Ripper." In 1888, he murdered five prostitutes in London's notorious White Chapel district. The crimes sent shock waves throughout Victorian England. Dr. Thomas Neil Cream was a diabolical, ruthless serial killer who hunted women through North America and Great Britain. Prostitutes were his ultimate targets. In criminal abuse of women by sexual killers, the victims are not always strangers. A married woman named Beryl had a daughter, Geraldine. When Beryl got pregnant by her husband but wanted an abortion, she told her neighbor, John Christie. Christie volunteered to perform the abortion. Instead, Christie raped Beryl, killed her, and then killed Geraldine. It did not end there. Christie also murdered his own wife. He lured many prostitutes to his apartment, raped them, and killed them. He then dumped their bodies in his closet. In a different approach in the 1890s, Theo Durrant, who was a medical student and Sunday school superintendent, murdered his girlfriends, one after another.

In another twist, H. H. Holmes, like Otokoto of Nigeria, built a terror mansion in Chicago to lure female tourists. Not all women that entered the mansion left alive. He killed 27 of them. In 1959, in London, England, "Jack the Stripper" roamed Duke's Meadows, on the banks of the river Thames in Cheswick, West London. It was a popular area for unconventional sexual practices. There he lured women, raped them, and strangled them. He killed a total of eight young women (http://www.trutv.com/library/crime/index.html).

Like H. H. Holmes and Otokoto, Bela Kiss of Budapest kept an apartment for traveling women to stay. He took out advertisements in the local newspapers in Budapest. Many young ladies spent some time in Bela Kiss's home in Cinkota. Many of the women stayed and left, but Bela Kiss murdered 24 of the women. In Dusseldorf, Germany, between the 1890s and 1931, when he was executed, Peter Kurten strangled many women and sadistically perpetrated many other heinous crimes (Masters and Lea 1963).

Rape-murderers span the pages of the history of sexual psychopaths. Melvin Rees was a brutal serial rapist who murdered many women. In the same vein, a warehouse clerk, William Lester Suff, raped and murdered 13 prostitutes in Southern California. He was convicted in July 1995 (http://www.trutv.com/library/crime/index.html). Young women are very trusting the first time they meet a handsome man, and most of the serial killers take advantage of the women's vulnerability. Ted Bundy was a handsome man and was very charismatic and ambitious. Underneath the charm was a demonic monster. He killed 40 young women and girls as young as 12 years old in a space of four years in the 1970s. Before he was caught, he appeared a normal political juggernaut.

Finally, like Ted Bundy, on the South Side of Chicago lived a man who appeared to be a law-abiding American citizen, Richard Speck. Living in a quiet apartment complex were eight nurses in training who were rooming together. Richard Speck killed all of them. He was caught when a ninth nurse in training in the complex "wedged herself under a bed and went undetected. Her description of the intruder with 'Born to Raise Hell' tattoo on his arm" led to Speck's arrest.

There is no biological or psychiatric explanations for the crimes of all of these men discussed above. Their crimes were not motivated by insanity or neurosis. Rather, it is my assertion that certain sadistic and monstrous crimes are motivated by evil forces for which we have no empirical proof. The logical basis of this assertion is that the scripture tells us that, in the time Christ, evil spirits possessed some people, tormented them, and made them commit certain crimes and evils against humanity. Since Christ was crucified, the world has not ended, and the evil spirits and angels of God have not left the world. Therefore, it should not be unexpected today that satanic spirits could enter the mind of a person and make him commit heinous crimes. Science avoids this line of explanation because it is based on an assumption that cannot be investigated. However, evil spirit possession is a logical assumption based on historical precedence. When Jeffrey Dahmer killed young boys, ate some of their body parts, and saved some in his refrigerator, he was not operating under a disease of the mind. I believe he was possessed by some negative entity, as were Ted Bundy, Richard Speck, Melvin "Sex Beast" Rees, and others.

Sometimes, serial killing can be a result of neurosis or psychopathy or mean-spirited, depraved-heart murder. Jerry Jones may fall into this category. In Calhoun, Georgia, in the United States, it is alleged that Jones was trying to hurt his girlfriend, Melissa Peeler, who was trying to end their relationship. He had a 10-month-old daughter with Peeler. On January 7, 2004, Jones killed Peeler's parents, her sister, and their 10-month-old daughter. After the killings, he kidnapped three other children, including two of his own, and drove off to an unknown destination. When the police discovered the bodies of the Peelers, a regional manhunt ensued in search of Jones and the three missing girls. The next day, a speed chase ensued when the police spotted Jones driving along Interstate 75 North toward Tennessee with the three girls. Jones crashed his car into a utility pole in East Ridge, Tennessee. He shot himself in the face, but he did not die. The police pulled out the three girls, who were unhurt. Jones spent some months in a prison hospital. During the jury trial in Gordon County, Georgia, on May 2, 2008, Jones pleaded guilty to all the charges. Despite his guilty plea, the Gordon County District Attorney Joe Campbell sought the death penalty, and the jury gave it to him (*Chattanooga Times Free Press* 2008).

It is not religious fanaticism that made some serial killers concentrate on killing prostitutes, because some serial killers killed many women who were not prostitutes. Instead, the serial killers engaged in their murders because of an inner force that they could not control. This postulation is supported by the painful admissions of Edmund Kemper, which go as follows:

> It was an urge…A strong urge, and the longer I let it go the stronger it got, to where I was taking risks to go out and kill people, risks that normally, according to my little rules of operation, I wouldn't take because they could lead to arrest. (http://www.trutv.com/library/crime/index.html)

Edmund Kemper's assertion is reminiscent of testimony by an Attica Prison (New York) inmate. I was giving a lecture to 22 Attica Prison inmates in the spring of 1992 under the auspices of the Consortium of the Niagara Frontier that was offering associate and bachelor degree programs in the prison. The lecture was on the causes of criminal behavior. I observed, after some interrogation of the class, that 18 of the 22 inmate students were serving 25 years to life for murder. During one of the class lectures, I asked the class, "Why do some offenders kill a total stranger without any altercation?" The whole class shouted, "Ohhh! Dr. Ebbe, you don't know what you are talking about." One of the inmates silenced the class and said, "There are times you feel like killing somebody and the feeling keeps you in a state of inquietude. Your only living option is to kill somebody and that's the only thing that can cool you off." Every inmate in the class shouted, "Yea!" in acknowledgement. It was a shocking revelation to me that day, a theory not taught in college.

The question is, where does the destructive feeling come from? Why is it that not everybody gets that type of feeling? That feeling, undeniably, goes to support the idea of evil spirit aggression and possession. I believe that Satan wants human blood and can make his angels enter the minds of some human beings to perpetrate monstrous crimes.

Family Violence

Some married men have been described as abusive husbands. There are factors that precipitate family violence and the consequent abuse of the woman. Among the factors that lead to family violence are sexual infidelity, money matters, denial of sexual access, drunkenness or alcoholism, drug abuse and addiction, sharing of domestic chores, sharing of the children's needs, type of friends or associations, and lack of mutual respect.

When a husband grows suspicious that his wife is having an affair, he may hire a private investigator without his wife's knowledge. When the husband gets all of the facts and presents the facts to his wife and his wife presents an irrational defense or totally denies it with irrefutable evidence, some men may lose their temper and beat the woman. Conversely, a woman may have a similar suspicion of her husband. The problem in a husband and wife relationship is that, when a wife accuses her husband of having an extramarital affair, some men use a violent response to cover it up. He beats the woman and tries to make her not raise such a question again. This often leads to a divorce.

Money is said to be the root of all evil, and in a marriage, this is not an exception. Some couples do not know how to merge the love they have for each other with their incomes, even when both have decent incomes. One is greedier than the other, or both are greedy and very stingy with their incomes. In such a situation, share of the family expenses becomes an issue of conflict. Violence may ensue in trying to come to a compromise. When there is no compromise, one may opt out of the marriage. If there are under-age children in the union and the woman wants to end the marriage, some men may resort to intimidation, threats, and violent physical harm to make the woman reconsider divorce.

When the family income is from only one source, that is, the man is working and his wife is a homemaker, money is less likely to be a source of violence. It can be a source of violence when the husband is not giving his wife enough money for household needs and little money for his wife's personal needs. The situation in which money is not the source of wife abuse is a situation in which neither the husband nor the wife is stingy or extravagant. However, some husbands withhold money from their wives when the women are not working or are working part time.

Drunkenness, alcoholism, drug abuse, and drug addiction are the most inevitable causes of family violence. When one party or both parties in a marriage are engaged in any one of the above bad habits, arguments and violence reign in the family's daily life. Drunkenness and being high on drugs can lead to unprovoked arguments and fights. The degree of destructive effect family violence has on children in the family is inestimable.

There are husbands who refuse to help in household chores. They leave everything to their wives, even when their wives are working full time. A simple complaint by a wife to her husband triggers a violent response. Husbands who try to act as bosses to their wives and refuse to help in domestic chores are mostly men with low self-esteem. Their minds are full of pride and arrogance. They are more prevalent among blue-collar workers and college graduates without self-respect.

Who takes the kids to school, picks them up, and takes them to sports activities can be a source of family arguments and abuse. A good husband and father takes delight in taking his kids to school and accompanying them to sports as far as his work schedule allows him, but there are some husbands who are nonchalant about their kids' sports and school activities. Their wives have to bear the brunt of the responsibilities.

The last factor to be discussed here about the causes of family violence and abuse of a woman is the type of friends both the husband and wife keep. The type of friends kept by either party can affect the marriage relationship positively or negatively. When one party has friends that the other does not countenance, the rational reaction is to tell the other to disassociate himself or herself from the friendship. This can be a battleground for the parties.

Unmistakably, there are female-precipitated abuses. Some wives or girlfriends lose their temper and strike at their man. The response from the man becomes more physically violent than what the woman started. Although some men can endure a slap on a cheek from their wives and walk away, others will reply by beating their wives beyond recognition.

Socioeconomic Factors

There is an inextricable connection between making money and women. In effect, men all over the world, for centuries, have exploited women to achieve their personal ends. Women are human beings, but when some men want to exploit them for economic ends, they apply Machiavellian means: "the end justifies the means." Both western and non-western societies have, all along, treated women like commodities.

Like an inanimate commodity, women are often moved from one location to another. The movement of women from one city to another and from one country to another for the purpose of employing them in criminal activities, legal and illegal brothels, or using them as slaves, is a crime against humanity and a violation of their civil rights. Unmistakably, trafficking in women for slave labor, pornography, and forced prostitution has become a horrifying modern-day social problem (Ebbe 2007). Enormous hardship, pain, and suffering are created for women illegally recruited, transported, and employed against their will in legal or illegal businesses. Also, their relatives wait in vain at their home of origin, thinking that their loved ones were taken away for meaningful employment and will return soon. They discover later that their loved ones were living in perpetual servitude or are even dead. This is an inexplicable abuse of a human being.

Some families are disorganized when one of their members is fraudulently taken away for several months or years without hearing anything about her. Very often, we read about women and children illegally transported out of their homelands for slave labor, pornography, child labor, or forced prostitution. Unfortunately, some of the women and children trafficked are killed for their "body parts" (Ebbe 1999, 2003, 151–152).

Every now and again, we hear about missing children or adults. The question is, where are they? What happened to them? The answer is, some are killed for their body parts, as mentioned above, sold into slavery, deployed in pornographic activities, forced into prostitution, sold to brothel owners, or made sex slaves for the rich and powerful. Unmistakably, illegally transported women very often end up being described as "missing persons."

There is a lot of profit in human trafficking, especially of women and girls. The United Nations estimates that the revenue from human trafficking ranges between $7 and $12 billion. Because there is no national or international systematic study or records of trafficking in persons, estimates of the volume of the trafficking vary from government to government, from agency to agency, and from one international organization to another (Ebbe 2007).

There are various explanations about the characteristics of the women who are trafficked. Some studies describe the trafficked women as victims (Bertone 2000; Doezema 2000; Gushlulak and Macpherson 2000; Bales and

Robbins 2001; Hyland 2001; Bales 2002; Adepoju 2005; Brennan 2005; Laczko and Gozdziak 2005).

Most of the women trafficked and abused in the process are single, divorced, or separated, with or without children, in refugee camps, poor widows, unemployed school graduates, school dropouts, local prostitutes, marginal hairdressers, or local bartenders, to name a few. There are various sociological theories that explain exploitation, criminal abuse, and trafficking in women. In explaining the etiology of this horrendous crime, we can look at the impact of "criminality and economic conditions" (Bonger 1916), poverty (More 1516), anomie (Durkheim 1964; Merton 1968), hedonism (Beccaria 1819; Bentham 1967), social control (Hirschi 1969), class and crime (Chambliss and Mankoff 1976; Quinney 1977), greed (McCaghy 1980), globalization (Esadze 2004; Laczko and Gozdziak 2005; Okereke 2005), and the sudden collapse of the Soviet Union.

Starting with criminality and economic conditions, Bonger asserted that, when a society is divided into "haves" and "have-nots," the have-nots will try to get even with the haves. In other words, when the economy is bad, some individuals who are determined to survive but have lost their expected rewards will try alternative means, however illegitimate. In many developing countries, the economy has been in a state of depression since the 1970s, without an end in sight. Consequently, trafficking in women from developing countries to more advanced countries for prostitution, illegal house service/maids, pornography, slave labor, and sexual slavery becomes an alternative moneymaking mechanism. In more advanced countries, greed (McCaghy 1980) drives the rich and powerful to get richer by employing cheap labor of illegal aliens, very often illegally and fraudulently transported women.

Furthermore, domestic conflicts and wars in some underdeveloped economies emanating from post-independence tribal struggles for control of the government, wholesale corruption, and crony capitalism and democracy created social disorganization and anomie (Merton 1957; Durkheim 1964) in those countries. In effect, there is a breakdown in law enforcement because social control mechanisms are weakened to a point of lawlessness (Hirschi 1969). In these developing countries, especially the former colonial dependencies, intertribal or interethnic conflicts gave rise to dictatorships and predatory states. The police are then used to protect the dictatorial and predatory state's political agenda at the expense of crime control and safety of the private citizens. The large mass of population of unemployed and destitute hang around, hopelessly, at the mercy of the fraudulent human traffickers. Some young men and groups, in such dictatorial regimes, find single women and children, struggling for survival, as easy targets for trafficking exploitation.

Poverty is not a universal theory of crime; poverty cannot explain crime in all cultures. However, poverty explains a significant amount of crime in developed, industrialized nations, and, to a small degree, in poor nations.

As Thomas More (1516) put it before British Parliament, if a man has determined to be alive but his basic needs are not provided, he must steal. In the same vein, the economic conditions of some developed and underdeveloped nations produced high waves of unemployment of both skilled and unskilled individuals in the 1980s and early 2000s. Consequently, many university and high school graduates engaged in all types of transnational crimes, including transnational trafficking in women. Beccaria (1819) and Bentham (1967) of the Classical School of Criminology asserted that man is hedonistic. In effect, man will continue to seek pleasure, wherever he can find it. Therefore, hedonism and greed combine to spur some middle-class and upper-class individuals in Western, Eastern, and Central Europe, America, Canada, the Middle East, Africa, South America, Japan, and Australia to import innocent, illegally transported women and children to serve as housemaids or sex slaves or to perform slave labor for them in sweat shops and other enterprises (Ebbe 2007).

Immediate Causes of Trafficking in Women and Consequent Abuses

Natural disasters and wars in Asia, Africa, Eastern Europe, the Middle East, and South America, from the 1960s through the 1990s, including the sudden collapse of the Soviet empire, left many women destitute in their own countries. Consequently, the traffickers saw the women as being vulnerable to exploitation and thus made false promises to take them to countries where life would be better for them. This was helped by the fact that some of the women actively sought escape from the hopelessness of life in their own country (Ebbe 2007).

Wars and natural disasters created opportunities for the emergence of transnational human smuggling and trafficking. Additionally, these war- and disaster-torn countries are in parts of the world that are traditionally poor. In Southeast Asia, Cambodia is one of the least developed nations in the world, with a per capita income of $280 per year. Most of the workers in their garment factories are single women between the ages of 18 and 25. Most of them were born and raised in provinces where there are no job opportunities at all. These women receive, on average, $40 a month, and they are forced to pay a six-month procurement fee of $240 to obtain the job. They bear the stress of having to send money home to their parents and loved ones and to get out of debt in Cambodia (Ebbe 2007). In effect, these single women are pressured to prostitute themselves to meet their family obligations, as well as to pay the rent and transportation to work. With loneliness, long hours of work, poor living conditions, poor nutrition, and lack of meaningful guidance, many of them fell prey to Western sex tourists and organized crime traffickers who make false promises about great lives in America, Germany, the United Kingdom, Canada, Italy, and France. Many of these women run from the frying pan into the fire.

In Southeast Asia, especially in Cambodia, girls under 18 are made to work 16 hours a day in village factories. In Phnom Penh (the capital of Cambodia), the home of the country's garment industry, 90 percent of the workers are women. These women get little money or have no money left after paying their bills. The exploitation of women is not only found in Cambodia. The same situation is present in Gabon and Equatorial Guinea in Southwest Africa, where boys and girls are forced to work in plantations without pay. Those who are paid are under bonded labor. They end each month in debt to their master. Some of them, who voluntarily entered these two countries and wanted to go back to their home countries, could not because they did not have the money for transportation (Ebbe 2007).

Another factor that contributed to the trafficking of women is globalization. The idea of shared political policies, culture, trade, and regional treaties that eliminated demand for visas at the international borders, such as among Economic Cooperation of West African States nations, the European Union, North Atlantic Treaty Organization nations, and North American states, made trafficking women across international borders very easy.

In fact, legislation without stringent enforcement of the law is tantamount to criminalizing the masses. When laws are made to control a certain aberrant behavior but the laws are not enforced, it makes some people in the society commit other crimes far and above those prohibited. This is because individuals in such a society have the belief that the violations will not be enforced. Traffickers in women know that law enforcement officials are not stringent at enforcing the law in developed and developing countries, especially when it is a matter of protecting sexually abused women. Additionally, some of the law enforcement officials are corrupt. For some people, there is no fear in beginning such a criminal activity because they are aware that the system of social control is weak.

Finally, the collapse of the Soviet Union created newly independent states that were thrown into an open-market economy without planning. Unemployment reached 70–80 percent in some areas (Bertone 2000; Esadze 2004; Tyldum and Brunovskis 2005), and more than 80 percent of the unemployed are women. Many of them had to find their way out of the quagmire by voluntarily or involuntarily heading toward Western European countries, the Middle East, America, Canada, or Australia.

The trafficking in women and children today is a product of supply and demand. Rich countries lure women and children to their territories, and the poor countries are ready to supply them. The rich and the poor are involved in this criminal enterprise. That is why controlling trafficking in women and children has become a wild goose chase.

Modus Operandi of the Traffickers

Reports from Eastern and Central Europe, South and Central America, and Southeast Asia show that the traffickers target poor, helpless, single women in underdeveloped countries, countries at war or coming out of war, or countries emerging from natural disasters. The traffickers make false promises to the women, painting a rosy picture of life in Western Europe, the United States, Canada, Israel, Australia, or Japan. To many of the women, the offer is like winning the lottery. Unfortunately, they did not know that they were heading toward a tortuous and agonizing adventure (Ebbe 2007).

In all studies of trafficking in women and children, the traffickers promised the women high wages and good working conditions in the advanced economies. To their innocent victims, they name the great cities of London, Paris, Frankfurt, Munich, New York, Chicago, Los Angeles, Atlanta, Milan, Rome, Amsterdam, and Geneva as their destinations. For the unsuspecting women, it sounds like a dream come true. These are women who are looking for ways to escape their hopeless existence in their home countries.

The traffickers and their middlemen go to towns and villages, small cities, and even churches to recruit their victims. The type of employment that they promise the women are services in restaurants as a waitress or bartender, nanny, model, housemaid, or work in salon shops. In Southeast Asia, Russia, and Ukraine, the traffickers may prepare bogus contracts and sign them with the young women to give the deal legitimacy (Richard 2000; Esadze 2004). In Russia, South and Central Europe, and East and Southeast Asia, the traffickers advertise for female service jobs available in various countries in Western Europe, the United States, Canada, Israel, and Italy. Also, some traffickers collaborate with travel agencies and match-making agencies to recruit their victims. The traffickers provide travel documents. Some of the travel documents are genuine but are obtained through bribing corrupt embassy and immigration officials (Ebbe 2007).

In all source or origination countries, some women are kidnapped and smuggled into the United States, Western Europe, Australia, or Japan. These kidnapped women are the typical women that are sold two or three times to different brothels. The voluntarily and fraudulently trafficked women are the ones that very often end up in debt bondage because the trafficker decided to exploit them by requiring them to pay $10,000 to $50,000 before they would be free to live on their own. Kidnapping and using threats and intimidation are some of the methods of recruitment in all origination countries. For instance, according to intelligence reports (Richard 2000), in a 1997 trafficking case in California, a 22-year-old Chinese woman was kidnapped in China and smuggled to California on a Taiwanese fishing trawler without any travel documents. She was forced to work as a prostitute in Los Angeles and continuously "confined, raped, and tortured."

In Nigeria, "Pat," a 21-year-old female, a high school graduate in the town of Bini, was fraudulently recruited by her mother's close friend "Grace" to work in the latter's hair salon in Milan, Italy. Below is part of Pat's paraphrased testimony before the United States Immigration Court in New York City.

Between July and August 1999, Grace visited Pat's parents four times in very gorgeous attire. Pat was never present when Grace spoke to her mother. After the visit, Grace invited Pat to her house in Bini. Grace then asked Pat what she was doing for a living. Pat replied that she was experienced in hair care, but she presently had no job. Grace offered to take Pat to Milan, Italy, to work in the former's hair salon. She told Pat that she had spoken to her parents and they had agreed. Grace also told Pat how great life would be in Milan and how she could make a lot of money and help her poor parents. Grace gave Pat a rosy picture of the life that she would have in Italy. She told Pat that there were other Nigerians settled in Italy and that there was a much higher standard of living there, with a far more promising future. The way Grace looked and talked spelled confidence, success, and only positive things awaiting Pat.

Pat decided to go with Grace and told her mother. In October, Grace and Pat left Benin City for Milan, Italy, via the Republic of Benin and Paris, France. In Milan, they took a train to the Padova station. Pat said little throughout the entire trip, because she found the experience unsettling. "I felt like a fish out of water, taken out of my familiar pond and finding it hard to swim in the ocean," she testified.

When Grace and Pat arrived at a location, Grace approached a man who seemed to be waiting for her. Both talked out of earshot and both came to where Pat was waiting. Grace introduced the man to Pat as her husband "Christopher." They loaded up their luggage in Christopher's car and drove for perhaps 20 minutes, before reaching an apartment, on the second floor of a four-story building. The apartment had only one bedroom, which Grace and Christopher shared. Pat slept on a thin foam mattress on the floor in the sitting room. Grace spoke to Pat in Bini language and spoke English with Christopher (an Igbo). The following morning (a weekday), Grace and Christopher went out, leaving (and locking) Pat in the apartment. When they returned, Grace told Pat that she needed to renew her salon license and that was why she was gone all the time.

On the next day, Grace disappeared, leaving Christopher and Pat in the apartment. At night, Christopher raped Pat several times after beating her for resisting. He told her that he paid 50,000,000 lira (equivalent to $25,000) to bring her to Italy, that she had to prostitute herself in the street until he recovered his money. He added that he would be with her in the street to protect her. When Pat asked him about Grace, he said that Grace had gone back to Nigeria to bring another woman and added that Grace was not his wife.

According to Pat, when she refused to be a prostitute, Christopher beat her so badly, coupled with starving her, that she nearly died. At long last, Pat agreed to become a prostitute for Christopher. Christopher started taking her to the street at night, where Christopher collected money from men and Pat had to have sex with the men in their cars. Pat testified that, after she had had sex three times, on three different occasions with one of the men, when Christopher was out of earshot, she told him how she had been brought to Italy and that she wanted to run away, that Christopher was raping her every day and night no matter how tired she was, and that Christopher had seized her passport. The man told Pat that anywhere she ran to in Italy that Christopher would find her and might kill her. But he told Pat that he was going to find a Christian organization (a nongovernmental organization [NGO]) that would help her leave Italy. According to Pat's testimony, the man did exactly as he promised. He collected Pat's full information, such as name, date of birth, and nationality. Within a week, he told Pat the night that the escape would take place and that the NGO obtained a passport and arranged with an airline to take her to the United States.

On the night of the planned escape, Christopher and Pat went to their usual location. Pat's "escape man" had arranged for another man to lure Christopher's attention away from him and Pat when they entered his car to have sex. When the escape man and Pat entered the former's car and pretended to be having sex, the decoy presented himself to Christopher as the next man to have sex with Pat and led Christopher to a corner. Then, the escape man drove away with Pat through a different direction to the NGO's designated rendezvous. That night, Pat was taken to the airport and flown to the United States. At JFK International Airport, she was detained and taken to New York's immigration detention camp. The United States Immigration Service gave her a deportation order. Pat contacted a relative in Boston, Massachusetts, who helped her get an attorney and apply for asylum. The U.S. Immigration Court denied the application and ordered deportation. Pat and her lawyer appealed to the U.S. Immigration Court of Appeals. Before the Appeal Court hearing, Pat's lawyer, by happenstance, spoke about the case to a professor at American University in Washington, D.C. The Professor told the attorney that she should look for me, that I published an article in the *Trends in Organized Crime* journal in 1999 entitled *Political-Criminal Nexus: "Slicing Nigeria's National Cake": The Nigerian Case*, which asserted that, if such a trafficked woman was deported to her country of origin, she would be killed by those who trafficked her out of the country within two weeks of her return. I was consulted to testify. I testified by an affidavit in 2001 before the U.S. Immigration Court of Appeals. After reading my affidavit and comparing it with the defendant's testimony, the appeals court sent the case back to the lower court, where the case started (which had not read my publication and testimony). At the lower court, after reading my testimony, Pat was granted asylum in the United States.

The case of Pat is typical of the modus operandi of the women and children traffickers in Southeast Asia, Russia, Latin America, and Eastern and Central Europe. In Nigeria, the traffickers are in a category of organized crime called "419" (four-one-nine). They range from two to five members specializing in fraudulent schemes. During the passage from the origination country to the destination country, these women are raped and sexually abused, especially when the trafficker provided the money for the international flights and local transportation.

The most heart-rending abuse of women is when a man lures a woman into prostitution and becomes her pimp. The pimp greedily takes all the money. To keep the prostitute under absolute control, he drugs her repeatedly so that the prostitute just works for the drug, while the pimp keeps all of the money. If the prostitute complains, she is beaten and raped. Sometimes, these prostitutes are robbed, stabbed, humiliated by the customers, and rendered penniless by their pimps.

Conclusion

The etiologies of criminal abuse of women and children are inherent in social systems of all societies, and some of these causes are inevitable. Elimination of poverty is an abortive dream in a state of capitalist mode of production. The class structure of societies, the inherent dependency of women and children, the power element in men's nature, the padrologies of pedophilia and nymphomania, the insurmountable hedonism in human nature, the greediness of some men and women, the pugnacious temper of others, the incorrigibility of some children, and the insurmountable sexual appetites and pervasiveness of both sexes are among the factors that make criminal abuse of women and children inevitable in modern society.

References

Adepoju, A. 2005. "Review of Research and Data on Human Trafficking in Sub-Saharan Africa." In *Data and Research on Human Trafficking: A Global Survey*, edited by F. Laczko and E. Gozdziak. Geneva: International Organization for Migration, pp. 75–90.

Bales, K. 2002. "The Social Psychology of Modern Slavery." *Scientific American* 286(4):80–84.

Bales, K., and Robbins, P. T. 2001. "No One Shall Be Held in Slavery or Servitude: A Critical Analysis of International Slavery Agreements and Concepts of Slavery." *Journal of International Affairs* 2(2):18–37.

Beccaria, C. 1819. *On Crime and Punishment*, translated by E. D. Ingraham, 2nd ed. Philadelphia: Philip H. Nicklin.

Bentham, J. 1967. *A Fragment on Government and an Introduction to the Principles of Morals and Legislation*. Oxford: Basil Blackwell.

Bertone, A. M. 2000. "Sexual Trafficking in Women: International Political Economy and the Politics of Sex." *Gender Issues* 18(1):4–18.

Bonger, W. 1916. *Criminality and Economic Conditions*, translated by H. P. Horton. New York: Dryden Press.

Brennan, D. 2005. "Methodological Challenges in Research with Trafficked Persons: Tales from the Field." In *Data and Research on Human Trafficking: A Global Survey*, edited by F. Laczko and E. Gozdziak, 17–34. Geneva: International Organization for Migration.

Chambliss, W., and Mankoff, M. 1976. *Whose Law? What Order? A Conflict Approach to Criminology*. New York: Wiley and Sons.

Durkheim, E. 1964. *Division of Labor in Society*. New York: Free Press.

Ebbe, O. N. I. 1999. "The Political-Criminal Nexus: Slicing Nigerian National Cake: The Nigerian Case." *Trends in Organized Crime* 4(3):29–59.

Ebbe, O. N. I. 2003. "Slicing Nigeria's National Cake." In *Menace to Society: Political-Criminal Collaborations around the World*, edited by R. Godson. New Brunswick, NJ: Transaction Publishers.

Ebbe, O. N. I. 2007. "The Nature and Scope of Trafficking in Women and Children." In *Global Trafficking in Women and Children*, edited by O. N. I. Ebbe and D. K. Das. Boca Raton, FL: CRC Press/Taylor & Francis Group.

Esadze, L. 2004. "Trafficking in Women and Children: A Case Study of Georgia." Paper presented at the ISPAC of the U.N. Crime Prevention and Criminal Justice Programme held in Courmayeur, Mont Blanc, Italy.

Garrett, J. 2008. "Jerry Jones on the Run." *Chattanooga Times Free Press*, May 6.

Gushlulak, B. D., and Macpherson, D. W. 2000. "Health Issues Associated with Smuggling and Trafficking of Migrants." *Journal of Immigrant Health* 2(2):67–78.

Hirschi, T. 1969. *The Causes of Delinquency*. Berkeley: University of California Press.

Hyland, K. F. 2001. "The Impact of the Protocol to Prevent, Suppress, and Punish Trafficking in Persons, Especially Women and Children." *Human Rights Briefs*, http://www.wcl.american.edu/pub/humanright/brief/index.htm.

Laczko, F., and Gozdziak, E., eds. 2005. *Data and Research on Human Trafficking: A Global Survey*. Geneva: International Organization for Migration.

Masters, R. E. L., and Lea, E. 1963. *Sex Crimes in History: Evolving Concepts of Sadism, Lust-Murder, and Necrophilia—From Ancient to Modern Times*. New York: Julian Press.

McCaghy, C. 1980. *Crime in America*. New York: Free Press.

Merton, R. K. 1968. *Social Theory and Social Structure*. New York: Free Press.

More, T. 1516 and 1949. *Utopia*, translated by H. B. S. Ogden. New York: Appleton/Century Crofts.

Ojukwu, D., and Grace, A. 1989. "Justice for Sale." *African Guardian*, July 10.

Okereke, G. O. 2005. "The International Trade in Human Beings: A Critical Look at the Causes Factor." *Contemporary Criminal Justice Review* 21(86):4–17.

Ola, Olaniyi. 1989. "Who Killed Dele Giwa?" West Africa, March 27–April 2: 468.

Quinney, R. 1977. *Class, State, and Crime: On the Theory and Practice of Criminal Justice.* New York: David McKay.

Richard, A. O. 1999. "International Trafficking in Women to the United States: A Contemporary Manifestation of Slavery and Organized Crime." Washington, DC: DCI Exceptional Intelligence Analyst Program, Center for the Study of Intelligence.

Tyldum, G., and Brunovskis, A. 2005. "Describing the Unobserved: Methodological Challenges in Empirical Studies on Human Trafficking." In Data and Research on Human Trafficking: A Global Survey, edited by F. Laczko and E. Gozdziak. Geneva: International Organization for Migration.

The Scope and Causes of Criminal Abuse of Children

3

OBI N. I. EBBE

From ancient to medieval times, child abuse has been a part of human development. There were no national laws protecting children until the 19th century. As far back as the Roman times, children were the chattels of their father. They depended solely on his decision as to whether they should live or die (Bala 1989). Unmistakably, even before the Roman times, there was a tyrannical rule of the husband over his wife and of the father over his children. Under the Civil Code of Napoleon Bonaparte (1804), the family was sustained as "the unit and bastion of moral discipline and social order, and gave it a basis in power by reviving the *patria potestas* of ancient regimes: the father was awarded full control over his wife's property, and full authority over his children until they came of age" (Durant and Durant 1975). A father could have his children imprisoned on his own word alone, and he could deny his son getting married until he was twenty six years of age. In the same vein, he could prevent his daughter from getting married until she was twenty one (Durant and Durant 1975).

In the fourth century, infanticide was practiced in many parts of the world. Despite the opposition of the Roman Catholic Church, it was still practiced in Europe, Africa, Asia, and other parts of the world. Under the Protestant Reformation, religious doctrines unequivocally emphasized the relevance of a parent's responsibility "to rid children of their innate wickedness." In effect, whippings were made common and acceptable mechanisms of punishing a child.

Children continued to have less freedom until 18th century social philosophers John Locke and Jean Jacques Rousseau challenged both the Roman laws and the Code of Napoleon, arguing that children are innately innocent and susceptible to social corruption. They further postulated that the state had to be the guardian of children and that it was the state's responsibility to protect society's overall economic welfare and moral values.

The idea of *parens patriae* is that the state acts as the parents of the child and the state should not punish the children for their criminal behaviors or delinquency. Instead, the state should help the children to control themselves and prevent further juvenile delinquent acts. This philosophy of the state being the guardian of the child is strictly applied in western societies. In non-western societies, it was imported by the colonial hegemony.

The customary norms of non-western societies have always been that the parents discipline their children according to immemorial customs and traditions. From the Middle East to far eastern Asia and from Africa to South and Central America, parents discipline their children without state intervention.

The non-western societies are less industrialized and less urbanized than western societies. Undeniably, family cohesion is stronger in non-western societies than in western societies. Consequently, the rate of juvenile delinquency is higher in western industrialized countries than in non-western countries (Ebbe 1984, 1989, 2006). As a result of a high degree of family disorganization or a high degree of broken homes in western societies, child abuse is more prevalent in western nations than in non-western societies. This is because, in non-western societies, informal control mechanisms still apply in both rural and urban areas (Ebbe 1988, 1992, 2006).

Furthermore, the degree of child abuse across nations varies according to the degree of alcoholism and drug abuse in the families. Alcoholism and drunkenness, which are common features of industrialized countries, are very highly limited in most non-western societies. Certain forms of child abuse such as child abandonment, rape of a child, sexual molestation of a child, and incest are not common features of non-western societies. However, child labor, corporal punishment, assignment of roles too hard for the child's age, pledging a child for money borrowed (collateral), and child betrothal to get dowry to solve family financial problems are typical behaviors defined as child abuse in developed nations. However, in most non-western countries, those child deployments, from child labor to child betrothal are not regarded as abuses. Those forms of child dispositions in non-western societies are the inevitable outcomes and adjustments to the economic conditions of the society. Neither the parents and children nor society as a whole see such deployments of the child as child abuse.

Dependency and Vulnerability

Children are dependents of their parents or guardian until they are eighteen in most jurisdictions. They have no income and no residence of their own. Even children who work for wages in non-western societies give all of their wages to their parents. They live under the roof of their parents and must abide by the rules set by their parents. In non-western societies, no matter how draconian the rules are, the child remains with his parents and abides by those rules. In western countries, if the rules and conditions at home are not convenient to the child, he might head to the streets and run away from home and become vulnerable to abuse by drug peddlers and pedophiles.

The dependency of a child makes him vulnerable to abuse by any adult or other juveniles. In western elementary and high schools, especially in the United States, where school teachers, headmasters, and principals are barred from using corporal punishment to discipline a child, bullies frighten and hurt weak students and sometimes make them drop out of school. In most non-western societies, if not in all of them, when a bully threatens or hurts another child, he is given 6–12 lashes. In effect, bullying other children is not a common feature of schools in non-western societies. In fact, in Nigerian high schools, for any act of bullying, the student is dismissed from school indefinitely. Nigeria does not allow such cases to appear in its courts. Such cases are dealt with by the schools and parents. That is the way it is in most non-western countries.

Traditional Authority of Father and Mother

In all societies, customary standards and traditions guide parents in taking care of their children. Most parents love their children and try to provide for them. However, there are persons who should not be parents. Child neglect is a common feature of bad parenting. The case of Dave Pelzer referred to in Chapter 2 is a case example. His father had no moral courage to protect him from sadistic and monstrous treatments meted out to him by his cruel mother. Some parents all over the world do not know when to stop in a process of flogging their son or daughter. What should have been a minor disciplinary spanking becomes child abuse. In fact, in the 1970s, in Nigeria, a father was persistently provoked by his 12-year-old son so that he lost his temper and punched his son directly in his left eye. The young boy fell down and cried bitterly. That eye is deformed today. There was no 911 call or police intervention, even though 911 emergency assistance is available, because such outside interference is not a feature of the Nigerian social system. The father's action against his son was beyond customary discipline; that was child abuse.

Similarly, some mothers are not so kind to their children. Some mothers slap a 10-month-old baby for crying. Does that make sense? No, it does not. A 10-month-old baby cannot articulate why she is crying. Breast feeding is a normal expectation of all mothers in Nigeria up to the eighth or ninth month. In 1990, a mother refused to breast feed her five-month-old child, and refused to give her Similac or even water from 6:00 a.m. to 11:00 a.m., left the baby crying, and unattended, and forbade her husband from picking up the baby. That is depraved-heart child abuse. We have mothers who shake and throw a crying baby up and down as a way to make the baby stop crying. That also is child abuse.

Babies and children of alcoholic and drug-addicted mothers are neglected by their mothers more often than babies and children of non-alcoholics and non-drug addicts

Based on ethnographic observations, child abuse is inversely related to social class and level of education. Unmistakably, child abuse is more prevalent among the poor than among the rich. The poor are frustrated, and frustration leads to aggressive behavior. When a parent is frustrated about life around him or her, any minor deviancy of a child is negatively responded to out of proportion.

There are fathers and mothers who are insatiable about the behavior of their children at home. The more the child tries to satisfy the parents' expectations, the more she receives disapproval from one or both of them. For some children, this is torture. She comes to believe that her parents do not like her no matter what she does. This is emotional and psychological abuse. Children like to be praised. When they make a mistake, correctional measures should be in a rational manner, because children are very sensitive about approval or disapproval of their actions by their parents.

Nonbiological Parents or Guardians

When a child is living with a nonbiological parent or parents, it is like fishing in a large river. You do not know what type of fish you are going to catch or whether you are going to catch any fish at all. The child in such a family lives at the mercy of his guardian. Children in foster homes have a lot to tell about their experiences. Some have very good Christian foster parents, although some in the United States have nonchalant monsters who just want to use the child placed under their care to get a handout from the government.

Some children living with nonbiological parents are often starved to a point that some of them start to look for a way to escape. In fact, some have committed suicide. The worst treatment to a child is failing to feed her fully. Denying a child a meal as a form of punishment is an unpardonable abuse. Unfortunately, some nonbiological parents or guardians are pathologically wicked to their foster child, whom they view as a servant. There are house servants who cook their masters' food, but the wives of their masters will never allow them to have enough to eat. In the 1950s, as a house servant, my master's wife lied against me. I wondered why she lied against me, and I could not comprehend it. I was flogged repeatedly by my master for more than five minutes for something I did not do. I was only eight years old. I decided to run home to my parents who lived 22 miles away. When I had gone six miles, I was stopped by an ambush of my master's wife and a godson of her husband. My master was my father's first son and my half-brother Michael, and my half-brother's wife realized that my father would send her back to her parents if he saw the strokes of lashes on my back for a false accusation against me. My half-brother's wife made me realize how wicked some nonbiological parents could be to their servants or house maids.

Negligent Society

In many parts of the world, including rich and poor countries, there are street boys and girls. They are homeless. Why are children homeless in a country of plenty? Some of the children are homeless because either both parents are deceased and no relative is available to take care of them or they ran away from home to another city and roamed about as a result of a drug problem. Sometimes, their families are too poor to keep them at home, as is the case in Southeast Asia and some parts of India, Myanmar, and Thailand.

In countries such as Cambodia, Thailand, and Myanmar, children scavenge through discarded rotten food and clothes in stinking, open city dumps. What a national disgrace! Why can't the government of these countries force these children into an institution and take care of them? A country that allows the existence of homeless children is a travesty. In fact, homeless children are a magnet for international traffickers in women and children. Children's homelessness is a national abuse of children and contributes to the creation of a criminal market for sexual exploitation and molestation of children by adults and international sex tourists (Ebbe 2007).

Sexual Abuse of Children

Rape

Rape is defined as sexual intercourse with a woman without her consent. Therefore, any sexual intercourse with a female who is under 18, in most jurisdictions, with or without her consent, is defined as statutory rape. Undeniably, any sexual intercourse with a girl under 17 years of age, in most jurisdictions, is an abuse of the child. A girl who is not 17 or 18 is regarded as a minor who has not reached the age of reason so as to give consent.

In the same vein, any boy under 17 in some jurisdictions is a minor, and any sexual encounter with such a boy is defined as sexual molestation or sodomy. In fact, any sexual encounter with a boy is an abuse of the child. Sexual molestation and statutory rape of boys and girls have become common crimes in the United States.

In many non-western countries such as Myanmar, Thailand, and Cambodia, poverty has caused many male and female juveniles to make themselves available as street prostitutes. The use of cars as sexual rooms on the streets has become a global phenomenon, especially in European and North American cities.

Incestuous Fathers and Kin

Incest is an abomination in almost all cultures, but incestuous relationships between a father and a minor daughter are an empirical reality. In 1986, I gave a lecture in one of my classes at Delta State University in Cleveland, Mississippi, on "Index Crimes and Part II Crimes" and touched on the taboos surrounding incest. After that class period, one of my female students came to my office and told me that incest is a fact of life in the United States. Next, she pulled aside part of her gown and bra on her left chest area. What I saw was a deep scar that was approximately one-half inch deep. "What's that?" I shouted in astonishment. "My father shot me when I was 12 years old," she replied. "Why?" I asked. "He had been having sex with me since I was 9 years old, which was a painful molestation and exploitation. So when I was 12, I told him that I was going to tell my mama, and he shot me," she concluded. I was in total shock. I had never seen a victim of incest until that day. Since that time, I started reading crime columns in various newspapers. Since then, I have read about a lot of cases of incest in the United States.

Before the advent of European systems of punishment, among the Igbos of Nigeria incest was one of the abominations for which the customary disposition of the offender was to dedicate him to the gods, in which he became an untouchable or an outcast (what the Igbos call *osu*). This was worse than the death penalty. Furthermore, Igbos do not allow marriage between a man and a woman until after the third cousin; otherwise, it is an incestuous marriage and is declared null and void and *ultra vires*.

The father of the Delta State University student victim of incest was an alcoholic, she told me. Over the years, I have found out that, for the most part, cases of incest in the United States are caused by alcoholism or drunkenness and drug abuse. Some fathers, brothers, uncles, and first cousins sexually abuse their minor sisters and brothers and other relatives in the United States while under the influence of a controlled substance or alcohol.

In April 2008, a 72-year-old civil rights activist was convicted of incestuous rape in Alabama, when his 15-year-old daughter testified against him. In Amstetten, Austria, a 73-year-old man, Josef Fritzl, imprisoned his daughter in a cellar and sexually abused her repeatedly for 24 years (from 1984 to 2008). According to the victim, Elisabeth F., 42 years old as of April 2008, her father had been having sexual intercourse with her since she was 11 years old, and fathered her six children, all hidden in the cellar. When Elisabeth went missing in 1984 and the police investigated, Fritzl lied to the police and told them that his daughter had joined a cult. At some point, it is alleged that he impersonated Elisabeth in a phone call to his wife (*Chattanooga Times*

Free Press 2008). Fritzl was able to accomplish his criminal sexual scheme by being authoritarian. He banished his daughter and the children to the basement. His tenants were warned that the cellar was off limits and that nobody should take photos of the windowless, soundproofed rooms where he confined Elisabeth and the children. Austrian police said that three of the six children were registered with authorities and that they lived with their grandparents, but the other three children were held captive with their mother. The six children, three boys and three girls, ranged in age from 5 to 20 years old.

Josef Fritzl's sexual drive that compelled him to imprison his own daughter, despite his wife's presence in the household, attests to the motivation for some men to pay money to kidnap girls so that they can be locked away in private houses just for their sexual pleasure. It also attests to the prevalence of underground brothels in North America and Europe, brothels in which underage girls are dumped (28–30 of them at a time) in a 12 × 10 square foot room and forced to have sex with men two to three times their age (Ebbe 2007). On April 16, 2008, CNN reported that, in New Orleans, Louisiana, one Patrick Kennedy raped his eight-year-old stepdaughter. Based on court cases in the United States, stepfather-stepdaughter incestuous relationships are on the rise.

The same factors that are involved in precipitating father and daughter incestuous relationships also explain similar relationships between stepfathers, brothers, and half-brothers with stepdaughters, sisters, and half-sisters. Alcoholism, drunkenness, drug abuse and addiction, gross immorality, and poor judgment also account for these incestuous relationships.

A Sexually Obsessive and Perverted World

Traditionally, sexual intercourse was exclusively for procreation. In 1896 in Ada, Ohio, an 18-year-old woman (then defined as a "girl") was publicly condemned and hanged on an oak tree because she was pregnant without a husband. The stump of the oak tree and the rope with which she was hanged were preserved at the Ada central cemetery up to 1983, when I took a picture of it. Today, in the United States, Great Britain, Germany, and in most industrialized European countries, unwed mothers are maintained with taxpayers' money. The United States does not actively attempt to reduce the proliferation of unwed mothers. In effect, there are some women in the United States who bear children as an occupation, because she is put on "Section 8" or Aid to Families with Dependent Children (AFDC). Unfortunately, there are women in the United States who have four children, all from different irresponsible fathers. These unwed mothers produce sons who become irresponsible fathers and daughters who bear children as an occupation. In this type of environment, in which there are many sons and daughters without fathers, incestuous relationships abound between first cousins. In a sex-saturated society like the United States, genealogical limits of choice of sexual partners are virtually thrown out of the window, and the people are thrown into a legitimization crisis as to what is moral and immoral in a sexual partnership.

On Thursday, April 3, 2008, the NBC evening news reported that 90,000 children in the United States were abused in 2006. Based on local records, most of the abuses involved sexual molestation, statutory rape, or sodomy. On April 10, 2008, the Children's Advocacy Center, in the medium-sized city of Chattanooga, Tennessee, placed 477 pinwheels in the ground in front of the center at Vine Street. According to the office coordinator at the center, the 477 pinwheels represented the 477 alleged child abuse victims who the center helped in 2007. According to the center and police investigations in the city, "5 out of 6 cases of child abuse go unreported." Based on the records of the Children's Advocacy Center, 25 percent of abuses were by parents or stepparents, 23 percent were by relatives, 23 percent were by someone else the victim knew, 4 percent were by parents' boyfriends or girlfriends, and 25 percent were by total strangers (*Chattanooga Children's Advocacy Center* 2008). The data show that 75 percent of the abuse cases were perpetrated by someone the child knew, and nearly half were family members. Additionally, sexual and physical abuses scored the highest frequency in the data.

Sexual norms are being violated every day in almost every part of the world, especially in the United States and Europe. According to a research report at Emory University's Jane Fonda Center for Adolescent Reproductive Health, "Teens are bombarded by sex in media." The study indicates that "an average teen is exposed to sexual messages in the media five hundred thousand times by the time he or she is 18 years of age" (*Chattanooga Times Free Press* 2008).

The high demand for sex by both men and women has reached epidemic proportions. Most families can no longer control their girls and boys, and many adults are setting bad examples. In America, we may have exceeded the immorality of Sodom and Gomorrah in our sexual pervasiveness.

Institutionalization of Juvenile Offenders

In various countries, orphans and juveniles who commit certain offenses are institutionalized. There are orphanages all over the world, and many countries have reformatories or juvenile correctional facilities. These institutions are centers of child abuse. Many of the institutionalized boys and girls are abused by their keepers sexually and physically. Also, some of these institutionalized children, who have no parental or guardian connection, are sold into slavery or severely mistreated at the institution to the point that they run away, join a population of homeless street kids, and become hookers. Unmistakably, some are trafficked to the underground world of sexual orgies and debauchery. They will never be seen again or never be recognized by someone who knew them.

Unfortunately, in institutions for children, when they are sexually abused, children are afraid to report the abuse to another person. In developing countries or third-world societies, there is another form of child abuse. The most painful type of abuse of children is giving them tasks that are too hard for their age. Furthermore, many are forced to work longer hours with little or no food in these third-world countries, and they are housed in very unsanitary conditions. Authorities in those countries do not care for the health of the children.

In juvenile correctional facilities all over the world, one can see so many incorrigible children. They have "devil may care" attitudes. These types of kids are the most frequently abused physically. Sometimes, the custodians use "denying them regular meals" as a mechanism to bring them under control. Some incorrigible kids are bullies, and, whenever they are penalized by the custodians, they turn around and abuse other kids.

The Economics of Child Abuse

One of the most important causes of child abuse is economic conditions. All over the world, parents, guardians, and relatives can abuse their own children to achieve an economic end. In Southeast Asia, some parents sell their children to get money to feed other children in the family. Also, some parents in Southeast Asia and depressed economies in other parts of the world guide their minor daughters into prostitution to survive (Ebbe 2007).

Undeniably, even in some industrialized, wealthy countries like the United States, some mothers take their 15- to 17-year-old daughters on prostitution trips, hopping from bar to bar and from brothel to brothel as a means of economic survival (Ebbe 2007). It does not matter to the mother whether her minor daughter likes the business or not. The child is simply coached and brainwashed to believe that she and her mom have no other way to survive other than to sell their bodies. Some of these crooked mothers demand an extra amount of money from their own boyfriends for them to have sexual activities with their minor daughter or daughters.

Unmistakably, some prostitutes in third-world countries of Africa South of the Sahara, Central and South America, India, and Southeast Asia who have daughters introduce their daughters into the life of prostitution before the child is 12 years old and demand higher amount of money than usual from their clients to take the virginity of their daughters (Ebbe 2007).

The basic principle of capitalist business is to maximize profit. In effect, child labor and child slave labor are rife throughout Asia, Africa, and Central and South America. Children are not paid as highly as adults when they work for wages in third-world countries. Also, in third-world economies, children are often deployed in slave labor. They are not paid at all. The employer purchases the boy or girl from a trafficker or from a parent or guardian (Ebbe 2007). Throughout the cocoa and rubber plantations in West Africa and Southwest Africa, including Equatorial Guinea, child labor and slave labor have been rife since the colonial times.

The incidence of child labor is typical of very populous Asian countries. According to the *Chattanooga Times Free Press* (2008), more than 100 children are taken from suspected slave work conditions in factories near Hong Kong. The Chinese government is investigating whether hundreds or probably thousands of children from poor southwest regions of the country were sold to work as slave laborers in fast-growing coastal factory urban centers. Government officials from Southern Guangdong province claimed to have "rescued more than 100 children from factories in the city of Donguan, a huge manufacturing center known for producing and exporting toys, textiles and electronics (*Chattanooga Times Free Press* 2008). According to the *Chattanooga Times Free Press*, the children were between the ages of 13 and 15 and were often tricked or kidnapped by employment agencies working in the indigent region of Western Sichuan province. Some of the children are said to be working 300 hours a month for a very little amount of money. A report from Shanghai, China, confirms that "some children are even sold by their parents, who often don't have any idea of the working conditions."

Throughout developing countries, employment of children by parents and relatives to do adult work as a means of economic survival is a normative practice. Like a mother subjecting her daughter to prostitution as a means of survival, some fathers and mothers allow their sons and daughters to be involved in what amounts to slave labor to add to the family income to survive. This state of affairs is rife and inevitable in overpopulated countries like China, India, and Indonesia and depressed economies like those in Nigeria, Sierra Leone, Gambia, Cameroon, Chad, and Sudan.

Sex in Cyberspace

The abuse of children has been taken to cyberspace. Many children are lured into pornographic postures, which are then posted on the Internet. Child pornography, especially for teenagers under 17, is a fast-growing business on the Internet. As a result of poverty, some single mothers make their children available for pornography and pornographic displays in cyberspace. There is no second thought about how the child will feel when she grows up and sees a pornographic photo of herself. Like teenage prostitution, some juveniles are enticed to pornography with money.

Children from Indonesia, Thailand, Cambodia, and other parts of Southeast Asia are the most exploited in the pornographic market. Sex tourism does not stop with having sex with minors. Some of the adult male sex tourists from western societies have been caught with pornographic photos of the boys and girls they victimized. Unfortunately, there are markets for child pornography. Furthermore, some sex tourists and Chinese mafia mobs (Yakuza, Triads, Yardies, and Tongs) ship videos of child pornography to North America and Europe.

Third-world countries have no market for child pornographic videos and photos. Although some third-world countries, especially Indonesia, Taiwan, Thailand, Cambodia, and India, use their children in pornographic videos and photos, those videos and photos are virtually not sold in the same countries. For instance, anybody coming or returning to Nigeria from another country found with a pornographic magazine, whether an adult or child pornographic magazine, is arrested at the port of entry and sent to a nearby jail without trial.

In many third-world countries, especially countries in Africa and the Middle East, pornography is unthinkable, because their customary norms and traditions prohibit sexual deviancy and pornography is unimaginable.

In the United States, unlike adult pornographic images, the First Amendment does not protect the possession or distribution of child pornography. Images that depict children engaged in sexual conduct is "a category of material outside of protection of the First Amendment" (*New York v. Ferber*, 458 U.S. 747, 1982). The First Amendment protects child pornography in the area of images in a medical textbook that displays child's genitalia (http://www.adultweblaws.com).

Unmistakably, the United States Code provides very stiff and severe penalties against sexual exploitation of children and child pornography (Protection of Children against Sexual Exploitation Act of 1977). Title 18 of the United States Code governs child pornography, Sec. 2251 governs sexual exploitation of children, and 18 U.S. Code, Sec. 2256 defines child pornography as follows:

> …any visual depiction, including any photograph, file, video, picture, or computer or computer-generated image or picture, whether made or produced by electronic, mechanical, or other means, of sexually explicit conduct, where—
>
> a) the production of such visual depiction involves the use of a minor engaging in sexually explicit conduct;
> b) such visual depiction is, or appears to be, of a minor engaging in sexually explicit conduct;
> c) such visual depiction has been created, adapted, or modified to appear that an identifiable minor is engaging in sexually explicit conduct; or

d) such visual depiction is advertised, promoted, presented, described, or distributed in such a manner that conveys the impression that the material is or contains a visual depiction of a minor engaging in sexually explicit conduct...

The U.S. Federal Statute also defines a "minor" as "any person under the age of 18 years" and "sexually explicit conduct" as actual or simulated, as follows:

a) sexual intercourse, including genital-genital, oral-genital, anal-genital, or
b) oral-anal, whether between persons of the same or opposite sex;
c) bestiality;
d) masturbation;
e) sadistic or masochistic abuse; or
f) lascivious exhibition of the genitals or pubic area of any person....Sexual intercourse and bestiality (sex with an animal) seem pretty clear—if your website displays images that a prosecutor believes involve minors engaged in sexual intercourse or bestiality, expect to be prosecuted. . . .

The U.S. law punishes child pornography with imprisonment of 15 to 30 years and may involve a fine. Still, some people are not deterred by the severity of punishment imposed by the U.S. laws. Even American citizens and immigrants who are involved in sex tourism face severe penalties in federal courts when they return to the United States, because such acts are in violation of Chapter 109A of the federal statute.

The United States crackdown on sex tourism gave rise to increased sex in cyberspace with minors within the United States territory. Cell phone sex talk with minors has grown beyond control in the United States and Japan. Some television investigative journalists have been able to entrap many shameless adults more than once who were trying to physically engage in sex with minors. The intended sexual encounters usually started in cyberspace.

Undeniably, there are criminal groups who specialize in arranging for telephone sex talks between their clients and girls who are 14 to 17 years of age. Telephone sex talk has become a very big business in North America and Europe, and it is very difficult to control. In fact, there are very few countries with laws controlling telephone sex talk. The problem is, how can one government agency monitoring such conversations know when such talks involve a minor? Besides, when a minor is involved, it is a deviance between two consenting individuals. Therefore, it is very hard to control such a crime in cyberspace, because there is no complainant.

Children and young girls involve themselves in cybersex because there is a clear degree of anonymity that dispels shyness and shame. Some adults exploit these children without some parents knowing that their minor daughter is involved in sex talk over the phone. Some young girls who ran away from home to become child prostitutes started with sex in cyberspace.

Globalization and Criminal Abuse of Children

Globalization is the relaxation of requirements in international communication among the nations of the world in land, sea, and air travel, including integration of economic activities, trade, culture, and political systems. Globalization is an attempt to create a global village through treaties and social cultural exchanges. In effect, international traveling visas have become easily obtainable.

The jet age and the computer, cell phone, and Internet revolutions have brought the nations of the world very close to each other. In effect, crime in cyberspace, including sex in cyberspace, has become a multibillion dollar industry. Undoubtedly, children have become the victims of globalization. According to the United Nations International Children's Emergency Fund (UNICEF), more than one million children are missing every year. The rate of international kidnapping, stealing, and selling of children rises every year.

Globalization has created a large market for child prostitution. Undeniably, globalization, in combination with natural disasters such as tsunamis and earthquakes, wars in many parts of the world, and the collapse of the former Soviet Union, made child prostitution inevitable in many parts of the world. Unmistakably, there is no country in the world that is immune to child prostitution, including the wealthy nations and the religious Middle East.

Conclusion

As far back as written accounts record, children have been abused by their fathers, mothers, stepfathers, stepmothers, guardians, brothers, sisters, and kin. Not even in the Roman Empire were children treated with any degree of presumed innocence. The Roman emperors and the Roman society were sadistic and cruel, and children were not excluded from their cruelty (Masters and Lea 1963). Unfortunately, generations transmit their cultural practices and traditions to the next generation. In effect, some of the primitive values of the Dark Ages have found outlets in the minds of modern man.

In this vein, the Civil Code of Napoleon was not sympathetic to women and children. Before the Code, women and children were treated just like in the Dark Ages. The code did little to ameliorate the tyrannical rule of the husband over his wife and of the father over his children. The code, in agreement with Roman law, gave the husband full control over the family as a pivotal machinery of moral discipline and social order.

Children have always been dependents, and they are vulnerable to all sorts of abuses in the hands of their parents, guardians, kin, and strangers. Parents and guardians have traditional authority over the children. In modern times, many parents have abused their exclusive authority by drowning their children, setting them on fire, strangling them, or beating them to death. Some nonbiological parents take advantage of their children, too. They receive public aid to take care of children, but they do not use this money for its intended purpose. Still others beat and starve their charges to death, whereas others sexually molest and emotionally abuse them.

In many countries of the world, both rich and poor ones, some children are neglected. The most heartrending is when children starve in a country of plenty. Sexual abuse of children worldwide has reached epidemic proportions. Incestuous fathers and kin are on the rise; those who should protect the children are the ones who are destroying them.

The world has become sex obsessed and perverted, making Sodom and Gomorrah look saintly in the eyes of contemporary society. Institutionalization of juveniles in correctional facilities and orphanages has made them supply centers for pedophiles, sex tourists, and human traffickers.

The security of children all over the world has been jeopardized by economic conditions, globalization, and advances in cyberspace technology. In the next chapter, the way to eliminate the dangers women and children face in modern society is delineated.

References

Associated Press. 2008 "In Amstetten, Austria, 73-Year-Old Man Fathered Six of His Daughter's Children." *Chattanooga Times Free Press*, April 10.

Bala, N. 1989. "Double Victims: Child Sexual Abuse and the Criminal Justice System." Paper presented at the Annual Education Institute, Criminal Law Program of the Canadian Bar Association–Ontario.

Durant, W., and Durant, A. 1975. *The Age of Napoleon: A History of European Civilization, 1789–1815*. New York: Simon and Schuster.

Ebbe, O. N. I. 1984. "Ecological Distribution of Juvenile Delinquency in Metropolitan Lagos." *International Journal of Comparative and Applied Criminal Justice* 8(2):187–198.

Ebbe, O. N. I. 1988. "The Juvenile Justice System in Southern Nigeria." *International Journal of Comparative and Applied Criminal Justice* 12(2):191–204.

Ebbe, O. N. I. 1989. "Crime and Delinquency in Metropolitan Lagos: A Study of Crime and Delinquency Area Theory." *Social Forces* 67:751–765.

Ebbe, O. N. I. 1992. "Juvenile Delinquency in Nigeria: The Problem of Application of Western Theories." *International Journal of Comparative and Applied Criminal Justice* 16(2):352–370.
Ebbe, O. N. I. 2006. "The Juvenile Justice System in Nigeria." In *Delinquency and Juvenile Justice Systems in the Non-Western World*, edited by P. Friday and X. R. Monsey. New York: Criminal Justice Press.
Ebbe, O. N. I. 2007. "Introduction: An Overview of Trafficking Women and Children." In *Global Trafficking in Women and Children*, edited by O. N. I. Ebbe and D. K. Das. Boca Raton, FL: CRC Press/Taylor & Francis Group.
Masters, R. E. L., and Lea, E. 1963. *Sex Crimes in History: Evolving Concepts of Sadism, Lust-Murder, and Necrophilia—from Ancient to Modern Times.* New York: Julian Press.
New York v. Ferber. 1982. 458 U.S. 747.

4 Control and Prevention of Criminal Abuse of Women and Children: Domestic and International Approaches

OBI N. I. EBBE

Modern man is a civilized man compared with man in ancient and medieval societies. In modern times, the Enlightenment thinkers coupled with the provocative writings and ideas of John Locke (1632–1704), Jean Jacques Rousseau (1712–1778), Jeremy Bentham (1748–1832), Cesare Beccaria (1738–1794), and Charles Montesquieu (1689–1755) brought about legal and political civilization. These Enlightenment thinkers restored the dignity of man from the sadism and absolutism of the medieval and early modern monarchies. In fact, all of them, especially John Locke and Jean Jacques Rousseau, profoundly recognized the innocence of the child.

Informal Control Mechanisms

In rural towns and villages of third-world countries, custom and tradition have determined routine behaviors for men, women, and children. The social structure and close kinship residential patterns allow brothers, sisters, uncles, and cousins to immediately intervene when an adult is physically battering his wife, sister, son, or daughter. Nobody pulls a gun or knife against a relative or a stranger who intervenes to make peace, when a person is manhandling or beating up another. Police are not invited into family violence. Neighbors stop the conflict and settle the problem according to their customary standards.

In urban centers of many third-world societies, residential patterns are according to ties of consanguinity. In effect, family conflicts are settled as if the family were living in its rural village. Children in third-world countries can be corrected or protected by any relative, neighbor, or concerned stranger in situations of physical abuse.

In most of these third-world countries, especially those of Africa, Asia, and the Middle East, incestuous abuses of women and children are customarily an abomination punishable with ostracism and expulsion from the society. In some of these societies, before the offender is expelled, he must pay a heavy fine. In many parts of Africa, especially eastern Nigeria and western Cameroon, the expulsion is preceded by setting the man's house ablaze.

In traditional Igbo society of Nigeria, before the advent of the Europeans, an incestuous offender, as mentioned earlier, was dedicated to the gods and became an *osu* (untouchable)—a thing set apart, an outcast, and an abomination himself. This Igbo method of punishing incestuous offenders was condemned and stopped in the late 1800s by the Christianity of the European colonial hegemony (Achebe 1959).

Still, some informal control mechanisms are preserved in many other aspects of human deviancy in third-world societies. For instance, in 1996, one Otokoto and his son, Obidiozo, had a three-building hotel (three, five, and six stories each, one behind the other) in the Amakohia part of the city of Owerri in the Imo State of Nigeria. It happened that Otokoto had been selling human body parts since 1976. In 1996, he had his guards at his hotel lure a 12-year-old orange hawker to the hotel under the pretence that they wanted to buy oranges from him. The boy happily responded. When the boy, with his merchandise on his head, walked into the central lounge of the hotel, the guards immediately grabbed him, closed his mouth, and carried him to their upstairs killing room, just like the guards of Countess Elisabeth Bathony or Catherine La Voisin in the early 1600s. They killed the boy, took his liver, head, genitalia, and a few other body parts, and buried the rest of the body in Otokoto's private graveyard in his village near the city.

After one month, a relative with whom the boy lived reported that he had not come home, and the police in Owerri launched a search for the boy, whom many people knew in the city for hawking oranges. With a tip from "area boys" (unemployed city vigilantes), the police confronted Otokoto, and, after torturous interrogations, he allowed the police to search his hotel. The police found a freezer filled with all kinds of human body parts, camouflaged with goat meat.

Otokoto and his son were arrested, and the police demanded to know where the bodies of the men, women, and children whose body parts were in the freezer had been buried. Then Otokoto took them to his village of birth and orientation and showed them where he buried the bodies and camouflaged the area with newly planted orange trees.

The moment people in Owerri learned what Otokoto's business was and that he was arrested by the police, they did not trust the police. In fact, in the traditional way, they went and burned the three hotel buildings and bulldozed the walls. Next, they went to Otokoto's village of birth and drove away all of his parents, uncles, and close cousins. Otokoto's relatives had to move to Lagos, Nigeria, which is more than 400 miles from their village home

(Anueyiagu 1997; Eke 1997; Ebbe 1999, 2003, 2007). Otokoto and his son were convicted by the Nigerian formal justice system and executed.

Religious Intervention

Mainstream religions have strong doctrines protecting women and children. Every major religion prescribes standard rules of conduct between husband and wife, parents and their children, and members' fair treatment of others, including children. As Emile Durkheim put it in 1958, "Society is religion and religion is society." Every religion has the responsibility of protecting children, because children are the future of every society and the future of every religion.

Unfortunately, some religious sects and cults abused women and children, too, as pointed out in previous chapters. The role of religion, as an order-maintaining institution in individual homes, is stronger in underdeveloped countries than in more advanced economies.

Criminal Codes of Nations

Every member country of the United Nations (UN) has laws protecting women and children. The only problem is that the laws are not enforced equally stringently in all countries. The U.S. Code Sec. 2251A prohibits "selling or buying of children." Also, every state in the United States has laws against spousal abuse. In the United States, some men have found themselves behind bars for battering or assaulting their wives. Simple assault and aggravated assault are taken very seriously in the United States, especially when the victim is a woman or a child. Unfortunately, in underdeveloped countries, the police are not very sympathetic to the woman when she is battered by her husband. Very few cases of family violence reach the courts in underdeveloped countries.

The issue of sexual exploitation of children all over the world has prompted the UN to take immediate control measures since the 1970s. The UN convened the Convention on the Rights of the Child and, over a period of 10 years (from 1979 to 1989), got input from delegates from all societies, religions, and cultures. On November 20, 1989, the UN General Assembly unanimously adopted the Convention on the Rights of the Child. In unequivocal terms, the convention condemned sexual exploitation of minors in prostitution, exploitative use of children in pornographic performances and materials, abduction, sale, and trafficking of children, and all sorts of unlawful sexual practices (United Nations International Children's Emergency Fund [UNICEF] 1999). All member countries of the UN, who were signatories to the resolution, based their laws against child sexual exploitation on this document.

After the Convention on the Rights of the Child, the First World Congress against Commercial Sexual Exploitation of Children was convened in 1996 in Stockholm, Sweden, to develop strategies for an international response to the epidemic of child prostitution and trafficking (Klain 1999). The 1996 convention called for governments and national, regional, and international nongovernment organizations (NGOs) to be involved in the fight against the commercial sexual exploitation of children. The convention also sought cooperation for the prevention of the exploitation of children, the protection of children, and the recovery and rehabilitation of rescued children (Klain 1999).

The Second World Congress on Commercial Exploitation of Children was held in December 2001 and was hosted by the Government of Japan in Yokohama. It was attended by representatives of 35 UN member states who did not attend the First World Congress. The main purpose of the Second World Congress was to ensure that the 159 member states who were signatories to the accord strongly committed themselves to the agreed line of action and check into loopholes in the designed lines of action to fight against commercial sexual exploitation of children (End Child Prostitution, Child Pornography, and Trafficking of Children for Sexual Purposes, ECPAT 2001; also see http://www.ecpat.net/EI/index.asp).

Virtually every country in the world has been alerted to the hideous crime of child prostitution and trafficking. Many countries that are destination or supply countries have passed severely punitive laws to slow down the influx of sex tourists and protect their children from sexual exploitation, but the fundamental etiologies of child prostitution make the protective efforts of the governments a futile endeavor.

The governments of Southeast Asian countries have passed legislations and set up special law enforcement units to tackle the problem of sex tourism to prevent foreign "child sex tourists" from sexually abusing and exploiting their children (Klain 1999). Furthermore, the Czech Republic has passed a law for prosecuting persons who are engaged in child trafficking. The Criminal Code of Germany was amended in 1993 to allow prosecution of Germans who travel for the purpose of sexual exploitation of children, regardless of where the act occurs (Klain 1999). In the Crime (Child Sex Tourism) Amendment Act of 1994, Australia criminalizes sexual intercourse with a person younger than 16 years of age whether in Australia or outside of Australia (http://www.missingkids.com).

In West Africa, countries such as Nigeria, Ghana, and the Ivory Coast have set up government strike forces that track down individuals and organized crime groups who engage in trafficking in human beings domestically and internationally. These countries also have NGOs who team up with the government strike forces to rescue children and women who are being smuggled out of the countries.

The Role of NGOs in Controlling Criminal Abuse

The lure of children into prostitution has deeply touched many religious organizations and other NGOs. These women and children, who are subjected to the life of prostitution are, invariably, denied their basic human rights when pimps force them to sell their bodies anytime and anywhere with indignity. Under this state of affairs, many individuals, Christian groups, and associations of women have established organizations to save children who are entrapped in this hideous sexual enterprise.

Today, there are many NGOs in every industrialized country and in every major developing country in Africa, Asia, Europe, and North and South America designed to fight exploitation of women and children. These NGOs have worked with governments and UN agencies, such as International Organization for Migration, UNICEF, International Labor Organization, International Scientific and Professional Advisory Council (ISPAC) of the United Nations Crime Prevention and Criminal Justice Programs, United Nations Office on Drug Control (UNODC), World Health Organization, United Nations Interregional Crime and Justice Research Institute (UNICRI), and the UNODC Global Programme against Trafficking in Human Beings (GPAT), to come up with viable solutions to end or ameliorate ruthless trafficking in women and children for sexual exploitation, slave labor, child labor, body parts trading, and sex bondage.

Although many societies still have a long way to go, the UN, governments, and humanitarian NGOs, including Amnesty International, are determined to control and prevent this inhuman trade (Ebbe 2003). The UN, through UNODC, has set up a program to deal with human trafficking. GPAT was designed by UNODC in collaboration with UNICRI and was launched in March 1999 to assist member states in their efforts to combat human trafficking, especially women and children. GPAT targets the involvement of organized crime syndicates in human trafficking and promotes the development of effective methods to catch perpetrators (Ebbe 2003). Although GPAT assists UN member states in cracking down on human trafficking, the key components in its efforts are data collection, assessment, and technical cooperation. With the cooperation of UNICRI, data are collected on various smuggling routes and the methods used by organized criminal syndicates for trafficking in women and children. GPAT also keeps a database containing trafficking trends, routes, and information about victims and traffickers to assist policy makers, practitioners, researchers, and the NGO community (Ebbe 2003) (http://www.humantrafficking.org).

Furthermore, UNODC gives direct assistance to specific countries that are ravaged by poverty and human trafficking. Presently, UNODC is helping the Vietnamese judicial system and law enforcement agencies improve their ability to combat human trafficking in Vietnam. Also, some agencies of the UN have given grants to many NGOs for fighting against this global sexual abuse of women and children.

In the United States, the National Center for Missing and Exploited Children (NCMEC) is open 24 hours a day to receive information on exploited children. NCMEC solicits reports of child sexual exploitation (1-800-843-5678 or www.cybertipline.com) and advises the public to call the police whenever a victim is identified. NCMEC reminds, "a child lost to prostitution is still a missing child" (http://www.cybertipline.com).

In support of NCMEC, the U.S. Congress mandated CyberTipline as a mechanism for reporting "cases of child sexual exploitation, including child pornography, online enticement of children for sex acts, molestation of children outside the family, sex tourism of children, child victims of prostitution, and unsolicited obscene material sent to a child" (http://www.cybertipline.com).

The united efforts of the NGOs, the UN, governments, other agencies, and investigative journalism have helped tremendously in making arrests and reducing the rate of trafficking in women and children for slave labor, prostitution, and wholesale exploitation of children.

Obstacles to Effective Control of Criminal Abuse

The persistence of abject poverty in different parts of the world, caused by poor economic conditions, sporadic occurrences of natural disasters that drive people out of their homes, civil wars and totalitarian regimes that create refugees, and globalization weaken all of the efforts made to prevent and ameliorate the degree of trafficking in women and children. Furthermore, all member states of the UN are not on the same page when it comes to enforcement of the laws promulgated to eliminate criminal abuse of women and children. Many third-world countries are not good at stringent enforcement of their laws because of wholesale corruption. Furthermore, in advanced economies, plea bargaining weakens the seriousness of the offense and the effectiveness of the reduced penalty for the crime.

Undeniably, the existence of legalized brothels in many wealthy countries impedes effective control of sexual abuse of women and children. Those wealthy countries where there are legalized brothels in Europe, Asia, and Australasia are the destination countries for trafficking in women and children, whereas Southeast Asia is the destination for child sex tourism because their governments need the tourists' western currency to boost up their economy. In Africa, South America, and Mexico, brothels are illegal but they operate without any meaningful government intervention. In poor countries, like those in Southeast Asia, no reason for stringent enforcement of the laws against prostitution, even underage prostitution.

In third-world countries, even a lawmaker may own some illegal brothels, with girls as young as 13 years old. It is illegal, but no police officer will venture to make arrests or try to close the brothel. Brothels can be seen in many streets of large urban centers of third-world nations. In advanced economies, many families are broken. Many of the young girls leave home to find the happiness that is no longer in their own homes. Many of them are into drugs and alcohol, making them unmindful of death in their pursuit of happiness. Unmistakably, obstacles to effective control of criminal abuse of women and children are ubiquitous. There is no country in the world that is free from various obstacles that impinge on effective control of criminal abuse of women and children.

Conclusion

Physical, emotional, and sexual abuse of women and children have been in existence from time immemorial. Modern existence has ameliorated the degree of some of those abuses. However, modern society is still haunted by the ghosts of the Dark Ages. Peter Kurten, Countess Elisabeth Bathony, Catherine La Voisin, Jack the Ripper, Zingua of Angola, Ted Bundy, Charles Manson, John Wayne Gacy, Andrei Chikatilo, and Jeffrey Dahmer are all modern day slaughterers of women and children. Modern society, however, has developed laws and mechanisms to control and apprehend monstrous sadists and pedophiles and has succeeded in driving them underground.

Mass education is essential in cutting down the sexual appetites of men and women worldwide. Children need meaningful education about the modus operandi of traffickers in women and children. Governments must have rigid limits about cybersex or ban it completely. Governments, religious organizations, and families must band together to cut down the spread of sexual deviancy across the globe. The UN, governments, and NGOs are fighting hard to control this monstrous sexual epidemic, but their efforts thus far are not enough. They must enact more stiff measures than those already in place.

It is a mistake for anybody to think that trafficking in women and girls will be eliminated. There is too much money involved in the practice. Trying to eliminate trafficking in women is like trying to eliminate drug smuggling when the market is so readily available. Trafficking in women and girls involves billions of dollars annually. Cooperative efforts are needed among governments to bring the crime to the lowest minimum. However, international policy makers should note that, in a situation in which some government leaders run with the hare and hunt with the hounds, controlling trafficking in women and children is impossible (Ebbe 2003, 2007). Additionally, prostitution network associations are opposed to anti-trafficking laws in countries with legal brothels. These are some of the obstacles in fighting trafficking and criminal abuse of women and children. Despite the obstacles to control and prevent the criminal abuse of women and children, we cannot give up trying to stop the criminals, because protecting women and children from criminal sexual exploitation ensures a humane society and a better posterity.

Finally, law enforcement agencies of all nations must be made morally responsible in enforcing the laws against trafficking and abuse of women and children. Punishment for involvement in trafficking in women and children by a law enforcement officer should be made as severe as to include a life sentence without parole. Many countries have passed legislations against trafficking in women and children, but there is no stringent enforcement of those laws.

Additionally, nations of the world should tackle the problem of poverty. The UN and more developed countries should help to reduce poverty in many regions of the world if trafficking and abuse of women and children is to be reduced. This approach is necessary, because some poor parents sell some of their children whereas others encourage their daughters to engage in prostitution as a way to survive poverty. Absolute poverty can lead to depraved-heart crimes and acts of mindboggling complexity.

Governments all over the world should develop strict screening methods for legally licensing adoptive parents. So many children have been killed, raped, starved, sold, emotionally destroyed, and sexually exploited by adoptive parents. Penalties for an adoptive parent abusing a child should be made more severe than presently in statutes, and a speedy trial and disposition of the offender is a key to the effectiveness of the penalty. Government authorities should be wary when allowing a single person to adopt a child; it has not been proven that lesbians and homosexuals adopting children contribute positively to a moral society.

This study has provided some insight into the history and present global scope of criminal abuse of women and children. It is not possible to cover all aspects of abuse of women and children because of cost and time. Also, this account presents an international perspective. It is therefore possible that some areas of abuses of women and children have not been covered in the first part of this book. This weakness, however, has not obliterated the relevance of this scholarly endeavor. The second part of this book presents case studies of criminal abuse of women and children in selected countries of the world.

References

Achebe, C. 1959. *Things Fall Apart*. New York: McDowell Obolensky.

Anueyiagu, A. 1997. "Nsukka Gripped by Otokoto Saga: A Six-Year-Old Boy Escapes Kidnap." *This Day*, January 4.

Ebbe, O. N. I. 1999. "The Political-Criminal Nexus: Slicing Nigerian National Cake: The Nigerian Case." *Trends in Organized Crime* 4(3):29–59.

Ebbe, O. N. I. 2003. "Slicing Nigeria's National Cake." In *Menace to Society: Political-Criminal Collaborations around the World*, edited by R. Godson. New Brunswick, NJ: Transaction Publishers.

Ebbe, O. N. I. 2007. "Introduction: An Overview of Trafficking Women and Children." In *Global Trafficking in Women and Children*, edited by O. N. I. Ebbe and D. K. Das. Boca Raton, FL: CRC Press/Taylor & Francis Group.

Eke, E. 1997. "Ripples of Otokoto Rock Aba." *The Guardian*, January 12.

End Child Prostitution, Child Pornography, and Trafficking of Children for Sexual Purposes. 2001. http://www.ecpat.net/EI/index.asp, accessed May 6, 2008.

Klain, E. J. 1999. *Prostitution of Children and Child-Sex Tourism: An Analysis of Domestic and International Responses.* Alexandria, VA: National Center for Missing and Exploited Children.

National Center for Missing and Exploited Children. http://www.missingkids.com, accessed May 6, 2008.

Perspectives from Europe

II

5 Criminal Exploitation of Women and Children: An Austrian Perspective

MAXIMILIAN EDELBACHER

Facts on Austria

Population

Austria is a democratic republic and, since January 1995, a member of the European Union. Covering an area of 84,000 square kilometers, Austria is a relatively small country situated in the heart of Europe. Of its eight million inhabitants, 750,000 are foreigners.[1] Austria's capital, Vienna, is situated in the eastern part of the country and has a population of six million.

Political Structure

Austria became a democracy in 1945. After the end of World War II, Austria was possessed by the winners of the war. In 1955, Austria became free. Today, four parties are active. The People's Party and the Freedom Party are conservative parties and built a coalition government. The opposition parties are the Social Democratic Party and the Green Party.[2]

Security Structure

The Austrian Police are headed by the Federal Ministry of the Interior. They are divided into two departments: (1) the federal police that operate in 14 large cities, and (2) the federal Gendarmerie that operate in the rural areas, the state police, and the criminal police.[3] The majority of police officers are employed by either the federal police or by the federal Gendarmerie (Pavol and Czeslaw 2001) and have a strength of 16,051 and 15,083, respectively. The complete security structure will be changed. The idea is to unify the police and Gendarmerie. Eventually, there will be only one force, the police.

Constitution and Policing

After the breakdown of the Austro-Hungarian monarchy, the Austrian Federal Constitution was established in 1920 by Kelsen and was essentially modified by a Constitutional Amendment in 1929. Therefore, today the constitution is a federal one. Austria consists of nine "Bundesländer" (federal provinces). Jurisdictions are divided between the Federal Government and the nine Bundesländer. Communities form a third force. The main principles of the constitution are the separation of powers and protection of human rights. Legislation, administration, and the judiciary are separated from each other (Edelbacher and Norden 2000). Police and security institutions are bound to administration and the judiciary. The justice system is based on the fundamentals of investigating the material truth.

Crimes in Austria

Until the fall of the "Iron Curtain" in 1989, Austria had a rather stable crime situation. Afterward, the first wave of crime between 1989 and 1992 showed an increase in the number of crimes. In 1992, more than 504,000 crimes were reported, an increase of more than 100,000 cases than five years earlier. The second wave of crime showed the challenge of the quality of crime. Organized criminal groups from the former Eastern Bloc countries, especially from Russia, tried to establish themselves in Austria. Today, Austria is confronted with a third wave of crime. This is a wave of quantity of crime, because Austria is situated on the border between rather poor and rich countries.

Crime Development

In Austria, since the fall of the Iron Curtain in 1989, crimes increased steadily, with short periods of decrease. In 1992, it was the first time that more than a half million crimes appeared in Austria. Since the conservative government took over in 2001, crime increased dramatically, and, in 2003, more than 660,000 offenses were reported. The clearance rate dropped dramatically, to less than 40 percent. That had never happened in Austria. There is usually a clearance rate of 49–52 percent.

Table 5.1 Crime Statistics by the Ministry of the Interior

Year	Austria	Vienna
1999	493,246	154,296
2000	516,929	163,210
2001	522,710	180,026
2002	591,784	211,547
2003	654,381	258,929

Source: Aahs Manfred, Austrian Ministry of the Interior, Official Statistics of Registered Offenses in Austria and Vienna in the Years 1999–2003.

Table 5.2 Violent Crimes: Crime Statistics by the Ministry of the Interior

Year	Austria	Vienna
1999	32,008	9,706
2000	34,311	10,246
2001	29,606	9,070
2002	31,348	9,399

Source: Aahs Manfred, Austrian Ministry of the Interior, Official Statistics of Registered Offenses in Austria and Vienna in the Years 1999–2002.

Violent crimes do not show such a clear picture. There are always "ups and downs" in the appearance of violent crime. Murder cases decreased greatly since 2002, especially in Vienna. The situation is very different with violent crimes. Although demographic statistics show a drop in the percentage of people under 25 years, violence is on an increase. A multitude of factors are responsible for this development, including an increase in unemployment, worsening of living conditions, higher percentage of foreigners (especially illegal immigrants), and less social coverage for poorer people.

Crimes against Women and Children

The society and the political authorities became very much aware that violence against women and children is a main threat and that something has to be done about it. In 1999, legal measures against "violence in the family" were passed in the parliament to repress and prevent violence against women and children (Gerald 2002). Two approaches were considered. In the first one, to prevent danger in a family or partnership, a new legal measure was implemented in the security law by passing Art. 38a SPG (Security Law), the so-called "Wegweisung": "advice by the law enforcement authorities (police or gendarmerie) to leave the home." A second amendment was passed, called "Betretungsverbot": "advice by the law enforcement authorities (police and gendarmerie) not to enter the home for a certain period of time (one to two weeks)." The second amendment was implemented in the civil law to protect vulnerable family members against violence. In the "Exekutionsordnung," the amendment was in place to empower the civil judge to give an order against the suspected offender of "Einstweilige Verfügung," following Art. 382b, Part 1 EO not to enter the home for a certain period of time. The law enforcement authorities have to ensure that this order will be fulfilled.

Since the implementation of these legal amendments to prevent violence against women and children, the crime statistics of Vienna demonstrate the picture shown in Table 5.3.

Table 5.3 Crime Statistics of Police Activities in Vienna against Violence in the Family

Repressive/Preventive Measures	1999	2000	2001	2002	2003
	By police				
Peace regulation (Streitschlichtung)	866	1,667	1,911	1,910	1,303
Advice to leave the home (Wegweisungen)	416	712	790	1,133	4,803
Verdict not to come back to the home (Betretungsverbot)	556	942	1,051	1,542	1,702
	By the courts				
Verdicts by the courts	182	274	276	358	417
Court procedures	117	173	269	324	376
Police activities after court verdicts	21	17	22	10	11

Source: Crime Statistics of the Federal Police of Austria (Vienna Headquarters), published in the yearly *Vienna Police Reports*, 1999–2003.

Violence in Relationships

Statistics show that violence in relationships and families is on the increase, but that does not mean an absolute increase in violence. It can be the consequence of more awareness in the society. It is estimated that about one-third of the violent activities happen against women and children.

Violence against Women

More than 50 percent of marriages end, and more violence in partnerships and marriages has been registered. Victims are primarily women and children. In Austria, we have university researchers studying the victims and the extent of violence against women and children. The term "violence against women" means any act of gender-based violence that results in, or is likely to result in, physical, sexual, or psychological harm or suffering to women, including threats of such acts, coercion, or arbitrary deprivation of liberty, whether occurring in public or private life. "Violence against women is a manifestation of the historically unequal power relations between men and women, which have led to domination over and discrimination against women by men and to the prevention of women's full advancement" (United Nations 1996).

Violence against Children

Children are just as often as women to be victims, especially in families with different ethnic backgrounds. It happens often as a clash of cultures. Very often, we see that men coming from other cultures do not understand the fact that women and children are not their "property" and that they cannot do "what they want" with them.

Exploitation of Women and Children in Connection with Organized Crime

Prostitution and gambling were always cornerstones of criminal activities, especially of organized crime. Since the fall of the Iron Curtain, trafficking in human beings became a bigger challenge for law enforcement agencies and criminal justice agencies. Austria, for many years, was a border country between the poorer and the richer parts of Europe. Since 1989, legal and illegal migration and trafficking in human beings increased dramatically. The threat of organized crime has changed societies, especially in the field of immigration. Each year, more than three million people move between and within continents. A lot of this legal and illegal immigration is connected with the exploitation of women and children. They can be exploited as employees, but very often they are exploited for sexual purposes. For example, the activities in the "red-light" districts have been organized by criminal groups for decades. Prostitution in streets, night clubs, bars, brothels, massage parlors, and escort services are in the hands of criminal organizations. This "night life industry" cannot survive if women from foreign countries will not work in Austria. In Austria, there are about 650 night clubs; about 200 of them are situated in Vienna. Prostitution is regulated by the laws of the nine provinces. In eight of the nine provinces of Austria, prostitution is legalized, and about 2,800 prostitutes are officially registered. The representatives of the Bundeskriminalamt Austria assume that three times more prostitutes are active in Austria.[4] In the field of prostitution and trafficking of women, the classical indicators of organized crime can be found. Because of the legal system, it happens that criminals often are charged only with Sec. 217 of the Austrian Penal Code (Strafgesetzbuch [StGB]) and not for being a member of a criminal association, following Sec. 278a of the Austrian Penal Code, because Sec. 217 StGB has higher sanctions than those of Sec. 278a StGB. The actual trend is that trafficking in women primarily is linked to Eastern Europe, Asia, and now South America. Most of the prostitutes from Romania, Bulgaria, Belarus, Moldova, and Slovakia are working in the night clubs and in the streets. Prostitutes from Asia, especially from China, are working in massage salons. It is estimated that 75 percent of the active prostitutes are registered in Austria. This is indicated by the advertisements in the newspapers, which show how many contacts are offered.

Experience of the PC-S-CO of the Council of Europe[5]

Trafficking in Human Beings for Sexual Exploitation

Trafficking in human beings is defined as all acts and attempted acts involved in the recruitment, transportation within and across borders, purchase, sale, transfer, receipt, or harboring of a person involving the use of deception, coercion (including the use or threat of force or the abuse of authority), or debt bondage for the purpose of placing or holding such person whether for pay or not, in involuntary servitude (domestic, sexual, or reproductive), in forced or bonded labor, or in slavery-like conditions, in a community other than the one in which such person lived at the time of the original deception, coercion, or debt bondage. This definition recognizes that the core elements of trafficking in human beings constitute violations of human rights. These are deception, coercion, force, or debt bondage. The nature of the labor and services is not relevant to the qualification of such an exploitative and abusive situation as trafficking. This definition therefore does not confine itself to prostitution but also includes, among other things, the exploitation of domestic workers, sweat shop labor, and forced marriages. For the purpose of understanding trafficking in human beings for sexual exploitation, the clear distinction between smuggling of and trafficking in persons has to be elaborated. The feature of exploitation and usage for criminal purposes, despite the smaller relative size of the problem, makes trafficking in persons as serious, if not more serious, a problem than smuggling of persons. An interesting observation from the field is that the majority of people being smuggled is actually male, whereas human traffickers more often concentrate on females.

Council of Europe Report

The following member countries of the Council of Europe reported trafficking in human beings for sexual exploitation.

Austria: The problem of trafficking in human beings for sexual exploitation is still at a high level. There are more than 600 brothels in Austria, and more than 90 percent of the women are coming from foreign countries, especially from the former dependencies of the defunct Soviet Union.

Bulgaria: Forty-two criminal groups were involved in trafficking in human beings for sexual exploitation.

Finland: Sixty-three cases of pimping were reported; 74 different individuals were suspected of these crimes. Although the activities have been tightly organized, it is not a large-scale business.

Germany: Organized criminal groups are still very active in night life activities, but, in the past three years, the number of criminals involved in these activities is decreasing.

Greece: Criminal organizations investigated for being involved in trafficking in human beings totaled 31, mainly Greek and Albanian. Investigations were performed for 205 suspected offenders involved in illegal trafficking in women; in addition to those who were Greek, the offenders were also foreign nationals such as Albanians, Bulgarians, Russians, Romanians, Ukrainians, and Iraqis. The organizations broken up usually have a small number of members (three to six). Last year, an increase was noted in the participation of female criminals in such trafficking groups, many them aliens, who were victims in the past and are now offenders themselves (Ebbe 2007).

Hungary: Business opportunities inherent in prostitution have increased. More and more organized crime groups have given up this area of criminality and look for more profitable activities.

Luxembourg: A great majority of prostitutes are coming from Russia, Ukraine, and Bulgaria. Organized groups from Brussels, Metz, and Hamburg are involved.

The Former Yugoslav Republic of Macedonia: Several channels for illegal transfer of women into the country to sell or procure them for prostitution have been established. Criminal activities have been extremely intensified for the illegal transfer of women of foreign nationality. Facilities where prostitution takes place have been differentiated, and persons that are involved in this type of illegal activity have been connected to foreign organized criminal networks.

Moldova: Two hundred thousand to 300,000 persons are connected to trafficking in human beings. Moldovan women are well known to be involved in prostitution activities all over the world.

The Netherlands: In its second report, the office of the National Monitor on Human Trafficking updated the national statistics relating to human trafficking up to and including 2001. In 2001, 132 cases relating to human trafficking were registered with the Public Prosecutions Service. In 27 of those cases, the victims were minors. One can observe that those suspected of human trafficking in 2001 were increasingly also often guilty of other criminal offenses, especially property offenses (35 percent), drug trafficking (27 percent), arms trafficking (13 percent), and migrant smuggling (10 percent). Of the victims, 49 percent were from Bulgaria, Ukraine, Russia, Nigeria, and Romania. In 2001, the majority of the suspects came from the Netherlands (42 percent), (the former) Yugoslavia (12 percent), Nigeria (7 percent), Albania (5 percent), and Bulgaria (4 percent). The number of unaccompanied minor asylum seekers fell sharply from 5,951 in 2001 to 3,232 in 2002. The main countries of origin of the asylum seekers were Angola (854), Sierra Leone (392), Guinea (199), China (177), and Togo (147). The reduction in the number of asylum seekers can largely be attributed to the new Aliens Act (April 1, 2001) and the tightening up of policy. Young girls still sometimes make use of the asylum procedures to go to the

Netherlands without realizing that they will be forced to work as prostitutes. It is above all human traffickers who deliberately abuse the procedure for this purpose (*National Monitor on Human Trafficking* 2003). On the basis of the nationality of the victims, one can distinguish two types of criminal groups. Eight criminal groups were involved in human trafficking from countries of the former Eastern European Bloc. Five groups brought women to the Netherlands from Central Africa (primarily Nigeria). In the first category, the victims were always adult women, whereas the second category included both adult and underage women. In all the investigations, the women and girls were lured to the Netherlands under false pretences. Thus, they were under the illusion that they were going to work in the hotel and catering sector or that they were going to study in the Netherlands. Some of the Nigerian women/girls were forced to come to the Netherlands, because their parents had accumulated a large debt with the criminal group. In the Netherlands, and sometimes even on the journey, the women/girls were put under severe psychological and physical pressure, extending from rape to the provision of a bare minimum of food. Voodoo rituals were often employed to force the Nigerian women/girls into prostitution and subsequently to keep them there. In one investigation, the criminal group was involved in both the trafficking and smuggling of human beings. In this inventory, human trafficking was virtually always the core activity of the criminal association. False papers were used to get the women/girls into the Netherlands. Eight criminal groups produced the false papers themselves (nearly always as a subsidiary activity). Some associations procured false residence permits to give the women legal status. These women were then frequently employed in legal sex clubs. Very few criminal groups were engaged exclusively in human trafficking and/or forgery. For example, the associations were also active in the trafficking of hard drugs (in four investigations), theft, and/or vehicle crime (each in three investigations). The women did not always end up in the Dutch prostitution sector. A number of the criminal groups put the women to work in other European countries. All the criminal groups engaged in both transportation and exploitation of the women and girls. Most groups were also involved in the "recruitment" of their victims. Because of their illegal status, the women generally worked in illegal prostitution zones (so-called "tippelzones"), clubs, or the escort industry.

Norway: Today, there seems to be a professionalization in the infrastructure around prostitution and trading in women, connected with criminal organizations, which invest the profit from this enterprise in other forms of illegal activity. An increase in Eastern European women on the prostitution market has been recognized, in which criminal ringleaders apparently take the profit. Albanians, who were formerly known for drug dealing and illegal gambling, have not become involved in activities connected to trafficking in women.

Romania: There has been a noticeable diversification of the ways in which illicit activities are hidden. Along with the classical covers of night clubs, casinos, artistic managers, and modeling agencies, others such as babysitter or taking care of and accompanying sick persons are now covering up what is, in reality, prostitution at the client's domicile. The categories of women who become victims of the panderers will know such a diversification. As a rule, the prostitution and pandering networks have very close relations with other crimes in the field of organized criminality, more often with drug trafficking. The modalities of recruiting will continue to be maintained at the same level, and those of getting out of the country will know other types of border-crossing routes to perfect the actions and the professionalization of the traffickers by endowing them with communication logistics and modern transportation means for recruiting, transporting, hosting, and guiding the migrants.

Child Pornography

Child pornography includes the production, distribution, exportation, transmission, importation, intention, possession, and advertising of child pornography. As practical experience shows, the Internet is used extensively for providing and selling pornographic materials. Child pornography, sexual services, and advertising contacts on the Internet are a growing problem. Basically, there are only a small number of reports on child pornography. Four member countries of the Council of Europe have sent the following reports.

Croatia reports a total of 31 criminal offenses of exploiting children or minors for pornography, and 19 criminal offenses of introducing children to pornography were noted. The existence of any organized crime groups dealing with child pornography were not proved.

Greece was concerned with one criminal group composed of six members of Greek origin that trafficked material over the Internet. The offenders also profited at the expense of unsuspecting Web site visitors, interrupting their connections with the Internet service provider and connecting them, unawares, with foreign telecommunication operators, for access to other pornographic Web sites.

Luxemburg was involved internationally in one Internet case of child pornography investigation.

The Netherlands reported that two investigations were concerned with production or possession of child pornography. In one case, a number of pornographic pictures of young children were found in the course of a house search. The second investigation did involve production. Children came to a studio, where, at first, they posed for normal clothing advertising brochures. It was not until later that nude photos were taken of the children. The photos probably circulated in pedophile networks. The suspects in this investigation originated in the Netherlands and Belgium.

The United Kingdom (the National Criminal Intelligence Service) reports that the number of child sex offenders cannot be told. More than 18,000 individuals, the vast majority of them men, are currently registered as sex offenders. This figure includes those responsible for offenses against adults. However, the Sex Offenders' Register holds the details only of those offenders convicted, cautioned, or released from prison for proscribed child and adult offenses after September 1997. A recent U.K. law enforcement investigation (Operation One) revealed that a significant proportion of the 7,000 U.K. subscribers are unknown to the police. This points to the limitations of the registration system as a guide to the level of child sex offending in the United Kingdom.

The Impact of Child Pornography on the Victims

The psychological impact on the victims of child sexual abuse varies from case to case. For some, there may be no outward sign of the abuse having affected them, but for others, it has resulted in alcoholism, petty crime, mental health problems, and, in extreme cases, suicide. Experiencing abuse as a child is also a risk factor that may influence whether someone becomes an offender. However, there is no proven causal link, and there are a number of other risk factors.

The Profile of Child Sex Offenders

Child sex offenders do not fit a standard profile. They come from all social and ethnic backgrounds and any walk of life. They have varying levels of intelligence and interpersonal skills. Some are obsessive collectors and keep detailed diaries and pictures of children and catalog their activities and fantasies. In the United Kingdom, by far the majority are adult white men. Although women make up only a small percentage of offenders, a large number knowingly or otherwise facilitate child sex offenders by providing access to their children or overlooking abuse. This usually occurs when the women themselves are vulnerable, either economically or emotionally. Some offenders have a preference for children of a particular age, sex, or appearance, whereas others will target any child. Most offenders in treatment programs report that they became aware of a sexual attraction to children before the age of 18.

Targeting and Controlling Victims, Including "Grooming"

Most identified child sex offenders act alone. Organized groups are relatively rare. However, there is extensive criminal networking. Offenders network to exchange indecent images and fantasies, to gain access to victims, and to justify and "normalize" their offending. For example, networks provide positive reinforcement that child pornography is acceptable. Where offenders are able to establish relationships with like-minded individuals, for example, through being imprisoned together, it is possible for networks to form. However, the arrival of the Internet has changed the nature and extent of networking. The Internet makes it possible to network on a much wider scale and, if security measures are taken, with less risk. Online guides to all aspects of child sex are available. Some have hyperlinks to bulletin boards, information about chat rooms, where information technology expertise and access or grooming techniques are shared, and passwords or pass phrases are given to access pornography.

The Nature and Extent of Organized Child Sex Offending: Networking

Most online child sex networks are hierarchical in structure and are secretive, with access by invitation only. Individuals may be approached in chat rooms and invited to join a network. Often, there is a vetting process, with status and trust being gained by evidence of illegal activity. Protecting themselves against law enforcement is a key concern, and some online child sex offenders openly discuss methods of keeping their activities from the police. There is also evidence that online networks undertake counterintelligence activity, researching techniques used by the police and Internet watch groups by debriefing people who have been arrested. Some members are aware of surveillance techniques and take steps to avoid being followed. If an offender puts members of the network at risk, perhaps by the unauthorized passing on of images, he is likely to have his computer targeted with viruses or denial of service attacks.

Grooming through the Internet

Some child sex offenders use Internet chat rooms (or ICQ/instant messaging) to target and groom children, looking to encourage children to supply indecent images of themselves or text of a sexual nature or ultimately to meet in person. A number of offenders have shown themselves adept at manipulating the children they contact, winning their trust by pretending to understand and share their interests and feelings. The anonymity of the Internet allows adult offenders to misrepresent themselves as young children or more often teenagers, making it easier for them to establish a bond. In some cases, children have been duped into meeting with offenders, who have then attempted to abuse them sexually, oftentimes successfully.

Images of Child Abuse

Some experts believe the viewing images of child abuse allows offenders to normalize their sexual feelings and break down any barrier of guilt and fear that prevents them from physically offending. Whatever the precise link between viewing images and committing child sex acts, possessing the images is an offense in itself. Moreover, the demand for new images encourages producers to find new victims or to repeat the abuse of existing victims. Production of images usually involves abuse of a child, but some images of adults are altered through a process known as "morphing." The Internet has enabled a rapid growth in the publication of computer-based images of child abuse and their global distribution. Computer-based images of child abuse have now largely replaced printed material.

The Internet Watch Foundation (IWF) disseminates intelligence on Web sites containing images of child abuse to law enforcement and liaisons with U.K. Internet service providers so that the illegal material can be removed from their servers. In 2002, the number of reports made to the IWF increased by 64 percent. More than half of all illegal Web sites known to the IWF are hosted in the United States, but the number in Russia has more than doubled from 286 to 706. However, sites may be hosted in one country and managed from elsewhere. This creates significant difficulties for law enforcement, not least of which is identifying and tracing the victims' identity or the location of the abuse. However, the National Crime Squad's Childbase initiative is an attempt to tackle the problem by analyzing seized images. It is impossible that a relatively small number of offenders, either individually or operating in networks, are responsible for the production of large quantities of child pornography. Some may distribute it for pleasure rather than profit via newsgroups, peer networks, fileservers, nonpayment Internet sites, and community groups. However, the potential profits to be made from selling images of child abuse online has also attracted serious and organized criminals. Advances in Internet technology mean that it is now used to real-time videorecord abuse simultaneously to a number of viewers. With the development and spread of digital technology, intellectual property crime offers potentially lucrative opportunities for serious and organized criminals. In particular, the cracking of security features integrated within products paves the way for the sale of pirated copies of software, games, music, and films. Serious and organized criminals have always sought fast and secure means of communication with each other.

E-mail, Internet chat rooms, and instant messages offer new options, as do Web-based and client server mail accounts, Web sites, and message boards. These methods can be used to coordinate criminal activity, locate victims, and make new criminal enterprises. They provide speed of communication and relative anonymity. There is evidence that some serious and organized criminals are exploring the use of the Internet to communicate. When combined with the communication systems and methods outlined above, encryption tools offer an additional level of security to serious and organized criminals in terms of data they store and exchange. The indications are that organized criminals are increasingly using sophisticated and high-powered encryption tools to protect themselves.

Legislation and Anti-Trafficking Policies in Austria

Anti-Trafficking Policies

Austria has set priorities for a long time in anti-trafficking policies. More than a hundred years ago, on May 18, 1904, Austria signed the international agreement in combating trafficking in women (Internationals Abkommen zur Bekämpfung des Mädchenhandels). A lot of activities were oriented against trafficking in human beings as an abhorrent and worrying phenomenon involving coercive sexual exploitation, slave labor, and exploitation for domestic servitude between 1904 and 2003. The Austrian Ministry of Justice and the parliament have signed the Palermo Convention and the three protocols. In preparation of the adoption of the United Nations Convention, the articles in the relevant Austrian laws about trafficking of human beings have to be changed. Furthermore, a new Procedure Code is being discussed in the parliament, in which the rights of victims shall be extended. The non-governmental organization "White Ring" (Weißer Ring) has taken the lead in arguing for the strengthening of victims' rights.

Legislation

In the Austrian Penal Code, there are provisions against violation of the sexual dignity of a person (Sec. 201 ff). Sec. 216 StGB deals with the exploitation of victims by pimps. The legal understanding of sexuality in the penal code is based on the understanding of the previous centuries and following the moral and ethical guidelines of the Catholic Church. A more modern approach can be seen in the legalization of prostitution in the competence of the provinces.

Sec. 217 of the Austrian Penal Code Dealing with Traffic in Human Beings (Federal Law Gazette 1974/60)

Sec. 217 (1) states that a person who procures or recruits another person, who may already be devoted to prostitution, to pursue prostitution in a state this person is neither citizen of nor regularly sojourns in, is to be sentenced to imprisonment from six months to five years; a person who commits these offenses professionally is to be sentenced to imprisonment from 1 to 10 years.

Sec. 217 (2) provides that a person who induces another person (Para. 1), with the intent that this person pursues prostitution in a state he or she is neither citizen of nor regularly sojourns in, through deceit about his intention to move to a different state, or coerces this person by force or perilous threat to do so, or transports this person to a different state by force or exploiting his or her misconception about his intentions is to be sentenced to imprisonment from 1 to 10 years.

Austrian Code of Criminal Procedure (Strafprozessordnung) as Amended by Federal Law Gazettes No. 526/1993, No. 1 105/1997, and No. 1 153/1998

Sec. 162a (1) states that, if it is to be feared that the interrogation of a witness will not be possible during the trial proceedings because of factual or legal reasons, the investigating judge has to enable the prosecutor, the injured party, and the accused as well as their counsels to participate in the interrogation and to examine the witness. Sec. 249 and 250, Parts 1 and 2 are to be applied *mutatis mutandis*. The investigating judge may arrange for acoustic or visual recordings.

Sec. 162a (2) provides on behalf of the witness, particularly with respect to his low age or his mental or physical condition, or on behalf of the establishment of the truth, that the investigating judge may limit the possibility to participate in such a way, that the parties and their counsels can exercise their right to interrogate without being present at the technical means of video-audio transmission. The investigating judge may appoint an expert for such an interrogation, particularly if the witness has not yet completed 14 years of age.

In Sec. 162a (3), the person mentioned in Sec. 152, Para. 1, Subpara. 3 (persons under 14 years) has to be questioned by the investigating judge according to Para. 1 and with limited participation of the parties (Para. 2), if they could have been harmed in their sexual sphere by the punishable act of which the accused is suspected. The person mentioned in Sec. 152, Para. 1, Subpara. 2 (relatives of the suspect), Subpara. 2a (persons who could have been harmed in their sexual sphere), and Subpara. 3 (persons under 14 years of age) otherwise are to be questioned by the investigating judge in that way (Para. 1 and 2), if they demand so.

Sec. 162a (4) states that, before the interrogation, the investigating judge has to instruct the witness about his rights according to Para. 3 and about the fact that the protocol can be read out and that video and audio recordings of the interrogation can be displayed in the trial proceedings even if he refuses to give evidence in the future proceedings. These instructions and any comments about them have to be recorded in protocol; they can also be performed by the expert (Para. 2). The age and the condition of the witness have to be taken into consideration for any instruction.

Other Relevant Laws

Beside these legal provisions in the Austrian penal and the procedural codes, there are legal provisions in the security police law and in the immigration law. These provisions are used as the legal framework of conditions for the operation in the intervention center.

Interagency Cooperation: Institutions involved in measures to prevent and control trafficking in human beings are criminal justice institutions such as the Ministry of Justice, the prosecutor's service, the courts, the Ministry of Finance with the customs service, the Ministry of the Interior, gendarmerie, the police, the Ministry for Health Care, regional services responsible for health care, and nongovernmental agencies. In the prosecutor's service and in the courts are specialists who are adept at dealing with organized crime issues. In the Ministry of the Interior, the Bundeskriminalamt Osterreich and regional organizations (Bundespolizeidirektionen and Landesgendarmeriekommandos) deal with organized crime and anti-trafficking measures. Although there exists no special task force dealing with anti-trafficking, basically good cooperation between all these agencies is performed.

Forms of Cooperation: Because policing is completely federally organized in Austria, relatively little formal interagency cooperation has developed. On the one side, there are legal advisers to cooperate formally between law enforcement agencies and the criminal justice system, especially dealing with the fundamental rights of persons and the human rights perspective. On the other side, there exists a network among the prosecutor's service, the investigative judges, and the law enforcement agencies (Gendarmerie, customs, and police), and necessary cooperation takes place immediately.

Formalization of Cooperation: The cooperation between law enforcement agencies, the prosecutor's service, and the investigative judge is based on the procedure code. Law enforcement agencies have to report all their investigation activities to the prosecutor's service. The prosecutor's service decides how a case will proceed. The prosecutor's service decides whether the investigation should be stopped, continued as "Vorerhebungen" (preliminary investigation), or whether it should be continued as a "Voruntersuchung" (judge's opening investigation). If it is necessary to interfere with the fundamental human rights of the accused, the competent judge, "Gesetzlicher Richter," has to decide how this will be accomplished (search, wire tapping, arrest, or warrant).

Legal Basis for Cooperation (Cooperation Agreements): The legal basis for this cooperation is the Austrian Constitution, in which the fundamental splitting of powers and the duty of support ("Amtshilfe") for organization of public administration is defined. The law for the competence of the ministries, the special laws for the criminal justice system, and the competent ministries with all agencies is written in the constitution.

There exist cooperation agreements in the field of international cooperation by the Republic of Austria, the Ministry of Foreign Affairs, the Ministry of Justice (extradition treaties), and the Ministry of the Interior, both bilateral and multilateral. In Austria, the cooperation with nongovernment organizations is based on treaties. The selection of partners for cooperation and the criteria used for the selection process are already experienced in other fields (for example, in the field of domestic violence): trust and confidence.

Cooperation of Victim-Witnesses with the Criminal Justice System, Experiences with Victims of Trafficking as Witnesses: Austria has a long tradition of supporting victims of international conflicts. When Austria became free again in 1955, it was confronted immediately with the Hungarian Revolution in 1956 and later with the Revolution in the Czech Republic in 1968. Austria acted in conflict situations, placing strong priority on supporting refugees and victims. This principle was extended to victims of trafficking. The priority therefore is to care for the victims, and, second, to ask and see a victim of trafficking as a witness.

Measures to Protect Victim-Witnesses, Witness Protection Programs in General: Two different ways of witness protection were developed in Austria: so-called "little witness protection" and "full witness protection." The easier way for law enforcement agencies is to provide victims with the little witness protection, which is based on the internal directive of the Ministry of the Interior for law enforcement agencies and in the criminal justice system on the procedure code. The full witness protection can be provided only by the Bundeskriminalamt Osterreich, but it is used very seldomly only under specific circumstances. It is based on internal directives and international treaties with Ministries of Internal Affairs of other countries by the Ministry of the Interior of Austria.

Procedural Measures to Protect Victim-Witnesses during Investigation, Court Proceedings, and Afterward: As explained above, the legal basis for the criminal justice agencies is found in the procedure code, Sec. 162a. All other measures have to be covered by the responsible authorities of the Ministry of the Interior and the acting law enforcement agencies.

Nonprocedural, Specific Protection Measures for Victim-Witnesses: These measures are practically oriented, for the most part. If somebody is in danger of becoming a victim, law enforcement agencies have to ensure that the identity of the potential victim is withheld. They must ensure that the home, work, and school addresses of the victim and the victim's family members are kept secret and that there is no confrontation between the witness and the offender at the court. Very often, potential victims need exemption of the alien law to be allowed to stay in Austria and to show up at court. Law enforcement agencies have to provide the potential victim with personal security measures. Another issue is the increase of cyber crime, pornography, and Internet crime.

The Austrian Criminal Justice System

General Features

The Austrian Criminal Justice system is based on the main principles of following the "material truth" and the freedom of the judge in fairly evaluating the evidence. Although there are changes in the development of the law and formalism is becoming more and more important, the desire to experience and learn the truth at trial is stronger than the serving of a sophisticated promotion of formalism. Because of their outstanding importance, the following principles have been incorporated into the constitution:

- The guiding principles of Austrian procedural law
- The principle of the independence of judicature
- The right of having criminal proceedings conducted by the "legal judge"

The principles are closely connected. Only complete independence of the courts from the influence of the state administration guarantees the protection of the citizen from the state's power. Judges are independent, which means they are only bound by the law. Instructions or any direct or indirect attempts to exert influence by anyone (e.g., the president of the court or the Minister of Justice) are illegal. To guarantee this position, judges are appointed for life and cannot, in the normal course of things, be removed from their court and transferred to another court without their consent. To complete this concept of judicial independence, a case cannot be taken away from the judge under whose jurisdiction it comes pursuant to the rules of procedure (a set of rules distributing the workload among all the judges of a certain court, fixed by a body of judges of the court every January for one year).

Principles of Accusation

In most European countries, criminal proceedings are formerly governed by the principle of inquisition, i.e., the functions of judge, defense counsel, and prosecutor are exercised by the same person. In Austria, this principle has governed criminal proceedings until 1873, when, following the ideas of the French Revolution, these roles were assigned to different persons. In the Anglo-American system, the public prosecutor and the defendant act as parties and the court decides only on the strength of the evidence provided by the two of them. In continental Europe, a different form of procedure developed. Here criminal proceedings can only be initiated and continued on request made by a prosecutor (public, private, or subsidiary). The preliminary investigation is conducted by a judge and not by a party. This concept of "investigating judge" has been abolished by most European countries.

Principle of Oral Proceedings and Principle of Direct Proceedings

These two principles are closely connected. The law demands that all relevant evidence be examined by the ruling court. Witnesses have to testify at the trial, court experts must give their opinions in court, etc. The reading of depositions made previously, e.g., before the police or during the preliminary investigation before the investigating judge, in the course of the trial, is the exception to the rule and is therefore only allowed under certain restricted preconditions.

Principle of Public Trial

The issue of publicity of the trial as an alternative to a "judicature in camera" was raised during the French Revolution and the Revolution of 1848. Today, it is an expression of an "open" judicature that allows control by the general public and the media during the trial (but not during preliminary investigation). Exceptions can be made, e.g., to protect people or their reputation. TV and radio transmission, taking photographs, or video filming during the court sessions is forbidden.

Principles of Participation by the People in the Legal Decision

In Austria, lay judges play an important role in the trials in which major offenses are involved. Minor cases are tried by one professional judge. When the court is faced with a serious crime, two lay judges and two professional judges decide on guilt and penalty together. In the case of the most severe crimes, a body of eight lay judges (the jury) decides the verdict. The sentence is fixed by the eight lay judges and three professional judges together. Unlike the American system, Austrian law does not demand unanimity. A (simple) majority of votes suffices. The votes of the professional judges and the lay judges carry the same weight. In the case of a draw, the milder sentence prevails. When the professional judges feel (unanimously) that the jury has erred, they can suspend the verdict. Then the case has to be tried again, by a different jury. Appealing the verdict is only possible under certain very restricted preconditions. Rarely ever is the verdict of the jury set aside by the second instance (the Supreme Court). The Austrian system, with its extreme emphasis on lay participation, is unique in continental Europe. Additional principles governing court proceedings in criminal cases can be found in the Code of Criminal Procedure.

Principle of Prosecution by the State

In principle, prosecution is a right of the state. The authorities have the duty to prosecute, if there is reasonable evidence that an offense has been committed. This duty to prosecute is called the principle of legality. The question whether the trial is appropriate or economical can never be an issue. In this uncompromising form, it is unique among Europe's legal systems.

Principle of the "Material Truth"

The court has to take all necessary evidence and to consider all the circumstances of the case *ex officio* without being bound by the motions of the public prosecutor or the defendant. In the beginning of 2004, the changing of the procedural code was discussed in the parliament, and the new procedural code was implemented in 2007. One important question was, shall the principle of material truth be changed? The answer was no.

Principle of Free Evaluation of the Evidence

Only evidence that has been obtained under circumstances in violation of rights protected under the Declaration of Human Rights (e.g., by torture) is not admitted in the trial. The Austrian penal code knows no binding rules on the evaluation of evidence. The judge decides on his assurance. Of course, he has to give the reasons for that assurance, and the judgment has to be based on the evidence taken in the course of the trial. Only a full assurance or, at least, a "probability that borders on certainty" carries a verdict of guilty. In the case of doubt, the defendant has to be acquitted (*in dubio pro reo*, for "when in doubt, in favor of the accused").

Juvenile Law

How juvenile law is structured is of high importance when dealing with cases of violence against women and children. Very often, in both cases, the juvenile law has to be used to justify such cases. How is a victim treated? How efficient is the witness protection? How can victims be supported waiting for the trial and after the trial? Because an increasing number of cases involve victims of foreign countries, it is necessary to build trust and confidence. For example, victims of many Eastern European countries have no confidence in law enforcement agencies, because they suspect a lot of corruption.

In Austria, special legislation in the field of juvenile justice has a long and distinguished tradition. As early as 1852, special provisions for juveniles were introduced in the penal code. The age of criminal responsibility was fixed at the age of 10. Juveniles between the ages of 10 and 14 who had committed a minor offense were handed over to their parents for further "treatment." "Nonviolent education" obviously was not an issue at the time. Major offenses were punished by detention lasing from one to six months. From the age of 14 upward, juveniles were treated like adults. Until the age of 20, neither the death penalty nor a life sentence could be imposed. They were substituted with sentences from 10 to 20 years. It was Franz Klein who, in 1907, first tried to establish an independent juvenile justice system. As a result of this famous politician's special interest in that field, a multitude of provisions improving the position of juveniles in criminal proceedings were introduced between 1905 and 1908.

The legal representatives were given certain rights: appointment of a defense counsel became mandatory for grave offenses, and pretrial detention was only possible under certain limited conditions. The political troubles of this period, which eventually led to World War I, prevented Klein's draft, which he presented on May 12, 1907, from passing parliament. Immediately after the end of World War I, special courts for juveniles were established (25.1.1919 StGB1.1919/46). At the time, specialized judges applied adult criminal law to juveniles. In 1923, Germany introduced a juvenile justice act. Following this example, Austria adopted its first juvenile justice act on July 18, 1928. This law was the first to contain special provisions for juveniles in both the fields of statutory and procedural law. As a guiding principle, the legislator stated that legal punishment was only one method among several others and was, by no means, the only or even the best way to deal with juvenile delinquency. The judge was instructed to substitute legal punishment by other educational means wherever possible.

After having virtually been suspended during the period leading up to World War II, the law was reintroduced in 1949 and amended in 1961. In the following 27 years between then and 1988, the year that saw the current juvenile justice act pass parliament, a great deal of work has been invested in this area, mainly by the practitioners of law who work in the field. Much of this effort has gone into drafting a new juvenile justice act. Because a development as described here is unique, at least in the history of Austrian legislature, the description will be detailed. The spirit behind it can only be called revolutionary. The way it was chosen was uncommon, to put it mildly. The guiding idea was that, beside the traditional tracks of criminal law based on treatment or punishment, a third one should be opened up based on the principles of reparation, reconciliation, and mediation as both the means and end of penal law. For various reasons, the first bill dedicated to these principles did not pass parliament at the beginning of the 1980s. The frustration caused by this development, or, to put it better, caused by the very lack of any development, coupled with the general dissatisfaction with the available measures, led to unique experiments.

In 1984, a group of highly motivated juvenile judges, public prosecutors, and probations officers in three Austrian provinces took matters into their own hands. They started to apply the aforesaid principles in their work. Fortunately, there was one provision in the "old juvenile act" that was wide enough to allow experiments within its boundaries. The limits were stretched rather shamelessly, but it worked and allowed the participants in this exciting endeavor to test their ideas in practice and to develop concepts in particular in the field of extrajudicial compensation. Surprisingly enough, this experiment, which challenged more than one principle of Austrian criminal law hitherto deemed immovable as a rock, did not cause much opposition in the beginning. The reason was probably that, at the time, most of the conservative judges, apt to oppose any new approach, simply did not catch on to the importance and the impact of what was happening. When they finally did, things had developed far enough to be irreversible. The advocates of this development were lucky in one respect: it was the right thing at the right time. The years before 1988 had seen a decrease in the number of juvenile delinquents. No spectacular crime committed by a juvenile made the headlines. The political events that led to the opening of the borders toward Eastern Europe, the fall of the Iron Curtain which was to bring with it many real and many imagined security problems, were yet to come.

Another important factor that contributed to the ultimate success of the experiment was that it was done professionally from the start. Right from the beginning, the Vienna Institute of Sociology of Law and Deviance was commissioned to evaluate the available data. This provided the participants with findings and in-depth information to give to the media. When they had success, they publicized it, so politicians no longer hesitated to endorse it. On October 20, 1988, the New Juvenile Justice Act passed parliament. The following years saw an overwhelming acceptance of the new provisions by both the general public and the practitioners of law. That is why, in 1992, another experiment was initiated, this time in the field of adult penal law.

In some provinces of Austria, the project Extrajudicial Compensation in Adult Criminal Cases was started by selected courts on nearly all (court) levels. Once more, a provision of the penal code was used to experiment within its limits. The experiences of this model project and the know-how acquired by the judges and public prosecutors working in the juvenile justice system led to the incorporation of "diversion" into the Penal Code for adults in 1999.

Law against Violence Security Law Amendment

Security Authorities Verdict to Leave and to Forbid the Entering of Home

Art. 38a (1) provides that, if there arises special fact, especially because of a previous dangerous aggression, and it is expected that a dangerous attack will be started again against life, health, or freedom, official security authorities are allowed to advise a person, from whom the danger is expected, to leave the home and forbid them to enter the home or the surrounding area, for a certain period of time, where the endangered person (partner) is living. They have to advise the offender which rooms he is not allowed to enter; this advice has to be structured to reach an efficient prevention.

Art. 38a (2) states that, under the conditions of item 1, the official security authorities are empowered to give an order against a human being to forbid the entering of a certain area. Enforcement by the authorities of this advice is not allowed. If a verdict not to enter a home was given, the authorities have to take care to respect the private life of the suspected person in relevance to the offense. The authorities are empowered to take all keys to the home from the suspected person but must give him the opportunity to take all necessary goods for living and support all opportunities of finding new accommodations. If there is a necessity for the suspected person to come back to the home, this is only possible in the presence of the official security authorities. End of the verdict.

Art. 38a (3) states that if the verdict of forbidding to enter the home was given, the official security authorities have to take care to ask for an address of the suspected person, to create the possibility of informing him about the ending of the verdict, or to inform him about the "giving of a judge verdict." If the suspected person does not react to this advice, the new verdict or the suspension of the verdict has to be repeated until the suspect understands. The suspected person has to be informed about this procedure.

Art. 38a (4) stipulates that official security authorities are obligated to inform the victim of the possibility to continue the security verdict by a second verdict of the judge, if necessary.

Exekutionsordnung: Prevention of Violence in the Family

Art. 382.b (1) states that the competent court has to release a verdict for a certain period of time against a person who is aggressive and endangers the personal integrity or psychological health of a near relative or partner living in the same home. The person must leave this home or not return if the continuation of living together is a danger and the victims are asking for this verdict.

Art. 382.b (2) states that if the danger continues and the victims make the request again, the competent court has to release a so-called "Einstweilige Verfügung" to continue the security and prevention measures.

Is the Law against Violence a Success Story?

To our knowledge, there exists only a limited number of research studies about violence in families. As far as it is known, one-quarter to one-third of all women in the world are victims of men's physical power. A prevalence study about the extent of violence against women from the University in Bielefeld, Germany, shows that 42 to 56 million women are victims of violent crimes in the European Union. In 70 percent of all cases, not only are women victims of violent crimes, but children, too, are victims of this violence.

A Dutch study proved that the yearly cost of violence in families is more than 200 million euros.

The Law as a New Measure against Violence

The new measures against violence in the family are principally a success story. Since the implementation of the law, more women and children trust the police and report cases of violence. The burden of intervention is on the side of the law enforcement agencies, as statistics show. The increase in the number of cases of intervention do not necessarily mean that violence is on the increase. It shows that people are more sensitive about these problems and ask for more help from law enforcement agencies.

Prevention Measures

Intervention Center. Philosophically, violence is the number one thing that terrifies people; it is a disease. The Vienna Intervention Center against violence in families is an accompanying measure assisting the Federal Law for Safety in Families. The Intervention Center started its activities and services in February 1998. Nine members serve in the Intervention Center. The Ministry of the Interior and the Ministry of Health support the Intervention Center yearly with half a million euros. Without the excellent work of non-government organizations, the law enforcement activities never would have such continuing success. Because the Intervention Center takes care of the victims, promotes the suppression and prevention of violence, and implements the new amendments to the laws, it is a success story. Women and children who become victims know where to go, to get support, therapy, and help. The Vienna model is implemented in all of Austria and will be an important measure to get control of the phenomenon of violence against family members.

Advisory Center: Because prevention of crime is the central issue in policing, a special unit was founded to care for victims of sexual exploitation of women and children. In cooperation with the Ministry of Justice, a victim-friendly procedure was developed to protect victims from direct confrontation with defenders and offenders in the court procedure. Another issue was to strengthen the awareness of children from potential dangers inside and outside of families. Findings indicate that children perceive the risk of sexual abuse much higher if they participate in a prevention program. Basically, children's perceptions of the likelihood of being sexually abused is quite low. A prevention program can change this risk perception, and therefore the "Vienna City Cops" started such a program several years ago. This program was enthusiastically accepted by children, parents, and teachers.

Notes

1. *Austria Facts and Figures 2004* (Vienna: Federal Press Service), p. 6.
2. Ibid., p. 10.
3. Ibid., pp. 68ff.
4. Bundeskriminalamt Österreich, Statement for the Council of Europe, Best Practice Survey Cooperation against Trafficking in Human Beings, Vienna, Spring 2003.
5. PC-S-CO is a group of specialists on criminal law and criminological aspects of organized crime of the Council of Europe (Strasbourg). Members include Maximiliam Edelbacher (Austria), Tom Vander Beken (Belgium), Kauko Aromaa (Finland), Drago Kos (Slovenia), Michael Levi (United Kingdom), and Toon van der Heijden (Netherlands), who acts as chief of the group. The Secretariat of the Council of Europe is headed by Alexander Seger.

References

Ebbe, O. N. I. 2007. "The Nature and Scope of Trafficking in Women and Children." In *Global Trafficking in Women and Children*, edited by O. N. I. Ebbe and D. K. Das. Boca Raton, FL: CRC Press/Taylor & Francis Group.

Edelbacher, M., and Norden, G. 2000. "Challenges of Policing Democracies: The Case of Austria." In *Challenges of Policing Democracies: A World Perspective*, edited by D. K. Das and O. Marenin, 215ff. Amsterdam: Gordon and Breach.

Kartusch, A., Knaus, K., and Reiter, G. 2000. *Bekämpfung des Frauenhandels: Studienreihe des Ludwig Botzmann Institutes für Menschenrechte*, edited by M. Novak and H. Tretter, vol. 9. Vienna: Verlag Österreich.

United Nations Population Fund. "Trafficking in Human Misery." (http://www.unfpa.org/gender/violence1.htm (accessed March 24, 2009).

Criminal Exploitation of Women and Children in Germany

6

ROBERT F. J. HARNISCHMACHER

Introduction

Of all forms of violence, rape and sexual abuse of women and children are the most terrifying crimes. The experience of being raped or sexually exploited can have adverse psychological effects on the victims and their families. Besides the trauma of experiencing sexual violence, these victims are further humiliated by authority figures such as doctors, police officers, judges, and lawyers. Adding to this trauma is the tendency for observers to hold these women and children partially responsible for the attack. The tendency to blame these victims for their victimization has been approached from many disparate directions and by various methodologies.

Women's and children's bodies are objectified in all forms of pornography. That is, these persons are depicted as objects whose sole justification for existence is the sexual pleasure of the male viewer. The more violent forms of pornography common today depict women and/or children being violently abused and degraded. Such images include rape, bondage, torture, physical and psychological brutality, sexual exploitation, and, in some cases, murder, all for the purpose of the sexual stimulation of its male participants and male viewers. Although people sometimes disagree with a unified definition of pornography and often disagree with a solution, there is growing acknowledgement that the drastic increase in the production, distribution, and consumption of pornography is a cause for grave concern. The newer wave of sadistic pornography is a cause for alarm. The fusion of sexuality with violence and degradation of females and children has harmful effects on all societies and exacerbating effects on victimization of women and children. By associating male sexual arousal with brutality against women, women become real or potential victims of violent crimes, particularly violent crime of a sexual nature.[1]

Explicit violence has been steadily increasing in recent years. Statistics show that rape and sexual abuse rates have been steadily increasing. Researchers viewed 26 porn films; of these, 21 had rape scenes, 16 had bondage and torture scenes, two had films of child molestation, and two featured the killing of women for sexual stimulation. The examples are endless, beyond imagination, and very difficult, at best, to confront. In Germany, police crime statistics for 2000 recorded a total of 15,581 cases of child abuse that came to police attention, as well as cases of sexual abuse of wards and 1,596 cases of possession/undertaking to gain possession of child pornographic materials. This is a 2 percent increase in the cases of child sexual abuse that became known in a 1999 report. In contrast, the sexual abuse of wards decreased by 12.5 percent, and possession and undertaking to gain possession of child pornographic materials decreased by 14.6 percent.

The police crime statistics of 2000 also show that 96.8 percent of the suspects identified are males. Looking at all sexual offenses, including those whose definitions do not specify any protective age limit (Sec. 177 and 178 of the Criminal Code), a total of 19,719 children were registered as victims in 2000. Of these, 76.3 percent were girls and 23.7 percent were boys. Despite the slight rise in the year under report (2000) compared with the same period in 1999, the data of the police crime statistics suggest that sexual offenses targeting children are decreasing in the long term. The victims' figures remained relatively constant over recent years. Although it is true that police registered an increase in perpetrators of child abuse from 1990 up to 1997, this is attributable, on the one hand, to higher detection rates and, on the other, to the growing propensity to report such offenses that is a result of the public being sensitized.[2]

In 2004, approximately 20,000 children are reported in police crime statistics as victims of sexual exploitation and violence. As a result, on April 20, 2004, Germany established the Federal Ministry for Family Affairs, Senior Citizens, Women, and Youth in Berlin. The ministry has started a huge campaign fighting sexual exploitation of children, youngsters, and women. The motto is "Seeing, Doing, Helping." This prevention campaign has the goal of awakening and informing members of the society, families, schools, and so on. This criminal phenomenon should be controlled officially with the assistance of organizations for protecting children and women, political institutions and parties, police agencies, and all human beings willing to help. The media can help to influence public minds and opinions. Furthermore, the ministry gives informative material for all of Germany. It provides examples of help for children, women, and youngsters. One can contact the ministry from everywhere, as can other institutions and organizations. When the ministry was established in 2004, there was a mass education tour through cities such as Hamburg, Frankfurt, Munich, Magdeburg, Leipzig, and other regional centers and stations. The message of the tour was, "Sexual violence is an absolute crime! It shouldn't hurt to be a child."

One can observe more violence in German cities. The number of offenses in Germany increased (in 2003) in series three times. The police registered approximately 6.6 million offenses after 6.5 million in the year before, with a 3 percent increase in violent crime. The number of serious offenses such as murder, homicide, robbery, or rape grew to 200,000.[3] In 2003 in Berlin (the capital of Germany), there were 733 cases of rape, the highest in the past 10 years in Germany. Also, there was an increase in sexual abuse of children, with almost 24 percent over the previous year. Frankfurt/Main led the list of all cities in violent crimes. For every 100,000 inhabitants, there were 17,159 registered offenses in Frankfurt/Main, 16,620 in Berlin, 15,698 in Hamburg, 15,200 in Düsseldorf, 14,600 in Bremen, 14,200 in Cologne, 10,900 in Dortmund, 15,400 in Leipzig, 9,800 in Essen, and 9,181 in Munich. Stuttgart is the most secure city in Germany.

The Sexual Exploitation of Women

Americans and Germans regard rape as one of the most serious crimes (Adler, Mueller, and Laufer 1991). In developing societies, premarital coitus is frowned on but tolerated if the couple intends marriage. In western countries, there has been an increase in tolerance of premarital coitus, and in some societies, it is almost normal.

Rape is the crime of a man having sexual intercourse with a female who is not his wife without her consent, or recklessly whether she consents or not. The requisite intercourse requires penetration but not necessarily emission. It is a defense that the woman consented, but consent obtained by force or threat, fraud, or impersonation of her husband or lover is not consent, and there is no consent if the woman was asleep, drunk, or drugged. Rape is also recognized with a female who is mentally defective (Walker 1980).

Rape and sexual assault are violent crimes. They are inherently a crime of violence, an exercise of power. Oddly, as Susan Brownmiller (1975) forcefully argues, rape really started as a property crime. Men as archetypal aggressors (the penis is a weapon) subjugated women by the persistent threat of rape. That threat forced each woman to submit to a man for protection and thus to become a wife, the property of a man. Rape then was made a crime to protect one man's property, his wife, from the sexual aggressions of other men, but even that view regards rape as a violent crime against the person, one that destroys the freedom of a woman (and nowadays of a man as well) to decide whether, when, and with whom to enter a sexually oriented relationship (Brownmiller 1975). This offense hurts, suddenly and dramatically, the life of this subjected woman. Rape and other forms of sexual violence may function as tools of social control through which men keep raped and non-raped women in a state of perpetual fear. The fear of sexual assault is argued to limit women's freedom of movement and make them more dependent on men for access to public places (Brownmiller 1975). Fear, however, is not the only effect rape has on the victim. A rape survivor's response to trauma may be physical, emotional, and/or behavioral. Rape trauma syndrome may include intense fear, anxiety, depression, suicidal ideation, inability to trust, increased feelings of vulnerability, sexual dysfunction, guilt, shame, rage, increased substance abuse, sleep disturbance, fear of men/women, and phobic reactions. Other immediate reactions include denial, guilt, hostility, and distorted perceptions. Rape survivors need an average of 18 months to recover from psychological symptoms associated with the rape itself (Brownmiller 1975).

The Bundeskriminalamt (Federal Office of Investigation) has noticed through scientific research that most cases of rape and sexual duress occur between 9:00 p.m. and 3:00 a.m. or between 6:00 p.m. and 8:00 p.m. All violent sexual offenses were committed in the evening and night hours. The nonviolent sexual offenses, such as sexual exhibition, occur during the morning and in the early afternoon (Baum 1986). In the past, the respected sexual act occurred only in the bedroom, and sex was not discussed in public. Today, one can see and compare illustrated papers, special sex magazines, the boulevard press media, and televised programs. In almost every public square and shopping center, there are sex shops and theaters for pornography and "peepshows," making the distribution of videos into private hands so easy. Nowadays, there seems to be no feelings of shame or embarrassment for those who watch or buy these films. In fact, this only serves to justify the abhorrent behavior of pedophiles, sex maniacs, and nymphomaniacs, allowing them to subdue women or men without feeling immoral and to do it like the heroes of their rape fantasies.

Rape victimization is characterized by a relatively high "dark figure" of unreported cases. Rapes in which victim and victimizer know each other or have some personal relationship tend to be reported less than those involving total strangers. There are also reasons to believe that they might occur more often indoors (in the offender's or victim's residence) than stranger-to-stranger rapes. As a result, spatial patterns based on officially recorded rapes may tend to underestimate the proportion of those occurring in the home of the offender or victim and to overestimate those occurring on the street (Fattah 1991). However, often a clearly and forcefully spoken "No" by the victim will give her a fighting chance. Thirty percent of these criminals said that the victim's determined "No" had frightened them. The University of Kiel characterizes five types of rape offenders:

(1) The uncontrolled, egocentric, and simple-minded offender with an aggression for sex to satisfy his sexual drives has relations with women that are regularly not personal, constant, or with affectionate respect. Such men constitute 30 percent of the offenders.
(2) Some young offenders experience late puberty, are shy, have problems with themselves, and are often lonely persons with their own

way of living. Their sexual wishes and imaginations are not fully mature, and adult sexual drives push them but they end up being refused by females. Therefore, rape is a step for solving their "sexual electricity" in combination with their internal stress. They constitute 10 percent.

(3) Frustrated, jealous offenders with conflicts of dominance see rape as the only option, which occurs toward the end of the relationship. They constitute 10 percent of the offenders.

(4) The brutal, cruel, woman-hating man as a macho type is sexist, a weak lover, an egocentric person, and a playboy, who expects every woman to be willing to have sex with him at any time. Such men constitute 30 percent of the offenders.

(5) The psychosexually abnormal offender is sadistic and has woman-hating feelings. This destructive sexuality makes this type of offender a sexually perverse criminal in the traditional sense. He constitutes 10 percent of the offenders.

Criminality in Connection with "Night Life" (Pimps and the Trade with Prostitutes)

In Germany, we do have to live with a new form of "slavery of men," that is, the trade with women and children for the "red-light scene." Regularly, women will be asked by citizens in their own countries, mainly in the East European countries, Africa, and Asia, whether they would like to go to Germany to do jobs, for example, as a nurse, translator, cook, or au pair. They are persuaded by the traders and smugglers with the promise of the salary they should get, but very few of the potential victims seems to know that the promises will lead to prostitution. They do not have a realistic grasp of the most terrible human conditions in the "red-light scene" and the possibilities of earning money. In reality, they will make a very low level of income because the swindlers and pimps take so much of the money.

It is important to know the backgrounds of these women. They have financial needs, and often, the women have a family and children at home. These criminals offer very simple work, and their threats of violence in all forms terrify the women. Because the women want to succeed financially, they yield to the threats of the determined traffickers. The women are enslaved, with no chance for their own identity. When they arrive on German soil, their passports are in the hands of their pimps, and they are threatened because they are brought to Germany with false visas, passports, and false letters of invitation. Travel agents in their home countries colluded with the traffickers as a means of getting quick money. One weapon of these criminal organizations is the "pseudo marriage" with a German "husband." Once in Germany, they are told that they do not have a chance at getting a legal job. Therefore, they have to become a prostitute to pay their debts, which includes high fees for a passport, visa, and flight tickets, as well as fees for the smugglers. If they do not obey, rape is one of the instruments for breaking the spirit of these women. They are now outlaws in the hands of pirates of criminality and their unwilling tools. Some women develop Stockholm Syndrome. To survive, the victims do their very best to please their captors, and they try to adjust to the painful life they are forced to live. They follow their instinct for survival in this cruel world of violence. They are victims, and victims have to seek opportunities for a rescue in such situations.

Furthermore, these women do not have traveling papers and money, they do not speak the German language, and they do not know the area. They fear the German government agencies and the police because they are in Germany illegally. They are controlled by their criminal pimps and have no other social contact other than other illegally transported women. They are isolated. Moreover, it is a fact that NATO Kosovo Force soldiers have forced women and girls from the Baltic states to come to Kosovo. Women and girls, some as young as 11 years old, are sold into sex slavery. They are coming from Moldavia, Bulgaria, and Ukraine but from Kosovo, too. The price in the European market inhuman trade is between 50 and 3,500 euros.[4]

Women from the Baltic states and Eastern Europe are riding by car to Germany, and they are sold for between 1,000 and 3,000 euros. In locations near Eastern Europe, it is not very expensive because of low transportation costs. The trade is very lucrative because there are many women, young females, and even children, ready for the exchange.

Thai girls and women have expensive flights by airplane. They are coming from Bangkok to Berlin, for instance, with false visas. They often have had a pseudo marriage in Denmark with a German. These women have lots of debts, often more than 40,000 euros. Berlin is, since the German reunification of the two German regions in 1990, a melting pot of a lot of women prostitutes from Russia, Bulgaria, and Turkey, to name a few. They are always accompanied by their pimps and criminal organizations out of their home countries. The trade in women as victims is highest in Berlin, Hamburg, Frankfurt/Main, the Ruhr District, the Benelux states, Austria, and Switzerland. They are "brown rats and travelers" in the sense of their criminal "undertakers." They are interested in the region around Berlin because chances of more profit are greatest as a result of the simplicity and naivety of the people. The former east part of Berlin is good for new brothels. According to police in Berlin, more than 8,000 women are working as prostitutes, and 70 percent of these are from foreign countries; 70 percent of these are from a newly independent state of the former Soviet Union. Every second, a prostitute is coming from an Eastern European country. These persons (approximately 4,000) make a daily money income of 250 euros per prostitute. Annually, that is a tax-free winning of 360 million euros. The women only get a small part of the money. This is the reality of the new slavery market.

Police Experts' Warnings before the European Union Extension

May 1, 2004, was a very important day in Europe when 10 new member countries joined the European Union. The European Union now has 25 member states in Europe. The population of Europe has grown by about 20 percent, now reaching 450 million citizens (compared to 290 million in the United States). The power of the European economy has grown by 5 percent.[5]

With the growth of the European Union, Germany has become the paradise for Eastern European criminal organizations, groups, gangs of pimps, and mafia structures. Additionally, there are thousands of illegal red-light district workers and prostitutes from the new European Union countries, the Baltic states, Poland, Tschechia, and Slovakia who work legally in the true sense of European law in Germany. Police experts estimate that, since 2004, more than 140,000 prostitutes from Eastern Europe are in Germany illegally. They do not have permission for their stay, but a lot of them do not need such permission after May 1, 2004. Now they can offer their work legally in dwellings and residences, in call houses, and on the streets. A prostitute from Tallinn, Estonia, said, "In Germany, I can earn 10 times more than in Estonia. I'll go to Germany, seeking a fine sex club!" The legal problem is that the persons behind these women are not breaking a law, as in years past, because German laws against aliens have been relaxed. Women trafficking was the main reason that police were watching organizations and gangs and making raids on criminal traders and smugglers of human beings. This new legal situation is a huge problem in the future control of the sex industry. Now the prostitutes have the status of freelance workers. They do not need permission to take employment. They only need employers.

One may think that the brutality against the prostitutes in the red-light sphere will increase, but this is not so. Now the gangsters are after the relatives and the family members of these women. The new freedom for travelers means that Germany will be confronted with more than 60,000 criminals from the European Union's new member states. All criminals registered in the computers based on the Schengen Information System has been effaced. So to say, the German police officers of the German Federal Border Guard and Federal Border Police now have to bid their former criminal clients "a very good day and a good trip" because there are no more remarks about a forbidden entry into Germany and the European Union. In the past few years, the mafia and other organized crime groups from newly independent states have become citizens of the new European Union member states or of offshore states (such as the colonies of Great Britain), hence enlarging their criminal radius. This makes it impossible to track criminal beggars, the children trained for theft and robbery, murderers, smugglers of stolen cars, pimps, bank robbers, burglars, and men of oppression, violence, assault, rape, and sexual abuse of children.

It is not accurate when politicians in Germany and Europe say that nothing has changed since May 1, 2004. The opposite is true. Eastern European criminals can now do their criminal activities very easily. Since May 1, 2004, all these persons are now citizens of the European Union as a result of Art. 17 of the European Union. We are losing our quality standards for the security of the interior of Germany.

Sexual Abuse of Children

The term "abuse," as in "child abuse," "wife abuse," or "elder abuse," is frequently encountered in the criminological, victimological, psychological, and gerontological literature. It seems to be gaining greater popularity with the passing of each day. When abuse can be objectively established and measured, such as in cases of physical, sexual, or financial abuse, one finds that the type of victimization involved already constitutes a crime under the provisions of "assault," "assault and battery," "aggravated assault," "sexual assault," "indecent assault," "theft," "fraud," "forgery," and "breach of trust," among others (Fattah 1997).

The numbers of sexual child abuse offenses are alarming. The increase is dramatic. Although sexual offenses against children are specifically outlined in the Criminal Code, child sexual abuse may be generally defined as any sexual exploitation of a child, whether consent is given or not. Some examples of exploratory questions might include the following:

- Who wakes the child up in the morning?
- Who in the family sleeps with the child?
- When the child has a bath, who helps her?
- Who babysits the child when her parents are away?
- What are special activities that the child shares with members of her family (mom, dad, siblings, offender)?
- Does the child share any "secrets" with anyone that might make her feel uncomfortable?

Sexual abuse of children is a daily reality. There are more experiences of incest than broken legs and appendicitis. At young ages, children (both male and female) are victims of incest. From five years of age and older, girls have an 80–90 percent chance of being victims of incest. It is almost always persons they trust and believe in, persons in their lives they really love, who will abuse them. All children are vulnerable, regardless of class, age, sex, race, or family situation. It is terrible to mention it, but most sexual abuse takes place within a trusting relationship. Always the offender takes advantage of the child's innocence, dependence, fear, and his or her position of power in the child's life. Often the abuse begins at a very young age with fondling and is kept secret through bribes, threats, and special attention. It can continue for years, eventually escalating to penetration or oral sex.

The world is full of strangers. How frightening it must seem to a child who has been taught that all strangers are dangerous. A child's molester is much more likely to be someone with whom the child is familiar, someone who belongs to the child's household. Most strangers do in fact have the welfare of children at heart, but children can be tricked. "It's best to be careful with people you're not sure about!"

Clues That Show a Child May Be a Victim of Sexual Abuse

Physical signs include the following:

- Difficulty in walking and sitting
- Discomfort going to the toilet
- Genital or rectal bleeding
- Frequent urinary infections
- Bloodied or torn underclothing
- Bruises, bleeding, or cuts to vaginal or anal areas
- Unusual or offensive body odors
- Bruising in unusual places such as armpits and mouth
- Throat infection
- Things placed in the rectum or the vagina

Behavioral and emotional signs include the following:

- Regression to more babyish behavior, such as wetting the pants and rocking
- Inexplicable hostility and aggression
- Frequent unprovoked crying
- Obsessive masturbation
- Reenactment of the abuse in play
- Poor concentration
- Displaying sexual knowledge that should be outside a child's experience

- Fear of particular places and people
- Withdrawal, depression, or anxiety
- Changed eating habits, such as appetite loss or problems with chewing or swallowing
- Changed sleeping habits, such as bedwetting, nightmares, fear of being left along, and crying in the night
- Psychosomatic illness
- Too frequent bathing
- Wearing too many layers of clothing
- Artwork depicting sexual behavior that is abnormal for a child
- Inexplicable attention-seeking behavior

Girls abused by trusted persons often end up in a future career in prostitution. The story of Jennifer in Dortmund is a good example. Raped by her uncle when she was 12 years old, she became a streetwalker for a pimp when she was 13, and then slave of a brothel and erotic club members. At 14 years of age, she was lonely, without money, desperate, and disappointed in life. About 80 children and youngsters with similar experiences were rescued and saved from this terrible situation in 2003 in Dortmund by "The Midnight Mission of Dortmund," a pilot model project. This is the tip of the iceberg. Many girls came to the mission with wounds, illnesses, and diseases such as syphilis, pox, gonorrhea, and clap, and many feared that they had AIDS. Their reports about their "clients" are very cruel and terribly inhuman (see http://www.standortdortmund.de/mitternachtsmission).

Although our understanding of the problem of child abuse has indeed increased, we need to know a great deal more about the offense before we can reduce its occurrence. Interpersonal violence is learned at home and transmitted from one generation to the next. Studies demonstrate that children who are raised by aggressive parents tend to grow up to be aggressive adults. Other researchers have demonstrated how stress, frustration, and severe psychopathology take their toll on family relationships. A few researchers have also explored the role of body chemistry. One investigation ties abuse to the tendency of males to secrete adrenaline when they feel sexually threatened. The relationship between domestic violence and the use of alcohol and drugs has also been explored. Abusive men with severe drug and alcohol problems are more likely to abuse their wives, girlfriends, and children when they are drunk or high and to inflict more injury (Adler, Mueller, and Laufer 1991).

We all share the duty of protecting the child. We should be aware of the dangers facing children and protect them from the criminals. We have to do more against these criminal acts and stop trafficking in children. We should help the United Nations International Children's Emergency Fund fight trafficking in children worldwide. Lost and abducted children need our help. The traffickers of children are working very actively and like top professionals. Children and youngsters (male and female) from countries such as Moldova and Romania are displaced in the Baltic states, Poland, Tschechia, and Western European states. Girls as young as 12 years of age are sold for a good price to prostitution rings. Young children are trained and forced to engage in begging for money and stealing, and they are forced to work in adverse conditions that are not good for their age.[6]

Legislation

In the course of the follow-up work to the World Congress against Commercial Sexual Exploitation of Children and as part of the efforts to provide a comprehensive form of protection for the population, the Federal Ministry of Justice has examined the existing range of punishment as regards to the need to adapt it to a new interpretation of values. Action was taken in the form of the Sixth Law Reforming the Criminal Code, which went into effect on April 1, 1998. The provisions of this act include a more stringent penal assessment of cases of sexual abuse of children and the dissemination of child pornography publications as well as a significantly stiffer measure of sentence for these offenses.

Serious cases of sexual abuse of children have been treated, since April 1, 1998, as felonies rather than, as has hitherto been the case, as misdemeanors and also have been treated according to the severity of the punishable act in question, generally resulting in a prison sentence of a minimum of one, two, or five years, up to a maximum of 15 years, which is the maximum fixed-term prison sentence available in Germany. The previous range of penalties was between 1 and 10 years imprisonment that was applied to all cases.

With regard to cases in which children are sexually abused for the purpose of producing and disseminating pornographic material, the reform law has introduced a new category of crime for which a range of punishment of between 2 and 15 years imprisonment shall generally apply.

Furthermore, the act extends Sec. 5, No. 8, Letter b of the Criminal Code so as to improve the possibilities of criminal prosecution of Germans who sexually abuse children abroad (cases of so-called "child sex tourism"). From now on, such cases can be prosecuted by German judicial authorities, even if the German offender's base of existence is abroad.

With regards to the commercial and gang-structured dissemination of child pornography publications that portray actual or true-to-life events, the maximum prison sentence, as laid down in Sec. 184, Para. 4 of the Criminal Code, has been increased from 5 to 10 years. In addition to these measures designed to tighten up Sec. 176 and 184 of the Criminal Code, the sixth law reforming the Criminal Code has extended the penal regulations against the abduction of children as laid down in Sec. 235 of the Criminal Code and introduced Sec. 236 of the same as a new penal regulation against illegal trafficking in children. The aim of these measures is also to improve the means available to combat the sexual abuse of children.

Effective April 1, 1997, Art. 4, No. 4 of the Information and Communication Services Act of July 11, 1997, has already widened Sec. 184, Para 4 and 5, Sentence 1 of the Criminal Code (dissemination and possession or obtaining professionally or as the member of a gang, of child pornographic writings that reproduce an actual event) in such a way ("actual or true-to-life event") that cases in which, by all appearances, a real event seems to have been reproduced, but when it cannot be excluded that the representation is simulated, are also covered. This may be the case for virtual sequences that are distributed through the Internet. For clarification, Sec. 11, Para. 3 of the Criminal Code, to which the foregoing provisions refer, has been amended to include the term "data storage media" in Art. 4, No. 1 of the Information and Communication Services Act.

The federal government checks all provisions of the youth protection legislation for any need to amend the individual definitions of risk. In this context, the introduction of a new definition of crime is also being considered under which the representation of naked children and young persons in unnatural and sexually colored poses shall be regarded as causing persistent grave harm to children and young people. Consequently, the implication of listing them is objectionable, and the restrictions on distribution, passing on, and advertising shall apply even in the absence of previous listing. For media that convey a distorted picture of what are normal relations between young individuals and adults and are misleading about the limits of self-determination rights of children and young people constitute a serious risk to children and young people in that they compromise their possibilities to fend off sexual assaults by adults.

The Federal Criminal Police Office (Bundeskriminalamt [BKA]) in Wiesbaden has been addressing the problems brought about by the Internet. It does so by performing random searches and spot checks of sites. The aim is to detect offenses, identify the perpetrators, and thereby deter others from using the Internet for criminal pursuits, to prevent offenses altogether, or to make them harder to commit. The Federal Criminal Police Office continually monitors the Internet and other online services on a systematic and non-incident-related basis for contents that are of police relevance, especially child pornography contents, and to collect, secure, and record the evidence.

Insofar as investigations abroad involve the Federal Republic of Germany, liaison officers from the BKA are deployed on the ground. These officers are generally responsible for the exchange of information with the relevant authorities of the host country on matters related to combating the drug trade and organized crime. More than 53 liaison officers are currently working around the world, in 38 countries, where they are stationed at 41 different locations with the additional expansion of the network planned for the future. These Federal Office of Criminal Investigation employees stationed abroad also support investigations in child pornography and child sex tourism.

Conclusion

Rape and sexual child abuse and all forms of exploitation of women and children occur regularly, within every society and culture. To fight against the crime of abducting and trafficking women and children is not an easy task. It is a social taboo that is difficult to prevent. More publicity about the facts of sexual assaults is needed to dispel myths so that all victims, regardless of their gender or sexual orientation, can come forward to receive the help that they need without feeling that they will be ridiculed or blamed for their assault.

And let's remember the Police Officers' Freedom Bill for Children:

- Every child has the right to a drug-free environment.
- Every child has the right to be free from violence.
- Every child has the right to live free and protected from all forms of physical, sexual, and psychological abuse.
- Every child has the right to possess property without fear of theft.
- Every child has the right to a role model, such as a police officer, whose responsibility is to provide guidance towards a lawful path in life.
- Every child has the right to actively participate in youth programs offered by communities and law enforcement agencies.
- Every child has the right to enjoy life to its fullest, to achieve his/her dreams, and to become law-abiding and productive citizens of our society.
- Every child has the right to be protected against all forms of harassment and discrimination.
- Every child has the guaranteed right to equal protection under the law.

Notes

1. Hutchings, N. 1988. *The Violent Family: Victimization of Women, Children and Elders*. New York: Human Sciences Press, p. 133.
2. Federal Ministry for Family, Senior Citizens, Women and Youth. 2001. Report of the Federal Republic of Germany on the Occasion of the Multilateral Conference on the Protection of Children from Sexual Exploitation, Budapest, November, 20–21. Berlin, p. 11.

3. "Short Noticed by DPA." 2004. *Der Patriot*, April 24.
4. http://www.bild.t-online.de/BTO/meingeld/aktuell/2004/04/18/EU_Erweiterung_BamS.
5. http://www.bild.t-online.de/BTO/news/2004/04/26/huren_alarm/huren_alarm.template.
6. National Crime Prevention Council. 1992. *Protecting Our Children*. Washington, DC: International Association of Chiefs of Police, Crime Prevention Committee, p. 2.

References

Adler, F., Mueller, G. O. W., and Laufer, W. S. 1991. *Criminology*. New York: McGraw-Hill, pp. 236, 239.

Baum, L. 1986. *American Courts: Process and Policy*. Boston: Houghton Mifflin.

Brownmiller, S. 1975. *Against Our Will: Men, Women, and Rape*. New York: Simon and Schuster.

Fattah, E. A. 1991. *Understanding Criminal Victimization*. Burnaby, Canada: Simon Fraser University, p. 76.

Fattah, E. A. 1997. *Criminology, Past, Present, and Future: A Critical Overview*. London: St. Martin's Press, p. 61.

Walker, S. 1980. *Popular Justice: A History of American Criminal Justice*. New York: Oxford University Press.

7 The Nature and Extent of Trafficking in Women and Children in the United Kingdom

WILLIAM HUGHES

This chapter looks specifically at the operational response in the United Kingdom to the criminal enterprises involved in trafficking in women and children. Although it sets the overall context, it is an operational perspective. In common with European partners, the United Kingdom believes that there has been a rise in the trafficking of women and children over the past few years. What is unclear is the scale of the rise and the current level of activity. Much of the information to date has been patchy and anecdotal.

In 2000, a Home Office research study, "Stopping Traffic: Exploring the Extent of, and Responses to, Trafficking in Women for Sexual Exploitation in the UK," concluded that there were no accurate estimates available either nationally or internationally. The report identified 71 women known to have been trafficked into prostitution in the United Kingdom in 1998 but added that there was a hidden trafficking problem several times greater than they were able to document with certainty. They were able to estimate that the scale of trafficking of women into and within the United Kingdom lay within the range of 142 to 1,420 per year.

The issue of trafficking of children to the United Kingdom came to prominence in the mid 1990s, when an investigation focused on unaccompanied children arriving from West Africa who were thought to be in transit to other European countries. Monitoring of the routes used by the traffickers highlighted a small but steady flow. However, there is no reliable data to show that trafficking in children is a significant issue in the United Kingdom.

In London, police noticed a rise in foreign nationals involved in off-street prostitution. A snapshot survey performed in 1999 indicated that, in some sectors of the vice trade, notably off-street prostitution, foreign nationals made up a significant majority of prostitutes. Recent intelligence confirms this assumption. More recently, a successful operation against a trafficking ring gave insight into the potential scale of the problem. The arrest of the main trafficker in one organization uncovered an operation that had trafficked 60 women into the United Kingdom from Eastern Europe, mainly from the rural parts of Moldova and Romania. Assessments are currently underway to provide an updated profile of this sector in the United Kingdom and fill gaps in the intelligence picture. Some of the obstacles faced include the following:

- Under-reporting of the offenses by those encountering trafficked victims attributable to lack of awareness of the problem
- Lack of reporting by victims themselves for fear of reprisal by traffickers
- Confusion in identifying those trafficked from those who have willingly travelled and from those children who have arrived unaccompanied for immigration purposes

Understanding these distinctions is crucial to establishing the true nature and scale of the problem. Wrongly classifying individuals can lead to an inappropriate level of response.

Despite these gaps, the organized trafficking of women and children is now recognized as a major threat to the United Kingdom. The 2003 UK Threat Assessment places organized immigration crime high on the list of major threats and identifies human trafficking as, arguably, the most acute threat within the category because of the continuing exploitation involved and the frequent use of intimidation and violence.

Nature of Trafficking in Women and Children in the United Kingdom

Operations and assessments undertaken point to sexual exploitation as the predominant type of trafficking, although other forms have been encountered.

The increase of foreign nationals identified in the off-street prostitution trade in London is beginning to spread to other major metropolitan areas. Off-street prostitution is favored to overcome language difficulties. Although Eastern European nationals have figured heavily in operations to date, the actual spread of nationalities is extensive. Those encountered include nationals of Albania, Bulgaria, China, Croatia, Lithuania, Latvia, Moldova, Nigeria, Pakistan, Romania, Russia, Somalia, Sri Lanka, Thailand, Turkey, and Vietnam.

There are some women who have worked previously in the vice trade in other countries before their arrival in the United Kingdom. The movement of women across national boundaries and, perhaps, from vice trade to vice trade, gives a glimpse of the level of organization involved.

The recent dismantlement of a London-based trafficking ring gives a clearer picture of how the trafficker operates. The main trafficker recruited girls from rural areas in Moldova and Romania and lured them to the United Kingdom with promises of employment and money. Once in the United Kingdom, they were supplied to brothels to begin paying off the debt of bringing them here. The trafficker even married one of the girls to secure her earning potential, but she was required to work at the brothel on her wedding night. It was claimed that assault and rape were used to ensure that the trafficked women met their targets. The full extent of the trafficker's income has yet to be established, but several bank accounts already indicate an income of in excess of 1 million pounds. His activities came to light when two of the trafficked women escaped from his control.

Sexual exploitation is the most common form of human trafficking encountered in the United Kingdom, but other forms do exist. The use of women and children to partake in street crime such as aggressive begging and pickpocketing is not a new phenomenon. However, only anecdotal information suggests that women are being trafficked to the United Kingdom to provide this service to criminal enterprises.

Labor exploitation is a form of trafficking that affects women, children, and men. There has been little evidence of serious and organized criminal activity in this field beyond the organized use of illegal labor in service industries such as hotels and catering. However, it is an area that will be covered by legislation.

Perhaps the most pernicious example to come to light so far in the United Kingdom involves an ongoing investigation into the discovery of a child's dismembered torso in the River Thames. The assertion that the child was brought to the United Kingdom from West Africa as part of a ritual sacrifice is being seriously pursued by the investigation team. The trafficking routes are numerous and include the United Kingdom as a transit point as well as a final destination for trafficked women and children. Traffickers are well resourced and flexible, able to change routings and modus operandi quickly in response to increased measures taken against them. Circuitous air routings are used to avoid enforcement measures taken against them. Deception of visa staff, or the immigration officer on arrival, is a favored method of traffickers bringing small but regular numbers to the United Kingdom. Concealment in vehicles, the preferred tactic of the volume smuggler, is also used.

The Precipitating Factors of the Trafficking

The trafficking of women and children is not a new phenomenon. What has changed over recent years is the scale in terms of numbers and geographical spread. It has become a global phenomenon fed, in part, by an increasing demand within commercial vice trades.

There are many reasons, some causal and some that facilitate, but many that are interlinked:

- Availability of cheap travel and the opening of previously closed borders has led to an increase in the geographical spread of trafficking.
- Poverty and deprivation still provide the economic spur to trafficking. It is here that distinctions between trafficking and smuggling merge; the desire for economic betterment not necessarily for the victim but for the extended family remains a powerful push factor.
- Poor education and lack of awareness can enable the trafficker to deceive victims with the lure of a better life.
- The involvement of organized crime, driven by profit, creates a motive to continue their businesses. The victim becomes a commodity.
- Globalization of business that allows criminal enterprises to operate internationally.
- Technological advances, in which the development of the Internet and communication systems enable traffickers to respond quickly to demands.
- Weaknesses in legislation and procedures enable traffickers to operate in jurisdictions where they cannot be prosecuted and, if they are, provide little deterrent in terms of penalties.
- Lack of international cooperation between source, transit, and destination countries negates individual efforts.
- Lack of domestic cooperation between agencies can lead to the problem of "falling through the gaps," with no clear lines of responsibility and accountability.
- Lack of resources coupled with insufficient priority accorded to tackling the problem can lead to available capability being used on other problem areas.
- Increase in irregular migration can provide a screen for the activities of traffickers, making it more difficult to distinguish the victim of trafficking from a smuggled migrant.
- Political/religious upheaval is another driver whereby a vulnerable population will take risks to escape their current predicament.
- Mass population movements bring with them differing demands and opportunities for criminal gangs to exploit.

Strategies Developed to Counter this Menace

It appears clear that any response to counter trafficking in human beings (THB) requires a strategy that includes the following:

- A strong legislative footing
- Support to victims
- A multiagency operational response that relies on intelligence-led policing
- Preventive and reduction strategies
- Strong overseas partnerships

The United Kingdom has developed a multiagency and multilateral approach that addresses each of these areas. The United Kingdom is a signatory to the United Nations (UN) Protocol on Trafficking that supplements the UN Convention on Transnational Organized Crime. A subsequent European Union Framework Decision covered trafficking for sexual and labor exploitation and was adopted in July 2002. It commits European Union member states to introduce criminal sanctions covering trafficking for sexual and labor exploitation within two years of its adoption. The framework decision also sets European Union-wide maximum penalties of eight years imprisonment for these offenses.

The Nationality and Immigration Act of 2002 introduced a stopgap offense of trafficking for the purpose of controlling a person in prostitution with a maximum penalty of 14 years. This offense came into force on February 10, 2003. More comprehensive offenses for trafficking into, within, or out of the United Kingdom for the purpose of sexual exploitation have subsequently been included in the Sexual Offenses Act of 2003, with a maximum 14-year penalty. In addition, an offense of trafficking for the purpose of exploitation, including forced labor and organ removal, is included in the Asylum and Immigration Bill currently before parliament.

One of the main challenges in combating human trafficking lies in providing support to victims. Traffickers can secure the noncooperation of victims toward law enforcement with threats of violence, reprisals against their families back home, or exposing their often illegal residence status. The United Kingdom has been pursuing various options to ensure that victims of trafficking are properly supported. This includes looking at assistance to allow them to escape their circumstances and, in certain cases, help law enforcement against organized criminals. When they are willing to come forward to the authorities, we are looking at special arrangements for their protection. We will also consider whether it would be appropriate to allow them to remain in the United Kingdom. The government is working with the International Organization for Migration to establish a return policy for victims who are not entitled to remain or who want to return to their country of origin. This will help to ensure that those who return home are helped to reintegrate into their own community. A scheme for adult victims of trafficking has been introduced. This involves using a voluntary organization with considerable experience in providing specialized housing to victims of domestic violence and other vulnerable women.

Recognizing those who may have been trafficked is an essential element of any strategy. The United Kingdom has published a trafficking toolkit that provides a best-practice guide for immigration officers, police, and others who potentially may come into contact with victims of trafficking. In particular, it seeks to raise awareness of the difference between trafficking and smuggling and help those concerned to treat victims fairly. However, providing refuge and legitimizing their immigration status may still not be sufficient to persuade victims to provide evidence against the traffickers. The United Kingdom is considering whether it is possible to develop a victimless strategy to investigating human trafficking, that is to say, a strategy that does not rely on the evidence of victims to prosecute or disrupt the traffickers.

The basis of such an approach lies in intelligence-led policing and proactive rather than reactive investigations. Disruption also forms part of the strategy, finding the weak spot in an organization to target and using the widest possible range of legislative and administrative tools to do so. These may include financial investigation, asset seizure, and use of administrative immigration powers.

In 2000, the United Kingdom developed a multiagency operational response to tackle organized immigration crime. Known as "Reflex," this multiagency approach brings together law enforcement, the intelligence community, and government departments under a common strategy and shared objectives. It is chaired by the Director General of the National Crime Squad, the operational police organization responsible for spearheading the fight against serious and organized crime.

Reflex is responsible for tackling all aspects of organized immigration crime. Its overall aim is to reduce the harm caused by serious and organized criminality involved in people smuggling and human trafficking by doing the following:

- Raising the risks that the criminals must take
- Rendering their illegal businesses unprofitable
- Reducing opportunities for them to exploit communities

Led by intelligence, Reflex operational and preventive measures target those crime groups involved in the following:

- Volume facilitation of illegal migrants
- Human trafficking (in particular the trafficking of women and children)
- Running the criminal infrastructures that serve to both facilitate illegal entry and exploit the illegal population once in the United Kingdom

Building on the National Intelligence Model, Reflex has developed systems in which agencies share intelligence on traffickers, jointly consider the best tactics for disruption, and decide who is best placed to carry it out. The strength of such an approach lies in the varied backgrounds, expertise, and resources that different agencies bring to the table. It requires individual agendas and cultures to be set aside, an achievable outcome providing all agencies share in the success of operations. This cooperation extends to include joint operational teams in which police officers work alongside immigration officers, an innovative approach considering that immigration officers in the United Kingdom are civil servants and not from a police background. Wherever they operate, traffickers are motivated by profit. Identifying and seizing assets, disrupting the underground money flows, and making it unprofitable for the gangs to operate form a major plank of the approach of the United Kingdom. However, realizing profits from organized immigration crime does not always rely on selling a commodity at the end of the process. Effective action requires the successful blend of existing expertise with new thinking and tactics.

Targeting trafficking feeds into the wider strategy of asset recovery by the United Kingdom, the aims of which include the following:

- Make greater use of the investigation of criminal assets in the fight against crime.
- Recover money that has been made from crime or that is intended for use in crime.
- Prevent criminals and their associates from laundering the proceeds of criminal conduct and to detect and penalize such laundering when it occurs.
- Use the proceeds recovered for the benefit of the community.

Financial investigators are therefore being allocated to immigration crime teams, and a central Reflex money-laundering unit will target sophisticated illegal money flows that support trafficking and other forms of organized immigration crime. However, Reflex is not only about developing operations against trafficking and facilitators. Under its banner, a number of overseas partnerships have been developed, leading to systems and procedures being introduced or strengthened to help tackle trafficking at the source or along the transit routes. This in turn serves to reduce the opportunities for the traffickers to exploit.

A good example has been Reflex Romania, in which a partnership with colleagues in Romania has developed a unit based in Bucharest to disrupt illegal migration and trafficking flows from and through Romania and its neighboring countries. The creation of a central intelligence unit has led to a significant number of arrests and disruptions. During its first phase of operational activity, 105 criminal groups operating in this sector were identified, 48 were disrupted, and 90 individuals were arrested in relation to immigration or trafficking offenses.

A slightly different focus was used in partnerships working with Italian, Serbian, and Montenegrin colleagues. The main achievements in this project, known as IMMPACT 2, have been to build strategic working relationships with Serbian and Montenegrin colleagues and to provide specialist training on passenger analysis, forgery, and anti-trafficking measures, the latter delivered in conjunction with the International Organization for Migration.

Under Reflex, the United Kingdom continues to develop overseas partnerships with projects in Bulgaria and Macedonia currently underway. A network of overseas liaison officers specializing in organized immigration crime, including human trafficking, have been introduced to develop and sustain their joint work with overseas partners.

Issues of Interest

This chapter outlined the operational approach to tackling human trafficking by the United Kingdom. It did so from the perspective of considering human trafficking as part of the threat posed by serious and organized immigration crime.

Most countries now agree that we face a significant threat from criminal gangs involved in human smuggling and trafficking that are increasingly sophisticated, well funded, and dynamic. Organized immigration crime is a big business. Although it has brought new criminal groups to the fore, it has also seen others switch from other commodities in which routes, safe houses, and transportation can all be used and in which skills in forgery, counterfeiting, and money laundering can all be transferred. Although there are gangs who offer and operate an end-to-end service, our increasing knowledge reveals many loose alliances providing specialist services, helping the human cargo to be moved the next link up the chain.

The fight is not fair. We have laws, rules, regulations, and procedures to follow. It can take months, even years to achieve a change in policy. Flexibility is critical if we are to make any headway. We must exploit any weakness, think laterally to disrupt their activities, target their finances, and use an intelligence-led approach. Critically, we must avoid playing into their hands by creating additional internal barriers that restrict our actions.

The position of the United Kingdom is that THB and people smuggling can often provide two strands of organized immigration crime and that a joint strategy, which recognizes and acknowledges the key distinctions, is the most appropriate way forward. Otherwise, there is a danger of tunnel vision developing, with multiple strategies allowing traffickers to exploit differences in approach.

The distinctions between the two areas of criminality are clear in the legal sense. Trafficking is more of a victim-focused crime than illegal immigration. How victims of trafficking are identified, handled, supported, and, if appropriate, returned does need careful and separate consideration. This is recognized in the Protocol on Trafficking under the UN Convention against Transnational Organized Crime.

THB also encompasses various forms of exploitation. Although THB for sexual exploitation may be considered the most significant current threat to the United Kingdom, trafficking for labor exploitation and other forms cannot be overlooked. Although intelligence on this latter sector is limited, it is nevertheless important to recognize that the source countries for trafficking for labor exploitation may not be the same as those for sexual exploitation. It is recognized that THB is not wholly an immigration offense. Although it is true that trafficking does not necessarily have to involve a border crossing, the numbers of those trafficked within the United Kingdom is likely to be a small proportion of the total. It is more likely that either they will have been smuggled or deception was deployed to secure entry. It is tempting to portray traffickers and human smugglers as two separate criminal groups. There are criminal elements that do distinguish one from the other, critically the exploitative elements. However, this presupposes that those involved control the whole end-to-end process. Certain groups do exist that have the capability to do this. However, it is equally clear that this area of criminal activity is moving beyond the family business operated along strictly ethnic lines.

Mixed commodities of several nationalities are increasingly common, as are loose alliances of different criminal groups offering different specialist services. Elements of the trade, such as transportation, production of false documentation, and harboring at transit points, are provided by specialists operating as subcontractors to the main traffickers/facilitators. These criminals are motivated by profit and are unlikely to be concerned with the ultimate fate of the human commodity. This provides common ground for taking operational action against both sectors.

Although trafficking is considered to be a more heinous crime than smuggling, it is, nevertheless, inappropriate to consider those involved in smuggling as providing a form of illicit service industry. They are serious criminals, motivated by greed and who seek to use the humanitarian issues surrounding migration as a veil for their criminal behavior.

Additionally, it is not appropriate to consider that the relationship between a smuggler and a smuggled migrant ends once the person has reached his or her destination country. Unless the migrant has paid in full in advance, the smuggler will invariably continue to exert control until the balance is paid. In such circumstances, does the smuggler become a trafficker and the migrant a victim of trafficking?

There is a significant difference between a victim who has been trafficked and a migrant who has been smuggled. In legal and procedural terms, they require separate handling once they have been identified. However, in operational terms, especially when proactive intelligence-led investigations are being planned, the status of the human commodity may not be readily identifiable from the outset.

Furthermore, if the recruitment of the trafficked persons is carried out by force, then the situation is clear from the outset. However, many of those who end up as victims of trafficking began their journey in search of a better life and to provide money for the families they left behind. Either at the outset or at some point in their journey, they are deceived and find themselves working, for example, as prostitutes without any control over their earnings or workload. Indeed, they may have worked in the vice trade in their own country and may have known that they would be doing so in the destination country. Nevertheless, they find themselves being subjected to inhumane treatment. A similar scenario applies to those who are promised work in sectors other than the vice trade.

This blurring of motivation and consent makes it extremely difficult to separate the two issues at the outset of an investigation or even when an investigation is underway. Any operation must be intelligence led, based on solid crime analysis with a clear strategy to counter identified threats. At the center of this is an operational tasking group charged with managing activity and ensuring that intelligence flows are maintained. This approach supports the National Intelligence Model that law enforcement in the United Kingdom is developing to ensure a more proactive method for preventing and detecting crime.

Human trafficking is a serious organized crime. Operational activity against serious and organized crime must focus on the criminal rather than the sector or commodity if it is to stand any chance of matching the flexibility the criminals can demonstrate.

Perspectives from Africa

III

Criminal Exploitation of Women and Children: The Kenyan Experience

8

GABRIEL O. NDOLO

Introduction

Exploitation, in all its forms, has been with humankind ever since creation. In Genesis, we read that Satan took advantage of Eve to settle a score with God. This theme of exploitation is seen throughout the Bible. Even animals practice exploitation. For example, once lions conquer a territory, they kill all the cubs and then fertilize the females to perpetuate their hegemony.

Exploitation can therefore be seen as a natural way of life. It is based on inequality of the participating parties. So long as there is inequality, be it based on economics, politics, education, race, sex, or religion, there will be exploitation. As far as criminal exploitation is concerned, it is the weak that are susceptible. These vulnerable groups tend to be children (of both sexes) and women.

This study is about criminal exploitation of women and children in Kenya. The problem is discussed in the next section, and this is followed by the objectives of the study. Assumptions as well as the significance of the study follows, and the chapter ends with a summary.

A look at newspapers in Kenya reveals that there is a lot of exploitation of both children and women as far as crime commission is concerned. Examples include the following. On Monday, February 9, 2004, one of the dailies reported that gangsters used children of the age of 14 and 16 to transfer weapons across the capital city, Nairobi. On the following day, another daily reported that girls as young as 17, commonly known as "twilight girls," were arraigned in court charged with a criminal offense of loitering with immoral purposes (Sec. 182 of the Penal Code). It was also an offense under the Nairobi City Council bylaws to loiter with prostitution intentions.[1]

When asked why they were loitering, the girls said they needed the money for their upkeep as they had tried a new business, but the businesses did not do very well. Therefore, they had to make ends meet. Four days later, a female civil servant working with the Ministry of Lands and Settlement was charged with sexually exploiting a 16-year-old boy by inducing him to engage in sexual activities and causing him to abandon school contrary to Sec. 15 of the Children Act.[2] This section states that the following: "A child shall be protected from sexual exploitation and use in prostitution, inducement or coercion to engage in any sexual activity, and exposure to obscene materials."[3]

To show that the exploitation is not confined to nonrelatives, it was also reported on Friday, February 13, 2004, that a chief (a government administrator in charge of a location) had been jailed for seven years for raping his nine-year-old stepdaughter and infecting her with a disease.[4]

These examples show that criminal exploitation of women and children is almost a daily occurrence in Kenya. This is illustrated by the fact that there are more than 2,000 cases of rape (including attempted rape) reported every year. The figures also appear to be increasing, with the year 2003 recording 2,308 cases. Criminal exploitation is therefore rampant in Kenya and needs to be addressed, hence the objective of this study.

The objectives of this study are as follows: to look at the nature and extent of criminal exploitation of women and children in Kenya; to find out the reasons that contribute to this phenomenon; to examine the strategies that have been adopted by Kenya to encounter this menace, with a view of identifying the ones that have proved effective; and to explore any other issues of interest from the perspective of women and children's exploitation.

This study is guided by the assumption that the ones who are less powerful are the ones that stand to be exploited. The exercise of power in a social process helps to explain how different people can influence the behavior of others. French and Raven (1968) identified five main sources of social power that individuals can use to exploit others: reward (especially economic reward), coercion, legitimacy (or the use of one's position in the organization), referent or charismatic power, and expertise or knowledge. These five power bases are used to explain the reasons and extent of criminal exploitation in Kenya.

As early as the late 1970s, the office of the United Nations (UN) High Commissioner for Human Rights had been interested in the elimination of all forms of discrimination against women and children. In 1997, a convention on the elimination of all forms of discrimination against women was opened for signature, ratification, and accession by the UN General Assembly resolution 34/180 of December 18, 1979. This convention had 30 articles. They are the relevant articles that will be used to examine the strategies that have been adopted by Kenya to encounter the menace of women's exploitation.

Children have also been found to be prone to abuse. This led to a UN Convention on the Rights of the Child. Again, this convention will guide the discussion. Because Kenya is a signatory to all these conventions, it is now time to examine the strategies that have been adopted by Kenya with a view to identifying the ones that have been effective. This study is therefore very valuable at this stage.

Criminal exploitation can be defined as the unfair use of others to commit a crime for the exploiter's benefit. An example is when a parent lets his child be employed, and it is the parent that benefits. Other forms of exploitation are running brothels, tricking others to defraud, and rape, which is sexual exploitation.

Theoretical Framework

As stated previously, exploitation is only possible if the person exploiting has some form of social power over the person being exploited. These bases of social power as identified by French and Raven (1968) are reward, coercion, legitimacy, expertise, and referent power. Reward power is based on performing a criminal act hoping to gain some benefit, usually money. Most hit squads and so on do so because they expect to be rewarded.

Coercive power is based on one's ability to punish the other party for not meeting requirements. An example that comes to mind is a bank robbery or robbery with violence. What the criminal exploits here is his strength and the victim's weakness. Legitimate power is when a person in authority uses his authority to exert influence. An example is sexual harassment by a boss in an office. Expert power is based on the perception or belief that the individual has some relevant expertise or special knowledge that the person influenced does not have. An example is when one is conned of money on the strength that the conman has the power to "double" the money.

Last, there is referent power. It is based on the victim's desire to identify with or imitate the criminal. Examples are many, such as people being led to cut their own throats as well as defying law and order, like the Mungiki sect in Kenya, who brainwashed its followers to commit crimes because they are followers of a certain political party.

Quite a number of studies have been done in Kenya as far as criminal exploitation of women and children is concerned. Human Rights Watch or Kenya Human Rights Commission conducted most of these studies. These studies are on property rights violations, blatant disregard of labor laws, and abuse of human rights.

Property Rights Violations

Sec. 75 of the Kenya constitution deals with protection from deprivation of property. However, a study by Human Rights Watch (2003) documented many women's property rights violations, which are frequent and extreme when it comes to inheritance and division or control of matrimonial property. Rural widows told Human Rights Watch that their relatives took their property, including their land, homes, vehicles, livestock, furniture, and household items when their husbands died. Case studies were cited across the various ethnic groups on widows that lost their property to in-laws. Even Muslim widows, in which property rights are protected under the Islamic law, were not spared, as in the case of Amina Juma whose property was confiscated, including a pension fund, canoes, fishnets, a house, cows, and household items.

Examples were also cited from urban areas. Adhiambo Nyarkumabor, whose husband died of HIV/AIDS in 1998 and left her HIV positive with five children, went from being relatively affluent to destitute after her husband's family took her property. Although inheritance law provides that daughters and sons should inherit equally from parents, when there is no will, it is uncommon for women in Kenya to inherit property from their parents, as is the case for this Maasai lady who said, "A lady cannot inherit property." If they inherit at all, then they get less than their brothers.

Divorced women leave the marriage with nothing. One of those who were interviewed by Human Rights Watch said, "When I left home, I did not take anything, just the clothes I was wearing." When she later filed for divorce, she did not seek division of matrimonial property. "I just wanted to leave my husband. I am not interested in the other property," she lamented.

Married women also have very little control over family property. This is blamed on customary laws among some ethnic groups that dictate that "all property a woman acquired before or during the marriage belongs to her husband." This, however, is contrary to Kenyan law, which recognizes women's rights to own separate property during marriage.

Labor Laws and Human Rights Abuse

The Employment Act states that one should not work for more than 60 hours in a week. The constitution protects people from slavery and forced labor (Sec. 73) and provides protection from discrimination on the grounds of race or tribe, to name a few provisions. In its study, the Kenyan Human Rights Commission (2004) reported that, in the export processing zones (EPZ) in Kenya, there is blatant disregard of national labor laws and abuse of human rights, particularly of women, who form 70 percent of the workforce.

The report reveals tales of excessive production targets, broken homes, sexual harassment, exploitation, unfair dismissals, overwork, and underpayment in the factories. Workers are even denied leave in the spirit of minimizing production costs and maximizing profits.

The deputy managing editor of the *Daily Nation* (a leading newspaper in Kenya) puts it this way:

> The sister of a friend who had a degree in clothing and textiles was forced to resort to the EPZ when she could not find a job. Her pay, 2,500 shillings (about $30) a month. (This is well below the minimum monthly wage.) Her hours of work 6 a.m. to 6 p.m. six days a week.[5]

Sexual Abuse and Exploitation of Children

Sec. 15 of the Children Act of 2001 protects a child from any form of sexual exploitation and use in prostitution, inducement or coercion to engage in any sexual activity, and exposure to obscene material.

In its study on sexual exploitation of children in the Eastern and Southern Africa Region (2001), the African Network for the Prevention and Protection against Child Abuse and Neglect, United Nations International Children's Emergency Fund (UNICEF), reported that sexual abuse and exploitation of children is reported to be rampant in Kenya. This abuse is a result of poverty, rejection within the family, and children dropping out of school, as well as the breakdown of traditional family values. Prostitution is widespread among street girls who hawk or beg during the day but prostitute at night. It has to be noted that prostitution is not stated as illegal in Kenya; rather, according to Sec. 154 of the Penal Code, "living wholly or in part on the earnings of prostitution" is illegal. The report also states that abuse in school is common, and many girls are forced to drop out as a result of physical, verbal, and sexual harassments. Some girls are also forced to service teachers to avoid additional harassment or to receive passing grades. The children are also not spared as far as the agricultural sector is concerned. Here many girls are forced to provide sexual services to obtain work on plantations. The report concludes by saying that the myth of the curative properties of sex with children is an important factor in the growth of child prostitution. Child sex, the report continues, has also been promoted by tourism. This sexual exploitation includes both girls and boys. There are also accounts of poor families selling their children to tourists. Other centers in which child prostitution is rampant include military bases (Nanyuki) and refugee centers. As for child pornography, there is very little information on it in Kenya.

The study relied heavily on library research. This was supplemented by an in-depth interview using a questionnaire as a guide. The data required were basically on the nature and extent of criminal exploitation of women and children in Kenya, the reasons that contribute to this phenomenon, the strategies that have been adopted to counter this menace, and the ones that have proved to be most effective.

Key respondents dealing with women and children were questioned. These included a divisional police officer, priests in charge of a Catholic and an Anglican church, a provincial director of culture (which deals also with women's affairs), an officer in charge of a nongovernment organization (NGO), and a provincial prison's officer. Others were a provincial children's officer, an officer in charge of an approved school (reformatory), an area commissioner, scouts, and district and provincial probation officers. Also interviewed were a senior resident magistrate and a district social development officer.

A look at Kenyan newspapers reveal that there is a lot of criminal exploitation of both women and children. This exploitation is based on social power.

The bases of this social power include rewards, force, expertise, legitimacy, and identification. The more of these powers one has, the greater is the likelihood of them exploiting others.

Nature and Extent of Criminal Exploitation

The available literature tends to agree that there is a lot of criminal discrimination as far as women are concerned. This is captured by a report of the Task Force for the Review of Laws Relating to Women (1998) which stated that the current state of gender relations treats male dominance as legitimate, natural, obvious, and inevitable. The effect is to create a social power hierarchy, in the context of which women are, by and large, reduced to powerlessness, economic marginalization, social vulnerability, and cultural inferiority. From cases cited in the literature review section, women seem to be exploited when property rights are concerned. Those interviewed added also rape and domestic violence.

Quantification of the extent of criminal exploitation of women is difficult because most of the cases are never reported. However, it is believed that criminal exploitation is extensive as far as property rights abuses are concerned. Human Rights Watch states that these are not exclusive to one social class, ethnic group, or religion. Rape is also on the increase according to available records. As for domestic violence against women, it is debatable whether it can be classified as criminal exploitation.

Factors that Contribute to Criminal Exploitation of Women

Property Rights

As far as rights are concerned, women's limited ability to own and control property is a product of historical, political, legal, and social development. Historically, property rights were vested in the clan where women did not belong. Women's access to most property was through male relatives (usually husbands). Whereas men had tenure, women had only the right of use.

Politically, the issue of land has been discussed with emphasis on ethnic and social economic equality but not gender equality. In most cases, what happened historically is what was inherited after independence.

Legally, there was a debate in the 1960s about reviewing the rules of inheritance, and a commission was set up. The recommendations of the commission resulted in the Law of Succession Act of 1981. This act failed to come up with a uniform way of division of family property after divorce or separation. In 1985, a bill that would have specified a uniform method of recognizing spouses equal rights in division of property was shelved when members of parliament said it interfered with men's ability to "chastise" their wives.

Economic Development

Women are worse off than men. Their average earnings, according to the National Development Plan of 1997–2001, are less than half of the men. Only 29 percent of those engaged in formal employment are women, and they account for only 5 percent of registered landholders nationally. This, therefore, puts them at a point where they are likely to be exploited.

The strategies that have been attempted to address the criminal exploitation of women are basically legal. This started with the constitution of Kenya, which outlaws discrimination on the basis of sex (Art. 82[3]). However, Art. 82(4) exempts certain laws from the discrimination prohibition. It permits discrimination "with respect to adoption, marriage, divorce, burial, and devolution of property on death or other matters of personal law." These are areas that are vital to women's property rights. The Law of Succession Act of 1981 attempted to bring some uniformity to succession in Kenya, but it too contains several discriminatory provisions. It ended up giving greater rights to men than women. This led to Muslim protest, and so the act was amended in 1990 to exempt Muslims from this act. In an interview with a magistrate in a rural area, he had this to say: "The Law of Succession Act is applied only to the educated. If it is in the rural area, we don't want to interfere with community set up."

The constitution and other laws that address discrimination against women and property rights have not gone far enough. As such, NGOs such as Human Rights Watch and women's organizations have worked hard to fill the void. Their work involves representing women in legal proceedings as well as advocating for legislative and social changes. Through their efforts, a new draft constitution included Sec. 35, whose emphasis is on guaranteeing that women's rights be equal to those of men. This draft constitution is still under discussion.

Another strategy that has been used by NGOs is trying to empower women (especially bar maids and commercial sex workers) by providing them with alternative means of earning a living. These, however, are very selective and localized and are almost nonexistent in rural areas.

Children's Issues

As far as children are concerned, they seem to be criminally exploited in terms of child labor and sexual abuse, which includes defilement, underage marriage, and incest. Others include conveying illicit goods.

Child Labor

According to the International Labor Organization, 4 million (or 41.3 percent) school-aged children in Kenya are working. Girls are more disadvantaged than boys, because they are the ones chosen to do the domestic chores and therefore are readily available for domestic work in towns and urban areas. Child labor is therefore widespread, and this goes against the labor laws as well as the Children Act.

Sexual Abuse

Studies done by Population Communication Africa state that child exploitation exists in the form of child prostitution, incest, early child marriage, rape, sodomy, indecent assault, and defilement. It tends to be widespread given that a day hardly passes without this type of exploitation being reported. The culprits include strangers, boyfriends of the child's mother, relatives, especially stepfathers and close cousins, and even friends. In the *Sunday Standard* of February, 29, 2004, it was reported that 38 percent of children in Kenya today have been sexually abused by an adult by the time they reached the age of 18.

Child Pornography

Child pornography, according to a special report by the *Sunday Standard* of February 29, 2004, "is one of the major problems in Kenya today." This is because pornography can be accessed through Internet cafes, which are quite common. Unfortunately, the law in Kenya is very lenient on this. According to Sec. 20 of the Children Act, a convicted person is liable for a term of imprisonment not exceeding 12 months or to a fine not exceeding 50,000 shillings (about one month's salary of an upper-middle-class civil servant).

Conveying Illicit Goods

Children are also subjected to conveying illicit goods as well as getting into burglar-proofed houses because of the size of their bodies. It is not easy to quantify the extent because most of the children never get caught as a result of their innocent looks.

Reasons for the Exploitation

The major reason for criminal exploitation of children is poverty. This is what is cited by Population Communication Africa. The majority of those who are exploited are poor, and this forces their parents to use them to earn a living. This explains both sexual exploitation and child labor. Other reasons include broken families or family disagreements, when the father takes out his frustrations and commits incest with the daughter of his estranged wife.

A provincial children's officer added to the list of reasons "improper socialization," especially in slum areas, where children are exposed to sex at an early age. The law, until recently, treated rape as more serious than indecent assault. This again has been blamed for the persistence of this offense. According to End Child Prostitution in Kenya, people commit this crime because they know they can get away with it. Lack of institutional protection of children also leaves them vulnerable to exploitation. In certain communities (especially along the coast), sex with minors is culturally acceptable. In fact, it was reported that a health minister was shocked to see a 17-year-old girl with four children of her own in a hospital clinic.

Strategies

The strategies used in Kenya can be divided into two: namely, through legal and policy frameworks and through the NGOs. These NGOs, especially CARE Kenya, try to empower all children through nonformal education. Art. 34 of the UN Convention on the Rights of the Child calls for governments to take all measures to prevent the inducement or coercion of a child to engage in any sexual activity. It also calls for governments to prevent the use of children in prostitution, pornography, or other sexual activities. These issues have been addressed through the Children Act of 2001. If the draft constitution is passed, then Sec. 37 will protect the child against all forms of discrimination, including child labor. As far as the penal code is concerned, the law remained inadequate in regard to children's rights. This inadequacy in law was addressed through the Criminal Law (Amendment) Act of 2003. In this section, the sentence for defilement and other forms of sexual exploitation was enhanced.

In the same act, Sec. 124 of the Evidence Act was amended to allow for evidence from a child in a criminal case involving a sexual offense. Previously, a child's evidence needed corroboration by other material evidence.

Nongovernment Organizations

The strategy used by these organizations is basically educational, as is the case with CARE Kenya. UNICEF also educates street children in Kenya on HIV/AIDS. The Global March was also involved in creating awareness against child labor. These strategies seem not to have been successful. First, most of the sexual activities are not reported, and, if reported, they involve relatives. This makes it very difficult to obtain evidence that may lead to conviction.

Second, defilement cases are very difficult to prove. A court in Kenya, late last year, acquitted a rape suspect simply because the court wanted a DNA test to be done on both the victim and the suspect, something that a poor victim cannot afford. It is also poverty that drives poor families to hire out their underage children to be used as house servants. So unless poverty is effectively addressed, child labor will still continue.

The approaches of the NGOs also lack merit because educating girls once a week (as CARE Kenya does) on basic arithmetic, reading, writing language skills, and general knowledge is too little too late. This is because Kenya is not short of learned people, and educating a child on these basics will not make them competitive with others as far as getting employment is concerned. As for stiff sentences, criminologists have not agreed that a sentence of offenders, which is carried out far away from the public, will really deter others. So stiff sentences may help placate the relatives of victims, but whether it will reduce sexual exploitation is debatable. Rather than addressing the exploitation from the legal or academic perspectives, it should be addressed from an economic angle, because the root cause is poverty.

Conclusion

The objectives of the study in Kenya were to look at the nature and extent of criminal exploitation of women and children, find out the reasons that contribute to this phenomenon, examine the strategies that have been adopted by the Kenyan government to counter this menace, identify control strategies to see whether they have proved effective, and explore any other issues of interest from the perspective of women's and children's exploitation.

The nature of the exploitation as far as women are concerned is basically in property rights, especially on matters of inheritance. Another form of exploitation is on labor laws in which women are overworked and underpaid. They also suffer rape and domestic violence.

The extent of some of this exploitation and discrimination is difficult to quantify, but it is far in excess of what is reported either to the police or in the daily newspapers.

The contributing factors to this exploitation are historical, political, legal, and cultural when concerning property rights. The strategies that have been used to try to address these issues are basically legal, but they have not been successful. In response, NGOs have tried to fill the void by attempting to correct the wrongs that discriminate against women.

As far as children are concerned, the nature of their exploitation includes child labor, sexual abuse (of both boys and girls), and using them as conduits for illicit goods. The major reason for criminal exploitation of children is poverty. This explains why they engage in child labor and sex. The rise of slums and the increasing number of single parents also socialize children to early sex. Children also lack institutional protection, such as a minimum age for marriage. The extent of exploitation is widespread, with girls being more prone to it than boys.

Strategies that have been used are legal, but, because the reason for exploitation is poverty, legislation alone is of little help. NGOs have tried to fill the void. They half-heartedly address this by providing nonformal education to selected categories of children (e.g., house helpers), but this is too little too late. Another issue that needs to be addressed is child pornography. However, it is very difficult to control this because of the increase in the use of the Internet.

In conclusion, there is criminal exploitation of both women and children in Kenya. The major reason for this is poverty. The government as well as NGOs have tried to address these issues through legislation and trying to empower the exploited through education and rehabilitation of prostitutes through provision of alternative sources of earnings.

These measures have not been successful because poverty cannot be reduced through legislation alone. Approaching only a selected group, such as barmaids, and trying to empower them does not encompass all the issues.

Being a way of life, it is very difficult to recommend a universal way of dealing with the abuse of women and children. However, the following approaches are recommended. First, empower the women and encourage them to secure property in their own rights. This will protect them from property exploitation.

Second, enforce Sec. 7 of the Children Act of 2001, which calls for free and compulsory basic education in accordance with Art. 28 of the UN Convention on the Rights of the Child. This will make children not easily available for child labor. Finally, the government has to create employment opportunities for women and young persons. Efforts must be made to prevent single women and girls having children without a strong economic base.

Notes

1. *The People Daily*, February 10, 2004.
2. *The People Daily*, February 14, 2004.
3. Kenya Republic Constitution, Sec. 15, 2000.
4. *Daily Nation*, February 13, 2004.
5. *Daily Nation*, February 20, 2004.

References

Achieng, J. 1998. "Children Continue to Get a Raw Deal." Interpress News Service, January 20.

African Network for the Prevention of and Protection against Child Abuse and Neglect. 1999. Summary Report on the Global March against Child Labor (GMACL) in Kenya, January 14.

Commentator. 2004. "Teenagers' Involvement in Violent Crimes." *East African Standard*, February 9.

French, J. R. P., and Raven, B. 1968. "The Bases of Social Power." In *Group Dynamics: Research and Theory*, 3rd ed., edited by D. Cartwright and A. F. Zander. New York: Harper and Row.

Gopal, H. 2002. *Gender and Law: Eastern Africa Speaks*. Washington, DC: World Bank, p. 22.

Johnston, T. 2002. *Domestic Abuse in Kenya*. Nairobi: Population Communication Africa, p. 10.

Kameri-Mboyte, P. 2004. "Violence against Women in Kenya: An Analysis of Law, Policy and Institutions." International Environmental Law Research Centre working paper, no. 2000-1. Nairobi: International Environmental Law Research Centre.

Kenya, Republic of. 1997a. *The Constitution of Kenya*. Nairobi: Government Printer.

Kenya, Republic of. 1997b. *The Penal Code (Cap 63): Laws of Kenya*. Nairobi: Government Printer.

Kenya, Republic of. 1997c. *National Development Plan, 1997–2001*. Nairobi: Government Printer.

Kenya, Republic of. 2001. *Kenya Gazette*, supp. 95 (act no. 8). Nairobi: Government Printer.

Kenya, Republic of. 2003. *The Criminal Law (Amendment) Act*. Nairobi: Government Printer.

Nesaba, D. 2004. "Women Hardest Hit by HIV/AIDS." *East African Standard*, February 9.

United Nations Development Programme. 2001. *Kenya Human Development Report*. New York: United Nations Development Programme, p. 67.

Criminal Abuse of Women and Children in Benin

9

ANTOINE AZONHOUME

Introduction

Benin is a small West African country, surrounded by Nigeria in the east, Togo in the west, Niger in the northwest, Burkina Faso in the north, and the Gulf of Guinea in the south. It was a former colony of France, and it became independent on August 1, 1960. It covers an area of 112,600 square kilometers, with a population estimated at 60 million inhabitants (by the census of 2000), including 52 percent women, 48 percent men, and 49.2 percent young people below 15 years of age. About 70 percent of the population live in the rural areas and mainly carry out subsistence farming. In 2001, the rate of illiteracy and the percentage of children in full-time education were 35 percent and 4 percent, respectively.

Benin is a poor country, ranked 161st on the UN Human Development of 2008. The per capita gross domestic product is low: 121,000 francs per year in 2000. The industrial fabric is insignificant. The government draws most of its financial resources from cotton and services (customs, taxes, and air and sea transits).

At the religious level, most of the Benin people are animists, and the Vodoun cult is largely practiced, but it harmoniously cohabitates with some monotheistic religions, such as Christianity, evangelist sects, and Islam (http://www.gouv.bj).

Benin is a democratic country. It signed several international agreements and covenants in terms of the respect for human rights that it considers as capital values. Indeed, human dignity is inviolable. Any human being has the right to the respect of his life and to the physical and moral integrity of his person.

No one can arbitrarily be deprived of this right. Any individual has the right to the respect of the dignity inherent to his legal personality. All forms of human exploitation and debasement, namely slavery, the slave trade, physical or moral torture, and cruel, inhuman, or degrading sanctions and treatment are prohibited (Art. 4, African Chart of Human Rights). Despite its good political intentions and its strong will to back the above mentioned concepts, Benin cannot be considered as a country fully respecting human rights.

In general and like many other populations of the world, the Benin people violate the most elementary human rights every day. In particular, women and children are the victims of such violations because of the country's poverty and customs. Criminal human exploitation is reprehensible because it goes against the law and moral standards. Exploitation against women and children arouses horror and revolt, because it is turned against human beings who are weak and defenseless.

Following this reality, it is necessary to answer the following questions:

- What is the nature and level of women's and children's exploitation in Benin?
- What are the causes of this phenomenon?
- What strategies have been adopted to fight against this plague?
- What approaches have proved the most efficient?
- What are the other approaches to tackle the issue in Benin?

From north to south, Benin society is a feudal and chauvinist society. The absolute domination of man over woman and that of parents over children is a system of social values. In Benin, equality of all before the law proclaimed by the December 11, 1990, Constitution is the acceptable standard. So, we can easily understand why women and children, aware of their inferior social status, accept and undergo, with a heavy heart, various forms of ill treatment from their husbands, fathers, or employers. Below are some of the manifestations of these misdeeds.

Criminal Exploitation of Women

Physical Violence

Physical violence concerns physical abuses of women at home. These abuses comprise any kind of assault and battery used to punish the woman and to make her submissive at home.

Moral Violence

This is an offense against the personality and dignity of women. It is manifested through threats, insults, blackmail, humiliation, mockery, contempt, indifference, and all sorts of deprivations, all things that tend to place a woman in a situation in which she feels like an inferior human being without rights.

Sexual Violence

The uncontrolled sexual appetite of men often leads them to have reprehensible behavior toward women. Rape is defined as having sexual intercourse with a woman without her consent and is a practice that is commonplace in the society and in families. The number of rapes is unfortunately and constantly increasing in Benin, and this is so for two reasons: (1) the public, and particularly the victims, for a sense of decency or for fear of reprisals, refuse to denounce the perpetrators of these misdeeds; and (2) although rape is classified in the category of crimes, it has never been punished as such by courts in Benin.

The penalty inflicted is only correctional sanctions. This laxness of the judges, which is not far from impunity, does not enable the perpetrators of this infraction to appreciate its seriousness. Rapists, as a consequence, keep on raping.

Sexual Harassment

Sexual harassment, as a form of moral and sometimes physical violence, mostly exists in such locations as work places, companies, schools and universities, apprenticeship centers, hairdressing salons, and couture houses. Sexual harassment is manifested by repeated assaults on schoolgirls by teachers, employees, headmasters, and heads of training centers who, by their social or professional position, oblige through donations, blackmail, false promises, or other insidious means, women (especially young girls) to satisfy their sexual desires.

There is a typical case illustrating this form of sexual aggression described in a review titled "Pour une société sans violence á légard des femmes au Bénin":

> The phenomenon moves dangerously from work places to schools and universities where those in charge of educating young girls blackmail them for a sexual purpose. Such is the case of a female student who was harassed by her professor for three years with the threat of never getting her master's degree. To discourage her professor she was obliged to get pregnant from her boyfriend. But that did not solve the problem. She has never succeeded in passing the subject of this professor.[1]

This case occurred at the Faculty of Technical Science of the National University of Benin, Division of Chemistry-Biology-Geology.

Incest

Incest, a vile act that consists of having sex with one's own daughter, is frequent in Benin society, but only few cases are communicated to the police. Many others have never been reported for fear of covering the perpetrator's family with opprobrium or for fear of reprisals from the perpetrator.

Other Forms of Sexual Exploitation with Economic Coloration

It is useful to recall that the domination of man over woman, domination coupled with an outmoded conception of affective and marital life, leads a man to choose for his daughter the type of marriage that suits him, namely the one from which he draws personal advantages to the detriment of the will and liking of his daughter. According to police registers, the types of unions imposed on women are as follows.

Simple Forced Marriage: In a simple forced marriage, the young girl at the age of getting married does not have the choice of her husband. He is imposed on her by force whoever he may be: old man, young man, or handicapped man, it does not matter. She has to accept the choice made by her parent.

Marriage by Exchange: Marriage by exchange is practiced in some northern localities of the country. It consists of exchange between two families of their respective daughters to strengthen friendship ties or for reason of interfamily gratitude.

Marriage by Abduction: Marriage by abduction is the kidnapping of the young girl by her future husband with consent of the bride's family. Marriage by abduction is an act of physical and moral violence very traumatizing to a woman because, in most cases, the young girl does not know her husband until the abduction date.

Levirate: Levirate is a disguised form of forced marriage. It consists in obliging a widow to take for her spouse a member of the family of her departed husband. The foundation of this non-free union is to prevent the widow from leaving the extended family of the departed, taking with her as a consequence the children of the departed to another family. The woman is prevented from leaving because of the dowry received by her parents, which turns her into her husband's property for life, even after the death of her husband.

From all these types of marriage mentioned above, one important common characteristic is the total absence of the woman's will to freely make the choice of her husband. The choice of her husband and the working of her marital life are designed for her and imposed on her by other people. By doing so, she is deprived of the most passionate and exalting element in marriage: love.

Rites of Widowhood

According to the customs of some Benin southern regions, the widow should honor the memory of her late husband and appease his soul by performing the following ceremonies:

(1) Drinking mystical potions to give evidence of her innocence regarding the cause of the death of her husband

(2) Sleeping near the body of the departed before the burial
(3) Drinking the water from the washing of the dead body of her husband (in some extreme cases)
(4) Revealing, if need be, the names of the men with whom she committed adultery during the lifetime of her husband
(5) Living in seclusion for a few weeks, even months (a year among the Igbos of Nigeria), with the obligation of not taking a bath, combing herself, and getting dressed decently
(6) Weeping twice or three times a day to manifest her sorrow for her late husband[2]

Any widow who refuses to perform these ceremonies is widely considered responsible for the death of her husband, through bewitchment, poisoning, or betrayal (adultery).

The Foundation of Exploitation in Benin

To understand the reasons for the criminal exploitation undergone by women and children in Benin, one must seek to understand the mentality of the population at the social, economic, sociological, and religious levels.

The Flaws of Benin Society

Benin society, as a whole, is a society of gender discrimination. The education of women lies on an age-old tradition that considers them second-class human beings after men; a woman has to be obedient and submissive to a man. This is the sacrosanct rule of the strong sex over the weak sex.

Religious Beliefs

Women pay a heavy tribute to religious beliefs, sometimes absurd, such as widowhood ceremonies, the placing under forced residence of women for weeks during the "ORO divinity" ceremonies in Benin Yoruba areas, and voluntary or forced offerings of young girls to Vodoun divinities in ceremonies to become members.

Economic Distribution of Women's Labor

According to the customary law of most ethnic groups in Benin, women do not have the right to heritage. In addition, even if they helped their husbands in farm production, they do not take a total profit of it. They just receive a small part in compensation of their toil, enough for their survival.

It derives from the above that this sexual segregation is a direct element of women's pauperization, which is the maintenance of women's permanent economic dependence on their husbands or on men.

Other Elements of Women's Pauperization

Besides the fact that women are deprived of heritage and the fruits of their toils, they become poorer for the following reasons:

- Long period of widowhood and their ritual ceremonies during which women are neither allowed to go out nor to work
- Some husbands' refusal to allow their wives to work under the pretext of making them always available for housework and children's education
- Certain husbands unjustified fear of losing their authority over their wives if the latter, by holding jobs, could acquire their financial autonomy

Criminal Abuse of Children

Criminal abuses of children are numerous and include the following: kidnapping of children by criminals; abandoning children, causing them to become delinquents; inhuman physical treatments, including bodily injury and deprivation of many kinds (feeding or educational); and hard toils that largely exceed children's physical capacity. This is the case of 220 Beninese minors aged 7 to 13 years recovered by the Nigerian police in fine gravel and sand factories at Abeokuta in Nigeria, where they were used as workers by unscrupulous dealers.

Fraud Trafficking

Victims of fraud trafficking are usually street boys and village children. The dealer who recruits them proposes a future of better living conditions to their parents, but, once abroad, they are simply delivered to third parties who use them in all sorts of toil for insignificant remuneration.

Pawn Trafficking

Pawn trafficking consists of pawning a child in exchange for a granted loan. The child is used in the fields or in business by the lender. He is only returned to his parents at the term of the work contract furnished, which corresponds to the amount of the incurred debt by the borrower (parents).

Sale Trafficking

Sale trafficking is selling children (slavery) to third parties in exchange for money because the children are a product of rape or adulterous relationships. Another reason is if the children are considered as sorcerers; in other words, those whose first teeth grew from the upper gum or have six fingers or raised toes presenting a congenital malformation. Additionally, some children, especially those from the northern part of the country, are either executed or abandoned somewhere by their own parents.

Disguised Trafficking

Disguised trafficking consists of taking a child abroad by means of plenary counterfeited adoption documents and then disposing of the child for money in the destination country.

Contract Trafficking

Contract trafficking consists of placing the child with a third party against an amount of money corresponding to the duration of the investment and the child's age. In effect, children are exported like goods to neighboring countries by some groups of Beninese who live there. Among those countries are Gabon, Nigeria, Ivory Coast, Equatorial Guinea, Congo, and Cameroon. Some of those children face all kinds of abuses.

Abuses of Girls

Besides the different kinds of child abuses mentioned above, females are also subjected to the following crimes.

Educational Discrimination

Girls are generally excluded from the field of education by their own parents who think they are more useful for housework and small business than going to school. They are compelled to get married for the money (dowry). That is why, in a population of 60 million inhabitants, only 374,622 girls (13 percent of the national population) receive primary school education. Besides, girls more than boys are subjected to educational loss. The girls abandon school either because of precocious pregnancy or for social and economic reasons.

Excision Practices and Other Genital Mutilations

The odious practice of excision justified by certain cultures or religions in some Benin regions as a means of making women stand by their husbands is a kind of severe physical injury to them. In effect, genital mutilations entail severe consequences such as sterility, libido reduction or frigidity, and death caused by hemorrhage.

Rapes and Attempts on Modesty over Minors

Children are, most of the time, easy prey to sexual criminals who make them undergo any sort of sexual aggressiveness such as rape and attempts on modesty. Sometimes vicious people use tricks to obtain children's sexual favors by enticing them to debauchery by which naïve girls are easily introduced to sexual pleasure, begin to like it, and then finally get stuck in it.

Pedophilia

Another sexual deviance, pedophilia, already exists in Benin society. Many cases of sexual intercourse with children of less than eight years are noticed by competent state police services.

It is important to say precisely that those who carry out such villainous deeds benefit from the age of their victims, who do not put up any resistance because the children are incapable of resisting or are ignorant of what is going on around them.

The previous long list of criminal acts or deeds shows in reality moral and physical abuses undergone by women and children, presently still considered in Benin as instruments of carnal pleasure or inexpensive labor.

Controlling the Abuse of Women and Children

As far as the struggle against criminal abuse of women and children is concerned, Benin bases its restraining action on the following texts, conventions, and agreements: the United Nations' Universal Declaration of Human Rights; people and human rights African charter of June 27, 1981; the December 18, 1979, convention on the elimination of any sort of discrimination in consideration of women; the convention relative to human rights of November 20, 1989; the convention relative to slaves of September 25, 1926; the December 2, 1949, convention on the human trafficking repression and the third party's prostitution abuse; the additional convention relative to the abolishment of slave traffic and similar institutions and practices of September 7, 1956; marriage authorization, marriage minimum age, and marriage convention of November 7, 1962; the convention against torture and other cruel and inhuman penalties or treatments; the convention concerning children's worst labor forms prohibition of June 17, 1999; the child's rights and good living conditions African charter; the December 11, 1990, constitution; Bouvent Penalty Code; the 61-20 law of July 5, 1961, relative to minor's displacement out of the national territory; and the 95-19 decree of June 21, 1995, concerning the modality of issuing administrative authorization as far as minors younger than 18 years old going out of the national territory.

The System of State Control over the Criminal Abuse of Children

The state police service, bound to the home secretary (Ministry of Interior), has the following goals: protection of adolescents and children by means of maladjustment prevention; the investigation of crimes and offenses committed by underage persons (those younger than 18 years old); and investigation of underage persons who are physically and morally in danger and abandoned.

Adolescence, Childhood, and Family Board

It is a structure under the control of the minister for family, social protection, and solidarity. It ensures adolescents' and children's safeguard and protection. It also participates with underage protection brigades in the struggle against any types of violation of children's rights, namely, child trafficking and physical and moral ill treatments.

Other Civil Service Organizations

Besides the aforementioned two civil services, many other institutions, nongovernment organizations, and associations provide their intellectual or financial help to the protection of children's rights and more generally of human rights in Benin, including the United Nations International Children's Emergency Fund, Benino-Belge Red Cross, the Carrefour d'Ecoute et d'Orientation des Soeurs Missionnaires de la Charité, the foundation Regard d'Amour, the Association de Femmes Juristes du Bénin, and the Soeurs Salesiennes. The results obtained, as far as the struggle against criminal abuse of minors is concerned, are the fruit of civil structures and other private institutions' miscellaneous actions. However, the more effective for repression of perpetrators of crimes and offenses against women and children is the one that is launched by the Benin police. For this purpose, the adopted strategy to face the plague consists of establishing children's trafficking prevention structures because the trafficking is the starting point of most of the abuses to which they are subjected. So, organizations called "supervising brigades" post guards in the most affected areas of children subjected to trafficking to look after security of the children and prevent their recruitment by traffickers.

Other Solutions

It is important to note that the deeper reason why some provide their children to traffickers is poverty. It is established that children subjected to trafficking are from poor rural areas, where domestic agriculture is not sufficient to feed the inhabitants. In urban centers, it is again children from poor areas that are affected by this trafficking. It derives from the aforementioned analysis that poverty is at the heart of child trafficking.

Another solution to the problem of trafficking in children is to restrict the number of children per Beninese family to two or three. Such birth restriction will have multiple benefits:

(1) The love for two or three children, the care and the control over them, will obviously be more qualitative than the case of a family of 15 children. In a large family, the departure of certain children does not unbearably preoccupy the family, and their absence is even sometimes considered a relief for already overburdened parents.
(2) Also, in a family of two or three children, parents are generally better able to provide, even if it is modestly, for their progenies.

In the short term, improvement in Benin's economic conditions will eliminate trafficking in women and children for slave labor and prostitution, because trafficking in women and children is a struggle against poverty. For this strategy to be effective, it needs some essential immediate measures such as development partnerships, international aid, and a national economic reorganization capable of furnishing jobs to the population and raising the purchasing power of the impoverished in small towns and rural areas.

Conclusion

From Benin's natural, economic, sociocultural, and religious organizations come the criminal deeds committed by its inhabitants. Their origins come from a mentality and a culture of the Beninese people. That is why any economic, moral, and physical errors attributed to women can be explained by the inferior social status conferred unjustly to them by Benin society. Likewise, the different forms of trafficking to which Benin's children are subjected have one explanation: the poverty of their families.

On the whole, to fight against the criminal abuse of children, Benin society has to be one in which human rights are actually respected, but this goal cannot be achieved without a real revolution of mentality and culture and without the creation of an economic superstructure to fight against poverty. When there is a will to combat this kind of physical and moral delinquency, criminal abuse of women and children will be eliminated. It does not need to be said that it is more a duty for the Beninese, rather than a simple will, to fight against this vice. Human rights have to be respected as a starting point in protecting women and children from perpetual bondage to men.

Notes

1. Women in Law & Development (WiLDAF) Benin newsletter. 2003. June, 15–16.
2. These requirements for widows are common in many ethnic groups in Africa south of the Sahara.

10 Criminal Exploitation of Women and Children: Domestic Workers in Kenya

VICKY KARIMI

Introduction

Exploitation of women and children takes various forms in different countries. In Asia, South America, and parts of Africa, it is usually in the form of trafficking. Women and children are smuggled and sold into slavery for bonded labor, child labor, and sexual exploitation, including prostitution and pornography.

In Kenya, it mostly takes the form of labor. Women and children enter the labor market mainly as casual laborers, domestic servants, and agricultural workers. The exploitive terms of service for these two groups are glaringly evident. Their conditions of work depend solely on their employers' status and goodwill. Legislation, when it exists to protect these marginalized groups, lacks proper enforcement, with the end result that the exploitation of women and children as bonded laborers in Kenya is prevalent and commonly accepted in the culture.

Kenyan society's definition of gender roles has resulted in the feminization of domestic labor. Although there are male workers in the country, especially in other sectors of the labor force, their population is hardly comparable with that of women and girls employed in Kenyan homes as domestic workers. It is primarily with these two vulnerable groups that this chapter is concerned. This chapter will therefore focus on domestic labor of women and children in the country.

The Kenyan government has identified this problem and sought to address it through legislation, partnership with organizations that seek to eliminate child labor, and other long-term strategies. This chapter will also examine the success of these efforts and will make recommendations on ways to eliminate exploitation of women and children in the labor market in Kenya.

Legal Framework

International Law

The United Nations' Universal Declaration of Human Rights[1] declares the following:

(1) Everyone has the right to work, to free choice of employment, to just and favorable condition of work and protection against unemployment.
(2) Everyone, without discrimination, has the right to equal pay for equal work.
(3) Everyone who works has the right to just and favorable remuneration ensuring for himself and his family an existence worthy of human dignity, and supplemented, if necessary, by other means of social protections.
(4) Everyone has the right to form and to join trade unions for the protection of his interests.

The African Charter on Human and People's Rights[2] further acknowledges an individual's right to work under "equitable and satisfactory conditions." Kenya, a party to both of these instruments, has a duty to ensure that the conditions stipulated therein are present in its labor market. That has hardly been the case.

There still exist a number of international instruments to which Kenya is not a party, which, if ratified, would enhance the protection of labor rights in the country. Kenya has yet to ratify one of the most important International Labor Organization (ILO) conventions,[3] "the freedom of association," which provides workers and employees with the right to establish and join organizations of their own choice with no previous authorization.

Also interesting to note is that, of the 181 International Labor Organization conventions, Kenya has ratified only 47, or approximately 25 percent of the total.[4]

National Laws

In Kenya, labor is mainly addressed under The Employment Act[5] and The Regulation of Wages and Conditions of Employment Act.[6] However, the main problem with the current labor regulations in the country is that the national laws are insufficient in some respects, for example, with regard to persons employed on a casual basis to whom certain labor rights, such as benefits on termination of employment and maternity leave, do not apply.

When the laws are sufficiently in place, they lack proper enforcement and serve as an ideal that many employers do not try to achieve. Ignorance of the labor laws cuts across the board in Kenya from the workers themselves to government officials. This, coupled with the need for labor in all spheres of everyday life in the country, makes the use of the Kenyan legal system, with regard to labor in Kenya, very selective.

In the case of domestic workers who are the subject of this paper, national laws hardly recognize them. The factors that contribute to this are mostly their ability to be unionized and the private nature of their work. National laws are usually only resorted to in extreme cases, for example, the numerous reports in the Kenyan media on assault cases by employers on their mostly female employees. This is a group marginalized even by the law.

Objectives

This paper is intended to discuss the nature and extent of criminal exploitation of women and girls in Kenya in the domestic labor sector, determine the reasons that contribute to this phenomenon, identify the strategies that Kenya has adopted to counter this problem and their effectiveness, and make relevant recommendations.

To achieve these objectives, the study will examine the legal framework, both local and international, in which labor issues are addressed and compare these with the current situation, the background of domestic labor in Kenya, the nature and extent of exploitation of women and girls in domestic labor, what measures the government has taken to eliminate the problem, and give relevant recommendations.

Domestic Labor in Kenya

Who Is a Domestic Worker?

A domestic worker is defined as "any person employed wholly or partly in any private household in any one of the following capacities, namely cook, house servant, waiter, butler, baby-sitter, valet, footman, chauffeur, bar attendant, groom, gardener, garden laborer, laundry-man, or watchman/guard."

In common Kenyan language, they are referred to as maids, house girls, houseboys, or ayahs. Their job descriptions are not at all as clearly defined as envisaged by the law above, in which a single individual performs all of the specified roles and any other conceivable position of labor that may arise in the household.

In the case of women, they are usually those who have dropped out of school mostly as a result of poverty, biases against the education of girls, or teenage pregnancy. In the case of children, it consists mainly of boys and girls from poor families who have become another source of income to their families, either out of a genuine attempt by their families to give them a better life or by commercialization of child labor.

It has not been possible to accurately assess the number of girls and young women forced into domestic labor in Nairobi, but it is in the thousands.[7] Most urban homes in Kenya have at least one house helper either living with the family or who comes to the house on a regular basis. What is clear is that the majority of domestic workers in Kenya are women and girls.

A Brief Background

Historically, paid domestic labor originated in the colonial period. As in all patriarchal societies, there existed in Kenya a marked division of labor across gender lines. It is interesting to note that domestic labor in colonial Kenya was mainly the purview of men. It was the male members of the family who left their own homes, mostly in the rural areas, to work in white households as a means of earning a livelihood.

The post-independence period saw the feminization of domestic labor in the country, with more women joining the workforce and gradually constituting the larger percentage of domestic workers. A more recent and worrying trend has been the entry of children, especially girls, in large numbers into this sector. Commercialization of domestic child labor has become rampant.

Domestic labor has therefore largely taken on a female character and is seen as "women's work." Currently, the number of male domestic workers can hardly be compared with that of women and girls. The erroneous feminization of gender roles together with social constructs of what work should be done by which gender have been the largest contributors to this new development.

The Nature of Domestic Labor

Domestic labor is "invisible." It is unregistered and does not form part of the national employment statistics. It is restricted to the private sphere of the home. The work "private" is used here to denote space that is not generally accessible to the public. Society regards a home as a private domain in which the inhabitants can, if you may, create their own rules. Any problems or disputes are to be solved "internally" with minimal outside interference. Both the law and cultural norms support this position.

Consequently domestic workers exist in isolation from other groups of workers who operate in more public spheres, such as offices, hotels, and educational institutions, which not only renders them invisible but also excludes them from the discursive spaces accessible to those other groups. Also as is the nature of most private relationships in which one individual has power over another, domestic labor is relatively easy to exploit, manipulate, and subject to abuse.

Terms of Service of Domestic Workers

Legal Provisions

Kenyan law has certain provisions regarding the terms of domestic workers. It provides that the workers are entitled to the following terms of service: basic minimum wage (revised from time to time), free housing accommodation or housing allowance at 15 percent of their salary, a maximum of 45 working hours per week, overtime payment, one rest day weekly, leave on national holidays with full pay, 21 days of annual leave with full pay, compassionate, sick, and maternity leave, and warning and procedural termination of employment.

The warning system requires that an employee whose work is unsatisfactory should receive two written warnings. The second warning should be copied to the branch secretary of his union. The assumption is that the workers in the defined categories are able to be unionized. However, studies indicate that the ability of a household worker to be unionized is more in theory than in practice (Lunghals 2002).

The Current Situation

A study that was conducted on a sample of 34 household workers from both the rural and urban areas (Lunghals 2002) shows the current situation to be a far cry from that one above. Of the 34 household workers who participated in the study, none had a written employment contract. In all cases, the worker and the employer were initially connected through a third party who mostly did the negotiations for them. More than 50 percent said that they had arrived from the rural area for their first employment. All had an average daily activity schedule that combined many household duties. In urban areas, these revolved around cleaning, cooking, and childcare whereas in rural areas, digging, grinding flour, and attending to animals were common.

Most of the subjects had never had any annual leave with pay let alone additional national holidays. Eight of 34 of these workers were nonresidents, and they reported to work between 7:30 and 8:00 a.m. and left between 5:00 and 6:00 p.m., an average of eight to nine hours a day. These women went back to their homes where they still had to do their own housework. The other 26 live-in workers started their days between 5:00 and 6:00 a.m. and ended at about 10:00 p.m., an average of 14 hours a day. Remuneration ranged from 500 to 1000 Kenyan shillings (Ksh) in the rural area and 800–2,000 Ksh in the urban areas. Payday was not definite, and payment was occasionally done in installments. None received any form of house allowance. There was no question of maternity leave because pregnancy equaled termination of employment. Dismissal was verbal and arbitrary. Thirty-two of the workers had a negative attitude toward their employer and complained of overwork and underpay. They found it unfair that they were expected to perfectly perform all the duties assigned to them, some of which they had no previous form of training in. None enjoyed the full benefit of all the terms and conditions of service stipulated by the law. All hoped to save up some money and start some kind of business.

An analysis of the information above clearly brings out the extent to which exploitation of domestic labor is prevalent in Kenya. The wide acceptance of such terms of employment by both the employer and the employee has made it even worse. These terms of employment are neither just nor favorable. Wages are too low, especially for people who have families to support, rest is inadequate, and working hours are much longer than those in other sectors. Duties are also not specialized. Employment is of a temporary nature and easily terminated. The entitlement to leave days is also not honored.

These conditions apply to all domestic laborers as a collective group. It is important to examine the two different groups addressed in this chapter and the vulnerabilities they encounter individually.

Women in Domestic Labor in Kenya

Domestic work is considered a female role in the system of division of labor based on gender. Most domestic workers are therefore women. This way of thinking has led to a disregard for women's services and a regard of their labor as "non-work." Consequently, female labor in Kenyan homes is largely undervalued and not adequately compensated.

Most women working as housemaids come from a poor background and often have dependants in the form of siblings, parents, or children back home. They usually lack sufficient education to enable them to seek employment in other sectors. Their only option is to remain in domestic labor for most of their lives. The only change that may occur is that of working in different households. Society regards the home as private. In the "privacy" of these homes, women are particularly vulnerable to certain forms of abuse. The most common are physical and sexual abuse.

Physical Abuse of Domestic Workers in Kenyan Homes

The relationship of employer and employee is of such a nature that one person has unlimited power over another. It is, in fact, comparable to the older forms of master-servant relationships. This power dynamic leaves a lot of room for abuse and exploitation.

Stories abound in the media about employers who have physically assaulted their employees to the extent of the matter becoming a police case.

The punishing of employees in the home is what brings about such abuse. To vent their own frustrations, employers verbally abuse, hit, beat, and even whip their housemaids and house servants.

Probably such employers consider domestic workers as "lesser beings" or inferior beings. In effect, they treat them with disrespect because this happens behind closed doors and is hidden from the wider public. Whatever the proposed justification, physical violence against domestic workers is wrong and is an abuse of their right to physical and emotional security.

Sexual Abuse of Domestic Workers in Kenyan Homes

It is also common for domestic workers to be sexually molested by male members of the family. If such abuse is reported, workers are not usually believed, and, the family, including the women in the household, side with the male members. The workers are then either dismissed or subjected to continued abuse. Such sexual exploitation often results in life threatening consequences of physical, psychological, and social development, including threats of early pregnancy and maternal mortality. When pregnancies occur, because of limited options, workers seek backstreet abortions, which could result in death or serious damage to their reproductive health.

The transmission of sexually transmitted diseases, including HIV/AIDS, is a high risk in this situation. Most of the workers who undergo such abuse suffer mental and psychological torture for years.

Children in Domestic Labor in Kenya

The exploitation of child labor in Kenyan homes is rampant. This violates their right to education, rest, and play. They are literally denied a childhood to make other people's lives more comfortable. The tasks assigned to them are difficult and include cleaning, cooking, washing, ironing, looking after children, and fetching and delivering items. However, what makes children's domestic work slavery is not the tasks but the conditions under which they work.

Typically, they are the first to wake up and the last to go to bed at night. Despite working such long hours, they are rarely the direct recipients of any pay attributed to their work. In one survey, 78 percent of child domestic workers were found to be only paid "in kind."[8] This amounts to servitude by any definition. These children usually have other siblings at home who also depend on their income. There is also the common culture of rural relatives "lending" their children to city kin to "help" with household duties. The problem with this situation is, that apart from denying the children a normal childhood, the labor sometimes goes unpaid or where wages are paid, they go to a third party. There is clearly no firm minimum age for admission to employment in Kenya. This is especially true of the domestic arena, with children as young as eight and nine years of age already working as housemaids or house boys.

What is particularly sad about the presence of child labor in Kenyan homes is that they are even more "invisible" than their older counterparts. They have almost no capacity of self-expression and can rarely seek redress. They, as do all children, fear being punished and are not usually the ones to describe to strangers about episodes of violence or sexual abuse. It takes a great deal of time and confidence building before they can do any such thing. Many are the times when neighbors have to intervene, when abuse is suspected. By this time, the abuse has usually reached disastrous proportions.

Because this type of work is conducted behind closed doors, the child is also vulnerable to physical and sexual abuse. Studies of girls working as housemaids have found that many reported being sexually abused in most of the houses in which they have been employed. These events have the effect of traumatizing these girls for life.

The following is an article that appeared recently in the local daily newspaper and that reflects the present nature and extent of child labor in Kenyan homes.

Scarred by Child Labor

Many children are wasting away their childhood working in urban households as domestic servants. Writes Dorothy Otieno (2003),

> The wounds have healed but the scars on Alison's face, hands and back remind her of the time she spent working as a house girl for her aunt under harsh conditions. For two years, with little provocation, her aunt used to beat her. "Even when her children erred, she would beat me," says the 13-year-old.
>
> Her aunt once beat her so severely that she fainted. In panic, she took Alison to hospital but lied to the doctor that the child had been sick. Until early this month Alison was one of the 166,016 children working as domestic laborers in Kenya according to the recent statistics from the Ministry of Labor. The fourth born in a family of six, Alison accompanied her aunt from her rural home in Kisii six years ago after her aunt convinced her mother—a widow—that she was going to educate the girl along with her children. But on arrival, the idea of taking her to school was discarded and Alison became the house servant. Every morning she would wake up at 5 a.m. to prepare breakfast. When her cousins woke up she would help to dress them up and clean their clothes after they left for school. She ended up doing all the chores. Her only free time was when she went to church on Sunday, which was only allowed after intervention of her uncle. "My aunt was very mean to me but my cousins and uncle treated me better," she says. Once when she was being whipped, neighbors saved her and threatened to take legal action against the aunt. The family moved to another neighborhood and the abuse continued. One day, her 11-year-old cousin destroyed things in the house and her aunt beat her with a ladle. "I bled all over," she tearfully recalls. A neighbor rescued her, nursed her wounds and

> then took her to a shelter for abused and battered women and children. Since she left Kisii when she was in Standard Two, she has never seen her mother and siblings. Alison was never paid any wages for her services and she does not know whether her aunt has sent any money to her mother. It has become common for poor rural folk to send young children to urban areas to work as domestic servants in the belief that they are handing them over to surrogate families. "Although there are young boys working as domestic servants, the bulk of child workers are girls aged 10–14," says Mary Kezzah, a Ministry of Labor official.

Edward Ouma, Head of Programmes at Children's Legal Action Network (CLAN), says that in the course of his work he has rescued children in domestic labor as young as five or six years old. Most children have little time to rest, whereas others work for no pay and are abused. "Child laborers face a multiplicity of abuse. They undergo emotional, verbal and physical abuse," says Ouma. Attesting to this reality is the case of Eunice, the second born in a family of five children, who left her home in Kisii at age six with a neighbor who promised to educate her in the city. For six years, the 13-year-old waited for her guardian to fulfill her promise as she worked in the house. It was only last year that she started school after a Good Samaritan offered to pay for her education. She is in Standard Two. Eunice was saved from her employer after the man of the house attempted to sexually molest her. When she resisted him, he threw her out, accusing her of backbiting him. "He took my clothes and threw them outside the house," she recalls. A neighbor who witnessed the expulsion took her to a social worker in Kibera. Before that day, Eunice's life was all work with neither play nor pay. "I would not leave the house unless I was running an errand," she says. She made a friend in church to whom she narrated her woes. The friend introduced the girl to her mother, who offered to take her to school. "Most of my clothes are donations from neighbors," she says. She is happy to be in school. Many urban employers receive child laborers from rural areas through family and friends. "This year alone CLAN has dealt with 86 cases of domestic child labor," says Ouma. "Some of the children are abandoned by the employers after they have outlived their usefulness," he says. Kezzah says the crisis occasioned by HIV/AIDS is reversing all the gains," she says. Ouma claims that many Kenyans still do not know what constitutes child labor. He says children who are exposed to labor and abuse have low self-esteem. Kezzah and Ouma say the introduction of free education has reduced the number of children in domestic child labor, but the war is not yet won. "It is one thing for the government to declare free primary education and another to take into account the interests of children with special needs," says Kezzah. "If the child cannot afford uniforms, food and other basics, education will remain inaccessible. We should give the young ones a chance to be children," she says.

Main Reasons for Abuse of Women and Children in Kenya

Poverty

One cannot fail to see the correlation between poverty in Kenya and exploitation of women and children. It is poverty that makes these people leave their homes to seek employment and that makes them endure the harsh working conditions and even abuse. Most domestic workers come from a poor background and are a source of support for their families.

Previously, before the introduction of free primary education, poor parents even considered it better to have their children work as domestic laborers in other peoples' homes, because this would mean that they lead a better life than they can provide for them. Any lasting measure to eradicate this problem must first address poverty.

It is no wonder then that the Kenyan Government, with its National Poverty Eradication Plan, intended to run from 1999 to 2015, has recognized as its first objective the need to address the burden of women's workload and seek to redefine gender roles in labor so as to encourage proper valuation and compensation for their labor. Illiteracy and lack of high levels of education are also factors arising from the poverty of these women and children.

Invisibility

The nature of domestic work renders this group of workers invisible. The distinction between "public" and "private" in Kenyan society makes it practically impossible to access the home. Abuse and exploitation thrive on this invisibility. The lack of a space where the workers can unionize or have their needs addressed puts them in isolation from other groups. The isolation of women each in a private home works against them.

The almost complete lack of data and documentation on the state of domestic labor in Kenya does not help the situation. It is hard to address the problems of people who are not visible, and society does not give recognition to the problem.

Perception of Gender Roles

The commonly held perception is that domestic work is a woman's duty that is naturally assigned to her by virtue of her sex. That is the reason for the large population of girls and women engaged in domestic labor. This perception is so ingrained in the society to the extent that female domestic workers do not undergo any formal training, because they are assumed to inherently know how to do all the duties assigned to them.

It is hardly possible to examine this issue properly without taking a gender-sensitive perspective. Any effective fight against female domestic labor exploitation must therefore first address society's perception of gender roles as the root of the problem and seek to change this misconception.

Weak Laws

Kenya is signatory to and has ratified various international instruments that address labor rights. However, it has yet to ratify certain key instruments that would go a long way in this fight. To do so would show government commitment and goodwill. It is also not enough to have agreements on paper; implementation is crucial. There is need to domesticate these agreements and incorporate them into national laws.

Kenya also has in place a national legislation to deal with this problem. However, in some regards, these laws are weak and do not suffice. When they are sufficient, they lack proper enforcement mechanisms. This defeats the purpose of enacting them in the first place, and the spirit of labor laws that seek to eradicate all forms of oppressive labor is lost in this way.

Government Efforts to Curb Exploitation of Labor

The Kenyan government has sought to address this problem mainly through international and national laws. The state has signed a memorandum of understanding with the ILO and various ILO/International Programme on the Elimination of Child Labor programs are being carried out. The state has also established a National Steering Committee on Child Labor. Kenya is also a signatory to the Convention on the Rights of the Child and has practically translated this into domestic law through the new Children's Act. In the government's National Poverty Eradication Plan intended to run from 1999 to 2015, there is a recognition of the need to have "women's heavy workload and drudgery reduced." The activity or long-term strategy through which this is to happen is by mounting gender sensitization campaigns to encourage men to share more in women's work.

In May 2003, the Government requested ILO assistance to review labor laws in the country through a task force that was appointed by the attorney general to harmonize domestic legislation with the various international labor standards that Kenya has ratified. The factor that the new government has introduced, which has begun to make significant change to the elimination of child labor in Kenya, is the introduction of free primary education. The president of Kenya has reiterated often in many public forums that all children of school-going age should be in school and that no one should keep a child of school-going age in the house for any reason. This includes child labor.

Recommendations

The government must come up with campaigns not only to sensitize men to share more in women's work but also to alter the conception of traditional sexual divisions of labor in the country. A shift away from society's perception of housework as non-work is encouraged.

These workers should be given a forum in which they can have a voice, an effective channel for redress and improvement of their terms and conditions of service. This would take the form of a union for domestic workers.

The employment of children as domestic workers in Kenya should be outlawed with the aim of abolishing child labor in Kenya. Civic education on national labor laws should be carried out to educate the employees and their employers on the rights and responsibilities that go with domestic employment.

There is therefore dire need for a comprehensive study to assess the situation of current domestic child labor in Kenya. There is an absence of information and data on this subject. A clear and enforceable legal age for domestic workers should be clearly established. There is also a need to allow labor inspections even in the "private" sphere of the home to counter this menace. Finally, there is need for provision of spaces where workers who are victims of sexual abuse and exploitation can seek recovery, rehabilitation, and integration.

Notes

1. Universal Declaration of Human Rights, Art. 23.
2. The African Charter on Human and People's Rights, Art. 14.
3. ILO Convention, No. 87.
4. "Beauty and Agony," Kenya Human Rights Commission Report on the working conditions on the flower plantations in Kenya, 2001.
5. The Employment Act, Cap. 226, Law of Kenya.
6. The Regulation of Wages and Condition of Employment Act, Cap. 229, Law of Kenya.
7. "Kenya Helps Young Domestics to Escape Abuse and Exploitation," CARE International Report, 2002.
8. UNICEF Innocenti Digest on Child Domestic Work, May 1999.

References

Lunghals, R. H. 2002. "The Gender Issues in Domestic Labor Focus on Uasin District, Kenya." *Daily Nation*, March 31.

Otieno, D. 2003. "Scarred by Child Labor." *East African Standard*, November 12.

11 Criminal Exploitation of Women and Children: A South African Perspective

LINDIWE MTIMKULU

Introduction

Violence against women and children in South Africa must be analyzed against the backdrop of the history of the country. Apartheid, many years of oppression and discrimination, poverty, high unemployment, and the many different culture and language groups are a few of the factors that need to be considered. The seriousness of the problem has, since 1994 (when the first democratic government in the country came to power), been acknowledged at the highest levels of government. This is evident in many speeches, policy statements, strategies, and legislation. "The compound effect of patriarchy, and colonialism has left African women a legacy of deprivation almost unparalleled in the rest of the world," Cheryl Gilwald (2002), South African Deputy Minister for Justice and Constitutional Development, said in an address on national Women's Day.[1]

The Department of Justice in a special publication on human rights commented that it was a sad and ironic fact that, in a country known for its progressive constitution, the rights of women and children continue to be abused.[2] It is not easy to obtain statistics on criminal exploitation of women and children in South Africa, largely because of underreporting. There are various reasons for this, a major one being the shame women experience in describing assaults particularly of a sexual nature. Another reason is that women are scared of loosing financial security. In a country in which unemployment is high and poverty abounds, the loss of even a meager income is serious. "Many women fail to report abuse, because they are afraid they will be unable to support their families and will have no accommodation should their husbands be arrested," states Beatrice Ngcobo, Deputy Chairperson of the Commission for Gender Equality.[3] However, available statistics do indicate that the incidence of violence directed at women and children is a reason for serious concern.

Statistics on domestic violence, specifically, are more difficult to establish. According to the Institute for Security Studies in South Africa, research results generally confirm that violence against women is most likely to happen in the home, a supposedly safe place for women (Rasool et al. 2002). Government and nongovernment organizations are actively pursuing options to assist women survivors of violence.

The past 10 years of democracy have provided our country with a consolidation of lessons learned from the past. In the process, we have developed practices that should have a positive effect on the reduction of violence and crimes against women and children. We have attempted to inculcate a culture based on the recognition of improving the quality of life for humanity and human rights. We have indicated areas requiring priority for transformation and improvement through our policies. We have also initiated steps (with ranging levels of success) to integrate our practices in a bid to improve the delivery of services to victims of violence and crime case management. This integrated approach has also served to recognize the limitations placed on effective prevention and control of crime and violence by relying on a single entity. Interventions have tended to be program directed to address a number of aspects. This includes systemic weaknesses that require improvement and designing action plans for new innovations. It has been necessary to highlight interventions in which to invest for purposes of producing lasting benefits for those who will live in the South Africa of the future.

In 1995, the Republic of South Africa (RSA) ratified both the United Nations Convention for the Elimination of Discrimination Against Women and the Convention of the Rights of the Child (1989). The ensuing years since ratification have brought most of the policies and laws in line with the principles expounded in these international instruments. Other key developments within the global and regional spheres that have assisted in guiding focus for the RSA on issues of violence against women and children include the following:

- Beijing Declaration and Platform for Action (1995)
- The Southern African Development Community Addendum to the Gender and Development Declaration of 1997; the latter also known as the Addendum for the Elimination of Violence Against Women and was adopted in 1998
- The African Charter on the Rights and Welfare of the African Child (ratified by the RSA in 1999), developed by the Organization of African Worst Forms of Child Labor Convention (1999) and ratified by the RSA in 2000
- The International Labor Organization (ILO) Worst Forms of Child Labor Convention (1999), ratified by the RSA in 2000

An Integrated Approach to Reducing Crimes and Violence against Women and Children

Since the adoption of the National Crime Prevention Strategy (NCPS) in May 1996 by the cabinet, the RSA has deliberately engaged in an integrated approach to crime reduction that takes into account operationalizing joint ventures with role players who can influence a range of factors that provide opportunities for crimes and violence to occur.[4] This framework has also been applied to analysis of crime factors and strategy development regarding the criminal exploitation of women and children. Factors that affect the criminal exploitation of women and children in South Africa range from the social and economic to criminal justice system-related matters.

The integrated program implementation and problem-solving approach to crime reduction has continued into the second administration (commencing in 1999) of a democratic RSA and is governed mainly through the Justice, Crime Prevention, and Security (JCPS) Cluster as well as the Social Cluster of government. Government departments and ministries jointly identify priorities for action, engage in strategic planning, undertake action planning, and monitor the implementation of those strategies. When required, departments engage communities, nongovernment, and not-for-profit organizations in these joint ventures. The office of the presidency coordinates the clusters with assigned lead departments for cluster chairing and key programs.[5] The justice, crime prevention, and security ministries and departments include those for Justice (court management and prosecutions), Safety and Security (police and secretariat), Correctional Services (correctional facilities, offender control, and offender management), Social Development (social workers, social security, and population development), Home Affairs (citizenship regulation and identification), Foreign Affairs, the South African National Defense Force, and the Intelligence Community.

Crimes against women and children are priorities of the NCPS and remain priority areas of the JCPS and Social Clusters. The priorities of the Social Cluster focus on women and children in social service delivery and developmental and investment programs. These programs are also reflected within the South African Police Service (SAPS) Strategic Objectives and Priorities.

Crime and violence against women and children are the focus of a number of interdepartmental programs supported by departmental action. These programs are interdependent and complement each other. Each has a succinct focus and cannot be "collapsed" into one program with one approach. It is therefore important to understand not only the relationship and interdependencies but also the different approaches and focus areas of each program.

During November 2002, the directors general of the Social and JCPS Clusters approved a proposal for the strategic redirection of work relating to social crime prevention and moral regeneration. The reduction and addressing of crimes and violence against women and children is a key element of these issues. Activities covered deal with the following priority areas: rape, child abuse and neglect, and domestic violence.

This chapter has three parts. First, it provides a context for understanding criminal exploitation of women and children within the RSA. Press coverage on the issue (between January 2003 and February 2004) is also discussed. Second, it provides specific strategies that have been used. Data that provide a comprehensive impact assessment of these strategies are not yet available. The third part provides some indications as to why some strategies may be considered promising for the reduction of such exploitation.

Context of Criminal Exploitation of Women and Children in South Africa

According to the Oxford Dictionary, "exploit" means "take full advantage of, use (another) for one's own advantage and their disadvantage." When this is applied in the South African context, it becomes closely linked to principles contained in the Bill of Rights section of the Constitution and principles of normative customary humanity referred to as *Ubuntu/Botho*.

The Bill of Rights affirms the democratic values of human dignity, equality, and freedom of all people and protects these rights from violation.[6] Because the Constitution is the supreme law of the land, the implications are that any law or conduct that does not comply with its provisions is rendered invalid.[7] Principles of the Bill of Rights regulate not only the acceptable behavior of individuals but also become the basis for measuring activities of the legislature, judiciary, and administrative organs.

Ubuntu/Botho directly translates as "humanity." It relates to the treatment of others in a respectful humane manner, preserving their human dignity. Victims of intimate violence are predominantly women and children. These are crimes relating to sexual offenses, domestic violence, and child abuse. Definitions of these forms of criminal exploitation are to be found in various pieces of legislation to include the Criminal Procedures Act, the Domestic Violence Act,[8] and the Child Care Act. New sexual offenses legislation is currently being considered by the South African Parliament. The key effect of the latter bill has been to define sexual offenses in a wider sense that recognizes its various forms and the protection of children against commercial sexual exploitation.

The Annual Report of the SAPS provides some indications of the extent of violence experienced by women and children in South Africa during the period of March 2002 to March 2003. There also are other sources of information that indicate the extent of violence in previous periods. The key challenge remains in establishing the extent of other forms of criminal exploitation of women and children. Reasons include the fact that there is currently no legislative framework that specifically addresses human trafficking and its attendant forms of exploitation such as child labor. There are, however, developments in process in this regard.

The South African Law Reform Commission is currently conducting an investigation into the scope of application that may be required for comprehensive legislation regarding human trafficking. In the meantime, an integrated Child Labor Action Program has been drafted by the Department of Labor, in consultation with various departments. It is due for implementation. "Criminal exploitation" is also viewed in the light of the usage of children in criminal activities by older children or adults.

The first indication of the prevalence of domestic-related violence emerged with the first National Victims of Crime Survey (1998). This survey indicated that violent crimes are more likely to occur in or around a victim's home.[9] It also indicated that people are more likely to be attacked by those who are known or closely related to them.[10] This appears indicative of a significant incidence of interpersonal violence that is likely to be domestic in nature.

These findings are supported by the findings of a survey conducted by the Institute of Security Studies, the Centre for the Study of Violence and Reconciliation, and the University of Cape Town Criminology Department.[11] The survey revealed that women are more likely to be abused by their parents/spouses (59 percent) and relatives (18 percent) than by strangers (14 percent).

Newspaper Reporting Analysis of the Phenomenon

South African newspapers devote much space to crime reporting. It is, in fact, one of the issues in the country that receives priority coverage, alongside education, housing, HIV/AIDS, and, increasingly, the economy.[12]

Reporting on crime could be broken down into a number of focus areas, notably, organized crime, which includes drug trafficking, cash-in-transit heists, and vehicle hijacking, other serious, violent crimes, and crimes against women and children. The analysis of reports on crimes against women and children (including domestic violence) in newspapers for the period of January to February 2004 indicate that such crimes receive as much coverage as all other crimes, possibly even more. The frequency of reporting on abuse of women and children (including domestic violence) is higher than for all other crimes. Not a single day goes by that the printed press does not report on this scourge.

Criminal exploitation of women and children in South Africa, based on conclusions arrived at through newspaper monitoring for the period January 2003 to February 2004, including the following:

Crime Committed by a Person Known to the Victim: The newspapers reported rapes committed by parents, brothers, teachers, priests, lawyers, and even doctors and important personalities in the community.

Crime Committed by a Person Not Known to the Victim: Newspaper reports indicate that women and children become targets when they are playing outside, when women or girls walk to work/school/parties, and when women walk alone in the early hours of the morning or evening.

Rape of Minors, Including Infants: This is a highly disturbing phenomenon that has increasingly received media coverage in South Africa over the past two years. To aggravate the problem, an urban legend has it that having sex with a virgin or a baby either heals or prevents persons becoming HIV positive. Newspaper reports further indicate that children are mostly raped by family members. They are also raped by persons who look after them and neighbors.

Domestic Violence/Spousal Abuse: Reports about domestic violence indicate that it occurs when there are marital problems, when couples separate, and after arguments. Love triangles, jealousy, and infidelity are some of the main causes. Former husbands and boyfriends sometimes resort to violence. Statistics furnished by the World Bank, however, show that domestic violence is serious worldwide, and that, in South Africa, it seems to be less of a problem than in some other countries.

Child Abuse Other Than Rape: Child abuse is mostly committed by parents. Mothers are also charged with child abuse. Neglect and physical abuse are the most common types of abuse that occur. There has also recently been an increase in reports of women discarding babies.

Family Killings: Family killings are mostly committed by males, usually the father. Reporting is usually about the father killing his wife and children and then committing suicide. This often occurs after a breakup or in cases of financial problems.

Human Trafficking: Human trafficking suddenly started hitting the headlines in South Africa in 2003. Previously, there were hardly any reports of it. The International Organization for Migration's research into trafficking of women and children has found that women and children are being trafficked to South Africa from Africa, Eastern Europe, and southeast Asia. Russian and Bulgarian mafias also traffic Russian and other Eastern European women on South African visas fraudulently obtained in Moscow to upscale South African brothels. The women are promised jobs as waitresses, dancers, strippers, and hostesses in South Africa.

Newspaper reports correlate with key findings from police docket analysis trends. Intimate violence cases are as follows:

- Docket analysis reveals that a very high percentage of victims and offenders were known to each other at the time the rape occurred (50–80 percent of reported cases).
- A large percentage of rape cases are withdrawn at the request of the victim (40–60 percent).
- An analysis of rape cases registered on the Crime Analysis Statistics since February 2002 reveals that, in 41 percent of all the cases, the victims were aged 18 years.
- 14.1 percent of murder victims were female.
- 45 percent of arrestees in rape cases tested positive for drugs.

The implications are that victim support and public awareness of the need to report rape cases and assist the criminal justice process are key aspects of an anti-rape strategy. The development of an anti-rape strategy has necessitated a range of interventions to address domestic violence, substance abuse, and positive youth development.

Factors related to gender-based violence and child abuse include exposure to violence/sociopolitical factors, gender roles, the objectification of females, perception of manhood, consumerist lifestyles, violent role models, HIV/AIDS-related issues, financial and emotional dependency of the victims in relationship to the abuser, substance abuse, environmental factors that make it easier for violent crimes to be performed within geographical locations, and withdrawals by the victims in cases that render them vulnerable to repeat victimization.

Exposure to Violence/Sociopolitical Factors

There are indications that exposure to violence, particularly at an impressionable stage of personal development, contributes to perceptions of violent behavior being a normal way of dealing with conflict. This may lead to patterns of violence and, alternatively, patterns of compliance with regard to violence. To address this, skills for positive communication and conflict management become a factor in strategies for violence reduction.

In addition to this, the sociopolitical history of the country has eroded family and community life. Apartheid laws, migrant labor practices, and the culture of violence that developed through the struggle for freedom have separated, disintegrated, and marginalized many families and communities. Many young people have been and continue to be exposed to acts of violence that affect their emotional growth, their ability to feel emotion themselves, and the ability to feel empathy for others.

Gender Roles, Objectification of Females, Perceptions of Manhood, and Urbanized Consumerist Lifestyles

Research conducted in Alexandra, near Johannesburg, showed that the urbanized street-wise lifestyle of urban young people, based on consumerism and putting much importance on possessions, does tend to encourage the objectification of women and could lead to gender-based violence. Under such conditions, relationships are valued according to the extent to which the male partner can provide a range of material objects to the female partner. In the process, the female is perceived as an extension of his possessions and is expected to submit to his whims. Such relationships are sometimes characterized by accusations of infidelity that could lead to domestic violence and rape (Motsei 1997).

The same study also documents some perceptions young men have of manhood. These include that of a man as a partner who has to assert his control and power over the female partner. Furthermore, there is also a tendency to idolize gangsters who often have expensive, abundant possessions and use violence to assert their control over others.

The notion of an extravagant urbanized lifestyle being the ideal situation as a factor in crime and violence finds resonance in the SAPS Annual Report (2003) analysis in the following description:

> Sometimes the family/kinship support network is replaced in the urban areas by the peer group system with its associated extravagant youthful lifestyle (based on alcohol, drugs, expensive clothing, fast cars and girlfriends) which may create more needs amongst unemployed youngsters…All prolonged unemployment….may result in family tensions, arguments and fights…. It may cause increasing exploitation of children who cannot satisfy their basic needs or develop extravagantly expensive needs through their interaction with peer groups….And may as a result become involved in prostitution, the drug trade and other criminal acts.[13]

On the question of the impact of these matters on male self-image and men's relationship to women, the same report states the following:

> The development of a weak self-image—especially amongst breadwinners and men—because they cannot provide for their dependents is also a dominant feature. In reaction to this, a male will, in all probability, develop the projection of a macho-man image and lifestyle which includes alcohol and drug misuse, association with friends following the same lifestyle, the use of violence and abuse to achieve aims and the perception of and attitude towards women as being "inferior" or there to fulfill sexual needs.[14]

In addition to this, a conservative patriarchal worldview relegates girls and women to a position characterized by a lack of power and vulnerability.

When women and girls deviate from their expected role within social units of this nature, they may become targets for anger, sometimes in violent forms. Conversely, the colonial domination and the legacy of apartheid have contributed to disempowerment, demoralization, and poor self-esteem among men, as well as the emasculation of men. This may have led to their seeking a sense of power, control, and status through abusive sexual behavior and other forms of violence.

HIV/AIDS-Related Issues

There are indications of a myth that the rape of a child or elderly woman could cure HIV/AIDS. Although data relating to the extent to which this has contributed to the prevalence of child rape are not available, there are anecdotal indications that this myth may play a role.

There also are indications of a relationship between the fear of HIV/AIDS infection and domestic violence. The problem may arise from the male/female understanding of their roles with regard to relationships. In the words of Vetten and Bhana (2001), this is expressed as follows:

> Male cooperation is paramount in safer sex practices such as condom usage. But with men traditionally having greater influence over when, where and how sex takes place, this disadvantages women in successfully initiating discussion about safer sex practices or negotiating safer sex.

The authors add that, in a study conducted in rural and peri-urban KwaZulu Natal, a significant number of women in marital or permanent relationships accepted that their husbands or partners had other sexual partners but feared requesting the use of a condom, simply because it would elicit a violent response (Karrim and Mohnty 1998; Votten and Bhana 2001). Even if this may not necessarily be representative of the country, it could be indicative of other similar relationships.

Fear is also attached to accusations of infidelity. Such accusations have been known to be a key factor in fatal domestic incidents. Thus, this is no idle fear; it is based on the real risk of being seriously harmed.

Financial and Emotional Dependency of Victims

There are indications that dependency on the abuser is a factor that contributes to their remaining in abusive relationships. Often the abuser is the family's breadwinner. It may also be a factor when children are exploited by adults. Research has shown that children are more likely to be abused by persons they know than by strangers. The vulnerability of children in some neighborhoods makes them susceptible to abuse by adults and other children and young people more powerful than them, such as youth gangs. This does not, however, suggest that poverty directly causes child abuse but that poverty increases the risk of child abuse. Children may be forced into prostitution and other forms of child labor to survive. The issue of options made available to victims, who are usually women and children, is an aspect that informs some strategies.

Substance Abuse

Substance abuse is a risk factor for family life and the entire society. It contributes to crimes being committed on vulnerable groups. Parental substance abuse, specifically, is a major risk factor contributing to child abuse. Children whose parents abuse substances do not receive appropriate treatment and are more likely to be removed to and remain in foster care and children's homes.

Withdrawal of Cases

The withdrawal by victims of reported cases increases the risk of these forms of violence being repeated. As a result, policy directives for prosecutions and national instructions for police regarding rape place limitations on the circumstances in which these cases can be withdrawn. In terms of current policy, only the senior prosecutor can make the decision to withdraw a case.

Environmental Factors

Docket analysis has revealed links between environmental factors and places where rapes frequently occur. Issues such as the lack of passive surveillance of public places that victims have to move through during quiet hours of the day, lack of sufficient street lighting, and other aspects have led to localized anti-rape action plans that indicate specific measures by local municipalities to rectify the situation.

Strategies to Address Criminal Exploitation

The factors referred to in the previous section are taken into account when strategies are developed. Various measures have been taken to address the criminal exploitation of women and children. These have included law reform, improvements in the criminal justice system, and program development implementation and monitoring.

Law Reform

Within the past decade, new legislation that addresses some aspects of criminal exploitation has either been promulgated or is in the process of enactment.

The Domestic Violence Act (1998) provides a comprehensive definition of domestic violence. Highlights include the following:

- A definition of forms of domestic violence that includes, physical, sexual, emotional, verbal, psychological, and economic abuse. The elements of any other controlling and abusive behavior are also included.
- A description of the nature of affected relationships, which ranges from romantic partners to people in a perceived romantic or intimate relationship, to any relationship through blood, marriage, or adoption and people who share the same residence.

The Child Care Amendment Act (13/1999) enforces the protection of children against commercial sexual exploitation. Provision has also been made for law enforcement against perpetrators and those who own, lease, manage, or occupy property on which the commercial sexual exploitation of children occurs and fail to report such occurrence within a reasonable time.[15]

In the South Africa Law Reform Commission (SALRC) Investigation into sexual offenses and the Criminal Law (Sexual Offenses) Amendment Bill, some of the areas of the process and procedural law relating to sexual offenses addressed in the draft bill including the following:

- The creation of a category of vulnerable witnesses that include children and all complainants in sexual offense cases and affords them new protective measures, in addition to protective measures already provided for in the Criminal Procedure Act of 1977 (such as in camera hearings, the appointment of intermediaries, and the use of closed circuit television) (Clause 16). The prosecution is obliged to inform witnesses of the possibility to be declared vulnerable (Clause 15). The proposed use of a support person has been removed from the draft bill because of the financial implications in this regard.
- The abolition of the cautionary rules in relation to children and complainants in sexual offense cases, which currently requires or allows that such evidence should or can be treated with caution (Clause 20).
- Allowing evidence of the surrounding circumstances and the impact of sexual offenses upon a complainant to be adduced at sexual offense trials (Clause 19).

- The provision of medical care, treatment, and counseling to victims of sexual offenses (Clause 21). The cabinet has removed the proposed provision of treatment at state expense from the bill because of the financial implications in this regard.
- Drug and alcohol treatment orders and supervision of dangerous sexual offenders, which form part of the wide array of possible sentencing options (Clauses 22 and 23).
- Failure by any convicted sexual offender to disclose the fact of conviction for a sexual offense when applying for employment in the child-care field, which constitutes a criminal offense (Clause 26).

In accordance with the expanded mandate given to the SALRC investigation into sexual offenses to detail legislative and nonlegislative measures to address such offenses, the Ministers of Safety and Security, Justice and Constitutional Development, Health, Correctional Services, Education, and Social Development were requested, during 2003, to consider implementing the nonlegislative recommendations pertinent to each government department as contained in the Report on Sexual Offenses. This is receiving attention.

The primary aim of the nonlegislative recommendations is to draw the attention of critical role players within the criminal justice system and auxiliary services relating to their spheres of responsibility to varying standards of service and to basic service dilemmas. Aspects addressed are, among others, resourcing, intersectoral cooperation, training, awareness raising, and capacity building.

The Children's Bill addresses the issue of child protection in the following ways:

- It recognizes prevention and early intervention services as vitally important components of a future children's statute.
- Formal measures for the protection of children from abuse and neglect are the central focus of the Law Commission's discussion paper and the eventual Children's Bill. The discussion paper considers legal provisions and interventions designed to deal with situations in which specific children are being harmed, or are at immediate risk of harm, through abuse or neglect. Exploitation and abandonment, being forms of abuse and neglect, respectively, are included within the ambit of these protective measures. The discussion paper further addresses issues such as the protection of the health rights of children, their protection as consumers, children in need of special protection, and the protection of children affected by divorce or separation of their parents.
- It considers the issues of religious laws and customary laws affecting children. It further addresses international issues affecting children.

These include, among other things, intercountry adoptions, trafficking of children across borders, child abductions, and refugee children.
- A monitoring system to ensure the effective implementation of the new children's statute is also proposed.
- The discussion paper specifically addresses the care of sexually exploited children. In this regard, the recommendations made in respect of child prostitution, child pornography, and child trafficking focus on the child as a victim and in need of care. These are closely linked to the investigation of sexual offenses, which focuses on the criminal law aspects. Both these discussion papers therefore aim at addressing holistically and in an integrative manner child sexual abuse, albeit from different perspectives.

The Department of Social Development is the lead department heading the Children's Bill. The various other departments, including the Department of Justice and Constitutional Development, form part of the Intersectoral Steering Committee, which is planning for the implementation of the bill by way of costs and an action plan.

Programs and Services

Some of the key concerns of the NCPS are cycles of violence and reducing gender-based violence (Garner and Fagan 1997), bearing in mind that the domestic violence program was developed as one of the ways to tackle the generational cycle of violence as well as the cycles of repeat victimization and offending, by focusing on causes and opportunities.

Attributes of a "generational cycle" are that the exposure to or experience of violence, particularly at an early stage of growth, increases the likelihood of someone becoming a violent offender later on in life. Expressed another way, violence may be learned through childhood experiences (Garner and Fagan 1997).

The cycles of repeat victimization and repeat offending relate to the complex relationship within a domestic situation that makes victims vulnerable and gives offenders the opportunities to repeatedly batter (whether emotionally or physically) their victims. This complicated relationship has been explained through social theories. A common trend that runs through these social theories highlights an increasing debilitation and powerlessness of the victim against increased confidence and impunity of the offender.

The domestic violence program is an attempt to effectively break these cycles of violence through a continuum of interventions. A similar approach is used in addressing rape and child abuse through the Anti-Rape Strategy and Child Abuse and Child Neglect Steering Committees. By providing focus on victimization and offending and environmental factors, there is an attempt is influence these specific elements in an integrated manner.

The Child Labor Action Program provides a consolidated framework for action in relation to the exploitation of children in South Africa. Improving the effectiveness and efficiency of the criminal justice system is an attempt at increasing conviction rates and thus creating real deterrence to potential offenders.

Programs that deal with services to victims, although not exclusively serving women and children, also provide an integral service required by women and children who are victims of violence. The Victim Empowerment Program (VEP) plays an important role in supporting the victim as a witness in the criminal justice system and preventing further victimization as well as breaking the cycle of violence. The VEP is one of the existing priority programs implemented by government and nongovernment organizations at all levels but is also an element of each of the other priority programs. Victim empowerment for young male victims of crime can also be viewed as a preventive measure; as such, interventions break the cycle of violence overwhelmingly perpetuated by young men.

Programs aimed at dealing with offenders (in prison and through community corrections) further complement other programs. The restorative justice principles used by the Department of Correctional Services and the new approach to child justice reflected in the Child Justice Bill seek to reduce repeat offending and ensure the offenders can safely and productively return to their communities. Given the prevalence of recidivism, these programs are essential in both response to committed crimes and the prevention of future crimes and apply to all the priority crime areas.

The Children's Bill will also assist in the protection of children from violent crimes. An Interdepartmental Children's Bill Steering Committee under the guidance of the Department for Social Development has been formed.

Anti-Rape Strategy

An Interdepartmental Management Team (IDMT) comprising the National Prosecuting Authority and the Departments of Safety and Security, and Health and Social Development was formed in early 2000 to develop an anti-rape strategy. In early 2002, at the cabinet's request, this team co-opted the Departments of Education, Correctional Services, Treasury, and Government Communications. The Sexual Offenses and Community Affairs (SOCA) Unit of the National Prosecuting Authority leads the team on behalf of the Department of Justice and Constitutional Development, and the team has developed a strategic framework of action, approved by the cabinet in 2002. The IDMT promotes an information-based, data-driven approach to address rape and sexual offenses. The matrix of action comprises three streams of action (prevention, reaction, and support) across three pillars (deal with the crisis and promote and accelerate good practice).

The establishment of dedicated Sexual Offenses Courts and Thuthuzela Care Centers (multidisciplinary rape management centers) is in line with the anti-rape strategy. Various pieces of research are underway by the Sexual Offenses and Community Affairs Unit of the National Prosecuting Authority, the SAPS, and the Department for Correctional Services on behalf of the IDMT to continue and develop information-based action plans.

Prevention

Studies that would inform appropriate preventive activities regarding rape are in progress. This includes a study on offending with regard to both children and adults managed by the SOCA Unit, victimization research managed by the SAPS, and research into offenders that is managed by the Department for Correctional Services. This research incorporates docket analysis and interviews with affected respondents.

Reaction

A study of the leakages within the criminal justice system is required to allow the National Prosecuting Authority to determine why certain regions have high withdrawals and acquittals, and why other regions have high conviction rates. The IDMT is building on previous research to desegregate areas of high withdrawals and low convictions.

The Integrated Rape Portal Project has been initiated, which aims to develop technology that will supplement existing data collected by the SAPS and provide a more comprehensive understanding of rape. The idea is to develop technology that allows ease of data collection but ensure uniformity of information in rural and urban areas. The findings that will be immediately available will influence the type and level of service delivery for rape management.

Support

On the support pillar, a tender has been issued to audit support services nationally and to evaluate their efficacy. Their process will lead to the development of minimum standards.

Enforcement Policy on Child Labor: The Child Labor Action Program

An enforcement policy enhancing Sec. 43 of the Basic Conditions of Employment Act was developed in 2002. The strategy is two pronged:

- Arising out of the survey results as well as other research, a number of target groups or areas in which action needs to be taken have been identified, in both addressing the problem of child labor and

more broadly addressing the rights of children and protecting and promoting their future development.
- It also focuses on the legal steps to be followed by inspectors of the Department of Labor. All inspectors of the department of labor were trained in the enforcement policy.

This initiative is led by the Department of Labor and addresses a range of matters that affect the exploitation of children through child labor. By applying various international and regional instruments (including those of the ILO), the Child Labor Action Program (CLAP) provides a framework that identifies the worst and other forms of child labor and gaps in the domestic legislative and institutional frameworks and proposes critical interventions that are required.

The worst forms of child labor are listed as follows:

- All forms of slavery and practices similar to slavery
- The use of a child for procuring or offering of a child for prostitution, drug production, pornography, or for pornographic performances
- The use of a child for procuring or offering of a child for illicit activities, especially for drug production and trafficking
- Work that, by its nature or the circumstances, is likely to harm the health, safety, or morals of children (hazardous work)[16]

In terms of the latter, consideration should be given to the following:

- Work that exposes children to physical, psychological, or sexual abuse
- Work underground, under water, at dangerous heights, or in confined spaces
- Work with dangerous machinery, equipment or tools, or that involves the handling or transport of heavy loads
- Unhealthy working environments
- Work under difficult conditions[17]

Other forms of child labor that receive attention within the South African context include paid domestic work, agriculture, retail and wholesale, collecting fuel, or fetching water. The program provides time-bound steps that can be taken to limit the exploitation of children in this regard, improve their learning, and improve their access to leisure time and other activities necessary for their development. The CLAP is due for consideration by the Economics and Social Clusters.

Domestic Violence Programs

The importance of the domestic violence program in intervening early to reduce the cycle of violence cannot be underestimated. As both a response to existing high levels of domestic violence and a mechanism to reduce future violent crime, initiatives to reduce and react to domestic violence are critical elements. In this regard, an effective response to domestic violence can be considered as one of the interventions to address the culture of violence that contributes to rape and sexual offenses.

Outputs of the Interdepartmental Domestic Program are as follows:

- Policy directives of the Prosecution and National Instruction of the SAPS provide detailed guidelines geared at improving services for victims of domestic violence.
- Policy and strategy on the minimum standards for victims of domestic abuse shelters was completed and launched by the Department for Social Development in December 2003.
- Training for all relevant service providers (the police, social workers, health workers, and correctional officials) has been ongoing since 1998. The police have the basic duty to provide victims with assistance (which includes accompanying victims and protecting them when they fetch their personal belongings from a shared residence) and information on their options (applying for a protection order, laying a criminal charge against the alleged abuser, or both). Training content for the police has undergone phases and increasingly includes social context issues to enable the police to appreciate the complex dynamics in domestic violence cases and respond in accordance with victims' needs or provide appropriate support through referrals.
- The Integrated Training Package on Domestic Violence, tested at Lethlabile in February 2004, is a tentative service level agreement that has emerged indicating how the police, prosecution, court officials, social services, and health workers in this locality are going to provide services for victims of domestic violence.
- The SOCA Unit coordinates the development of an integrated training package.
- A Director of Services (produced by the Department for Social Development in partnership with the National Network of Violence Against Women) has been reviewed and made available for direct service providers to make referrals relating to services for victims of violence. This directory is designed to enable service providers to refer victims to other service providers as the need dictates.

Improving the Efficiency, Effectiveness, and Integration of the Criminal Justice System

There is continuing work to improve the efficiency, effectiveness, and integration of the criminal justice system. The successful prosecution of sexual offense matters is a national priority of the Department of Justice and Constitutional Development and the National Prosecuting Authority. A National Strategic Framework for the development of dedicated Sexual Offenses Courts has been drawn up as a matter of priority by the National Department of Justice and Constitutional Development, the National Director of Public Prosecutions, and the Lower Court Judiciary.

During the past years, the need for the expansion of the sensitive service rendered to children and to adult victims of family violence and sexual offenses was identified. This led to the approval of the establishment of the family violence, child protection, and sexual offenses (FCS) units on March 18, 1996. The SAPS continues to increase the capacity of its members through training (on investigations including crime scene management), increasing the numbers of their FCS units and child protection units (CPUs), and building the capacity for forensic analysis, including DNA. For the purpose of the activities of the CPUs, a person is regarded a child if he is younger than 18 years. The definitions of a child, as stated in Sec. 1 of the Child Care Act of 1983 (74/1983 as amended) and Sec. 28(3) of the Constitution of the RSA of 1996 (108/1996) serve as a guideline to determine age.

Some CPUs have since been transformed into FCS units. The objective is to transform all CPUs and establish FCS units, depending on available resources and the occurrence of crimes.

There are currently 27 CPUs and 21 FCS units at the main centers. Specialized individuals are attached to the local detective services to police crimes against children at the smaller centers. The FCS units and CPUs are specialized units for the investigations of family-related attempted murders and family-related assaults with intent to do grievous bodily harm. Regarding children, these units investigate rape, incest, indecent assault, attempted murder, assault with the intention to do grievous bodily harm, common assault (only if there were three or more incidents over a period of time, intrafamilial), kidnapping, abduction, and crimes with regard to the abuse/exploitation of children. Crimes with regards to the sexual exploitation of children and child pornography are also investigated, in which children are victims.

To coordinate SAPS inputs and responsibilities, with regards to the anti-rape strategy process, an internal team composed of senior management from the divisions of Crime Prevention, Crime Intelligence, Detective Services, and Evaluation Services was established at the national level. The role of this team is to ensure that SAPS responsibilities, which cut across all these divisions, are followed up and addressed at all levels.

To improve the Criminal Justice System's response to rape and convictions, the SAPS continues to invest in improving its investigative and forensic capacity.

The FCS units and CPUs achieved the following successes during 2002:

- A total of 1,406 cases were finalized in court concerning sexual offenses against children (under 18 years of age). Perpetrators were sentenced to a total of 7,946 years' imprisonment, including 84 life sentences, and fines to the value of 378,980 rand were imposed.
- A total of 314 cases involving adults were finalized. Sentences included five years' imprisonment, including eight life sentences, and fines to the value of 90,137 rand were imposed.

Training of SAPS members to improve the investigation of adult and child rape and sexual offenses continued in 2002. Ninety FCS unit members received specialized training in 2002, and resources were made available for the training of 300 additional FCS unit members in 2003. The SAPS also continued its programs to improve crime scene management and forensic services. With the assistance of the European Union, a project to increase the capacity of the SAPS to undertake DNA analysis commenced in 2002 and continued in 2003.

The SAPS has also engaged in the following practices:

- The mobilization of traditional leaders and religious leaders in raising awareness of the undesirability of gender-based violence in the Limpopo province. Issues relating to gender-based violence are addressed on an ongoing basis.
- A three-year program for the establishment of victim-friendly facilities as a strategy for the improvement of services to victims of intimate violence (including rape, domestic violence, and child abuse). Statements of rape victims on intimate and humiliating details are made in private environments that are comfortable to the victim.
- A process to develop, implement, and integrate a capacity-building program to provide police personnel with skills to work with young offenders. During 2003, a training curriculum for this purpose was developed and tested. Trainers who will act as facilitators for capacity-building workshops have also received training.
- Partnerships with the Departments of Education and Sports and Recreation, which have enabled young people to become conscious of the undesirability of gender-based violence. This has been conducted in support of the Safe Schools Program (led by the Department of Education) and the Young Champions Project (led by the Department for Sports and Recreation). In addition, youth outreaches to young

people are conducted through the Captain Crime Stop and Adopt a Cop projects.

Victim Empowerment

The VEP was established to improve the provision of services to victims. The VEP generally strives to enable victims to heal from the effects of their victimization, participate in a meaningful way in the criminal justice system, and prevent secondary victimization. Priority attention is given to victims with special needs. Members of the VEP and particularly its criminal justice partners are also mindful of the barriers to reporting, particularly on intimate violence matters, which may be attributable to intimidation, fear of secondary victimization by service providers, and feelings of alienation from the criminal justice system.

A South African Charter was finalized in 2003 with an attendant implementation plan for affected departments to implement. Departments affected include those of Justice, the Social Development, Correctional Services, Health, and the SAPS. Agreement has been reached on a framework for the development of a set of minimum standards for victim empowerment. The Victim Charter is expected to be submitted to the cabinet in time.

Features of victim empowerment services include the following:

- Improving facilities for victims of violent crimes at police stations, which continues to be a priority and is ongoing.
- Ongoing training of SAPS members through the victim empowerment training program. The training program is due for review.
- Three violence referral centers piloted at hospitals in the Eastern Cape, KwaZulu-Natal, and Mpumalanga. The information from the pilots will inform the development of a primary healthcare model.
- The Department of Health, in conjunction with the Department of Education, has been conducting ongoing training for educators and learners on violence prevention.
- Violence surveillance projects have been piloted in government mortuaries of five hospitals to form strategies for the effective prevention and treatment of violence.
- Skills training has been provided for clinic nurses and other healthcare providers to effectively prevent violence by assisting women with parenting skills and in early detection of violent behavior.
- Primary healthcare workers are trained in victim empowerment and trauma counseling.

- The Department for Correctional Services is implementing the restorative justice approach to the rehabilitation of offenders. The restorative justice approach is also being prioritized through the Intersectoral Child Justice Steering Committee and the planning for the implementation of the Child Justice Bill.
- A new parole board system that allows victims of crime to make inputs on the offender's parole hearing has been established.

The SOCA Unit of the National Prosecuting Authority has established several Thuthuzela Care Centers (multidisciplinary care centers) for rape victims at hospitals. The objectives of the centers are to reduce secondary trauma, improve the conviction rate, and reduce the cycle time to finalization of cases.

Thuthuzela (literally meaning "providing comfort") is a radical approach to rape care management. Beginning at the police station, rape victims are removed from the crowds to a victim-friendly room while they wait for an ambulance to transport them to the center. They receive comfort and crisis counseling from a trained ambulance volunteer while in transit to the hospital. At the center, they are ushered to a quiet, private space and are welcomed by the site coordinator. A doctor is immediately summoned to conduct a medical examination. Information is provided to the victim regarding the procedures to be performed, and she signs consent to the medical examination and blood specimens. She is then offered the opportunity to take a bath or shower and to change into clean clothes. During this process, an investigating officer, on call to the center, is summoned to take a statement. Thereafter, she receives appropriate medication and is given a follow-up date for additional medical treatment before being transported home. The process ensures that service providers are available to a victim from one location instead of being shuttled throughout the system.

A specialist prosecutor is involved in the investigative process from the outset. The prosecutor works with the investigator to ensure that all necessary information is gleamed from the victim during the first statement taking. Specialized investigators are linked to centers on standby so as to expedite and improve investigations. A case manager also ensures that the case is ready for trial within three to five months of reporting, thus ensuring speedy finalization. These cases are dealt with at the sexual offenses courts, which are designed to have two prosecutors, a dedicated magistrate, intermediary services, and a closed circuit television system to allow children to testify away from the court environment. All Thuthuzela staff are sensitized and offered compulsory multidisciplinary training on social contextualization, forensic evidence collection, investigative skills, leading expert evidence, and basic counseling.

Impact of Interventions: What Is Promising?

A comprehensive impact assessment is not available at this moment. There are, however, indications of promising practices that should be able to influence contributory factors with respect to cycles of rape, domestic violence, and child abuse. These include information-driven interventions that are developed on the basis of an analysis of factors that contribute to rape, domestic violence, and child abuse. This includes the Anti-Rape Strategy, Domestic Violence, Child Labor Action, and Child Abuse and Neglect Programs.

- Integrated victim service provision should enable confidence of victims in the criminal justice system to be increased, thus enabling these cases to be dealt with effectively.
- Integrated case management should ensure increased efficiency in the management of cases and increased conviction rates. The other effect of this should be to create deterrence by rendering effectiveness in case management.
- The mobilization of traditional leaders, religious leaders, and other positive role models particularly for young men. This should have the impact of regenerating positive values among young people that can be an investment in primary crime prevention. This is also linked to heightening awareness of principles of humanity (*Botho/Ubuntu*).
- Investments in the Urban Renewal Program and Integrated Sustainable Rural Development Program should provide opportunities for poverty alleviation and addressing environmental factors that may contribute to vulnerability with regard to victimization.
- Youth-focused crime prevention programs that are linked to the youth development framework of the National Youth Commission should provide an opportunity for positively channeling the energy of young people into developmental work. The "Young Champions" program provides one example of "edutainment" opportunities, i.e., education-through-entertainment for young people. Usage of programs in electronic media that focus on young people's positive value development, such as popular "Soul Buddiez" and Take 5 (for pubescent young people) and Takalani Sesame (for young children) provide examples of valuable socializing instruments that are guaranteed to grasp the attention of young people in a positive manner.

Conclusion

The finalization of such processes as the legislative framework for the trafficking of persons should enable improved monitoring of this phenomenon. A key challenge remains of the extent to which an assessment can be made on interventions. It is our hope that promising practices are emerging that can provide useful lessons for the reduction of criminal exploitation of women and children.

It was former South African President Nelson Mandela who said, "There can be no keener revelation of a society's soul than the way in which it treats its children." We hope and dream that South Africa, through all her dedicated efforts to establish a secure and safe environment for all its children, shows a soul that cares deeply.

Notes

1. Address by Cheryl Gilwald, South African Deputy Minister for Justice and Constitutional Development on National Women's Day, August 9, 2002.
2. Department of Justice special publication, "A Voice for the Victims: Protecting the Rights of Women and Children," pp. 22–23.
3. Ibid.
4. The NCPS provided a paradigm shift in the manner that crime reductions were addressed by the government of the RSA in that it acknowledged that effective crime prevention relied on the mobilization of partnerships that are beyond the criminal justice system to include social services, role players within the economy, local government, and civil society.
5. The National Commissioner for the South African Police Service chairs the JCPS.
6. Constitution of the Republic of South Africa (Act 18 of 1996), Art. 7, 9, and 10.
7. Constitution of the Republic of South Africa, Art. 2.
8. Sec. 1, Act 116 of the Domestic Violence Act of 1998.
9. Assault accounts for 55 percent of incidents and sexual offenses for 68 percent.
10. Assaults by partners/spouses/former account for 23.3 percent, boyfriends/girlfriends/former for 7.5 percent, relatives for 13.0 percent, and close friend for 19.3 percent. Sexual offenses by partners/spouses/former account for 20.5 percent, boyfriends/girlfriends/former for 1.6 percent, relatives for 15.8 percent, and close friends for 10.8 percent.
11. Women Speak Out, "Violence against Women in Three Cities," 1998.
12. W. Shreiner, interview with South African FM Radio, December 17, 2003.
13. SAPS Annual Report, 2003, pp. 24–25.

14. Ibid.
15. Insertion to Sec. 50 of the Child Care Act of 1983 (Act 74).
16. "Discussion Document: Toward a National Child Labor Action Program," 2002.
17. Ibid.

References

Garner, J., and Fagan, J. 1997. "Victims of Violence." In *Victims of Crime*, edited by R. Davis, A. Lurigio, and W. Skogan. London: Sage, p. 63.

Karrim, B., Abdool, O., and Molnty, T. 1988. "Women and AIDS: The Imperative for Gendered Prognosis and Prevention Policy." *Agenda* 39:15–25.

Motsei, M. 1997. "Perceptions of Young Men in Alexandra Township on Factors Leading to Gender-Based Violence" (unpublished research paper). Alexandra, South Africa: Asinsamang Domestic Abuse Prevention Training Center (ADAPT).

Rasool, S., Vermaak, K., Pharoah, R., Louw, A., and Stavrou, A. 2002. "Violence against Women: A National Survey." Tshwane, South Africa: Institute for Security Studies, 1.

Vetten, L., and Bhana, K. 2001. *Violence, Vengeance, and Gender*. Johannesburg: Center for the Study of Violence and Reconciliation, p. 10.

Trafficking of Women and Children in Nigeria: Slavery in the Modern Era

12

AGBONKHESE S. MOSES, OLUFUNKE J. ARUNA, AND MICHAEL FOLAMI

Introduction

In a democracy, all citizens deserve respect. No group can be singled out and identified as second-class citizens. The integrity of the individual is also a basic premise of human rights irrespective of the gender or marital status of that individual. At the same time, another basic premise of both democracy and human rights is tolerance of individual differences, whether those differences concern gender, race, ethnicity, religion, or ideas. There are "more slaves alive today than all the people stolen from Africa in the time of the transatlantic slave trade" (Bales 1999). Bales estimates that there are more than 27 million people today "enslaved by violence and held against their will for purposes of exploitation," and the number is increasing. A feature of the new slavery is that slaves become disposable once the slave holder has used them.

The trafficking of people for prostitution and forced labor is one of the fastest growing areas of international criminal activity. The overwhelming majority of those trafficked are women and children. An estimated one to two million people are trafficked each year worldwide, with over 50,000 going to the United States. Trafficking is now considered the third largest source of profits for organized crime, behind only drugs and guns, generating billions of dollars annually.

Although officially illegal in every country, a new form of slavery is arising because of globalization. Transitional companies switch their production to subsidiaries and subcontractors in the developing world and "take advantage of slave labor to improve their bottom line and increase dividends to their shareholders" (Bales 1999).

Areas where centuries of slave or slave-like traditions have existed are evolving into new forms. Common lands become concentrated in the hands of an increasingly wealthy elite. Cash crops for export replace subsistence farming. As a result, the poor become homeless, refugees, and powerless, and become vulnerable to enslavement.

A "Wild West syndrome" exists in which corruption and state forces protect slaveholders. Bales (1999) points out that today's slaveholders get "all the benefits of ownership without the legalities. Indeed, for the slaveholders, not having legal ownership is an improvement, because they get total control without any responsibility for what they own."

According to the Communication Initiative (The Advocacy Project) of July 2003,[1] Nigeria is referred to as the most "donating African country in the global sex industry." Nigerian women make up 70 percent of the 70,000 African victims of this trade. About 70 percent of these Nigerian women end up in Italy. The United Nations International Children's Emergency Fund (UNICEF) states that 80 percent of young women engaged in prostitution in Italy are Nigerians.[2] Global trafficking in persons generates annual revenues of between $6 and $12 billion. Two million women and children are trafficked each year.

The reasons for the increase in trafficking are many. In general, the criminal business feeds on poverty, despair, war, crisis, and ignorance. The globalization of the world economy has increased the movement of people across borders, legally and illegally, especially from poorer to wealthier countries. International organized crime has taken advantage of the increasingly free flow of people, money, goods, and services to extend its own international reach.

The Nigerian Situation

According to Inter Press Services (IPS) (2003),[3] more than 45,000 Nigerians are transported to Europe every year and forced to work in brothels. The lucky ones, who reach their destinations safely, often do so after encountering untold hardships on the way. According to the Nigerian police, several girls were roasted in the Sahara heat while trying to cross North Africa to Europe. To combat the trade, Nigeria is now getting tougher on human trafficking. It is imposing a life sentence on anyone caught trading in humans. "Any person who procures a girl or woman…to become a common prostitute either in Nigeria or elsewhere is liable to life imprisonment," says a new law on human trafficking. Additionally, the law, signed by the Nigerian president in 2003, prescribes a fine of 100,000 naira (about $1,000) for any Nigerian convicted of human trafficking. These penalties are a marked difference from previous laws on human trafficking, which handed out a jail term of just two years. However, for the law to be effective, human rights activists have urged the government to enforce it. When signing the bill into law, the president assured the people that the new law will be implemented to stem the tide of this modern day slave trade. Until recently, all laws on human trafficking and prostitution in Nigeria were scattered in various criminal codes and law books, and punishments for offenders were light and largely not enforced. The new law is a handiwork of nongovernment organizations such as Women Trafficking and Child Labor Eradication Foundation (WOTCLEF) founded by Titi Abubakar,[4] wife of Nigeria's vice president. It is a collation of all laws on human trafficking and prostitution in the various legal books of Nigeria. The old laws did not even mention giving assistance to victims. But this has been taken care of by the new law. Trafficking is an emerging problem worldwide. It is thriving in Nigeria because the punishment for offenders has been too light.

The WOTCLEF founder told IPS that human trafficking is an organized crime that needs to be fought with every available means, and culprits must be given the harshest of punishments. At the signing ceremony, an elated Mrs. Abubakar called for the setting up of a specialized organization to enforce the law and bring perpetrators to justice. "Our organization was motivated by the realization that the perpetrators of this heinous crime are specialists who have specialist routes, specialist language and specialist means of operation. To confront them with the same zeal of force, the need for a specialist organization like the National Agency for Trafficking in Persons Law Enforcement and Arrest, becomes inevitable," she said.[5] "Since three quarters of the Nigerian population are women and children, we should make their welfare and rights our priority. We cannot allow the issue of trafficking to be subsumed under the general duty of the police. The police have so much to do in fighting high profile crime like murder, armed robbery and advanced fee fraud," she said. "We shall not only catch traffickers, but assist to protect the victims," Abubakar said.[6] Human trafficking may not be a high-profile criminal act like drugs, but it is a crime that not only destroys the country's future but also the lives of its victims.

The 2001 UNICEF report estimated that one million children worldwide enter the multibillion dollar commercial sex trade every year.[7] Most of these children are caught up in child sex tourism. Most of the children are usually citizens of less developed countries such as Nigeria who are carried to developed countries to feed the sex tourism. Major causes of commercial sexual exploitation of children are poverty and armed conflicts, which have caused a rise in the number of trafficking cases as well as the spread of the crime to areas that were previously less affected, according to UNICEF. As part of the effort to check the menace internationally, a Europe-Africa summit was held in Brussels in October 2001, where countries agreed to draw up a plan of action against human trafficking. Part of the collaborative efforts in the fight against human trafficking across borders is the teaming up of the immigration authorities in Nigeria with their foreign counterparts. The exercise has yielded positive results. In 2003, it culminated in the deportation of 142 girls and young men from Italy, 160 from Spain, 59 from the Netherlands, 4 from the United States, 13 from South Africa, 6 each from Ireland, Cote d'Ivoire, and Niger Republic.

Despite the fact that the incidents of trafficking in woman and children in Nigeria had been going on as far back as the 1960s, the public recognition and focus on the issue heightened only since the mid 1990s. The recent awareness of trafficking in Nigeria resulted from the publicity generated by the deportation to Nigeria of trafficked persons for prostitution from Europe and the Middle East, which started in 1994.

Abhulmen (1999) noted that the increasing number of deportees who were trafficking victims of prostitution influenced the negation of the seriousness of other forms of trafficking such as child labor and slave labor trafficking. He argued that the definition of "trafficking in women" should be the movement of young girls of ages 13 to 18 from one country to another by road, rail, sea, or air for the sole purpose of prostitution. However, it fails to recognize trafficking for other forms of labor. In Nigeria, women and children, especially underage girls, are victims of trafficking for various forms of labor, including prostitution and sexual exploitation.

Types of Trafficking

In Nigeria, children especially are victims of both domestic and international trafficking in human beings. Internal trafficking of children takes the form of recruitment and transportation of children from the rural areas to the urban centers for different forms of labor under exploitative conditions. International trafficking of children is trafficking of children across national borders for different forms of labor, also under exploitative and slave-like conditions.

Domestic

For decades, children, predominantly from rural communities such as many parts of Akwa-Ibom and Cross River State, have been recruited by traffickers and trafficked to cities such as Lagos, Ibadan, Kano, and Port-Harcourt. Recruitment can include voluntary placement of children with traffickers by parents or guardians to be transported to the cities for labor. Sometimes the children, out of peer pressure, curiosity for city life, and/or lack of alternative opportunities, seek out the traffickers on their own.

Traffickers force domestic trafficked children into labor such as domestic service, shopkeeping, catering service, hawking, and prostitution. The conditions of labor are exploitative and slave-like. As domestic workers, for example, the children are subjected to 12 to 18 hours of cleaning, babysitting, cooking, and other forms of household chores and hard work. Such children are the first to get up in the morning and the last to go to bed in the household. Most of the children are denied any forms of formal or vocational training; they are poorly clothed and are kept in very low conditions of living.

International

Ojomo (1999) asserts that Nigeria constitutes a recruitment, transit, and destination center for international trafficking of women and children. Like the domestic trafficking, children also constitute the majority of the victims of international trafficking. As a recruitment center, Nigerian children are recruited predominantly from southeastern states, such as Akwa Ibom and Cross Rivers, and trafficked mostly by sea to Gabon, Cameroon, and Guinea to work in farm plantations. Children are also recruited from Shaki in Oyo State and trafficked to Guinea, Mali, and Cote d'Ivoire to work as hawkers and domestic servants. Not much research has been conducted on the forms of recruitment of this type of trafficking, but there is evidence that those recruited are children from a poor family background and mostly from rural communities. The mode of transportation, usually by sea, is mostly under deplorable conditions, comparable with the 18th century trans-Saharan slave trade.

Nigerian children are also trafficked to European countries and the Middle East for prostitution and sexual exploitation. The trend for the trafficking of Nigerians to European countries, especially Italy, Belgium, the Netherlands, Germany, Spain, and more recently, England, started manifesting itself in the 1980s but reached alarming proportions toward the mid and latter part of the 1990s up until now. Even without specific data, the few studies conducted show that thousands of Nigerian women and children have been trafficked to Europe, particularly Italy. According to the Nigerian ambassador to Italy, a survey indicates that more than 10,000 Nigerians are engaged in prostitution in Italy. This large number is buttressed by the declaration of the then Italian ambassador to Nigeria that Nigerian girls constitute 60 percent of all prostitutes in the sex trade in Italy (*News Magazine* 1999).

Most of the trafficked victims for prostitution are children at the time of travel. The recruitment of girls for trafficking en route to Europe are predominantly from Edo and Delta States. There are also records of recruitments from other states such as Imo, Enugu, Ogun, Anambra, and Akwa-Ibom. For the Middle East, particularly Saudi Arabia, recruitment of girls is predominately from Northern Nigeria, especially Kano, Kwara, and Kaduna States.

The usual bait for luring the Nigerian girls into trafficking for prostitution is a false promise of employment to earn much-valued foreign currency, vocational training, or marriage. Those trafficked to Saudi Arabia are usually offered an opportunity to perform the holy pilgrimage to Mecca, an Islamic injunction, and an opportunity for importation of high-profit items. With recent publicity, some awareness has been created as to the true nature of the employment, which is prostitution. Despite this information, many children still fall prey to traffickers through the active connivance of family members who coerce the children into trafficking.

Because of some sociological factors, such as the escalating level of poverty, lack of viable opportunities, fallen family values, the attraction to earn foreign currency that is more valuable than the local currency, and the desire to get rich quick, many parents and guardians will use any means to force their children into the trafficking ring. After recruitment, the victim and her family member are subjected to oaths of secrecy before traditional shrines. The victim's body parts, such as pubic hairs, blood, fingernails, and personal items such as pants, are collected and used for oath-taking rituals. The oath-taking ritual has a multipurpose effect on the victims, one aspect of which is to instill fear of terrible reprisals, such as death or madness, if the victim breaks the oaths.

The routes taken to the various destinations are dynamic and are as varied as the different syndicated gangs of traffickers. Some of the most common routes are from Nigeria through the neighboring countries of the Republics of Benin and Togo to Ghana or Mali, where orientation and change of identities are conducted for those traveling by air. Another route is through North African countries, such as Morocco or Libya, and through the Suez Canal to Britain and other parts of Europe. In recent times, there has been an increase in young girls claiming asylum in Britain but who are, however, lured into trafficking for prostitution in Europe. The porous borders in West Africa facilitated by the Economic Community of West African States Treaty allows easy passage for the trafficking of women and children from Nigeria and neighboring countries using Nigeria as either a recruitment center or a transit country to Europe.[8]

On arrival at destinations in Europe or the Middle East, the personal belongings of the trafficked children, including travel documents, are confiscated, and they are forced into prostitution and repayment bonds of amounts ranging between $30,000 and $50,000. This repayment schedule sometimes necessitates the children engaging in unprotected sex with 10 to 20 partners in a day. An average repayment lasts from three to five years, but some victims, especially those trafficked to Saudi Arabia, never get freedom from their bondage. The madams (female traffickers) may terminate the transaction prematurely to her benefit by alerting the European authorities that the victim is an illegal immigrant. This happens if the victims fall ill, contracts HIV/AIDS, or has almost completed the repayment schedule.

As far back as the 1960s, Nigeria has been the destination country of mostly children from neighboring Republics of Benin, Togo, and Ghana who are forced into domestic service. These children are between 5 and 18 years old and are recruited by traffickers most times with the consent of their parents or guardians and sometimes through kidnapping. After arrival in Nigerian urban centers in the southwest, such as Lagos and Abeokuta, the trafficked foreign children are forced to serve as nannies, housekeepers, shop attendants, merchandise carriers, and hawkers and are employed to do odd jobs in the informal sector. In the characteristic manner of trafficking, the conditions of labor are slave-like, with little or no benefits to the trafficked children. Some of the family members benefit disproportionately to the traffickers, who make most of the profit in the illegal trade. Most of the middle-class homes in city centers are found to engage children as domestic servants, and the streets are filled with children hawkers and head loaders, most of who are trafficked children from within and outside Nigeria.

Root Factors and Social Implications of Trafficking in Children

With the dwindling economy, especially since the dictatorship of the military regime in Nigeria, came the unprecedented escalation of engagement of children in labor. The trafficking trade has fed the labor industries, particularly the informal sector. Some of the root factors for the reenactment of this modern form of slavery have been attributed to poverty and its attendant consequences. Other factors include the devaluation of the local currency, which has made the acquisition of foreign exchange more attractive. In addition, the fallen standards of family values, lack of parental control, and general avarice for wealth have contributed immensely to the escalation of the illegal trade of trafficking in human beings.

The social implications are manifold on the development of the nation. The subjection of children to slave-like labor, some of which are the worst forms of labor, has seriously impaired the growth and development of Nigerian children, who are the bedrock of the society. The trafficked children are denied education, a basic standard of living, fundamental human rights, dignity, and freedom in negation of the Nigerian Constitution and international instruments for the protection of the rights of the child. In fact, the low level of societal perception of the status of children in Nigeria makes Nigerians virtually ignore the criminality of trafficking in children for forced labor. Undoubtedly, trafficking in human beings is a heinous crime according to Nigerian law and international law. Unfortunately, there has not been any recorded arrest and successful prosecutions and convictions of traffickers. In reality, the traffickers of children for labor other than prostitution are not regarded as criminals; hence, there is no record of any arrest of traffickers of children for domestic labor. It is of paramount importance for the Nigerian government and the society to take serious steps to address and find solutions to the issue of trafficking in children. A first step will entail the enforcement of all the covenants, particularly instruments such as the World Congress against Commercial Sexual Exploitation (1996), the Convention on the Rights of the Child (1989), the Stockholm Agenda, the Libreville Convention, International Labor Organization (ILO) Convention 105 on Abolition of Forced Labor (1959), ILO Convention 182 on the Worst Forms of Child Labor (1999), the Slavery Convention (1926), the Convention for the Suppression of the Traffic in Persons and of the Exploitation of the Prostitution of Others (1949), the Convention on the Elimination of all Forms of Racial Discrimination (1965), the Convention on the Elimination of all Forms of Discrimination against Women (CEDAW) (1979), the Convention against Torture and Other Cruel, Inhuman or Degrading Treatment or Punishment (1984), the Convention on the Protection of the Rights of All Migrant Workers and Their Families (1990), ILO Convention 29 on Forced Labor (1930), and the Protocol to Prevent, Suppress, and Punish Trafficking in Persons Especially Women and Children (2000).

Global Efforts in Eliminating Discrimination against Women

The recognition of these problems by the world community led to the adoption of a United Nations Decade for Women (1976–1985) and the CEDAW of 1979, which sets the standards for eliminating discrimination between men and women. The United Nations Decade for Women's three major themes are equality, development, and peace. Equality means elimination of what is by law or in the actual situation discrimination against women and full observance of the equal rights of women. The main international instrument promoting equality between the sexes is the CEDAW, which has been ratified by more than 115 countries. The convention now has an additional protocol allowing individual complaints before the United Nations Human Rights Committee in case of serious breaches. Development sought to integrate women into all development planning efforts, to eliminate their marginalization based on psychological, social, and cultural grounds.

Peace was mentioned because international peace has been disturbed by international tension and conflicts resulting in gross violation of the United Nations charter and in which women suffer most in times of crisis. The decade sought to address this problem. Furthermore, the draft Declaration on Violence against Women recently adopted by the United Nations condemns physical assault, sexual harassment, or psychological injury to women. The declaration then calls on governments to prevent, investigate, and punish every violent action against women whether committed by individuals or states and their agents.

Other measures taken to ensure women's empowerment is through the United Nations conferences on women and other meetings held since 1974, which address human rights, social economic, and development issues. The World Conference on Human Rights held in Vienna, Austria, in 1993 adopted the historic declaration that "women's rights are human rights." At the Population and Development Summit held in Cairo, Egypt, in 1994, thousands of women brought visible support and added strength to the new, widely accepted concept of women's reproductive rights. The Declaration and Program of Action arising from the World Summit for Social Development in Copenhagen, Denmark, in March 1995 contained very extensive and far-reaching commitments. They include the creation of an enabling economic, political, social, cultural, and legal environment that will enable people to achieve social development, eradicating poverty in the world, promoting the goal of full employment, social integration and full respect for human dignity, as well as achieving equality between women and men. By this, the Copenhagen Declaration effectively merged women's rights into the broader covenant on human rights and the central role of women into social development.

Recommendations

There is a need for deeper understanding of the issue of trafficking, its causes, and its elements, which often involve deception, coercion, force, giving or receiving of benefits for the purpose of prostitution, forced labor, slavery, or slave-like practices, and manifestations as human rights abuse and crime.

Trafficking in women should be distinguished from illegal migration, prostitution, and organized crime, and should not be tackled only as one of such issues per se but as a violation of human rights of the victims.

Poverty, ignorance, globalization, and gender discrimination are major causes of trafficking; therefore, poverty alleviation programs should be strengthened to tackle its effects particularly on women and programs established to counter the negative effects of globalization.

The National Coalition against Trafficking in Persons should strengthen its network and collaborate with governments and other partners to ensure respect for the rights of victims of trafficking.

Existing laws relating to trafficking should be strengthened through amendments to make them more comprehensive and adequate in conforming with the need to respect the rights of victims. Nongovernment organizations should identify problems aimed at creating awareness at national, state, and community levels and sensitize the populace on the harmful effects of trafficking in women. Calls for structure and facilities to be put in place to address the health, psychological, and social needs of victims of trafficking.

In entering into agreement with receiving countries, the Nigeria government should demand human rights standards in the handling of victims who are her citizens. Nigeria should implement international treaties that she has ratified and signed, such as the Convention against Transnational Organized Crime and the United Nations protocol to prevent, suppress, and punish trafficking in persons, especially women and children, supplementing the United Nations Convention against Transnational Organized Crime 2000. Law enforcement and judicial officers should be trained and sensitized on human rights standards for victims of trafficking. Government should make laws and policies that respect the human rights of victims of trafficking. Government should create an enabling environment and provide facilities that will encourage Nigerians to enjoy their rights in their country and create opportunities for youth development. Airport officials in Nigeria, as an origination country, should also provide full information on trafficking and where victims should go for help if they fall prey to traffickers.

Immigration laws should be relaxed in destination countries to reduce the incidence of women falling prey to traffickers, and embassies in destination countries should provide information, visa validity, and migrant rights to women who are likely to become victims of trafficking, when necessary, in destination countries.

Conclusion

There is continuing subordination of women in many societies, as reflected in economic, educational, and work opportunity disparities between men and women. Many societies still favor sons and view girls as an economic burden. Desperate families in some of the most impoverished countries in Southeast Asia sell their daughters to brothels or to traffickers for the immediate payoff and to avoid having to pay the dowry to marry off daughters.

There is a high demand, worldwide, for trafficked women and children for sex tourism, sex workers, cheap sweatshop labor, and domestic workers. In effect, traffickers are encouraged by large tax-free profits and continuing income from the same victims at very low risk.

The inadequacy of laws and law enforcement in most origination, transit, and destination countries hamper efforts to fight trafficking. Prostitution is legal or tolerated in many countries, and widespread. When authorities do crack down, it is usually against prostitutes. Penalties for trafficking humans for sexual exploitation are often relatively minor compared with those for other criminal activities, such as drug and gun trafficking.

The priority placed on stemming illegal immigration in many countries has resulted in treatment of trafficking cases as a problem of illegal immigration, thus treating victims as criminals. When police raid brothels, women are often detained and punished, subjected to human rights abuses in jail, and swiftly deported. Few steps have been taken to provide support, healthcare, and access to justice. Few victims dare testify against the traffickers or those who hold them, fearing retribution for themselves and their families because most governments do not offer stays of deportation or adequate protection for witnesses.

Notes

1. Communication Initiative, "The Advocacy Project," July 2003.
2. UNICEF Report, 2001.
3. IPS, July 28, 2003.
4. Titi Abubaka, address to WOTCLEF, 2003.
5. Ibid.
6. Ibid.
7. UNICEF Report, 2001.
8. *Daily Telegraph*, March 9, 2001.

References

Abhulmen, P. D. 1999. "Trafficking in Women in Nigeria: The Modern Slavery." Presented at the National Workshop of the Women's Consortium of Nigeria, Lagos, Nigeria, December.

Bales, K. 1999. *Slavery in the Modern Era: Disposable People—New Slavery in the Global Economy.* Berkeley: University of California Press.

News Magazine. 1999. Comments on international trafficking between Nigeria and Italy by the Italian ambassador. October 4, p. 44.

Ojomo, A. J. 1999. "Trafficking in Women and Forced Labor Migration." Presented at the National Workshop of the Women's Consortium of Nigeria, Abuja, Nigeria, October.

World Congress against Commercial Sexual Exploitation. 1996. Stockholm, Sweden, August 27–31.

IV

Perspectives from Asia, the Middle East, and the Americas

Criminal Exploitation of Women and Children in the Philippines

13

VICTOR LUGA

The Nature and Extent of Criminal Exploitation of Women and Children in the Philippines

Criminal exploitation of women and children, particularly prostitution, pornography, and trafficking, is a reality that faces the Philippine society today. A decade back, the country was known abroad as a center for child prostitution. This bad image was depicted in a Japanese pornographic magazine *Lalicon Land*. The translation was quoted as saying: "Manila and Cebu are the treasure islands of girl prostitutes. If you want to buy Lolita (young girls) but cannot afford to go to Thailand, Manila is the best place to go. Manila is within three hours from Narita (Tokyo) and does not cost too much. There are many 'Lolita' prostitutes and they are cheap."

Unfortunately, however, the number of Filipino women and children engaged in commercial sexual exploitation cannot be accurately ascertained. By the very nature of the activities, which is rather covert, only estimates can be made. The serious state of children exploited in prostitution, however, had been the subject of research by the End Child Prostitution, Pornography, and Trafficking for Sexual Purposes (ECPAT Philippines). The study showed that there were more than roughly 60,000 children victimized by prostitution in the country.[1] These data, generated a decade ago, remain unverified but, when set as a baseline, are expected to have risen higher than that estimate.

Commercial sexual exploitation among children is one of the most extreme forms of child labor. Some children who were sexually abused at home end up as sex workers. Children in tourist areas are lured into accepting attention from and providing sexual favors to pedophiles in exchange for cash or gifts. Parents condone the situation because they benefit from the children's "benefactors." Other children are lured to cities by promises of lucrative jobs but end up in brothels.[2]

Prostitution is relatively more prevalent in highly urbanized cities and a number of tourist destinations in the country. Because of its imperial location and huge population, metro Manila ranks first in the incidence of prostitution in the country, followed by large cities such as Davao, Debu, and

Angeles. Other places include well-known tourist destinations in Puerto Galera in Mindoro Oriental, Boracay in Aklan, and Pagsanjan in Laguna.

The commercially exploitative condition of women and children in the country has long been a cause for attention not only domestically but also internationally, where victims are also exploited as a result of the transnational crime of trafficking.

Eighteen is the average age of women/children exploited in prostitution. In recent years, however, research shows that the majority of male customers are looking for young teenagers because of their innocence and the likelihood that they would not be afflicted with sexually transmitted diseases, including AIDS, if they engage in sexual intercourse with young girls. In the process, more and more children fall prey to these so-called “child predators.”

Among the most common modus operandi and types of criminal exploitation of women and children are the following.

Street Sex Workers (Pick-Up Girls)

Pick-up girls hang around side streets at night waiting for customers to pick them up. They are also housed in small rooms inside the residence of their recruiter-manager. Outside, the pimp bargains with customers for a sexual encounter, whispering to male passersby, “Boss, babae, bata, gusto mo?” (Boss, you want young prostitute?)

This type of prostitution is available only for a limited engagement, usually three hours. However, if the customer wants a longer time or overnight service, they are open for such arrangements with a corresponding increase in payment.

Casa (Brothel) Girls

Casa girls are those who stay in a brothel whether voluntarily or by force to engage in prostitution. The owner (*amo*) or manager tends to the girls’ needs in exchange for sex-for-sale activities. The girls pay for everything they consume through deductions in their income per night from their total weekly income. Casa girls are mostly young, with ages ranging from 15 to 25 years old.

In a casa, 10 or more girls can be found. Recruiters lure these girls from remote barangays (villages) with promises of decent jobs in the urban areas such as Manila, Cebu, and Angeles. Out of shame, they often refuse to go back to their families. This type of prostitution is believed to be operated by syndicates and usually has a connection with some authorities.

Bikini Bar Girls

As the name would suggest, bikini bar girls entertain guests and customers by dancing on an elevated platform wearing skimpy bikinis or two-piece see-through apparel. Most of these girls are young but claim to be more than 18 years old when asked about their age.

Karaoke Bar Girls

These girls are employed as receptionists in karaoke bars and are usually called a guest relations officer. In contrast to bikini bar girls, karaoke bar girls wear decent clothes. Karaoke bar girls sit at the customer's table and assist in taking orders as well as encouraging the customer to sing. These women are young and attractive, always insisting, when asked how old they are, to be above 18.

A floor manager (*mama-san*) assigns a girl to a customer's table. Usually, these girls are not allowed by the karaoke bar management to go out with customers during bar time. If the girls agree to go out with a customer, she can only do so after the bar has closed but on her personal capacity and risk.

High-Class Prostitutes

This type of sex worker is said to live in exclusive condominiums in the metropolis. They do not deal with ordinary people. They entertain only a limited number of people.

International Prostitutes

Those involved in this type of prostitution are pedophiles. Their operation is usually to befriend Filipino minors, after which they pamper them with expensive clothes, jewelry, toys, food, and money, but, because of the Filipino custom of *utang na loob* (debt of gratitude), pedophiles are at liberty in exploiting the minors.

Aside from having sex with them, the pedophiles also take nude photos for publication in pornographic magazines abroad, notably Japan, Australia, France, the United Kingdom, and Germany. It is through these pornographic magazines that prostitution in the Philippines is promoted and encouraged.

Prostitution in Schools

Some girl students were reportedly engaged in prostitution in their own capacity to make a living for themselves, particularly for the payment of their tuition fees. In police parlance, the scheme is called "prosti-tuition."

Prostitution through the Internet

This type of prostitution has not yet been considered as very alarming in the country because it is only limited to people with access to computer technology. However, this does not preclude law enforcement agencies from devising ways to detect this computer-generated crime. So far, very few people have been caught engaging in this form of victimizing women and children. Usually, the law that is enforced to address this problem is Republic Act 6955 or the Anti-Mail-Order Bride Act.

Other Types

The commoditization of women and children is found to have also been taking place in massage parlors/saunas, hotels, commercial malls, and, in some instances, even military establishments.

Children at Risk of Other Forms of Criminal Exploitation

Children living on the streets, which is still prevalent in major cities of the country, will always be at risk of exploitation. They may feel constant humiliation from the more affluent passersby and experience low self-esteem and feelings of neglect. These feelings may push them to use drugs and eventually commit crime.

Children who stay on the streets most of the time develop behaviors and undertake activities that mainstream society considers "deviant." These problem activities include gambling, drug use (glue or paint thinner), and casual sex. The children are further exposed to possible abuse and exploitation and may resort to prostitution to support a drug habit.

During the 1996 World Congress against Commercial Sexual Exploitation of Children in Stockholm, Sweden, one group explained that the network of child sexual exploiters is composed of the "users," the "suppliers," and "protectors."[3]

Suppliers refer to the pimps, brothel owners, and parents who force children of both sexes to engage in prostitution and pornography. They also include individuals who engage in human trafficking, deceiving parents and children into thinking that the children will get legitimate employment in the city. The protectors are some government officials, local politicians, or the police that protect the suppliers and allow them to operate.

The users depicted in most of the literature on child prostitution are foreign pedophiles arriving as tourists.[4] Undeniably, protectors can also be users. This shows the tendency of the activities of the members of the network to overlap. The user usually becomes a supplier. One person can be both user and supplier. The two protect each other's interests and function as protectors.

Dela Cruz asserted that the framework of the network/triangle of abusers reinforces the notion that "one need not have a direct hand in the actual abuse and exploitation for one to become a participant in the phenomenon of abuse. One need not have direct contact with the abused child either. By allowing ourselves to be enveloped by the culture of silence, fear, and apathy, we all contribute to the perpetration of child abuse."[5]

Sexual exploitation of women and children should be seen within the framework of this "triangular network of abusers." Dela Cruz and her colleagues said that dismantling the network of abusers is important in battling sexual exploitation of women and children.

What Are Factors That Contribute to This Phenomenon?

Prostitution among women and children is generally believed to be a result of poverty. The need to survive is a compelling force that drives adults to prey on children, especially girls who would soon be grown-up women. Poverty in itself breeds other ills, such as the increasing migration of people from rural to urban areas for economic pursuits. Family dysfunction and the breakdown of support systems and the shedding of traditional values that uphold strong family foundations are also some of the reasons why criminal exploitation of women and children abounds.[6]

Poverty and the concomitant factors of unemployment, landlessness, and armed conflict combine to deny the prospect of a secure future for many of these women and children and their families, especially in the most disadvantaged provinces of the country. They become a natural target for unscrupulous recruiters, procurers, and prostitution pimps, including organized crime syndicates having a network of local contacts. They use a combination of deception, false promises, and cash incentives to win over the parents or the child directly.

The heart of the problem is the exploitation by the powerful over the powerless, male over female, adult over child, devious over naïve, rich over poor, organized over unorganized. Urbanization, the colonial legacy, machismo culture, commercialization, tourism, military bases, and religious and cultural factors are among the main causes of child sexual exploitation. Materialism, consumerism, and patriarchy promote the idea of children as commodities.

Children are not usually subjected to HIV tests in the Philippines, but 18 percent of the street children contract sexually transmitted diseases. Many children in the sex industry are presumably infected. These sexually abused children are prone to experience "sudden attacks of anxiety and panic; act younger than their age; be depressed, sad and withdrawn."[7]

Another factor is the role of the media, which unwittingly capitalizes on sexual violence and eroticism such as exposure to pornography through indecent literature, information technology (particularly the Internet), movies, drug addiction, and alcoholism.

Control Mechanisms

The Philippines is a signatory to various international treaties and declarations aimed at addressing several issues on the protection of women and children from violations of human rights, among others. It has been a national policy of the Republic of the Philippines to recognize the equal rights and inherent human dignity of women and men as enshrined in the United Nations Universal Declaration on Human Rights, United Nations Convention on the Elimination of All Forms of Discrimination against Women, United Nations Convention on the Rights of the Child, United Nations Convention on the Protection of Migrant Workers and their Families, and all other relevant and universally accepted human rights instruments and other international conventions to which the Philippines is a signatory.

Another international instrument signed by the government of the Philippines and ratified in Congress is the Hague Convention on Inter-Country Adoption in June 1996. Earlier in 1995, the Philippines also presented several proposals to the Beijing Platform for Action on Women, which paved the way to addressing with greater intensity the issue of violence against women.

In the year 2000, the country became a state party to the United Nations Convention against Transnational Organized Crime, which aims among other things to protect innocent victims at risk of trafficking, the majority of whom are women and children. Being a party to this convention came on the heels of previous conventions on trafficking to which the Philippines was also a signatory, one of which was the first United Nations treaty to denounce trafficking in persons, the 1949 Convention on the Suppression of Trafficking in Persons and the Prostitution of Others. The country also took part in the formulation of the Association of the Southeast Asian Nations Plan of Action for the World Summit on Children in 2000.

In 2002, the Philippine Senate ratified two optional protocols to the Convention on the Rights of the Child on the involvement of children in armed conflict and on the sale of children, child prostitution, and child pornography.

Other international instruments that address women and children, to which the Philippines became a party, are the following: 1956 Supplementary Convention on the Abolition of Slavery, Slave Trade, and Institutions and Practices similar to Slavery; 1990 Vienna Declaration on Human Rights; 1993 Declaration on the Elimination of Violence against Women; 1997 Commission on the Status of Women and General Assembly Resolutions on Traffic in Women and Girls; 1997 International Labor Organization (ILO) Convention 138 Concerning Minimum Age of Children for Admission to Employment; and 2000 ILO Convention 182 Concerning Worst Forms of Child Labor.

The framers of the 1987 Philippine Constitution, to stress the importance of women, youth, and family relations, inserted several articles entirely concerned with recognizing the role of the family, the empowerment of women, and the right of children to special protection.

The subsequent sections, provided under Art. II (Declaration of Principles and State Policies) of the Philippine Constitution, state the following:

- ***Sec. 11:*** The State values the dignity of every human person and guarantees full respect for human rights.
- ***Sec. 13:*** The State recognizes the vital role of the youth in nation-building and shall promote and protect their physical, moral, spiritual, and social well-being.
- ***Sec. 14:*** The State recognizes the role of women in nation-building, and shall ensure the fundamental equality before the law of women and men.

Furthermore, under Art. XV (The Family) of the Constitution, the subsequent sections state the following:

- ***Sec. 1:*** The State recognizes the Filipino family as the foundation of the nation. Accordingly, it shall strengthen its solidarity and actively promote its total development.
- ***Sec. 3:*** The State shall defend the right of children to assistance, including special protection from all forms of neglect, abuse, cruelty, exploitation, and other conditions prejudicial to their development.

In pursuit of all these national policies on women and children, therefore, the state is giving top priority to the enactment of legislative measures and development of programs that promote the protection of women and children from all forms of violence and exploitation. Several domestic instruments, special laws in particular, were used and adopted to translate national commitment into concrete measures to make life bearable to women and children, they being the most vulnerable to crimes and lawlessness.

Among the laws enacted by the Philippine Congress to protect women and children are as follows: Republic Act (RA) 7610, An Act Providing Stronger Deterrence and Special Protection against Child Abuse, Exploitation, and Discrimination; RA 9208, Anti-Trafficking in Persons Act of 2003; RA 7658, An Act Prohibiting the Employment of Children below 15 Years of Age in Public and Private Undertakings; RA 8043, An Act Establishing the Rules to Govern Inter-Country Adoption of Filipino Children; RA 8353, Anti-Rape Act of 1997; RA 8369, Family Courts Act of 1997; RA 6955, Mail Order Bride Act of 1989; RA 7877, Anti-Sexual Harassment Act of 1995; RA 8505, Rape Victim Assistance Act of 1998; RA 7192, Women in Development and

Nation-Building Act; RA 8239, Philippine Passport Act of 1996; RA 8042, Migrant Workers and Overseas Filipinos Act; Act 3810, Revised Penal Code; Executive Order (EO) 64 (Series 1999), Creating the Philippine Center on Transnational Crime; and EO 209 (Series of 1988), Family Code of the Philippines.

With the passage of all of these laws, the government of the Philippines has made positive its effort to ensure that criminal exploitation of women and children is substantially being reduced, if not totally eliminated. Likewise, several special bodies have been created for the protection of women and children, the following among them:

- Council for the Welfare of Children, which coordinates the implementation of laws on children, formulates policies, and devises, introduces, develops, and evaluates programs and services for the general welfare of children and youth
- National Youth Commission, created pursuant to RA 8044, establishing a National Comprehensive Program on Youth Development
- National Commission on the Role of Filipino Women, which formulates policies and programs for the empowerment and general welfare of women
- Committee for the Special Protection of Children, created pursuant to EO 275, series of 1992
- Anti-Human Trafficking Council, pursuant to RA 9208, that addresses the problem of trafficking in women and children
- Violence Against Women Coordinating Committee, chaired by the National Commission on the Role of Filipino Women, composed of 15 government agencies that jointly address violence against women

National Initiatives against Trafficking in Women and Children

Although there are still gaps in policies, legislation, enforcement, and monitoring, the country came out with a tremendous response to address criminal exploitation of women and children through the following national initiative/measures:

(1) Philippine Plan for Gender-Responsive Development (1995–2025), a 30-year plan that aims to empower women, eliminate gender stereotyping, and protect women against all forms of violence, including the commoditization of women for sexual purposes.

(2) National Plan of Action against Commercial Sexual Exploitation of Children (CSEC) (2000–2004), a five-year plan in keeping with the commitment to protect a child's right as embodied in the United Nations Convention on the Rights of the Child, formulated as a

collaborative effort of government, nongovernment agencies (NGOs), and child participants prepared under the helm of the Philippine Council for the Welfare of Children.

(3) Philippine National Development Plan for Children (or CHILD 21), a strategic framework formulated in 2000 for the next 25 years that aims at ensuring that every Filipino child will be able to exercise her rights to survival, protection, development, and participation through one-third of her life cycle.

(4) Executive Order Creating the Philippine Center on Transnational Crime in 1999, which focuses on crimes of international dimension, including trafficking in human beings.

(5) Executive Order creating an Inter-Agency Council against Trafficking in Human Beings, Especially Women and Children, which paved the way to a stronger national plan of action against trafficking in women and children. Both executive orders were already superseded with the passage of RA 9208 (Anti-Trafficking in Human Beings Act).

Likewise, to give flesh to the country's active involvement in addressing the crime of trafficking, the Philippines served as a pilot area of the United Nations Project against Trafficking in Human Beings, which paved the way to raising the consciousness and enticing the active involvement of the different agencies directly concerned with addressing cases of trafficking in human beings.

Earlier on, the country was able to forge bilateral agreements with the United Kingdom and Australia to address the sexual exploitation of children and women through sharing of intelligence information and skills enhancement of the law enforcers in assisting women and children victims of crimes.

The Asian-European Movement (ASEM) Conference is an offshoot of a collaborative endeavor of the Republic of the Philippines and the United Kingdom for Asian countries and European nations to put up a strong stand against CSEC. It is an ongoing concrete initiative between the two countries on surveillance and monitoring of cases of children trapped in commercial sexual exploitation, an effort that moves forward the 1996 Stockholm Agenda.

The country, incidentally, has played host or is a co-party to various international events or agreements related to the criminal exploitation of women and children, including the following:

- 1998 Philippine-Belgian Pilot Project against Trafficking in Women, which has extensively covered the issue of trafficking in women in the country from three different perspectives: legal, socioeconomic, and sociocultural. It has key findings and recommendations that were endorsed by the National Commission on the Role of Filipino Women, among them, that trafficking in women is one of the priority issues that needs to be addressed.

- Fifth Country Programme for Children between the Philippines and the United Nations International Children's Emergency Fund, addressing Children in Need of Special Protection, particularly those engaged in commercial sexual exploitation.
- ASEM on Child Welfare Initiative Tripartite Planning Session held in Manila in March 1999. This meeting brought into finality the agenda for the ASEM in Seoul, Korea, in May 2000, in which 10 Asian and 15 European countries gathered together to address the global concern on CSEC.
- Asian Regional Initiative against Trafficking in Women and Children, March 28–31, 2000, in Manila. This ministerial meeting among senior-level government officials in the Asia-Pacific countries discussed the global phenomenon of trafficking in women and children.
- ASEM on Justice for Children in Makati City, March 3–5, 2003, which gave major focus to children in conflict with the law.
- ASEAN Seminar/Workshop on the Prevention of Domestic Violence in Markati City, August 22–29, 2003, which enhanced the capacities of Asian member countries to wage a holistic campaign to address the rising incidence of domestic violence across the region.
- In August 1996, the Philippines participated in the World Congress against Commercial Sexual Exploitation of Children, held in Stockholm. It culminated in the adoption of a "Declaration and Agenda for Action against Commercial Sexual Exploitation of Children."
- Five years after Stockholm, the country again participated in the Second World Congress against Commercial Sexual Exploitation of Children in Yokohama, Japan, in December 2001. The outcome document in the second Congress aimed to push for greater commitment and continuing mechanisms to address child prostitution, child pornography, and child trafficking for sexual purposes.

Law Enforcement Mechanisms

The Philippine National Police (PNP), the premier law enforcement agency in the land, has also established a foundation for its direct involvement in combating the criminal exploitation of women and children. Together with other concerned law enforcement agencies, the PNP has scored a number of milestones in the promotion and protection of women and children since its inception in 1991 following the passage of RA 6975. Several programs, projects, and activities were introduced, carried out, and sustained by the PNP as an instrument of the Philippine government to implement its commitment to international treaties and obligations for the protection of women and children.

In carrying out an arduous task of reducing, if not totally eliminating, the victimization of women and children arising from criminal exploitation of trafficking, prostitution, and pornography, among other crimes, a national law enforcement framework has been designed for the prevention, protection, rescue, recovery, and reintegration to address violence against women and children. The said law enforcement framework is culled in substance from the existing national government plans of action geared toward addressing the protection of women and children from various forms of commercial sexual exploitation.

The PNP, for this purpose, aimed to implement this blueprint of action within the next five years through its operating units, especially the Women and Children Protection Desk (WCPD), a specialized unit in every police station that has been mandated pursuant to RA 8551 (PNP Reform and Reorganization Act of 1998), to attend to and administer cases involving women and children.

The efforts of the PNP WCPDs, a best-practice model in Asia and the Pacific, are complemented by the establishment of a one-stop PNP Women's Crisis and Child Protection Center based in Camp Crame, which houses "under one roof" a multidisciplinary approach to addressing cases of children who fall victim to abuse and violence. Similar structures were established in Davao City and Legaspi City.

Also, the National Bureau of Investigation established its version of the PNP women's desk with its own Violence against Women and Children Division, which provides investigative services and rescue operations to women and children victims/survivors of abuse and violence.

Other than the regular anti-vice squads based in police stations, a task force composed of various agencies, headed by the Department of Labor and Employment, was organized. Dubbed Task Force *Sagip Batang Manggagawa* (Anti-Child Labor Rescue Operations), with the PNP among its members, the task force ably intensified the government drive against prostitution of children, which is one of the worst forms of child labor under ILO 182. Likewise, at the PNP National Capital Region, a regional office for the protection of women and children has been activated to respond to the victimization of women and children as a result of commercial sexual exploitation that includes white slavery, trafficking, pornography, and the like.

One of the PNP initiatives was entering into a multiorganization agreement in September 2001, with an information technology company, Integrate

Browsers Systems Inc., to help the police inform the public through the use of the Internet about reported cases of missing children who may have fallen victim to prostitution, trafficking, illegal adoption, and the like.

Incidentally, the PNP has also been conducting several training activities for police personnel to raise their awareness and to enhance the capacities of our duty holders dedicated to handling cases of child abuse and violence against women.

In the area of prevention, the PNP is also actively involved in the conduct of community dialogs, seminars, interagency collaboration, and even community organizing, which are all aimed at raising the consciousness of community members about the rights of children, preventing family/domestic violence, developing Filipino core values, and institutionalizing government measures to help eliminate the victimization of children.

The following are the program components and strategic activities being implemented by the PNP to address criminal exploitation of women and children (2001–2005).[8]

Prevention Program

Advocacy is seen as a core strategy in addressing the criminal exploitation of women and children. The police are exerting efforts to be more relevant and effective by planning, implementing, and evaluating a comprehensive advocacy program for women's and children's rights, particularly against sexual exploitation, slavery, debt bondage, and other forms of violence against women and children.

Program Objective

Increased awareness, knowledge, and skills strengthen the resolve of the police to protect women and children from becoming victims of crime. This may help the police generate broad-based support and participation from the NGOs.

Strategic Activities

Strategic activities include the following:

(1) ***Enhance national capacity for information, education, and communication (IEC) program design, management, and implementation.*** In view of the need to develop expertise in strategic IEC skills and facilitate continual capacity building in peripheral areas of the country, it is proposed that a particular police institution with the appropriate experience, mandate, and potential be strengthened through technical and financial assistance by other agencies and bodies, both local and international, to enhance its capacity to

become a primary resource and information center in the PNP on women's and children's protection.

(2) ***Intensify gender sensitization efforts on women's and children's right to protection.*** This should involve the police organization and a variety of target audiences at all levels of government and civil society, i.e., children, family, community, business sector, media, church, hotel and tourism industry, government, and NGOs. There is a need to make known this information to as many Filipinos as possible if we want to see an intensification of vigilance and escalation of advocacy down to the grassroots against the exploitation of human beings resulting from sexual abuse and exploitation.

Awareness-raising activities require all available interpersonal channels, including the mass media. Specifically, it involves a combination of tactics:

a) *Individualized approach:* personal contacts with the police at the station level.
b) *Direct appeal to specific groups:* political, traditional and religious leaders, government personnel, local chief executives, media/tourism/hotel managers, church leaders, and key local communicators.
c) *General promotion activities:* using the mass media by publishing articles about sexual abuse and exploitation of women and children in newspapers or magazines, broadcasting information via radio and/or television advertisements, and community assemblies.
d) *Development and production of appropriate information and motivational materials:* brochures, posters, and fact sheets, including pamphlets containing basic information on women and child protection laws (international and national) and their wide distribution to various users.

The advocacy and IEC efforts include training of trainers to expand the pool of police officers who shall eventually be tapped for some training programs on women's and children's protection.

(3) ***Integrate women's and children's protection systematically into PNP development planning, with special attention to victims and those at risk of sexual abuse and commoditization through prostitution, pornography, and trafficking.*** The government has always realized the importance of the protection of women and children and endorses, as a policy, the promotion of the family as a basic unit of the society and the welfare and participation of both women and children in asserting their rights and in contributing to the development of the nation. This stand is reflected in various official documents, including the constitution, and has been manifested by concrete sectoral actions.

The PNP must be responsible, therefore, for providing policy guidelines, standards, and technical assistance to lower units/offices in implementing an integrated, holistic, and comprehensive development program. In view of this, it is vital that women's and children's protection variables and agenda are mainstreamed into the development plans of the PNP to ensure priority attention, resources, and sustainability of program efforts.

(4) ***Incorporate modules on women's and children's protection, including gender sensitivity, in career courses and in-service training programs for all members of the PNP.*** This measure can be coursed through the Philippine Public Safety College, which serves as the training and education arm of the interior branch of the Department of the Interior and Local Government.

(5) ***Promote family and community empowerment to prevent criminal exploitation among women and children and other forms of abuse and violence.*** Creating awareness about protection of women and children and how it can be sustained is a task that should begin right at home and in the communities.

It is the family's role, as well as that of the community, to instill this consciousness into the minds of its members. It is through these units of society that awareness and respect of women's and children's rights is affirmed and where mindsets are shaped. The results of this endeavor will undoubtedly accelerate the momentum of police-community relations in advancing the cause of women and children and the role of the police as frontline advocates for the protection of women and children.

The effectiveness of community-based IEC for women and children can be enhanced at the family and community levels through capacity building that focuses on awareness raising and skills development. It emphasizes the right to protection of women and children and makes police-community action against commercial sexual exploitation and other forms of abuse and violence appropriate.

The police in this regard may consider as entry points the existence of day care parents associations, parent-teacher associations, and similar groups that can be tapped for this purpose.

(6) ***Help organize, activate, and strengthen local councils for the protection of children in accordance with PD 603 as focal points for protecting children from commercial sexual exploitation and other forms of child abuse, as well as for coordination and monitoring.*** Give appropriate and continuing capacity-building opportunities and support of experienced community organizing agencies and local government units; the local councils can become potent mechanisms for advancing the agenda of women's and children's

protection and facilitating coordination, integration, and monitoring of efforts for child protection at barangay, municipal, city, province, and regional levels.

Part of this activity is pilot testing, an effective mechanism or system for coordination, monitoring, and evaluation in selected regions in Luzon, Visayas, and Mindanao, with some functional local councils at different levels (barangay, municipal, city, province, and region). These results can prove useful in developing and fine tuning standard systems for coordination, monitoring, and evaluation of women's and children's protection at all levels.

(7) ***Design and implement a database system on violence against women and children to have timely and reliable information for formulation of plans, policies, and programs in the PNP.*** The indicators and data shall be integrated into the bigger women's and children's protection data collection and monitoring system within the PNP. The data will also serve as a basis for monitoring and keeping track of other women and children at risk of trafficking, prostitution, pornography, and other forms of commercial sexual exploitation.

(8) ***Undertake PNP research initiatives on law enforcement operations against sexual abuse and exploitation of women and children.***

Protection Program

The PNP recognizes the protection of women and children from commercial sexual exploitation as a vital element in addressing the problem.

Program Objective

The program objective is to improve the protection and rescue of children and women from victimization through commercial sexual exploitation.

Strategic Activities

Strategic activities include the following:

(1) ***Review and modify laws, policies, and procedures to protect women and children from commercial sexual exploitation.*** There is a need to review and modify existing statutory and policy frameworks to make it more relevant to the needs and situation of women and children involved in commercial sexual exploitation such as RA 7610 (Anti-Child Abuse Law), RA 8505 (Special Assistance to Rehabilitation of Rape Victims), RA 8043 (Inter-Country Adoption Act), RA 8369 (Family Courts Law), Republic Act 8559 (Domestic Adoption Law), and the latest law, RA 9208 (Anti-Trafficking in Human Beings Act).

(2) ***Enforce existing laws, policies, and programs to protect women and children and to prohibit the commercial sexual exploitation of women and children.*** Existing laws are not always as fully enforced as they should be. There is, therefore, a need to ensure in the future that appropriate actions are taken by the police for full compliance with these laws, that regulations are strictly enforced, that prosecution and disposition of violence against women and children cases are expedited, and that penalties are firmly imposed. A vital component of this endeavor is the conduct of periodic reorientation/orientation/training seminars on existing laws and policies to protect women and children from prostitution, trafficking, pornography, and other forms of abuse.

(3) ***Operationalize a child-friendly protection network system, which consists of the following elements.***
   a) Trained personnel, including judges, prosecutors/lawyers, police, doctors, and social workers
   b) Availability and accessibility of support services, including legal assistance and security measures, medical/psychological evaluation and/or treatment, and psychosocial support such as counseling
   c) A standard protocol for handling surveillance, rescue, and investigation
   d) Secure, safe, and child-friendly facilities for protective custody
   e) Effectively linked and coordinated councils for the protection of children at the barangay, municipal, city, provincial, regional, and national levels and other existing mechanisms

(4) ***Formulate a standard protocol.*** Establish a standard protocol on surveillance, detection, and rescue of children to ensure a systematic and child-friendly procedure in handling CSEC cases.

(5) ***Upgrade knowledge and skills.*** Upgrade the knowledge and skills of concerned staff in dealing with women and children victims, particularly on surveillance and rescue. A continuing professional and para-professional training of governmental organizations and NGO personnel should be pursued (police, social workers, judges, prosecutors, lawyers, local authorities, medicolegal officers, care givers, health/community workers, and tourism and hotel personnel).

Content will focus on the following: women and child rights; women and child protection laws; child development; interviewing/communication skills; gender sensitivity; dynamics of domestic violence/child abuse and commercial sexual exploitation; nonpunitive approach to dealing with women and child victims; conflict resolution; case management; team building and community organizing; and referral system.

(6) ***Strengthen surveillance, monitoring, and rescue mechanisms.*** Strengthen and mobilize the Barangay Councils for the Protection of Children (BCPCs) as the focal vehicles for the surveillance, detection, rescue, and monitoring commercial sexual exploitation of young women and children in partnership with the Barangay Human Rights Action Center Sagip-Batang Manggagawa, Bantay Bata, and concerned NGOs. Given the training and support, these community-based organizations or groups are in the best position to undertake surveillance, rescue, and monitoring of these cases at the community level because of their proximity and accessibility to children and families. The linkages of the BCPC with the municipal, city/province, regional, and national councils for the protection of children should be operationalized.

(7) ***Undertake studies on surveillance.*** Undertake studies on surveillance and rescue practices to support planning and program development concerning women and children.

(8) ***Intensify regional and international linkages to combat criminal exploitation of women and children.*** Collaborative efforts will be pursued in cooperation with the police, Bureau of Immigration, Department of Foreign Affairs, Interpol, and other regional or international authorities and NGOs such as ECPAT, Defense Children International, and Save the Children, for the purposes of monitoring child traffickers and pedophiles in a coordinated manner.

Recovery and Reintegration Program

The PNP proposes to adopt the following action agenda for the recovery and reintegration program during the plan period.

Program Objective

The program objective is to improve a long-term psychosocial recovery and reintegration program for women and children survivors.

Strategic Activities

The strategic activities include the provision of rehabilitative and support services to women's and children's desk officers to address the psychological trauma and other needs of women and children victims of criminal exploitation. Availability and accessibility of comprehensive services should be ensured from the time of admission until discharge. These new services by the PNP should be geared toward achieving early recovery and eventual return of the victims to the normal network of family and community relationships.

These services may include the following: temporary care in halfway houses/facilities; group counseling; family therapy and group work to cope with the effects of trauma; health-related services; referrals; vocational training; livelihood schemes; sports and recreation; leadership and value formation training; and other after-care services.

Additional strategic activities include the following:

(1) Making the police well versed in helping empower families to facilitate recovery and reintegration of the victims/survivors. This includes the empowerment of families of survivors of sexual abuse and commercial sexual exploitation, which is a vital element in the recovery and reintegration process. It includes linking families with formal and informal resources and providing capacity-building opportunities to enable, support, teach, and encourage family members to bring about positive change in their family.
(2) Empowerment-based practice with families of survivors to focus on the empowerment of families through collaborative relationships between the police and family members. It also includes capacity building among families and use of the resources that the family and community networks provide. Such practice with families and children will help families build on their own strengths, gain access to police services, and develop a stronger police-community partnership.
(3) Developing a PNP WCPD Manual on Psychosocial Care and Intervention for women and children victims of human trafficking and other forms of commercial sexual exploitation focused on case management and the team approach. The WCPD shall be the lead unit in the police stations performing this function because its personnel shall be trained to gain knowledge and expertise in handling cases involving sexual abuse and commercial sexual exploitation of women and children.
(4) Replication and/or conduct of pilot or demonstration projects of WCPD psychosocial interventions in selected police stations. Treatment models for women and child victims of trafficking as well as other successful alternative schemes should be documented for possible replication. Through this mechanism, the police may come to see how the problems of the concerned victims are similar to those of others. Through mutual information sharing, police and the victims can think critically about the internal and external aspects of the situation, they may establish relationships that will strengthen the resolve of law enforcement to fight for justice for the victims, and the police can also practice problem solving and interpersonal communication. They can also begin to notice common experiences that could help them collectively to understand and take action.

(5) Conduct studies on the impact of various police interventions and methodologies for psychosocial care to women and children victims. The study is not limited to the number of women and children and their families reached out to by the police but is more concerned with the effect of such programs on the lives of the victims and families reached.

Conclusion

There is a need for more effective and innovative approaches to detection, intelligence, and rescue operations and for a stronger collaborative effort between nations as well as between governments and NGOs to address the rising global phenomenon of criminal exploitation of women and children.

In the area of law enforcement, there is a need for technological tools and improved mechanisms to keep abreast with the transnational dimension of the problem. Additional police personnel, equipment, and other capability structures to fight against trafficking, prostitution, and pornography, among others, must be at the top of all priorities to carry out the mandate of existing laws. There is also a need for greater public awareness, including the development of duty holders, to promote the protection of women and children from all forms of harm and danger. Finally, there must be heightened attention on judicial processes and greater windows of opportunity for support and assistance from the NGOs to deliver the ends of justice and help rebuild the lives of women and children survivors.

Notes

1. ECPAT, Philippines National Report, 1994.
2. Dela Cruz, "Trust and Power," 2001.
3. Ibid.
4. ECPAT, Philippines National Report, 1994.
5. Dela Cruz, "Trust and Power," 2001.
6. "Tourism and Child Prostitution in Cebu: An Exploratory and Descriptive Research," 1994.
7. "Children and Youth Foundation of the Philippines," 1995.
8. Patterned after the Philippine National Plan of Action on Commercial Sexual Exploitation of Children.

Criminal Exploitation of Women and Children in India: Its Control

14

YATEENDRA SINGH JAFA

Introduction

This chapter deals with the nature and extent of the criminal exploitation of women and children in India, the reasons for such exploitation, the strategies adopted to counter this menace, and suggestions for improving the strategies.

India professes respect for women and concern for children. Her constitution and laws guarantee gender equality and protection to woman and children against abuse. In reality, innumerable women and children are exploited. The latest published police statistics (for the year 2001), on the national level, show that every hour one woman is sexually harassed, four women are molested, six women suffer cruelty by husbands and/or their relatives, two are raped, and a woman is killed in a dowry death (National Crime Records Bureau 2003a). Although the country's population grew 9 percent during the period 1995–2001, crime against women, including dowry deaths, torture of wives, rape, and sexual harassment, rose 24.25 percent (National Crime Records Bureau 2003b). There is also a large volume of trafficking in women and girls.

The majority of the children are neglected and many of them victimized. There are about two million infant deaths each year, and 1 in 11 children dies before reaching the age of five years. Of 160 million children younger than six years of age, 60 million exist below the poverty line. Fifty percent of children between the ages of 6 and 15 are out of school because of poverty and lack of access to educational facilities. Sixty percent of the girls are not in school. Official reports place the number of child laborers in India at 20 million; nongovernment organizations estimate it to be 111 million (Global March against Child Labour 2000). There were 3,132 reported cases of rape of children in 2000 and 2,113 cases in 2001. The registered cases of kidnapping and abduction of children were 711 in 2000 and 2,845 in 2001 (National Crime Records Bureau 2003h).

The instances cited in this chapter are illustrative of various forms of exploitation of women and children in India and have been selected from numerous well-documented cases.

Major Forms of Exploitation

Domestic Violence: Dowry Demands, Torture, and Deaths

The custom of dowry reflects the exploitative subjugation of women. Because of the social stigma attached to single young women, anxious parents try to buy bridegrooms for their daughters. Combined with this is the greed of husbands who, sometimes with the aid of family members, often inflict physical and mental torture on the wives to extract dowry from the wives' parents. Sometimes wives are murdered or they attempt to or successfully commit suicide to escape the misery.

The government has amended the existing laws to curb this crime. The penalty for demanding dowry is punishable by imprisonment for up to two years, and taking dowry attracts a minimum imprisonment of five years. A proven charge of cruelty to a wife by her husband or his relations imposes imprisonment for up to three years. An inquiry by a magistrate and a post-mortem examination are mandatory if a woman commits suicide within seven years of her marriage. If cruelty on the part of the husband or his relations is established in the event of the wife's suicide within seven years of marriage, then the court may presume that the husband or his relations abetted the suicide. However, these measures have not deterred domestic violence. From 1996 to 2001, the reported cases of dowry deaths increased 47 percent, torture by husbands and their relatives increased 41 percent, and cases under the Dowry Prohibition Act increased 8.5 percent (National Crime Records Bureau 2003c).

Some of the recent cases indicate the magnitude of dowry-related cruelty. In a case decided by the Supreme Court in 2001, a woman harassed over dowry threw herself in front of an oncoming train. She was devastatingly maimed for life and became a paraplegic (Supreme Court 2001). A man in the State of Gujarat tormented his 23-year-old wife for six years for dowry, and, in August 2002, assisted by his mistress, he chopped off her hands (*Hindustan Times* 2002b). On October 13, 2003, the Delhi police recovered the half-burned dead body of a 21-year-old woman, who had been hurriedly cremated by her husband and in-laws. They were arrested on the charge of murder and dowry-related harassment (*Hindustan Times* 2003c). A surgeon's educated son and his relatives in the State of Uttar Pradesh harassed his young wife for dowry. On January 2, 2004, they attacked her and cut off one of her fingers and some flesh from her cheek. They also grievously injured her four-year-old daughter (*The Hindu* 2004b). While deciding a dowry case in 2002, the Indian Supreme Court noted, "Daily, the demon of dowry is devouring the lives of young girls, who marry with high hopes of having heavenly abode in their husband's house" (Supreme Court 2002).

Sexual Exploitation: Rape and Molestation

The incidence of rape has risen almost seven-fold in the past four decades: from 2,487 in 1971 to 16,075 in 2001 (National Crime Records Bureau 2003b). In the year 2001, girls under 14 years of age constituted 12 percent and teen-age girls (14–18 years) 24 percent of the total number of victims: nearly 50 percent of the victims were in the age group of 18–30 years (National Crime Records Bureau 2003g). Incest rape increased 21 percent in 2001 over the previous year (National Crime Records Bureau 2003f). There were 28,939 registered cases of sexual molestation in 1996 and 34,124 in 2001, an increase of 21 percent (National Crime Records Bureau 2003c).

Educated and affluent men and so-called disciplined policemen and soldiers are increasingly being identified as rapists and pedophiles. A deputy inspector general of police in the State of Rajasthan has not been seen since 1997. It was alleged that he raped his security aide's wife (*The Times of India* 2002). In October 2002, an airport assistant manager was arrested in Delhi on the charge of raping a girl (*The Times of India* 2002c). The police filed a charge in court in September 2003 against an additional commissioner of the Delhi police on the charge of raping his maidservant in August 2002 (*Hindustan Times* 2003a). On September 23, 2003, a 54-year-old doctor was arrested by the police for the offense of raping a 13-year-old girl suffering from tuberculosis in his hospital in Delhi (*Hindustan Times* 2003b). On October 6, 2003, four army soldiers of the president of India's bodyguards gang-raped a 17-year-old girl in a public park in Delhi (*Hindustan Times* 2003d). On October 14, 2003, a 35-year-old Swiss embassy employee was abducted and raped in her car by two educated and well-dressed men in the highly protected car park of the best known auditorium in Delhi (*The Hindu* 2003b). Custodial rapes have also been reported. An employee of a government remand home raped a physically disabled girl at the remand home on September 21, 1997 (National Human Rights Commission 2001g). A 10-year-old girl was raped on July 10, 1998, in a government juvenile observation home in the State of Andhra Pradesh (National Human Rights Commission 2001h).

Pornography and Indecency against Women

In India, "Eve teasing" (sexual harassment or molestation of women by men) is common on public transport and around girls' schools and colleges, especially in Northern India. There were 4,689 registered cases of sexual harassment in 1996 and 9,746 cases in 2001, an increase of 100 percent (National Crime Records Bureau 2003c). There are also lewd representations of the female body in magazines and posters, and obscenity and suggestive vulgar sex on TV and in the cinema. Across the country, 662 cases were registered in

2000 and 1,052 cases in 2001 under the Indecent Representation of Women (Prohibition) Act, an increase of 49 percent (National Crime Records Bureau 2003d).

Female Feticide and Infanticide

Men in India generally prefer sons to daughters because they think that a son will perpetuate their family name. The vast majority of people, being poor and lacking social security, expect a son to look after them in their old age. Thus, in disregard of women's health, men use them as machines for producing children till a boy is born. Furthermore, many indigent parents prefer aborting a female fetus or killing a female infant for fear that they would be unable to afford a dowry for her or that she might fall into the clutches of traffickers. Medical professionals and quacks exploit the preference for sons to make money by aborting female fetuses; for these reasons, there is a sharp decline in the nationwide ratio of females to males in the age group of birth to six years (from 945 in 1991 to 927 in 2001, compared with the world average of 1,045 women to 1,000 men). On October 20, 2003, the registrar-general of India stated that the deficit in women was "spreading like cancer. A stage may soon come when it would be extremely difficult to make up for the missing girls" (*The Hindu* 2003c).

The federal government promulgated the Prenatal Diagnostic Techniques (Regulation and Prevention of Misuse) Act in 1994 to prevent the misuse of such techniques for illegal feticide. However, its implementation has been poor. In the public interest, in a litigation case decided in 2001, the Supreme Court directed federal and state governments to enforce the law stringently and laid down a mechanism for monitoring the activities of unscrupulous sex-diagnostic clinics. Reiterating these directives two years later, it observed that there was no change in the mind-set of the people, and discrimination against the girl child still prevails (Supreme Court 2003).

Trafficking in Women and Children

India is a major receiving country of trafficked women and children from Nepal, Sri Lanka, and Bangladesh. There are between 70,000 and 100,000 Nepalese prostitutes in India. Thirty percent of them are younger than 18, and a considerable number of Bangladeshi girls come to India to be domestic workers or prostitutes. Five thousand to 7,000 Nepali girls are trafficked every year to India (United Nations International Children's Emergency Fund 2002). Indian women and children are reported to be trafficked to the Middle East and the West for purposes of forced labor and sexual exploitation (U.S. State Department 2002). There is also a large amount of trafficking in women and children within the country attributable to poverty and the low social status of girls. Trafficked persons are pushed into domestic service, industrial or agricultural work, and the sex industry. "The practice of child prostitution has increasingly become associated with the involvement of organized crime" (National Human Rights Commission 1997c).

Despite the efforts of the National Human Rights Commission, the Department of Women and Child Development of the federal government, the National Commission for Women, and the United Nations International Children's Emergency Fund, it was reported in 1999 that the evil of child prostitution was "a vast and growing human rights problem" (National Human Rights Commission 1994c). Adolescent girls are the primary victims of trafficking. A study of the Central Social Welfare Board found that 40 percent of the sex workers in six major cities in India were girls forced into prostitution (National Human Rights Commission 2000a). According to a recent study, trafficking in minor girls from and within India has increased about 40 percent in the past decade, and many child prostitutes catch sexually transmitted diseases. It cited the report of two nongovernment groups working in this field that 40 percent of the 300 minors rescued in West Bengal in the past two years were HIV positive (*India Today* 2003).

Denigration of *Dalit* and *Adivasi* Women

Certain Hindu castes, now called *dalits*, that were socially, educationally, and economically backward were "untouchables," i.e., polluting. They were shunned by people of higher castes and considered fit only for menial jobs such as scavengers and shoe cobblers. *Adivasis* (tribal people) were also outside the caste system and therefore untouchables. Despite the statutory abolition of "untouchability," members of the erstwhile higher castes still abuse *dalits* and *adivasis*. Sometimes, greed for land triggers atrocities. *Dalit* and *adivasi* women become particular targets because to humiliate the women of a particular community is to humiliate the entire community.

Many police officers and other government officials harbor caste and gender prejudice. They ignore atrocities committed on *dalits* and *adivasis* and sometimes themselves victimize them. Criminal cases were registered in 1996 against a forest officer and four forest guards for taking four *dalit* women in custody, disrobing them, and beating them. The women were let off only after they agreed to pay 1,000 rupees (equivalent to $50) and surrender honey collected from the forest to forest officials (National Human Rights Commission 2001e). A *dalit* woman committed suicide in 1996 in the State of Kanataka following her rape by eight persons, including four police officers, and a 15-year-old *dalit* girl in the State of Uttar Pradesh committed suicide in 1998 after two firemen and a police constable raped her (National Human Rights Commission 2000d). While making an arrest in a *dalit* village in the State of Tamil Nadu in November 1998, police officials assaulted two women, who received serious injuries, and wrongfully detained 34 women, three of them with infants, for 18 days. It was viewed as "lawlessness on the part of the police" (National Human Rights Commission, 2001d). In June 1999, police officials in Gurgaon in the State of Harana stripped naked seven *dalit* boys between 7 and 12 years of age. The boys were paraded and beaten in the streets because their cricket ball had landed on the premises of a police officer (National Human Rights Commission 2001f).

Sati and Witch Hunting

Sati is an old Hindu custom, in which a widow immolates herself on her dead husband's funeral pyre as a manifestation of her conjugal love and fidelity. The British authorities abolished it in 1829. However, the practice has continued with social sanction. Sometimes an exploitative intent is detected in it. On August 6, 2002, a 65-year-old woman committed *sati* in a village in the State of Madhya Pradesh. The police arrested 15 persons, including the woman's two grown sons who were believed to be after their mother's property. A 50-year-old woman and her young daughter-in-law were gang-raped, paraded naked, and forced to swallow human excreta in the State of Jharkhand in July 2002 on the charge of practicing black magic. The police stated that the real provocation was that these women were thought to be obstructing the acquisition of land by some influential persons (*Hindustan Times* 2002a). Women's rights groups say that greedy priests, village chiefs, or relatives label women as witches to seize property. The All India Democratic Women's Association, a major women's group, issued a statement that, in both these cases, the "not so-hidden agenda is the control over the land that the attacked women may have a right to" (*The Hindu* 2002). The practice of witch hunting, however, largely exists in tribal areas because of superstition. Unofficial estimates are that at least 200 women are killed as witches across India each year.

Devdasi System

The *devdasi* system prevails in certain parts of the country (National Human Rights Commission 2000b). *Devdasis* (servants of God) are dancing girls attached to temples but generally seen as harlots. Their duties consist of dancing before the idols of gods. To ensure safe delivery, expectant mothers often vow to dedicate their children, if they would be girls, to the service of God. Some temples in south India are reported to be serving as brothels kept by priests (Shah 2000). The *devdasi* practice also exists in Belgaum, State of Karnataka, and the National Human Rights Commission is trying to eradicate it with the help of district officials (National Human Rights Commission 1999c).

Medical Experiments on Women

It was reported that the antibiotic erythromycin was illegally administered to 790 women in the State of West Bengal during the period from August 1999 to October 2002 to test its efficacy as a contraceptive. The drug was banned in India in 1998 after a Supreme Court ruling. The trial doses failed, and many subject women became pregnant. Medical experts have described this experiment as illegal, unethical, and a human rights abuse (*Hindustan Times* 2004b).

Condition of Muslim Women

Marriage under Islam is a simple contract made on a formal proposal of marriage from one side and its formal acceptance by the other, but a man can divorce his wife simply by uttering the word *talaq* (divorce). This leads to problems of survival for the woman, as highlighted in the well-known case of Shah Bano. When her lawyer husband refused to maintain her after the divorce, she filed a case in the State of Madhya Pradesh and won it in 1985 after seven years' litigation. However, the majority of divorced women cannot afford such a legal struggle. They have to battle through the courts of a judicial magistrate, sessions court, high court, and perhaps the Supreme Court, as was done by Shah Bano. Even if they finally win the case, they must get a decree from the magistrate's court for implementation of the court decision. A notice is issued to the husband. If he still refuses to pay, his immovable and moveable property is seized. If he has no such property, he can be arrested. If he persists in not paying after the arrest, he goes to jail for a period not exceeding one month for every breach of the monthly payment. If the husband chooses to go to jail, the wife ends up getting nothing.

Rich and aging Muslim males are reported to be marrying young girls from poor families for pleasure with the help of venal *kazis* (priests) and divorcing them after a short time. Such short-term marriages are said to be common in the old part of the city of Hydrabad, State of Andhra Pradesh. A decade ago, the marriage of minor girls from penurious Muslim families to oil-rich elderly Arabs had also come to be noticed in Hydrabad. The police and Muslim religious institutions took notice of this practice only after public outcry (*The Hindu* 2004c).

Child Labor

The Supreme Court observed in a judgment in 1997 that child labor was a major problem and had remained intractable. "As estimated by the Planning Commission on 1st March, 1983, there would be 15.70 million child laborers (14.03 rural and 1.7 urban) in the age group of 10–14 years and 17.36 million in the age group of 15–18 years. None of the official estimates included child workers in the unorganized sector, and therefore are obviously gross underestimates. Estimates from various non-governmental sources as to the actual number of working children range from 44 million to 100 million" (Supreme Court 1997). The National Human Rights Commission stated the following: "Despite the announcement of a National Child Labor Policy in 1987, the subsequent constitution of a National Authority for the Elimination of Child Labor (NAECL) and the undertaking of National Child Labor Projects (NCLP) in an increasing number of areas of our country, the goal of ending child labor remains elusive, even in respect of the estimated 2 million children working in hazardous industries who were to be freed from such tyranny by the year 2000" (National Human Rights Commission 1997a).

Poor families are forced to allow their children of a tender ages to work as domestic servants at exploitative wages. A survey in India noted that 17 percent of domestic workers under 15 years of age and 90 percent of the employing households preferred girls among them as servants (United Nations International Children's Emergency Fund 1997). Profiteers have organized this trade to meet the increasing demand of cheap labor in middle-class homes in metropolitan towns. On January 18, 2004, the Delhi police arrested three persons for the offense of illegal trafficking in minor children and rescued two girls. This was a racket by some people who gathered minor children from their parents in the State of West Bengal on the promise of getting them employment and forced them into various jobs in Delhi (*The Hindu* 2004d). Government officials are prohibited from employing minor children as domestic servants. However, many of them flout this ban. For instance, on January 11, 2004, a physically handicapped 11-year-old boy was rescued from the house of an official of a government-owned oil company. He was tortured by the official's family and forced to work as a domestic servant (*Hindustan Times* 2004a).

Bonded Labor

The Bonded Labor System (Abolition) Act of 1976 prohibits any form of forced labor, but the practice still flourishes. Bonded laborers are paid nominal wages and cannot discontinue work. They live in miserable conditions and are subject to restrictions, assault, and sexual exploitation. A bonded child is generally paid wages in consideration of a loan advanced to his parents. The bondage continues, because poor parents can rarely liquidate the loan. In November 1997, the Supreme Court directed the National Human Rights Commission to supervise work relating to the abolition of bonded labor (Supreme Court 1997). Accordingly, an action group headed by the chairman of the commission created a mechanism for identifying the districts where the problem was acute and for taking corrective steps. The commission found, after two years' work, that the implementation of the act had been inadequate. It recorded that the vigilance committees, established for identifying bonded labor, were nonfunctional in most states and no serious effort was made to identify bonded labor, although the existence of such labor, in as many as 100 districts across the country and in certain industries, was well documented (National Human Rights Commission 1999d). Reports indicate that there is only occasional identification and release of bonded laborers. The record of the National Human Rights Commission shows that bonded laborers who were rescued by its initiative in one year (1999–2000) included only 65 people in Jallandhar (State of Punjab), one family in Ratnagiri (State of Maharashtra), 29 people including women and children, in Gurgaon (State of Haryana), and 21 people including 13 children, in Sonebhadra and Allahabad (State of Uttar Pradesh) (National Human Rights Commission 2001i).

Child Sacrifice

Occasionally, children become sacrificial victims of superstition. In April 2003, a villager beheaded his own 10-year-old son in the State of Madhya Pradesh to please the goddess Kali. A childless couple sacrificed a six-year-old child in a village in the State of Uttar Pradesh to fulfill their desire to have a son (*Hindustan Times* 2003e). The hacked body of an 11-year-old child was recovered in November 2003 near a Kali temple in Muzaffarnagar in the State of Uttar Pradesh; a woman who wanted a son was suspected of having sacrificed the child (*Hindustan Times* 2003h). An emotionally disturbed woman in a village outside Delhi enticed a two-year-old child and bludgeoned him to death in December 2003 on the advice of a witch doctor to cure her husband's alcoholism (*Hindustan Times* 2003i).

Abuse of Women and Children by Police and Civil Servants

Police officials and civil servants frequently abuse their official authority in order to harass and exploit women and children. Deciding a case in 1995, the Supreme Court ordered the prosecution of police officials who subjected a married woman to physical and psychological torture calculated to scare her into abandoning her legal marriage (Supreme Court 1995). On July 2, 1998, two drunken police officials ordered a boy working at a roadside food kiosk to bring his mother. When the boy refused, they stripped him and branded him with a hot iron (National Human Rights Commission 1999f). In 1997, a woman visited a police station to inquire after her husband who was detained under suspicion of theft. She was asked to bring 2,500 rupees ($50) as the cost of the stolen goods. Later two policemen visited her at night and summoned her to the police station. They misbehaved with her, snatched 500 rupees ($10) from her, and beat up her 10-year-old son. Fourteen injuries were found on the boy's person (National Human Rights Commission 1999e). Illegal trade of indigent people, including women brought from the State of Bihar as laborers to the State of Punjab, was discovered in 1998 to be flourishing with the knowledge and patronage of the police and other authorities for the past 30 years (National Human Rights Commission 2001j). The police in the State of Bihar falsely implicated a woman in the murder of her sister-in-law. She remained in jail for 10 years until the court acquitted her in an impoverished and paralytic condition (National Human Rights Commission 2000e). The civil and police authorities in the State of West Bengal detained a three-year-old girl in police custody and childcare homes for about 10 years, merely because she was a witness in a murder case (National Human Rights Commission 2000f). A female witness in a criminal case was illegally detained in a police lockup at night in April 2001 in the State of Rajasthan. The State Human Rights Commission held the concerned police officials responsible for her physical and mental torture (*The Hindu* 2003a).

Raw Justice

Sometimes elected village bodies administer primitive justice against women. Five tribal women were beaten to death on July 29, 2002, by a village mob at a tea garden in West Bengal. The villagers suspected them of practicing witchcraft after a local man died of an unknown disease, and the village jury ordered the women to be killed (*The Times of India* 2002a). In July 2002, a village *panchayat* (elective body) in the State of Madhya Pradesh ordered the gang rape of a woman on a false charge of immorality. Her husband saved her in time. In October 2003, the High Court held that the fundamental right of this woman to live with dignity had been violated and ordered the state government to pay her 200,000 rupees ($4,000) as compensation (*Hindustan Times* 2003f).

Strategies Adopted to Counter Exploitation

The remedial strategies and mechanisms that exist for curbing the exploitation of women and children include constitutional and legal safeguards, statutory commissions for investigating and redressing the grievances of victims, executive action through law enforcement, rescue and rehabilitation, judicial redress, and public awareness programs. Nongovernment organizations are major players in fostering public awareness and rescue and rehabilitation efforts.

Statutes

The Constitution of India enjoins the social equality of people of all sexes, religions, castes, and communities and prohibits discrimination and exploitation in any form. There are laws to enforce these principles and impose punishment for their violations. Special laws have been enacted for the protection of women against rape, cruelty by husbands and their relatives, dowry demands, *sati*, immoral trafficking, forced prostitution, pornography, child and bonded labor, and atrocities on *dalits* and *adivasis*. Special provisions have also been incorporated into existing laws for similar purposes.

Permanent Statutory Commissions and Autonomous Bodies

The federal government has set up several commissions for the protection of the vulnerable sections of society. The National Commission for Women investigates violations of women's legal rights and makes suitable recommendations to the government for legal reforms. It has the powers of a civil court to summon and examine persons while investigating such matters. It promotes awareness of women's rights among the people through seminars and the dissemination of relevant literature. Twenty-one states have established State Commissions for Women for promoting women's cases. The National Commissions for Minorities, Scheduled Castes, Scheduled Tribes, and Backward Classes investigate injustice against minorities, *dalits*, and *adivasis*. The National Human Rights Commission has a wide mandate to safeguard the human rights of the people. Any aggrieved person may send his or her complaint to the commission free of costs.

Other Government Organizations

The federal government's Department of Women and Child Development, the Central Social Welfare Board, and the National Institute of Public Cooperation and Child Development work for the empowerment of women and the enhancement of women's and children's welfare through training and awareness-promotion programs. The Ministries of Social Welfare and Child Welfare run their own schemes for the welfare of women and children and assist the programs of nongovernment groups for the rehabilitation of victims. The Ministry of Labor runs the National Child Labor Projects in 100 districts across the country in 13 states for the rescue and rehabilitation of child laborers engaged in hazardous industries, and 50 more such projects will soon be started (*The Hindu* 2004a). The federal government and the International Labor Organization jointly fund such projects. Children get 100 rupees ($2) each month as an incentive for attending schools in addition to regular health examinations and midday meals.

District Administration

The district administration is directly responsible for identifying child and bonded labor, giving employment to families of victims of exploitation, establishing the National Child Labor Projects, arranging schooling for rescued children, and rehabilitating of victimized women and girls. As head of the district administration, the collector has the duty to implement the government's welfare programs for tackling all forms of exploitation at the grassroots level.

Police

The laws of the land have assigned the most crucial role to the police for curbing exploitation. Most forms of exploitation of women and children are cognizable offenses, in which the police can register criminal cases, arrest offenders, and charge sheet the cases in the courts. In some states, the police do proactive work for crime prevention against women and children. For example, the Juvenile Aid Protection Unit of the Mumbai Police identifies runaway girls and children and restores them to their parents before criminals can trap them. It deploys its personnel at the railway stations and bus terminals for this purpose. Many states have women cells and protection of civil rights units at the state police headquarters for handling cases of cruelty against women, particularly domestic violence against married women. Women cells attempt marital reconciliation and also get cases registered with the police in the event of actual crime.

Judiciary

The judiciary is the last resort of the victims. The trial courts at the district level decide all cases of crimes against women and children. Because the appellate courts mostly use the evidence marshaled in the trial courts for deciding appeals, any weakness in the prosecution at the trial stage can ruin a criminal case. The trial courts thus have a pivotal role in punishing crimes against women and children. The High Courts at the state level and the Supreme Court as the final appellate court decide appeals in such cases. They also have original jurisdiction for hearing public interest litigation on issues of public importance. Most cases of rape and murder of women including dowry deaths eventually reach the Supreme Court.

Civil Society

This segment of the people in India is active in detecting crime against women and children. The media highlight atrocities against women and children.

Nongovernment organizations promote public awareness about such atrocities, take up individual cases of victimization and seek redress through the police and other official agencies for registration of criminal cases and rescue of victims, and launch public interest litigation cases. They have been advocating changes in the laws relating to dowry and domestic violence. They also provide support to victimized women and children.

Success of These Remedial Measures

Executive, judicial, and other remedial actions are slow and inadequate. Therefore, they have only partially succeeded, and the work done so far can at best be called a good and promising beginning.

The Supreme Court has strengthened the legal foundations of reformatory work in India. It has boldly interpreted laws, enjoined duties on the government administrative bodies and the police, and administered exemplary punishment to criminals and erring civil servants. The National Human Rights Commission actively monitors and rectifies human rights abuses and prods the government and apathetic police and district administration into taking appropriate action in cases of exploitation. It investigates atrocities committed against women and children, rescues victims, seeks redress from the executive authorities by way of compensation, gets criminal cases registered against those charged with crimes, and promotes public awareness about human rights. Largely because of its efforts, the subject of human rights is now in the curriculum of schools and universities. It is actively engaged in sensitizing the police and other civil servants to women's and children's issues.

The commission promotes reform through action based on the Supreme Court rulings. For instance, the Supreme Court has identified certain hazardous industries, ordered a survey of child labor in such industries, and directed the offending employers to pay 20,000 rupees ($400) for every employed child into the Child Labor Rehabilitation-cum-Welfare Fund (Supreme Court 1997). Accordingly, the National Human Rights Commission launched a project in 1999 for locating and inspecting all the looms in the carpet-making belt of the state, identifying child and bonded laborers employed there, and rehabilitating children in special schooling facilities. It is doing similar work in other hazardous industries such as the glass industry in the State of Uttar Pradesh and the firecracker industry in the State of Tamil Nadu. By March 2001, the number of National Child Labor Project schools had grown to 346 in 11 child-labor-prone districts of Uttar Pradesh, and 19,807 children had been rehabilitated (National Human Rights Commission 2001c). However, this is extremely inadequate relief, considering that about 300,000 children are estimated to be working in the carpet industry (U.S. Department of Labor 1997). The National Child Labor

Projects have introduced 200,000 children to the formal educational system in 100 districts in the country. This hardly touches the fringes of the enormous problem of 20 million child laborers reported to be employed across the country.

Performance of the Criminal Justice System

The executive authority, including the police and the judiciary at the district level, are primarily responsible for implementing the laws and supporting the victims of exploitation. However, many criminal cases are not registered. Investigation and prosecution are weak, and court delays are enormous. Because the legal system is very slow and the conviction rate is low, many victims subsequently withdraw their statements, leading to the acquittal of the accused.

There are various reasons for the low registration of crime. Because the yearly crime statistics are the sole official measure of police performance in India, sometimes the police do not register crimes. Victims distrust the police because the police are indifferent to their grievances. Police investigations are vexations and mostly done by unskilled personnel, and the National Human Rights Commission held as false the report of the district police chief who absolved the culprits of guilt in the case of the forcible detention and sexual exploitation of a 24-year-old woman in the State of Rajasthan. The woman, who was undernourished, ailing, and traumatized, was rescued in April 1998, and a criminal case was registered against six persons (National Human Rights Commission 1999g). A human rights group undertook a study in the 1990s and found that none of the 22 officials of the Delhi police accused of rape had been convicted at the time of the study. The policemen were dismissed from service after departmental inquiries in seven of these cases, which occurred between 1989 and 1993. However, all of them were reinstated following judicial acquittals in criminal cases registered against them because the victims denied in the courts that they had been raped (People's Union for Democratic Rights 1994). A national daily recently published an eyewitness account by an officer of the Indian Forest Service who, on November 12, 2003, saw a mob beating up girls on a railway platform, stripping some of them, and raping one girl. "About six cops walked towards the train. They didn't act and the rape happened in their presence" (*Hindustan Times* 2003g). A survey conducted among students by Saheli, a Delhi-based women's group, found that 95 of 100 women said that they would not report an incident of sexual violence to the police as a result of a lack of trust, fear of additional complications, and negative publicity.

The rate and quality of disposal of cases by the police and the courts determine the level of satisfaction that the criminal justice system gives to the victims. The data given in Table 14.1 are relevant in this regard.

Table 14.1 Registered Crimes against Women in 2001

	Rape	Kidnapping and Abduction of Women/Girls	Dowry Deaths	Cruelty by Husbands and Relatives	DPA[a]	IRWA[b]
Disposal by police	93.1%	73.9%	92.7%	91.6%	89.7%	99.5%
Disposal by courts	17.4%	14.1%	18.2%	13.3%	17.1%	56.8%
Rate of acquittals	12.9%	10.1%	12.3%	10.4%	12.0%	2.5%
Rate of convictions	26.1%	4.0%	5.9%		3.0%	5.1%
Cases pending trial in courts	55,572 (82.4%)	42,748 (85.2%)	22,697 (81.2%)	145,920 (84.3%)	8,654 (80.9%)	703 (43.0%)

Source: NCRB. Crime in India 2001.

[a] Cases of Dowry Prohibition Act.

[b] Case of Indecent Representation of Women (Prohibition) Act.

Representation of Women Act

The low rate of convictions is attributable to defective police investigation, poor quality of prosecution, witnesses turning hostile, and victims themselves not wanting to pursue the cases. "Efficiency in police investigation is fundamental to criminal justice. A basic factor today is that there is a loss of public confidence in police investigations and the criminal justice delivery system" (National Human Rights Commission 1999a). The judiciary often passes strictures on faulty investigations. There is, however, little improvement in the investigative techniques of police, which rely more on oral evidence than forensic evidence. It is significant that even the conviction rate for rapes in police or judicial custody was zero in 2000 and 2001. Victims perceive the judiciary as unhelpful, too. The majority of cases of rape, dowry deaths, and cruelty against women get acquitted as a result of the stringent requirements of credible evidence. There are also enormous delays in the disposal of cases by the courts.

Certain sensational cases indicate police misconduct, their apathy toward crime against women, and the weakness of the justice delivery system. Mathura, a 16-year-old tribal girl, was allegedly raped by two policemen in a police post in the State of Maharashtra. On June 1, 1974, the district session judge acquitted the accused on the grounds that the girl was a "shocking liar" and habituated to sexual intercourse, and only intercourse was proved but not the rape. The High Court sentenced the accused to imprisonment, but the Supreme Court overturned the High Court's judgment and set the accused free on the grounds that there was no resistance from the victim and the alleged intercourse was a peaceful affair. In June 1980, six policemen molested a village girl, Maya Tyagi, and stripped her naked in the State of Uttar Pradesh. When her husband resisted, they shot him and his friend and falsely branded them as robbers. It took the judiciary eight years to decide this case. Bhanwari Devi, a 41-year-old woman working in the government's Women's Development Program in the State of Rajasthan, was allegedly gang raped in 1992 in her husband's presence by five men of the powerful Gujjar community for preventing a child marriage in defiance of an old custom. The police delayed the registration and filing of the case in court. The trial court acquitted the accused in 1995. It held that rape was a teenager's preserve and the middle-aged individuals accused were respectable persons, that the accused belonged to upper castes and could not have committed a crime against a *dalit*, and that the husband's testimony was unreliable because he had not fought off the rapists, which he was expected to do (*Indian Express* 1995). More than 12 years have passed, and Bhanwari Devi's appeal is still pending in the High Court. In view of these well-publicized facts, victims and their families regard the police as unreliable and any litigation as futile.

Additional Measures Required

The foremost requirements are to ensure greater accountability of the police, better policing of crimes against women and children, effective implementation of the welfare and rehabilitation schemes by the district administration, helpful trial courts, and speedy trials. It is also necessary to strengthen legal procedures and empower women.

Police Accountability and Attitudinal Change

The police, being directly responsible for crime control, are the strongest instrument for curbing criminal exploitation. The National Human Rights Commission says that far-reaching reforms in the police are required for improving the human rights situation in the country. "Regrettably, a situation has developed in which those who should be the protectors of such rights are, too often, the predators. The vast number of complaints received by the Commission each year alleging the violation of human rights by police personnel provides melancholy testimony to this" (National Human Rights Commission 2001). The commission has made specific recommendations that it considers essential for improving the quality of policing for protecting human rights (National Human Rights Commission 2001a). It issued guidelines in November 1999 to the state chief secretaries and directors general of police to sensitize the police officials during training and to discipline errant officials to minimize the abuse of the powers of arrest. It wrote to the state high courts and state governments to create a district complaint authority in each district to examine the grievances of the public. It also recommended the creation of a police complaints authority in the office of the state director general of police so as to have general oversight of the conduct of the police in each state. Because there is no implementation of these recommendations, police accountability remains elusive in India.

Reform in the Criminal Justice System

The National Human Rights Commission attributes the unsatisfactory state of the criminal justice system in the country to "docket-clogging; inefficient, unscientific police investigations; weak prosecution depending largely on oral evidence; and inept discharge of prosecutorial functions by unskilled prosecutors" (National Human Rights Commission 1999a). In 1999, the Law Commission of India advocated the establishment of special courts to try cases of rape and sexual abuse. Section 30 of the Protection of Human Rights Act (1993) provides for the establishment of human rights courts for effective trials of human rights violations. So far, such courts have not been constituted. Special courts for crime against women and human rights courts would provide judicial forums for victims and for securing speedy justice.

New Legal Provisions

Certain legal reforms can create a legal system that is sensitive to victims and tough on criminals. The federal government has approved the deletion of a humiliating provision in the Evidence Act that subjects a rape victim to questioning about her sexual past. In 2002, a task force set up by the government recommended changes to the Indian Penal Code aimed at broadening the definition of rape to all forms of sexual abuse. The act ought to be amended so as to deal effectively with the traffickers. After studying the state of child labor in the glass industry in Ferozabad, State of Uttar Pradesh, the National Human Rights Commission assessed that free and compulsory education was the only way to wean children away from work. It therefore advocates that the right to education be enforced as a fundamental right (National Human Rights Commission 1997b).

Economic and Political Empowerment of Women

Women can rarely support themselves economically if they try to get out of a bad marriage. Therefore, women's groups advocate a statutory provision of an equal share for women in inherited property. Moreover, Sec. 125 of the Criminal Procedure Code gives discretion to a judicial magistrate to fix the amount of maintenance for a divorced woman. However, because it is to be paid by the woman's former spouse, it may still leave her dependent on his whims. As the National Human Rights Commission has recommended, it should be fixed at 5,000 rupees ($100) per month (National Human Rights Commission 2001b). Lastly, there is a need to pass the long-pending Women's Reservation Bill, which seeks 33 percent reservation of seats for women in the parliament. Such an act will create gender balance in politics by placing an adequate number of women in positions of power and decision-making.

Conclusion

The Supreme Court and the National Human Rights Commission can only macro-manage reform. A responsive administration, police, a supportive justice delivery system, and prompt and adequate action against incompetent and guilty government officials are the basic prerequisites for minimizing criminal exploitation. Equally important is the need to foster the ongoing program of increasing public awareness of the issues concerning women and children and sensitizing officials at the cutting edge. At the initiative of the National Human Rights Commission, the Copenhagen-based International Rehabilitation Council for Torture Victims, the Indian Medical Association, and the Indian Law Institute organized the Seminar on Torture on September 22–25, 1999. They recommended India's early ratification of the United Nations Convention on Torture; revisions of national laws for effectively dealing with criminals and providing reparation for victims; intensified efforts by the government, national institutions, and civil society to promote a culture of nonviolence; respect for human rights; and sensitization of the political leadership to human rights issues (National Human Rights Commission 2000c). These recommendations indicate that the remedies and schemes for reforms will succeed only in a favorable environment to be created by the political leadership, executive authorities, police, and the civil society.

References

Global March against Child Labour. 2000. "Worst Forms of Child Labour Data: India." http://www.globalmarch.org/worstformsreport/world/india.html.

The Hindu. 2002. "AIDWA Protests against Violence." August 9.

The Hindu. 2003a. "Cops Indicted for Detaining Woman." April 8.

The Hindu. 2003b. "Swiss Woman Raped in Delhi." October 16.

The Hindu. 2003c. "When Girls Go Missing in Society." October 21.

The Hindu. 2004a. "50 More Districts under Child Labor Elimination Project." January 4.

The Hindu. 2004b. "Finger, Flesh Bitten Off for Dowry." January 10.

The Hindu. 2004c. "New Garb to Exploitation of Child Brides." January 18.

The Hindu. 2004d. "Human Traffickers Arrested." January 19.

Hindustan Times. 2002a. "Villagers Strip, Rape Women in Hazaribagh." July 7.

Hindustan Times. 2002b. "Man Chops Wife's Hands for Dowry." August 17.

Hindustan Times. 2003a. "Ex-DIG of Delhi Charged with Rape." September 18.
Hindustan Times. 2003b. "Doc Rapes Teenage Patient." September 25.
Hindustan Times. 2003c. "Police Recover Body from Pyre after Dowry Complaint." October 14.
Hindustan Times. 2003d. "One More Rape: Where Is the City Headed?" October 16.
Hindustan Times. 2003e. "Childless Couple Sacrifices Six-Year Old in UP Village." October 31.
Hindustan Times. 2003f. "Panchaya's Gang Rape Order: Teacher to Get Compensation." October 31.
Hindustan Times. 2003g. "Cops Watched as Mob Raped Girl, Looted Train." November 20.
Hindustan Times. 2003h. "One More Child Sacrificed in W. UP, Woman on the Run." November 23.
Hindustan Times. 2003i. "Woman Sacrificed Child to Cure Husband of Vice." December 12.
Hindustan Times. 2004a. "Tortured Domestic Help Rescued." January 13.
Hindustan Times. 2004b. "Illegal Tests Done on 790 Indian Women." January 18.
Indian Express. 1995. "Crime and Acquittal." November 28.
India Today. 2003. "Girls for Sale." Living Media India Ltd., K-9. New Delhi: Connaught Circus, pp. 16–19.
National Crime Records Bureau. 2003a. Ministry of Home Affairs. Government of India. *Crime in India 2001*, p. 5.
National Crime Records Bureau. 2003b. Ministry of Home Affairs. Government of India. *Crime in India 2001*, p. 15.
National Crime Records Bureau. 2003c. Ministry of Home Affairs. Government of India. *Crime in India 2001*, p. 16.
National Crime Records Bureau. 2003d. Ministry of Home Affairs. Government of India. *Crime in India 2001*, p. 34.
National Crime Records Bureau. 2003e. Ministry of Home Affairs. Government of India. *Crime in India 2001*, p. 256.
National Crime Records Bureau. 2003f. Ministry of Home Affairs. Government of India. *Crime in India 2001*, p. 258.
National Crime Records Bureau. 2003g. Ministry of Home Affairs. Government of India. *Crime in India 2001*, p. 259.
National Crime Records Bureau. 2003h. Ministry of Home Affairs. Government of India. *Crime in India 2001*, p. 283.
National Human Rights Commission. 1997a. *Annual Report 1996–1997*, p. 37.
National Human Rights Commission. 1997b. *Annual Report 1996–1997*, p. 40.
National Human Rights Commission. 1997c. *Annual Report 1996–1997*, p. 41.
National Human Rights Commission. 1998. *Annual Report 1997–1998*, pp. 46–47.
National Human Rights Commission. 1999a. *Annual Report 1998–1999*, pp. 20–21.
National Human Rights Commission. 1999b. *Annual Report 1998–1999*, p. 35.
National Human Rights Commission. 1999c. *Annual Report 1998–1999*, p. 36.
National Human Rights Commission. 1999d. *Annual Report 1998–1999*, p. 38.
National Human Rights Commission. 1999e. *Annual Report 1998–1999*, p. 73.
National Human Rights Commission. 1999f. *Annual Report 1998–1999*, p. 82.
National Human Rights Commission. 1999g. *Annual Report 1998–1999*, p. 83.
National Human Rights Commission. 2000a. *Annual Report 1999–2000*, p. 7.

National Human Rights Commission. 2000b. *Annual Report 1999–2000*, p. 9.
National Human Rights Commission. 2000c. *Annual Report 1999–2000*, pp. 71–72.
National Human Rights Commission. 2000d. *Annual Report 1999–2000*, pp. 127–130.
National Human Rights Commission. 2000e. *Annual Report 1999–2000*, p. 131.
National Human Rights Commission. 2000f. *Annual Report 1999–2000*, p. 132.
National Human Rights Commission. 2001a. *Annual Report 2000–2001*, p. 24.
National Human Rights Commission. 2001b. *Annual Report 2000–2001*, p. 65.
National Human Rights Commission. 2001c. *Annual Report 2000–2001*, p. 69.
National Human Rights Commission. 2001d. *Annual Report 2000–2001*, pp. 130–133.
National Human Rights Commission. 2001e. *Annual Report 2000–2001*, pp. 135–136.
National Human Rights Commission. 2001f. *Annual Report 2000–2001*, pp. 136–137.
National Human Rights Commission. 2001g. *Annual Report 2000–2001*, p. 146.
National Human Rights Commission. 2001h. *Annual Report 2000–2001*, p. 147.
National Human Rights Commission. 2001i. *Annual Report 2000–2001*, pp. 152–159.
National Human Rights Commission. 2001j. *Annual Report 2000–2001*, p. 160.
People's Union for Democratic Rights. 1994. "Custodial Rape: A Report on the Aftermath." In *Crime against Women: Bondage and Beyond*, edited by Centre for Women's Development Studies, 2002. New Delhi: Bhai Vir Singh Marg (Gole Market), pp. 49–54.
Reddy, G. B. 1997. *Women and the Law*. Hyderabad, India: Gogia Law Agency.
Shah, G. 2000. *Crime against Women and Police*, vol. 1. New Delhi: Vikas Publications, pp. 8–9.
Singh, D. 2002. *Human Rights and Police Predicament*. Delhi: Bright Law House, Chandni Chowk.
Supreme Court. 1995. *Arvinder Singh Bagga v. State of Uttar Pradesh*, AIR 1995 Supreme Court 117.
Supreme Court. 1997. *M.C. Mehta v. State of Tamil Nadu*, AIR 1997 Supreme Court 699.
Supreme Court. 2001. *Satvir Singh v. State of Punjab*, 8 SCC 633.
Supreme Court. 2002. *Vikas v. State of Rajasthan*, AIR 2002 Supreme Court 2830.
Supreme Court. 2003. *The Center for Enquiry into Health and Allied Themes (CEHAT) v. Union of India*, AIR 2003 Supreme Court 3309.
The Times of India. 2002a. "Villagers Beat Five Women to Death for Being Witches." August 1.
The Times of India. 2002b. "DIG Facing Rape Charge Is Absconding for 5 Years." August 28.
The Times of India. 2002c." Airport Official Held for Rape." October 24.
U.S. Department of Labor. 1997. "Sweat and Toil of Children: Consumer Labels and Child Labor." Quoted in Global March against Child Labour. 2000. "Worst Forms of Child Labour Data: India." http://www.globalmarch.org/worstformsreport/world/india.html.
U.S. Department of Labor. 2002. "Trafficking in Persons Report." Quoted in *The Hindu*, July 20.
United Nations International Children's Emergency Fund. 1997. "State of the World's Children." Quoted in Global March against Child Labour. 2000. "Worst Forms of Child Labour Data: India." http://www.globalmarch.org/worstformsreport/world/india.html.
United Nations International Children's Emergency Fund. 2002. "Child Protection from Violence, Exploitation and Abuse." http://www.unicef.org/programme/cprotection/focus/trafficking/stats.html.

15 Sexual Abuse in Taiwan: Multidisciplinary Criminal Case Processing

WANG SU-HUAN AND CHANG CHING-LI

> There was a case of sexual abuse in a religious organization reported by the Xi-Zhi-San-Bao Monastery yesterday. Of the 25 monks that were investigated, the eldest was only in his third year of middle school, and the youngest was in his second year of elementary school. One monk in particular begged in tears to the main prosecutor, "Don't ask me anymore! You're already the seventh person who's asked me about this. I don't want to think about it anymore. . . ." Some of the monks expressed that they had already been asked a total of 17 times. . . . The head prosecutor, Chen Wen-Qi, expressed that this was the second attack. . . . (*United Daily News* 2000)

Introduction

The description above is not out of the ordinary at all. In fact, this is an experience that is common to all victims of sexual abuse. As notably reported, Hsu Lu described the painful experience in the police station after she had been sexually abused in her book, *Survivor from the Black Night*:

> The female officer routinely pulled out her notepad, and asked me my personal information: "name?"; "address?"; "profession?"' . . . The officer was very serious and rushed. I suddenly realized that this was an official log. At that instant, I just wanted to escape. But the door was closed . . . The officer asked me about every event and detail, and I started to get a mental picture of the occurrence. I even tried to make up some rational sounding details for the memories that were utterly in pieces so that she could finish her log . . . When the officer asked me, "Did he rape you?", I violently shook my head. The officer asked again. My stomach knotted up, and I was in so much pain that I started to faint . . . I then told her that my stomach hurt, and asked her if we could stop . . . There were also cases from the Taipei Modern Women's Foundation help files in which the victim asked the researcher, "Why do I have to keep repeating myself?" The male cop asks me, then the female cop, then the doctor, then the nurse, and then the social worker asks me again! Then, just when I don't want to think about it anymore, the prosecutor asks me again. And who's next? The Judge, right? . . . Can I just get a little justice here? Are they really going to believe me?

> Maybe I'll go crazy before I ever see justice . . . Who's going to help me? (Taipei Modern Women's Foundation 1998)

This is an attack that occurred after the passing of the Law of Control and Prevention of Sex Violation, yet victims still did not get the respect and protection that they deserve. Is it because the system is incomplete? Is the law insufficient? How can it be that these people have to deal with so much pain, even after they were attacked? What can the government and people do so that these people can get a little justice?

Taiwan Sexual Abuse Crime Scenario Analysis

Sexual Abuse Occurrence

With the help of extensive promotion by female organizations, the Law of Control and Prevention of Sex Violation finally passed in 1997. This new law provided a regulated protocol for the processing of sexual violation cases, as well as protection for the victims in such cases. According to the crime statistics of the Criminal Investigation Bureau, National Police Administration, rape and gang rape cases processed by police stations during recent years (1997–2003) increased marginally, with an average total of 1,921 cases each year (Table 15.1). However, if this is compared with before the passing of the Law of Control and Prevention of Sex Violation, the number of cases

Table 15.1 Statistics of Rape/Gang Rape Cases Processed by Taiwan Police Organizations from 1991 to 2003

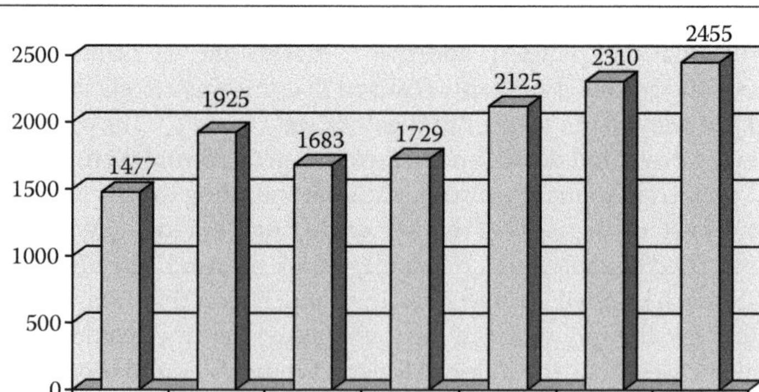

	1997	1998	1999	2000	2001	2002	2003
Rapes/gang rapes	1477	1925	1683	1729	2125	2310	2455

Source: Diagram information was received from crime statistics of the Criminal Investigation Bureau, National Police Administration; 2003 information represents initial statistics.

Table 15.2 Statistics on Rape/Gang Cases Processed by Taiwan Police Organizations from 1991 to 1997

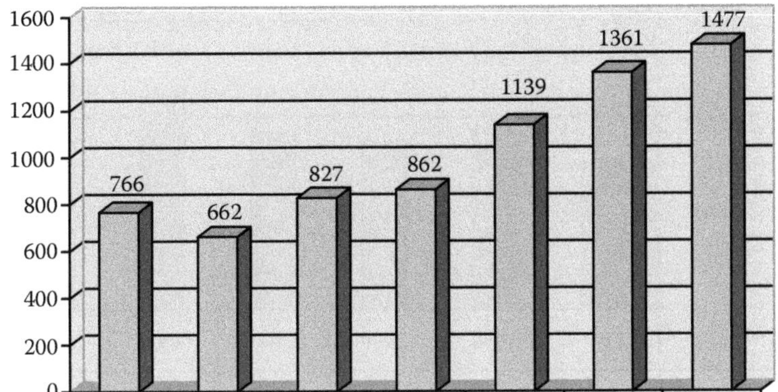

	1991	1992	1993	1994	1995	1996	1997
Rapes/gang rapes	766	662	827	862	1139	1361	1477

Source: Diagram information was received from crime statistics of the Criminal Investigation Bureau, National Police Administration.

has noticeably increased (Table 15.2). Why was it that the number of cases substantially increased after the passing of the law? One can find that the answer is because there have always been a high number of hidden violations.[1] After the law passed, one can see that the care shown by the vast governmental manpower and resources helped to gradually uncover the hidden cases (Fu-Yuan 2000; Ping-Wu, Guo-Yong, and Fu-Yuan 2002).

According to research by crime experts, the number of sexual violations is actually 7–10 times higher than that of reported cases (Fu-Yuan 2000; Guo-Yong 2000). Thus, one can ascertain that the average number of actual sexual violations occurring each year is approximately between 13,000 and 19,000. However, according to observations of the experienced sexual abuse counselors at the Modern Women's Association, the number of hidden violations could be considerably more than these figures suggest (Taipei Modern Women's Foundation 2002). From this, one can see the severity of sexual violation in Taiwan.

Gender of Sexual Violation Victims and Suspects

More than 95 percent of all victims of sexual abuse in the Taiwan area are women, and more than 90 percent of the suspects are males. Thus, one can see that there are rather extreme figures for the gender of victims and offenders in sexual violation cases. Detailed analyses are shown in Tables 15.3 and 15.4.

Table 15.3 Analysis of Gender of Sexual Abuse Victims in Cases Processed by Police Institutions in the Taiwan Area from 1997 to 2003

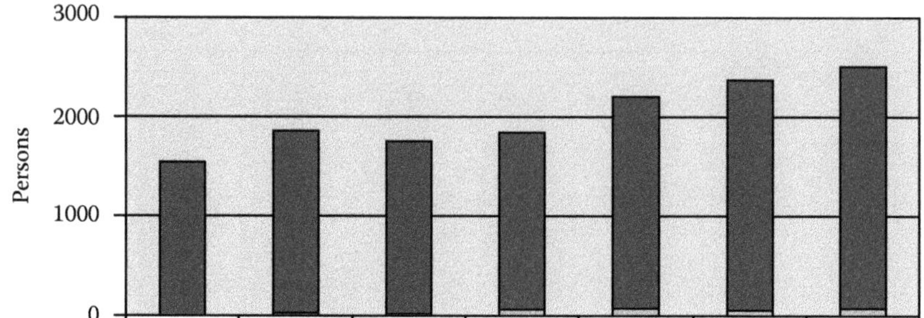

	1997	1998	1999	2000	2001	2002	2003
Female	1544	1832	1732	1778	2132	2317	2434
Male	0	27	22	63	74	57	75

Source: Diagram information was received from crime statistics of the Criminal Investigation Bureau, National Police Administration; 2003 information represents initial statistics.

Table 15.4 Analysis of Gender of Sexual Abuse Violators in Cases Processed by Police Institutions in the Taiwan Area from 1997 to 2003

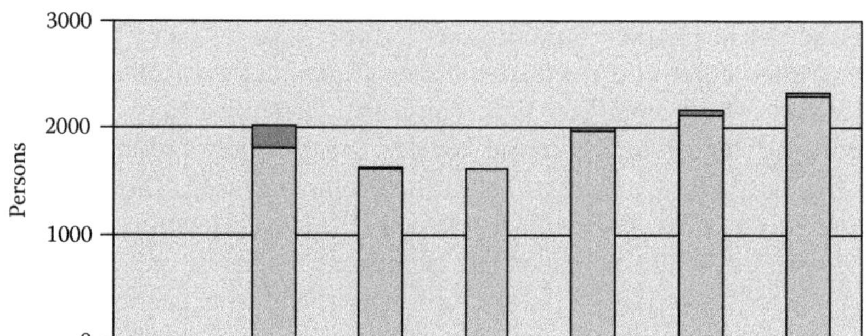

	1997	1998	1999	2000	2001	2002	2003
Female		213	21	13	30	48	31
Male		1806	1607	1607	1970	2120	2293

Source: Diagram information was received from crime statistics of the Criminal Investigation Bureau, National Police Administration; 2003 information represents initial statistics.

The Age Distribution of Sexual Abuse Victims and Offenders

Seventy percent of all sexual abuse victims in the Taiwan area are 18 years of age or younger. The greatest distribution of sexual violators is aged 19–23, and the second is 12–17, as shown in Table 15.5. The category of under six years old was not specified from the category of under 12 years old for the year of 1997 (see Tables 15.5 and 15.6).

One can see from the above information that, by adding in the hidden violations figures for the past seven years, the average number of violations each year could likely be around 13,000–19,000. The vast majority of victims are female, and the majority of violators are male. Also, the majority of female victims are students, children, and teens under the age of 18 years old.

Table 15.5 Age Distribution Analysis of Sexual Abuse Victims from Cases Processed by Police Institutions in the Taiwan Area

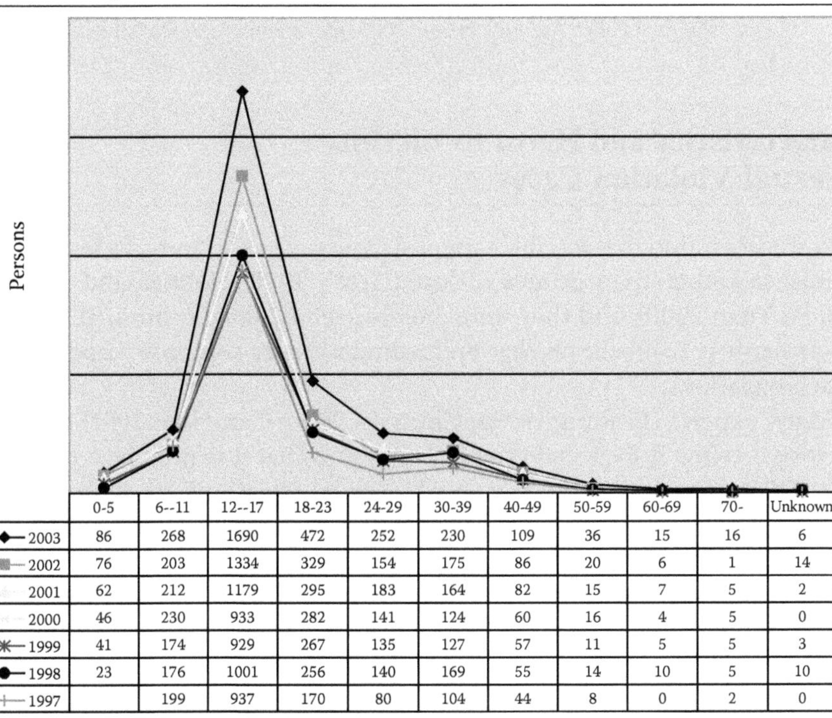

	0-5	6--11	12--17	18-23	24-29	30-39	40-49	50-59	60-69	70-	Unknown
2003	86	268	1690	472	252	230	109	36	15	16	6
2002	76	203	1334	329	154	175	86	20	6	1	14
2001	62	212	1179	295	183	164	82	15	7	5	2
2000	46	230	933	282	141	124	60	16	4	5	0
1999	41	174	929	267	135	127	57	11	5	5	3
1998	23	176	1001	256	140	169	55	14	10	5	10
1997		199	937	170	80	104	44	8	0	2	0

Source: Diagram information was received from crime statistics of the Criminal Investigation Bureau, National Police Administration; 2003 information represents initial statistics.

Table 15.6 Age Distribution Analysis for Sexual Violators from Cases Processed by Police Institutions in the Taiwan Area

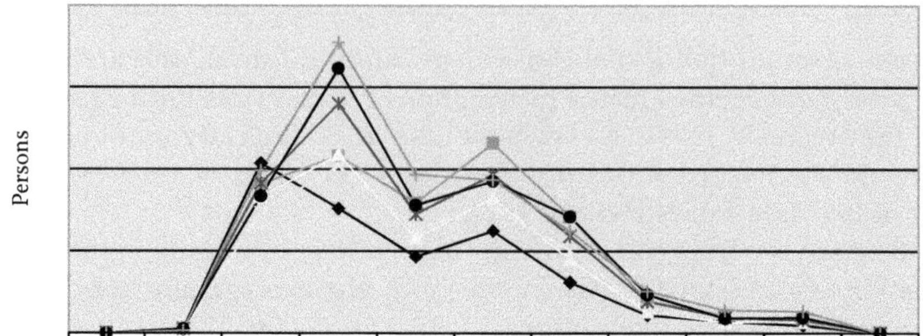

	0-5	6--11	7--12	18-23	24-29	30-39	40-49	50-59	60-69	70-	Unknown
1997	0	10	415	304	186	249	124	44	28	19	0
1998	0	10	364	433	317	464	284	78	43	26	0
1999	1	12	332	436	231	330	179	52	27	28	0
2000	0	4	294	408	255	306	201	58	41	53	0
2001	0	10	366	560	290	387	237	77	39	32	2
2002	0	10	334	646	312	371	284	94	36	38	0
2003	0	6	397	709	387	374	249	102	56	53	0

Source: Diagram information was received from crime statistics of the Criminal Investigation Bureau, National Police Administration; 2003 information represents initial statistics.

Characteristics and Harm to Victims in Sexual Violation Cases

Many studies found that forcible rape and gang rape cases were, by far, crimes of violence rather than crimes of lust (Groth 1979; Holmes and Holmes 1996; Fu-Yuan 2000), and they were mostly premeditated crimes. The Israeli scholar Amir (1979) believes that premeditated rapes compose 71 percent of all such violations.

Many experts (Li-Rong 1999a; Ching-Li 2000; Can-Huai 2001) contend that sexual crime is a special type of crime and that it is not just a crime of lust but also of violence. The reason why sexual violations are so horrible is not just because the violator makes contact with the private parts of the victim against her will but rather because of the violator's violent, abusive, and harmful methods with which the crime is committed. These actions cause the victim physical harm but can also create devastating emotional distress and distortion of self-awareness, resulting in the inability of the victim to function normally in everyday life. Added to this is the damage to the traditional Chinese precepts of female purity and reputation, which severely affect the victim's relationships in her social and family lives. Because of this, both foreign and Taiwanese experts believe that victims of sexual violations could likely experience great lifestyle changes and could even fall victim to rape trauma syndrome (Can-Huai 1999).

According to the experiences of many long-time counselors of sexual violation victims (Ching-Li 1999), one may find that rape trauma syndrome can definitely extend the harm done to the victim. The lingering effect can even last as long as 10 years. There are even some cases in which the victim is burdened by the experience for her entire life. Obviously, other factors play a vital role in the extent of the victim's recovery, such as personality, maturity, and support from friends and family. Likewise, obstacles such as depression, fear, anger, withdrawal, helplessness, and sexual problems caused by the experience influence recovery similarly.

Research about Concealing Sexual Violation

According to research by Chun-Jin and Chuan-Zhen (1992), the three major characteristics of the crime of sexual violation are (1) low report rate, (2) low conviction rate, and (3) high repeated offense rate. Why is it that the victim is unwilling to report the case and get her justice? According to the observations of Chun-Jin and Chuan-Zhen (1999) about workers involved with the Law of Control and Prevention of Sex Violation (including police officers, social workers, educational personnel, media personnel, and judiciary personnel), most of the workers feel that the main reason (cited by 73 percent) for why victims are unwilling to report their cases is because of "damage to personal reputation." The second most popular opinion was because of "fear of revenge from the violator" (50.2 percent). The third reason was "not wanting to remember the experience" (49.1 percent), and the fourth was "private settlement" (45.7 percent).

According to investigative research of sexual abuse victims in the Taiwan area by Xu Chun-Jin, it was discovered that the most common reason for not reporting the incident was "not knowing who the attacker was/lack of evidence," with 41.2 percent. The second highest "feel that it was a personal event, and are not willing to publicize it" or "feel that it wasn't a severe crime," each with 29.4 percent. The third most common reason was "fear of revenge by violator or other party," with 17.6 percent.

One can see from the above research that the primary reasons for victims of sexual attacks not being willing to report the incident were attributable to damage to reputation, lack of evidence, and fear of revenge. Associated scholars also further clarified the reason of unwillingness to report and found that the predominately female victims exist in a male-dominated society in which female victims are admonished for their circumstances. This makes females unable to muster the courage to come forward and seek help.

Even if they do seek help, they often face problems with physical issues, psychological issues, police investigations, civil lawsuits, and judiciary review. The number of personnel and institutions involved is staggering, yet these personnel of the so-called "sexual victim protection system" may lack the training necessary for them to clearly identify the victim's problems. This can cause them to manifest inappropriate attitudes or value systems and can even cause an imbalance in the entire system attributable to a lack of interdepartmental coordination. The bottom line is that this not only forces the victim to repeatedly relive the traumatizing event through the constant questioning by each of the separate institutions, but the victim is also in danger of becoming further traumatized from inappropriate lines of questioning. It is no wonder that sexual crime prevention experts estimate that the number of hidden offenses is several times greater than the reported cases (Ching-Li 1997a; Li-Rong 1999; Fu-Yuan 2000).

The Judicial Difficulty Faced by Sexual Abuse Victims

The Taiwanese criminal court code states that criminal activities should be based on witnessed facts. In criminal trials, the law requires that the necessary certainty for criminal activity must be "beyond a reasonable doubt," as termed by the American legal system. Because of this, should there exist a reasonable doubt, the presiding judge should seriously consider a verdict that would benefit the defendant (Su-Xian 2003). From this, one can see that the system is obviously sided against victims with incomplete evidence.

According to the Taiwanese judicial system, criminal cases are structured around verbal testimony and displays of related evidence. At the same time, by the very nature of sexual crimes, sexual violation trials have always tended to lack witness testimonies, and physical evidence is extremely scarce. In fact, the entire case is reliant entirely on the testimonies given by the victim and violator, the latter of which is extremely unlikely to freely admit that he is guilty of the crime. Because of this, sexual violation convictions are extremely difficult to obtain. In general, there are two types of evidence that can appear in sexual violation trials (Ji-Zhen 2002): (1) descriptive evidence, including victim testimony, witness testimony, and confession by violator; and (2) nondescriptive evidence, including hospital diagnostic reports of the victim (recording injuries and damage to hymen), a summary of the victim's medical case report, medical evaluation of sleeping pills, sedatives, or other medication used on the victim, medical reports pertaining to whether or not the victim will require psychological treatment (loss of sanity, and whether or not mandatory treatment is necessary), polygraph tests, DNA reports from the Criminal Investigation Bureau, suggestive reports from social workers or child protection case interviews, child protection case reports, social investigative reports, academic advisory information of the victim, telephone logs, handicap manual, torn clothing, weapons used in the crime, audio recordings, and video recordings.

In terms of descriptive evidence, the defendant would not normally confess to the crime but rather would give an oral defense in his favor and refute the crime evidence. As for the questioning of a witness by a prosecutor or judge during an investigation or sentencing, there are seldom many witnesses because of the private nature of the crime. Therefore, other corroborating evidence must aid the witness's testimony before the judge would give credence to such evidence. In terms of the victim's testimony, the judicial processes mainly involve live questioning of the victim and are irreplaceably important. Unfortunately, the victim is often unwilling to appear in court, or her testimonies lack stability as a result of personal relationships (in cases such as incest or other cases in which the victim knows the violator) or incomplete memories, which can cause the legal system to fail.

In terms of nondescriptive evidence, there are harms that the victim cannot guarantee are beyond a reasonable doubt. This evidence can vary greatly, depending on whether the victim sought immediate medical attention or whether there were changes in her condition, because they were examined after reporting the case. Some items with reports or logs of the victim conducted by other personnel can be used as corroborating documental evidence and vary in persuasiveness because of the circumstances of the individual. Some items do not apply to every case and may not be used as evidence at all.

One can see from the above information that sexual violation cases are more reliant on the testimony of the victim and violator and the performance of the involved parties during the trial than any other type of crime. If the involved parties are not adept at expressing themselves, such as children or mentally impaired individuals, they will appear rather ineffective in the judicial process. Moreover, the lack of direct evidence in sexual abuse cases (such as sperm or hair left by the violator, eyewitnesses, and video recordings from the crime scene) makes rulings in sexual violation cases even more difficult.

In addition, feminists and related experts (Ching-Li 1999; Tzan-Huai 1999, 2001) believe that the biases of our male-dominated society toward female sexual abuse victims cause more scrutiny toward victims in court than in general cases. Moreover, the courtroom personnel are more likely to be influenced by emotional and monetary problems, occupational stereotypes, and the conduct of the victim and violator, which can prevent them from clearly discerning the truth in such cases. What is also worth mentioning is that sexual abuse cases not only deal with the physical violation of the victim but also the resulting psychological trauma. This trauma can easily manifest itself as emotional barriers in the victim, which could prevent her from reacting in a rational manner, even causing her to lose control or "react in a defensive manner" (such as suppression, denial, transference, and reaction formation), which can make memory recall even very difficult. Because of this, the victim is likely to produce reverse or silent testimonies (Ching-Li 2000). This can create a lot more difficulty for a case that was already difficult to decide.

Research Methods and Definitions

Research Method and Information Collection

This is a continuous study based primarily on a collection and analysis of historical information. The information collected is mainly from government department meeting logs, research information, executive manuals, nongovernment organization publications, meeting logs, and media reports for the years 1999–2004. The object of this study is to understand the dynamic, historical process, and results of the case.

Definitions

Rape and Rape Victim

Rape refers to a person conducting sexual behavior without the consent of the other party. According to Art. 2 of the Law of Control and Prevention of Sex Violation, rape refers to crimes from Arts. 221–229 and 233 of criminal law, including forced intercourse, violently forced intercourse, forced lewd actions, violently forced lewd actions, or opportunistic intercourse, lewd actions, forced (violently forced) sexual intercourse, forced sexual intercourse with homicide or major injury, sexual intercourse or lewd actions to an underage child, using one's authority to force sexual intercourse or lewd actions, tricking others into sexual intercourse, forced sexual intercourse, or lewd behavior to a child under 16. In addition, other criminal laws are included: Art. 231, forced sexual intercourse or lewd behavior on another person; Art. 296, the sale, purchase, or detainment of a person for sexual intercourse or lewd behavior; and Arts. 332 and 334, forced sexual intercourse or lewd behavior during robbery. A rape victim is thus the victim of the above crimes.

Secondary Harm

Secondary harm refers to the harm incurred by a rape victim during the post-rape search for help caused by the disbelief, belittlement, misinterpretation, or querying of others. This type of harm is different from the harm caused by the initial incident and is called secondary harm (Can-Huai 2001).

Reduction of Repetitive Testimony

This refers to the reduction of repetitious narration of the attack and feelings of the victim during the querying process conducted by prosecutors, police officers, social workers, and medical personnel in the coordinated network.

Coordinated Network

This refers to the notion that all departments, institutions, offices, and personnel strive to collaborate and coordinate to protect the rights of the user of the services by integrating resources, information, and cases or project strategies, and avoid lapses, fragments, repetitions, and waste of resources in the system. Through this, the connections within the system can be strengthened, and the services can focus on the common goal of protecting the victim (Zhao-Rong 1987; Bi-Hui 1992; Jiao-Yu 1995; Zhi-Ling 1998).

Promoting the "Reducing Repeat Interrogation for Victims of Sexual Assault" Project

Project Content

Project Background and Objectives

With the passing of the Law of Control and Prevention of Sex Violation, a new door was opened in the protection of rape victims. The law clearly regulates that specific central and local institutions should be responsible for planning and promoting services to rape victims, therapy and counseling for sexual violators, and sex crimes education for the public. Because of this, the Sexual Assault Prevention Committee of the Ministry of Interior, as well as city and county sexual assault prevention centers, were consequently born.

However, the county and city sexual assault prevention centers have mostly been providing a more segmented type of processing service in which the social services, police, prosecution, and medical institutions work separately. This type of system seriously lacks effective communication, which causes repetitions, lapses, and delays in services to the rape victim. In fact, the institutions themselves are unable to use each other's resources and which can affect service quality and results (Ching-Li 1997; Li-Rong 1999, 2000; Fu-Yuan 2000; Shu-Qiong 2002).

To eliminate the secondary harm caused by difficulties in rape victim services, such as repetitive questioning, poor questioning, and lengthy investigative process, the Sexual Assault Prevention Committee plans to search for breakthrough decision-making policies for police and government processing protocols. The project was conceived in 1999, after having been discussed in 12 formal meetings and countless private discussions. After a year and a half, the Sexual Assault Prevention Committee finally reached a consensus among the various institutions within the system and formally began to implement the project in Taipei, Hualien, and Kaohsiung, in hopes that it could be used in all of Taiwan if successful (Domestic Abuse and Sexual Assault Prevention Committee, Ministry of Interior 2001a).

The project consists of the following three main objectives:

1. ***Integrate victim service systems.*** The project aims to integrate the four large victim service systems (prosecuting, police, social services, and medical institutions) so that the number of lapses in the system can be reduced and the victim can experience completely coordinated care.
2. ***Reduce repetitive testimonies by the rape victim.*** The project aims at the coordination of the four main departments through a collaborative questioning process, thus reducing the number of times that the victim has to recall the events of the incident, thereby reducing the victim's trauma.
3. ***Improve investigative speed and quality.*** The project shall implement video (audio) recording throughout the entire procedure, thus compensating for the victim's incomplete or lost memories attributable to the lengthiness of the investigation. In addition, there shall be social workers or professional personnel on site to assist with the questioning of the prosecutor so as to improve the quality and speed of the rape case processing.

In short, this project reduces the number of times that the victim is questioned through a coordination of the four institutions and helps to improve the speed and quality of the investigation by using video (audio) recording throughout the entire questioning process, thus completely protecting the interests and rights of the victim (Ching-Li and Mei-Xun 2003).

Project Characteristics and Range

This collaborative project is rather different when compared with other general projects. Some of its defining characteristics are as follows:

1. ***Collaborative.*** This project is different from other projects in that it attempts to integrate the four systems (police, prosecuting, social services, and medical). What is particularly special is that it conquers traditional task distribution and bureaucratic obstacles and attempts to structure its coordinated services around the needs of the victim.

2. ***Multifaceted.*** This project focuses concurrently on policy, execution, monitoring, and evaluation. The areas of policy and execution were regulated in this plan to facilitate its initial promotion. However, monitoring and evaluative systems were also created to ensure its quality and success.
3. ***Dual-tracked evaluation.*** This plan uses a dual-tracked evaluation system based on both female organizations and administrative departments. Monitoring, evaluation systems, and strategies are critical in maintaining the quality and effectiveness of a project. The Rape Prevention Committee boldly uses the professional evaluative and monitoring offices from the Modern Women's Foundation, which claims that advocacy is its duty. The project also combines administrative support and assistance so that the project may become even more objective and impartial. Project efficiency is also streamlined with the aid of an administrative department.
4. ***Centered on protection of the victim.*** This project was first created around the needs of the victim. Its procedures and services all help reduce secondary harm to the victim and it has been termed a new marker for human rights in Taiwan's judicial system. In addition, it has received the praise of the U.S. Department of State and has been listed in the 2001 Taiwan Human Rights Report (Ching-Li and Mei-Xun 2003).
5. ***Police department initiation.*** The Violence Prevention Team of the Rape Prevention Center (composed of detectives) was the first organization to promote this plan on behalf of authoritative and conservative police officers. This project has also become a great movement for human rights and shatters the stereotyped image of the "cold, inhuman police officer."

Project Range and Target

Project range refers to the institutions involved during execution. The project is currently designed around the medical therapy, social services, police investigations, and prosecuting services required by the victim. Although the court investigation is based around the rights of the victim, it could hinder the result if the system were to become overly large. It could also cause the institutions that were meant to be reformed to become faced with the problems of being linked together and lose their direction. The process is supposed to solve problems, not create them. Although the project is oriented around the integration of the four institutions (medical, social services, police, and prosecuting), it is not so rigid as to fail to consider the effects of the court verdict. After all, this project was intended to be a multiphased reform experiment in the rape prevention system. The only solution is to continually strive to protect the victim, while at the same time investigate future judicial system reform measures (Domestic Violence and Sexual Assault Prevention Committee, Ministry of Interior 2001a).

Currently, the project is not just centered around victims who are mentally challenged or under 16 years of age but also includes adult victims. The adult victim can apply for the protection of this program as long as social worker evaluations determine the adult to be suitable for the project and the subject is willing (Domestic Violence and Sexual Assault Prevention Committee, Ministry of Interior 2001a).

Project Procedure

Sexual violation case processing protocol is different from that of general cases, such as shown below.

Project Strategies and Timeline

Project Planning and Promotion Cycles

Based on the above information, the head of the committee developed and promoted a plan in hopes of resolving issues in rape victim protection and noticed that this plan follows a special lifecycle. The following section, in addition to summarizing the general lifecycle of the plan, also briefly describes some of its important focal points, strategies, and methods.

Birth (Initial Forming of a Case): After the passing of the Law of Control and Prevention of Sex Violation, the committee was the first entity focused on the organization and promotion of nationwide rape prevention activities. The committee members included not only public relations personnel but also scholars and nongovernment organizations. At the time, professor Chen Ruo-Zhang mentioned that the United States was demonstrating great results with its synchronous video questioning system and protection of child rape victims (Ching-Li and Mei-Zun 2003).

The director of the Violence Prevention Team at the time, Wang Pei-Ling, encouraged professor Chen Ruo-Zhang to lobby for the support of a similar system in Taiwan through committee nomination. After passing in the committee, private inquiries were made to central and local government institutions regarding their thoughts on this matter, including the Ministry of Justice Prosecutor, the High Court Prosecutor's Office, the Hualien Local Prosecutor's Office, the Shilin Local Prosecutor's Office, the Head Public Prosecutor, the Taipei Local Prosecutor's Office, the Taipei City Government Police Bureau Female Police Squad, the Kaohsiung County Police Department Young Squad, Hualien County, and the Kaohsiung County Sexual Assault Prevention Center personnel members. These people

Table 15.7 Reducing Repeat Interrogation for Victims of Sexual Assault Protocol Summary

	Reduced Testimony Protocol	General Protocol (before Implementation of the Reduced Testimony Plan)
Case collection and processing	Each sexual violation processing window type prevention center shall dispatch specially appointed case social workers to the location of the victim (questioning may not begin before the arrival of the prevention center appointed social worker).	Sexual violation report centers may dispatch social workers in shifts only if the subject is under 18 or if they specifically ask to be accompanied by a social worker (the victim could have already given statements at police or medical institutions before the arrival of the prevention center appointed social worker).
Examination, evidence gathering	The victim is provided with psychological support while accompanied by prevention center social workers or police officers and assisted by the hospital social worker to record injuries, as deemed necessary on a per-case basis. Project locations are outfitted with specialized hospitals that provide discrete, hospitable meeting room facilities for the investigation and recording processes.	Social workers or case processing police officers shall be dispatched in shifts to accompany the victim only if they are under 18 or specifically ask to be accompanied. Police officers shall arrange a meeting room in a police station for questioning and records after the injury examination and evidence collection processes.
Prequestioning interview and evaluation	The prevention center dispatches social workers to interview the victim before the police interrogation to evaluate the physical and psychological status of the victim and whether or not they are suitable for the procedure.	None
Time for questioning of the victim	The prevention center social worker determines a suitable time for questioning and requests additional professional personnel required (such as special education teacher or sign language interpreter) to assist the prosecutor and police officers in the questioning at the appointed time.	Immediate questioning

(Continued)

Table 15.7 *(Continued)*

	Reduced Testimony Protocol	General Protocol (before Implementation of the Reduced Testimony Plan)
Questioning	The prosecutor on duty and a commanding police officer (at least one female police officer among them) shall begin the questioning together, accompanied by the prevention center appointed social worker, and recording on video and audio throughout the entire process.	The police officer (usually female) begins taking notes without the direction of the prosecutor. If necessary, a victim can apply to be accompanied by social workers. No video or audio recording of the questioning process.
Crime investigation	Request the prosecutor's office to dispatch the prosecutor on duty to direct the questioning of the victim, not taking crime scene evidence collection, and suspect pursuit immediately after the case is received. The prosecutor takes immediate authority over the investigation.	Police institution begins the investigation based on the information provided by the victim or person responsible for reporting the case.
Delivery of investigatory evidence	The police institutions complete crime investigations, following the direction of the prosecutor, and deliver the related files and evidence (including victim interrogation videotape) to the prosecutor's office. The name of the prosecutor is notated on the documents.	After police institutions complete the investigation, the related evidence and files are processed by the prosecutor's office.
Separate case investigation	The original prosecutor of the local prosecutor's office takes responsibility for this, under the knowledge that the case information should not be relayed to the victim unless necessary.	The prosecutor responsible relays information related to the police investigation to the victim, suspect, and related parties, and questions them again.

Source: Domestic Violence and Sexual Assault Prevention Committee, Ministry of Interior, 2000.

later became important individuals in promotion of the project. Through this, the committee helped further define a general outline of the project, as well as which counties and cities in which it would be initiated.

In short, the project benefited from the environment in which it was created, but the help of certain key individuals was still essential to continue fighting to obtain support and project definition. The methods used include lobbying, official visits to key individuals and organizations, meeting proposals, and communication.

Childhood (Concrete Project Development): In an effort to obtain even more stable support and discussion to substantiate the project methods, the committee officials established project teams for discussion and analysis of project details and potential problems during execution. Project teams were composed of individuals including members of the central ministry, the Taipei Women's Hospital Director and gynecologist Dr. Jiang Qian-Dai, the High Court Prosecutor's Office, and the Modern Women's Foundation Executive Officer Chang Ching-Li (these individuals are also committee members), as well as head public prosecutors, police administration personnel, and social services management from local districts in which the project might be implemented in the future. At this time, the "Guidelines for the Reduction of Repeat Rape Victim Questioning" were also composed, providing a legal basis and model for future investigations.

Many problems were encountered during team meeting discussions, such as the numerous concerns expressed by public prosecutors and social service institutions, mostly resulting from the increase in workload for the two institutions attributable to their early intervention. The committee resolved this problem by having respected and experienced members from each integrated network explain the benefits of an integrated network, so as to keep the concerns and resistance of public prosecutors and social service personnel to a minimum.

After coordinating the prosecuting and social service systems, the project team brought in representatives from the Department of Health and local health departments during the fourth project meeting. However, the medical personnel did not intervene until rather late in the process, at which time the prosecuting, police, and social worker representatives had already reached a consensus on many issues. In fact, each of the concerns expressed by the medical institutions were abruptly answered by the public prosecutor, who provided the communication and explanation instead of the promoter (Domestic Violence and Sexual Assault Prevention Committee, Ministry of Interior 2000b). This dramatic outcome was rather puzzling if not amusing. In other words, the important strategy of the project's childhood was in establishing the project team, a stable support and discussion organization, devoted toward further solidifying project range and content, looking for advocates in related institutions to become advocates in this one, recruiting new members, and initiating the legal basis promoted by this project. The methods involved in this stage include meeting coordination, private lobbying, cooperation, and conflict resolution.

Teenage Years (Project Range in Its Establishment and Draft): In addition to more discussion and consolidation of the project legitimacy, the project phases, schedule, range, strategy, execution forms, procedure, and other notable points from the project procedure were further standardized. Because this was a multi-institutional, integrated project, implementing it throughout the whole of Taiwan could not be considered an easy task at all. Therefore, the project was designated for implementation on a trial basis in locations with relatively developed backgrounds in rape prevention, such as Taipei, Kaohsiung County, and Hualien County. Should the trial implementation prove successful, the project could be expanded over several phases during subsequent years. Planning for the trial phase was set for November 2000 and was to officially begin in January 2001. During this time, critical implementation strategies were drafted, including training programs, integrated networks, dual-tracked monitoring (monitoring by a women's organization and an administrative department), and research analysis (see below for details). During this time, important project standards and advisory items were drafted. In addition to the "Reducing Repeat Interrogation for Victims of Sexual Assault Project: Project Guidelines," this included "Questioning Guidelines," "Social Worker Interview Log," "Consent Forms," "Project Procedure," "County and City Government Processing Notice," "Police Institution Processing Notice," and "Victim's Rights" (Domestic Violence and Sexual Assault Prevention Committee, Ministry of Interior 2001a).

Many disagreements and conflicts arose during the discussion and regulation phase, which the committee resolved by reaching consensus in private negotiations but also in larger meetings, strategically led by nongovernment scholars, to help avoid the conflicting ideas in government institutions. For example, there were many conflicting opinions regarding target individuals for the project: the prosecuting institution felt that this project should target regulation Art. 15 from the Sex Crime Law, while the social service institutions felt that the trauma experienced by adult rape victims is no less important than that of child rape victims, advocating that they be included in the project service range. In such cases, when the two parties were unable to come to an agreement, nongovernment experts and scholars could take over and help the two parties think about the issue from the victim's perspective. In this particular case, it was finally decided that mentally challenged victims and victims younger than 16 years old would be the targets for services of this project. However, this did not include individuals who had been specifically evaluated as requiring this type of service. In other words, the important strategies used in the teenage years of the project included the drafting of project promotion strategy, the creation of the project's range, and the expansion of negotiating space. The methods used included private negotiations, persuasion, continued communication, using nongovernment experts, and alleviating conflicts.

Adult Phase (Confirming the Plausibility of the Project): At this time, project planning was already complete, but it was still necessary to verify the availability of the required fees, resources, and equipment, in addition to finalizing the details of implementation and motivating project personnel. Although the project was complete, it was still not ready for implementation. The people implementing the plan still felt unclear as to the specifics of the project's implementation. The plan was created under the notion of "protecting victims," but the executing personnel seemed to be confused about why the plan was the way that it was. The primary strategy of this phase was centered on resolving these issues by verifying that equipment and finances were intact, developing a video procedure process, creating outside opportunities, and quickly reaching a common understanding.

The strategy was to increase the probability of project implementation by making a project implementation video based on the discussions and procedures attained from previous phases, through the knowledge and resources of the Kaohsiung Rape Prevention Team (Domestic Violence and Sexual Assault Prevention Committee, Ministry of Interior 2000b). Also, dinner parties were held to encourage personnel in locations designated for project implementation, and press conferences were held to announce the importance and significance of implementing the project in counties and cities in the future. With this, the committee helped to motivate the public, glorifying and unifying each of the cities and counties.

Mature Phase (Official Project Promotion and Evaluation): The project began its full-scale city/county trial implementation and at the same time conducted monitoring and evaluative operations. During this process, a lack of familiarity with the teamwork, as well as the integrated process and methods resulted in constant promotional problems. Because of this, the training programs, post-promotional integrated network, and problem resolution monitoring systems such as network seminars, interdepartmental focused seminars, and the establishment of contact personnel and lists became essential during this promotional phase.

At the same time, the project entered its evaluative phase, in which opinions of project personnel and victims who used the services were collected through surveys, network seminars, and victim interviews. These opinions were provided as reference to project policy makers for the establishment and amendment of the project system and its measures (Domestic Violence and Sexual Assault Prevention Committee, Ministry of Interior 2001b) (details below).

Rebirth Phase (Project Reevaluation): An in-depth evaluation was conducted to see whether the project should be continued, expanded, or transferred to another area for implementation. Possible methods included strict evaluative and research methods, such as exact experimentation and design, detailed interviews of victims, and documental analysis. Information for this phase is incomplete because it is currently in progress, and no further explanation shall be given.

In general, the lifecycle listed above can be basically divided into two main phases: the planning and preparatory phase and the project implementation phase. The planning and preparatory phase includes birth, childhood, teenage, and adult phases. The project implementation phase includes the mature phase and the rebirth phase.

Project Structural Factors, Implementation Strategy, and Technique

The project lifecycle described above explains the progression of the project throughout time. Next, we shall delve into project promotion, explaining the structural factors, implementation strategies, and methods that we need to consider:

(1) *Structural factors*

(A) Legal statutes: Although there are many guarantees for the victim based on sex crime laws, there are no clear regulations for the reduction of victim questioning through collaborative or video-recorded interrogation of the victim. Therefore, in an effort to enforce project implementation, the rape prevention committee drafted the "Reducing Repeat Interrogation for Victims of Sexual Assault Project: Project Guidelines," which called for project implementation in Taipei, Kaohsiung County, and Hualien County starting in the year 2001. These guidelines have the legal weight of a government commandment, strongly enforcing the establishment and compliance of project teams and reducing unnecessary resistance.

(B) Manpower: Sexual assault prevention centers have already been established in each city and county, all of which have been outfitted with the basic required manpower. Because this case deals with collaborative interrogation, the social workers and prosecutors complained of an increase in workload attributable to their early intervention. However, in reality, social workers have always been required to accompany child rape victims 16 years old and under according to rape prevention regulations. In terms of the investigative duties of public prosecutors, the duties remain the same, whether completed sooner or later. This is why there have been no manpower increases planned for this project, except in the areas of training programs and integration, but there have always been manpower shortages in rape case processing. Therefore, county and cities should increase their manpower in this area to comply with the promotion of this project.

(C) Organization: There have been no new organizations established for this project. In principle, all of the organizations established after the passing of the Law of Control and Prevention of Sexual Violation have been regulated by the rape prevention center regulations in each city and county (Domestic Violence and Sexual Assault Prevention Committee, Ministry of Interior 1999). Such centers are responsible for the establishment of combined planning organizations, protection and help organizations, medical care organizations, and sexual assault and violence prevention organizations. In addition, sexual assault prevention centers must have a director (held by the mayor or county governor), an assistant director (held by the secretary general of the state or county), an executive secretary (held by the director of social welfare), and two secretaries (held by the director of the health bureau and the director of the police department). The main goal of this is to combine and integrate different institutions from within the city or county. Because the prosecutor's office is under the jurisdiction of the Ministry of Justice, it has always been an important part of this project.

(D) Fees: To ensure the purchase of all of the required equipment, training seminar spending, and to monitoring and evaluate spending, the rape prevention committee must produce a spending budget for each city or county targeted for implementation. However, because the Domestic Violence and Sexual Assault Prevention Committee is promoting this project, full financial support was provided during the first phase.

(E) Equipment and devices: A good project requires the use of good tools with which to implement it. Therefore, there must be a complete supply of equipment to effectively reach cost objectives. This includes suspect voice recognition systems, interrogation rooms for the combined use of prosecution and police personnel, video and audio recording devices, three-way video conference system, and fax machines.

(2) *Critical strategy and methods for project execution*

After the committee completed project planning, it was submitted to the three locations for implementation. In addition, the committee commissioned the Modern Women's Association to provide monitoring and evaluation of pre-execution training and execution, to ensure that the project was implemented as required. The training program, integrated network, dual-tracked monitoring, and research evaluation strategies conducted by the Modern Women's Association are as follows:

(A) Training programs
   (i) Training participants and content: The basic participants of the training program include specialized personnel, because they are required. The content of the training program includes the nature of rape, its mystery, possible victim responses, and violator characteristics. In addition to the processing skills required by each institution, training programs should include recognition of the roles of each institution in sexual violation cases, as well as conflict management methods.
   (ii) Educational training materials: Because the majority of personnel involved in project promotion are just ordinary people, easy-to-understand training manuals, video tapes, and integrated procedures have been developed to ensure smooth project operation (Domestic Violence and Sexual Assault Prevention Committee 2001a; Ching-Li and Mei-Xun 2003).
   (iii) Training methods: In addition to improved explanations of project implementation, training focuses on case discussion and analysis in an effort to aid personnel to apply these guidelines and standards. This can also help personnel to bring up any problems that they have during operations, as well as provide them with resources and discussions to resolve the problems. This is also an opportune time to adjust any impractical areas.
   (iv) Training instructors: Cross-departmental instructors shall be involved during training to familiarize students with victims' feelings and circumstances, for example, a police official assisting police officers and social workers, or a social worker assisting police officers or public prosecutors. In addition to reinforcing knowledge of other departments, this can also help establish trust between the different institutions, thus benefiting future collaborations.

(B) Integrated network: Change of attitudes and cooperativeness is a process that can be separated into developmental phases of a resistance phase, an adjustment phase, and a support (or separative) phase. Different methods and techniques are used in each phase.
   (i) Resistance phase: Some of the visible traits of the resistance phase are reluctance to use time and resources to communicate with the other members, reluctance to change, negative feelings, inability to have rational discussions with others, fear of inspection, and fear of being criticized.

It is difficult to avoid a great deal of negativity as a result of difference of opinion, professional knowledge gaps, and reluctance to change during meetings in the initial project planning phase or official project implementation, making it difficult to conduct rational discussions. However, the Modern Women's Association has made a special effort to focus on communication, emotional support, and consideration to reduce the occurrence of conflict and facilitate rational discussion (Ching-Li 2001).

(ii) Adjustment phase: In the adjustment phase, we are still faced with the conflicts arising from different opinions and standpoints from each of the different institutions, but there has already started to be a gradual understanding among the members. In fact, having many different opinions at one's disposal is not uncommon in the least and can actually be helpful when attempting a task. There are many different institutions involved in this project, including the Domestic Violence and Sexual Assault Rape Prevention Committee, police institutions, court systems, medical institutions, and social service institutions, and each is divided into the central and local government levels (for example, public prosecutors of the Ministry of Justice belong to the central government, whereas the Taipei Domestic Violence Prevention Center belongs to the city government). Therefore, the coordination and communication process is rather difficult. In addition to the communication principles described above, the following are methods also currently being used:

(a) Transcending rank: There is a nongovernment organization member acting as chairman for each meeting (official and unofficial). Even if a particular attendee holds a high rank, he is only considered as a participant during the meeting (he shares equal rank with the others). The main reason for this is an attempt to break down the rank system and create an equal, cooperative team. In addition, meeting participants are required to use regular language during the meeting. For example, the chairman, police officers, and others shall be addressed by their names and not by their ranks. Second, the opinions of low-ranking social workers and police officers shall be particularly noted as to show respect and increase their professional status within the system.

(b) Individual concentration: There will always be a few members showing resistance throughout project implementation. These individuals can be overly negative and can even start spreading antagonistic rumors and negativity. In this type of situation, one can individually communicate with the resisting parties, make clarifications, give them more responsibilities, continue to support them, and explain that the central government is determined to implement the plan and has passed ordinances governing its implementation.
(c) Partial unification: Because there are so many institutions involved in this project, if it seems impossible to quickly integrate them into a new team, one can first integrate institutions that are similar and then later integrate the other institutions. For example, prosecution and police institution operations can first be integrated and social workers introduced later, if successful.
(d) Formal and informal scenarios: During the formal network seminars, opinions are expressed orally by the involved institutions, and there are written reports clarifying project results and providing reform measures. Although these formal meetings are helpful in monitoring institutions during their later evaluations, several base-level opinions seem to get omitted. Therefore, informal-type scenarios can be used in such situations, such as private face-to-face or telephone discussions or focus seminars (gathering members from similar institutions and focusing on low-ranking personnel).

(iii) Support phase: After completing the previous two phases, the party responsible for execution can begin to acknowledge that the different institutions should be cooperating and that this cooperation can make their job even easier. The strategy critical in this phase lies in creating external opportunities that can reinforce the close relationship of the team. The method in which to do this is the selection of a particularly active or opinionated member as a lecturer for a portion of the training. This individual can share his positive experiences regarding project collaborations. In addition, large-scale observatory meetings or press conferences can be held, which can publicize project results and motivate its participants. Of course, a separative phase is also possible. The project could be canceled if the constant conflict between the different institutions cannot be effectively resolved and negative attitudes make it impossible to conduct rational discussions.

(A) Dual-tracked monitoring: During initial project planning, there was concern that the administrators responsible for monitoring could lose their impartiality or cause resistance. Thus, a dual-tracked monitoring system has been established, using the Modern Women's Association, in hopes that the intervention of a nongovernment institution can help assist with problem definition, clarification, and resolution. This system can help alleviate some of the possible setbacks and difficulties during initial product implementation. From this, it is apparent that monitoring is based primarily on problem solving. Therefore, the establishment of a problem-solving system has been a critical strategy during the promotion of this project. The problem-solving system used by the Modern Women's Association is described below (Ching-Li and Mei-Xun 2003).

(B) Establishment of integrated seminars: Seminar content was already touched on briefly in the descriptions of the different information collection methods. Seminar participants include the decision makers and leaders of each institution regarding sexual violation cases, nongovernment institution experts, and project executors. The purpose of these seminars is to provide an opportunity for improved communication and integration. Before the seminars, the members from each institution conduct a preparatory meeting so that concrete problems can be discussed during the cross-institutional seminar. After the discussions, institutions should produce problem solutions and time restrictions, and provide a written examination of whether or not the problem has shown improvement before the next meeting. Cross-institutional seminars should be held approximately once every two months.

   (i) Establishment of interdepartmental focus seminars: At this time, focus seminars can be conducted on various situations that could occur, including the uneven distribution of power between the institutions, issues that need to be examined in depth, or emotional problems of members that need to be addressed. During these focus seminars, the institution can thoroughly address problems or difficulties experienced by the executors of the project. In addition to alleviating some of these concerns, the group discussion and relationships can help the project team to reach a common understanding and can also help to improve their problem-solving abilities and resources. The leaders of the focus seminars include a member of the monitoring team, a meeting participant, and also an executor from one of the institutions, such as a social worker, police officer, or public prosecutor.

(ii) Establishment of a cross-institutional problem-solving officer (contact officer): Problems could occur in each different institution at any time during case processing. Sometimes an individual causes the problem; sometimes it is a procedural problem in one of the institutions. However, if the problem is put off until the next meeting, it could negatively affect the entire process. Therefore, these types of problems should be immediately discussed by a specially designated officer, for example, the director of the women and children protection team of the prosecution institution, the director or evaluator of the prevention center, or the captain or subcaptain of the police squad or young police squad. The negotiating personnel can then write out the problem on the special form or notify the other party via telephone, fax, or e-mail, based on the severity of the problem. If there have been actual negotiated solutions for the problem, agreements that a particular solution shall be used in the future should be in written form, so that the problem does not occur again.

(C) Research evaluation: This can be divided into process evaluation and result evaluation.

(i) Process evaluation: The objective of process evaluation is to obtain a clear understanding of the status of the implementation, as well as improve victim services. The focal points of process evaluation are as follows: (1) Does the project satisfy the victim's needs? and (2) Does the project's performance still adhere to its initial objectives? These two focal points have been monitored in logs from the beginning of the project's execution to ensure that all logs, documents, and case files can be tracked throughout the entire project implementation process (Martella, Nelson, and Marchand-Marelle 1999; Domestic Violence and Sexual Assault Prevention Committee, Ministry of Interior 2001a).

(ii) Result evaluation: The main purpose of result evaluation is to conduct a final project analysis and appraisal. This includes the four levels suggested by Martella, Nelson, and Marchand-Marelle (1999): (1) Has there been any improvement in the status of the participant? (2) Does the participant show any improvement when compared with individuals not participating in the project? (3) Does there seem to be a cause and effect relationship in project provision and results? and (4) Can the project results be generalized? Project executors can conduct evaluation studies during in-depth interviews of victims. They can help to describe the feelings of the victim, the attitude of the project executors, cause-and-effect relationships, and project effects throughout the entire service (Modern Women's Foundation 2003).

Project Results and Challenges

System Reforms: Promoting Specialized Rape Case Management (Prosecutors)

With regard to the unique nature of sexual violation, the Ministry of Justice intends to police and prosecute sexual violators, protect the victim, and assist the victim in the various problems arising from their public testimony, all of which require specialization and improved professional networking. In 1997, the Ministry of Justice ordered the establishment of a rape case task force, selecting experienced, mild-tempered, married prosecutors. Male task force members were to be accompanied by female court secretaries. A married female public prosecutor would be designated if necessary. In 1998, the Female and Child Protection Team was established, specializing in sexual assault, child and young adult sex prevention, domestic violence, and young adult cases. With the implementation, institutions began to cooperate by adjusting duty shifts, case distributions, and investigation directions. In an effort to get investigating prosecutors to intervene immediately during rape cases, 24-hour female public prosecutors were established by this project, for immediate rape case processing and direction. After investigation, the police department concerned submits the name of a public processor, at which point the prosecutor's office shall designate the original public processor as the official appointed prosecutor for the case, in an effort to maintain case consistency. The prosecutor shall then have precedence over police department notes and video recordings, thus avoiding repeated interrogation of the victim unless extremely necessary. In addition, in December 2003, the Ministry of Justice ordered that, starting on January 1, 2004, all prosecutors' offices should rotate "suitable for reduced interrogation procedure" on the case after receiving the case from the police institution, if deemed suitable for this project. Through this, prosecutors can benefit project evaluation, including tabulating of lawsuit and conviction rates, as well as determining whether the time required in related cases has been affected as a result of the reduction of victim interrogation.

Establishing Specialized Teams in Police Institutions and Improving the Reputation of Female Police Teams

1. In November 2001, with the "Reducing Repeat Interrogation for Victims of Sexual Assault Project: Police Institution Processing Notice," the National Police Administration regulated that all police institutions shall designate criminal investigative personnel to specialize in rape case investigation and evidence collection. The purpose of this was to effectively integrate the processes of victim interrogation recording, suspect apprehension, and onsite evidence collection.
2. In April 2002, the National Police Administration ordered the promotion of the "Plan for Female Police Squad Investigations in Major Female and Child Cases." Before project implementation, the female police squads from the young police squads in each county and city were only responsible for duties related to the protection of women and children and were not responsible for female victim safety investigations. Because of this, they were not functionally capable of doing so. However, after project implementation, female police squads or young police squads (women and children protection teams) were designated in six locations on July 1, 2002, to specialize in continuing investigations cases or sexual assault cases without suspects (not including lewd behavior), major domestic violence cases, human trafficking cases, forced child and young adult sex cases, and other female cases that have attracted the attention of the international media to help them improve their abilities in these areas.
3. On March 8, 2002, Women's Day, the National Police Administration announced that female police squads from each police bureau would officially be known as "women and children police squads." Because of the fact that the name "female police" is based on gender, there are many apparent problems for male officers on female police squads. This also causes the misconception that the police officers working in female safety are all female, which results in a negative long-term effect for female safety operations. Because of this, the National Police Administration decided to consider an adjustment of the facility of the aforementioned female police squad, and, after deliberation of suggestions from the public, officially changed the name of "female police squads" to "women and children police squads," and "female police teams" from the young police squad was altered to the "women and children squad."

Advances in Investigation Logs

A sample of a complete rape victim interrogation and computerized suspect is provided as a reference to all police bureaus, along with a great deal of technical and professional training for the interrogation procedure. This can help expedite, professionalize, and standardize rape case processing by police institutions. The sample contains a description of the procedure but also provides special reminders to police officers to make note of the emotional reaction of the victim in the records, in order to provide an accurate account of the victim.

Specialization of Local Prevention Centers and Establishment of Resource Networks

1. Designate a local domestic violence and rape prevention center to be used as a coordinating center for this project and then execute the original rape victim report system. After receiving telephone or fax reports from an associated institution, the designated personnel shall be permanently responsible for that particular case and interview the victim onsite. During this interview, the designated personnel shall provide emotional support, evaluate the victim's circumstances, and suggest a suitable time for interrogation. In addition, the personnel should give special consideration to the special needs of the victim and assist in contacting professional individuals to aid in the interrogation (lawyer, special education teacher, child psychiatrist, psychiatrist, or sign language interpreter) or transfer the case to specialized services.
2. To help resolve the burden on human resources in prevention centers, each area designated for project implementation should establish a specialized task force. For example, Taipei has hired additional personnel to be on call during non-office hours, including holidays and night hours. Moreover, personnel are responsible for making interview logs during the interviews of rape victims and then submitting these logs to the designated social worker for processing. In Hualien, because of its narrow area of jurisdiction and inconvenient transportation, social workers have to be separated by district. In addition, because of Hualien's long-term, relatively stable work force, police officers and social workers have begun to work in fixed teams during their interactions.

Laptop Computers, Wireless Communication Devices, and Vaginal Microscopic Cameras

1. The financial aid provided by the Ministry of Interior helps implementation districts purchase necessary equipment, such as laptop computers, wireless video/audio transmission systems, video

meeting systems, and digital camcorders and audio recorders, thus facilitating communication and collaboration during case processing.

2. After the passing of the Law of Control and Prevention of Sex Violation, the Department of Health has cooperated by improving the specialization of medical institutions during victim injury examination and evidence-gathering operations in sexual assault cases. The 157 specialized rape prevention hospitals in the Taiwan, Penghu, and Kinmen/Mazu areas help in the injury examination, evidence gathering, and medical treatment process in sexual assault cases. After project implementation, the number of designated personnel from each specialized medical facility was increased (social workers or nurses) to help victims receive medical attention, consult various hospital departments, and provide a hospitable, discrete medical environment. It is also recommended that the vaginal microscopic camera systems be used in the recording process as reference for the courts.

A Communication System for All Institutions, Government-Associated and Otherwise

At the beginning of this project, the Ministry of Interior held a deliberation meeting and invited representatives from each associated central government institution, including the Criminal Assembly (Judicial Yuan), the Youth and Domestic Service Assembly, the Ministry of Justice, the Department of Health (Executive Yuan), the Ministry of National Defense, the National Police Administration, local government representatives, and scholars. The purpose of this cross-departmental project meeting was to establish an open, free, multidisciplinary communication forum. Mutual understanding and trust was gradually established between the different institutions, focusing specifically on the victim of sexual assault cases. During these meetings, individuals hailing from different professional backgrounds listened to the opinions of others. As a result, police officers began to appreciate the efforts of social workers who provide psychological rehabilitation to victims, public prosecutors began to recognize the hard work put into evidence collection by police officers, and judges finally became cognizant of the unique nature of sexual assault cases and the effort put into them by the investigative teams. Meeting participants cast aside their personal interests and began to sincerely face the necessities of the cases at hand. Furthermore, they developed an awareness that their organization alone would not be sufficient to solve the various problems encountered by victims; opened their minds to the integration of medical institutions, social service institutions, police institutions, and prosecutor institutions; and became a model for cross-departmental integration in Taiwan.

Adding Military- and Youth-Related Sexual Assault Cases to the Project

There are different investigatory and review procedures for different types of defendants in the Taiwanese criminal prosecution system. For example, military-related cases are investigated by the military prosecutor's office and are submitted to a military court for review; youth (12–18 years of age) or child (under 12 years) cases are submitted to the youth court for review. As a result, this project cannot be applied to all victims in the same way. However, in an effort to offer complete project services, the Ministry of Interior gathered representatives from the Criminal Assembly (Judicial Yuan), the Youth and Domestic Service Assembly, the Ministry of Justice, the Department of Health (Executive Yuan), the Ministry of National Defense, the National Police Administration, and local domestic violence and rape prevention centers a year after the project first began implementation to comprise the phase-two project team, focused on the deliberation of military- and youth (child)-related case procedure. After three meetings, the team completed a revision of the "Project for Reducing Repeat Interrogation for Victims of Sexual Assault: Project Guidelines," and the Judicial Yuan drafted the "Project for Reducing Repeat Interrogation for Victims of Sexual Assault: Young Court Investigatory Matters." These were implemented in the military court and prosecuting systems starting on February on 15, 2003. Youth courts also began implementation in areas designated for project implementation.

Specialized Resources and Flexible Interrogation Schedules

As described above, rape case sentencing is largely dependent on the testimonies of victims or witnesses; however, in cases in which the victims are children or mentally challenged individuals, the language ability of the victim is rather limited. Likewise, there are no special procedures for the questioning of these witnesses by police officers or public prosecutors. This can make the procedure exceedingly difficult, and can even produce repeated or unclear testimonies, thus limiting case processing, and can be damaging to the victim. The "Project for Reducing Repeat Interrogation for Victims of Sexual Assault: Project Guidelines" specifically states that social workers shall evaluate the physical and psychological condition of the victim during an initial interview. If the victim has any special needs, they shall actively request assistance from specialists, for example, a special education teacher, a sign language interpreter, or a child psychologist. This project is very different from the old system in which the victim was immediately interrogated. In this project, the interrogation time is scheduled based on various requirements.

Examination, Thoughts, and Challenges of the Executor

Aside from the changes and challenges inherent in this project that were discussed previously, perhaps an even greater impact comes from changes in the value system, attitude, and mindset of the project executors. I personally have worked in the police profession for more than 10 years and am very aware of the great importance of traditional investigatory procedure in criminal investigations, not to mention that time efficiency and eliminating crime have been two core principles of police institutions for a very long time. Although the nature of sexual assault has been listed as one of the six types of violent crimes, also including murder, theft, robbery, kidnapping for ransom, and threatening others for the purpose of attaining wealth, the frontline police officers seem to lack training and education in the special nature of sexual assault or psychological condition of the victim (such as posttraumatic stress syndrome). Also, as a result of the traditional Chinese precepts that sexual assault cases are unlucky, there exists a psychological resistance to such cases, thus resulting in investigators who are very slow to advance in their professional training in this area. Because of this, we faced a lot of resistance during our initial promotion of this project. Other than this, the biggest challenge came from convincing administrators that empathizing with the victims can actually motivate them to cooperate with court investigations and increase their satisfaction with the legal system, thereby increasing the number of solved cases, as well as prosecution and conviction rates. This is why we have maintained from the beginning that project evaluation is an invaluable aspect of project implementation. This is why we have so much data with which to convince policy makers.

To ensure the smooth promotion of this project, the Domestic Violence and Sexual Assault Rape Prevention Committee hired the Modern Women's Association to conduct training, monitoring, and evaluation. To a certain degree, this also deepened the frontline workers' understanding of the project vision: to protect the rights of the weak, strengthen the confidence of advocators from each institution, and improve the integrated network relationships of different institutions through interaction and project implementation, thereby empowering their work and strengthening project foundations.

During the three years that the project has been implemented, we have seen police officers and public prosecutors become more compassionate. They have learned how to listen: the victim is not just a testifier in a criminal case, but she is a person who has been physically and psychologically traumatized. These individuals are not able to cast aside all outside influences in the judicial process and provide the victim with complete protection and care, however, they have started to integrate social work into their tasks. There are even some police officers who, in the victim's best interest, have actively sought out social workers to assist with finding accommodations or outside counseling for a victim. The committee has continued to provide training and integrated network classes and has required the National Police Administration to implement professional specialization and increase the specialization of female police officers in sexual assault cases, such that women can have an important role in current criminal law regulations. Many prosecutors and judges have observed that police officers who have undergone specialized training show both depth and credibility in the logs created following samples from this project. In cases in which there are inconsistencies, possibly for a variety of reasons, the police log can be considered as evidence and used by the court.

In their integrated network investigatory work during rape cases, public prosecutors make exchanges with different institutions and develop a lot of social-worker-type ideals. Because of this, they are able to win the confidence of police officers and begin to take control over the investigatory timetable right from the very start. This enables prosecutors and police officers to coordinate seamlessly in the investigation, thus making the victim the winner in the big picture.

Social workers also benefits from their close interaction with prosecutors and police officers. This can help them to see things from a legal perspective, as well as teach them to strive for efficient evidence collection and injury examination, learn to pay attention to the legal effects of testimony, and let the evidence do the talking. In addition, the specialized medical treatment, the role of nurses in injury examination, and evidence collection from this project have also helped medical institutions to become a part of the rape prevention network. All aspects of this system accommodate the needs of the victim, whether because of their hospitable, safe locations, or their sophisticated medical equipment.

However, the people benefiting most from this project are ourselves, the authors. This is because each time the project is implemented in a new area, each time we have a new participant, all of our previous effort is erased, and we must restart negotiations, fight for recognition, create a working consensus, and motivate each new center to fight for our ideals. In addition, one must constantly face people's doubts and resistance to change. However, the thing that has been the most difficult for us was the lack of funding and human resources. We thought about quitting on many occasions, but, in the end, this is not just an ordinary project. In fact, it was our vision to create a friendly legal environment that kept us going when the times got tough. We kept telling ourselves that setbacks are an unavoidable part of this cause, that others' doubt and resistance are just tests of our convictions. The lack of funding and manpower really helped to demonstrate our problem-solving ability.

We also learned patience and flexibility with our positive thinking, and our problems started to gradually be resolved. After grueling brainstorming, even the most difficult funding problem was solved using three different methods of government-based financial aid, appropriated reward money, and the revised "Ministry of Interior Social Welfare Expansion Services: Financial Aid Application Items and Standards."

Conclusion

Through the toil and suffering we experienced promoting this project through its infancy, childhood, and maturity, we were able to develop a deep understanding of the victim in sexual assault cases. What we really care about is not how many times they are questioned, but rather, how are they treated throughout the entire process? Do they receive support and assistance? Is a friendly, hospitable environment provided?

This project is still currently being promoted. Having its own lifecycle, the most exciting facet of the project is the integration of workers who are willing to establish a platform of truth through trial and error, conflicts, communication, and understanding. With this, the victims can sincerely address their own feelings, search for solutions, and motivate each other to grow in this dynamic process.

From 2001 to 2004, the plan was already implemented in 13 counties and cities, which is more than half of the number of government-regulated cities and counties in Taiwan.[2] We know that there is still room for improvement, but we shall continue to consider and solve different problems that can occur as a result of the different backgrounds, duties, and locations of project executors.

Looking back on this experience, we find that people are the most important factor in implementing a project and also the biggest asset to the project. The project is based on taking care of the workers so that they can stay motivated on their work and give their best effort. We have found that addressing the secondary impact of workers and helping avoid the exhaustion caused by the environment and job requirements shall be an area to focus our efforts in the future.

Of course, we also have to consider the following. How do we lobby for support from the judicial system? How can we obtain more specialized social worker and police manpower? How should we face the impact of the criminal court interrogation system on victims? These are some of the challenges inherent in this project, and, although we do not know how far it can go, we know which direction to take it. However, we are confident that it will have a chance to develop during its implementation, and we recognize that we have to keep persisting if we want to see changes in the system. We shall diligently make the necessary continued changes to the project along the way and do our best to protect the rights of disadvantaged individuals within the court system. "Protecting women and children from criminal sexual exploitation is an insurance to a humane society and a better posterity" (Ebbe 2008).

Notes

1. Hidden violations refer to sexual violations that were covered up after they occurred.
2. The Taiwan area refers to 25 government-regulated cities and counties in areas including Taipei City, Kaohsiung, Kinmen, and Mazu.

References

Amir, M. 1971. *Patterns in Forcible Rape*. Chicago: University of Chicago Press.

Bi-Hui, L. 1992. "Study of Integrated Social Security System in Taipei City Districts." Master's thesis, Dongwu University.

Can-Huai, W. 2001. *Study of the Utilization of the Reaction of Traumatized Sexual Assault Victims on the Judicial System*. Taipei: National Central University.

Ching-Li, C. 1997. "Difficulties and Directions for Sexual Assault Prevention." *Police Studies Journal* 2(3):1–13.

Ching-Li, C. 2000. *Integration and Evaluation of Personal Safety Resources for Women*. Special Publication from the National Women's Personal Safety Meeting. Taipei: Women's Rights Promotion Coalition, pp. 99–106.

Ching-Li, C., and Mei-Xun, L. 2003. "Project for Reducing Repeat Interrogation for Victims of Sexual Assault: Project Handbook." Taipei: Ministry of Interior.

Chun-Jin, X. 2000. "Investigatory of Criminal Experiment in the Taipei Area." Taipei: Ministry of Justice, National Police Administration, and Ministry of Interior.

Chun-Jin, X., and Chuan-Zhen, M. 1992. "Study of Types of Sexual Assault Criminals and Characteristics of Victim Personality." Taipei: Taipei City Research, Development, and Evaluation Commission.

Chun-Jin, X., and Chuan-Zhen, M. 1999. "Investigatory Study of Sexual Assault Circumstances in the Taipei Area." Taipei: Ministry of Interior.

Criminal Investigation Bureau, National Police Administration. 1997–2003. *Crime Statistics*. Taipei: Detective Bureau.

Domestic Violence and Sexual Assault Prevention Committee, Ministry of Interior. 1999. "Sexual Assault Prevention Worker Service Manual." Taipei: Ministry of Interior, pp. 12–18.

Domestic Violence and Sexual Assault Prevention Committee, Ministry of Interior. 2000. "Project for Reducing Repeat Interrogation for Victims Of Sexual Assault: Interrogation Videotape." Taipei: Ministry of Interior.

Domestic Violence and Sexual Assault Prevention Committee, Ministry of Interior. 2001a. "Project for Reducing Repeat Interrogation for Victims of Sexual Assault: Final Evaluative Report of Preliminary Project Implementation." Taipei: Ministry of Interior.

Domestic Violence and Sexual Assault Prevention Committee, Ministry of Interior. 2001b. "Project for Reducing Repeat Interrogation for Victims of Sexual Assault: Minutes of the Preliminary Project Implementation Evaluative Meeting." Taipei: Ministry of Interior.

Ebbe, O. N. I. 2008. "Control and Prevention of Trafficking in Women and Children." In *Global Trafficking in Women and Children*, edited by O. N. I. Ebbe and D. K. Das. Boca Raton, FL: CRC Press/Taylor & Francis Group.

Fu-Yuan, H. 2000. *Police Officers and Female Victims*. Taipei: Xin-Di-Wen.

Groth, A. N. 1979. *Men Who Rape*. New York: Plenum.

Guo-Yong, F. 2000. "Analysis of the Trauma Caused by Criminal Proceedings Interrogation in Rape Victims." *Taoyuan: Law Enforcement Publication* 3(31): 69–95.

Holmes, R. M., and Holmes, S. T. 1996. *Profiling Violent Crimes*. Thousand Oaks, CA: Sage.

Jiao-Yu, S. 1995. "The Administrative Reconstruction and Service Interrogation in Children's Welfare Institutions." 21-Century Children's Welfare policy dissertation. Taipei: 21st Century Association and R.O.C. Children's Welfare Association.

Jin-Li, C. 1999. "Sexual Assault Prevention Measures: Overall Yearly Evaluation." *Social Establishment Quarterly* 99:65–68.

Li-Rong, W. 1999a. "Study of the Establishment of a Women's Protective Network." Taipei: Department of Social Affairs, Ministry of Interior.

Li-Rong, W. 1999b. "Evaluative Study of the Sexual Assault Prevention in the Taipei Area." Taipei: Department of Social Affairs, Ministry of Interior.

Martella, R. C., Nelson, R., and Marchand-Marelle, N. E. 1999. *Research Methods: Learning to Become a Critical Research Consumer*. Needham Heights, MA: Allyn and Bacon.

Modern Women's Foundation. 1998. "Who Will Believe Me?" Taipei: Modern Women's Foundation.

Modern Women's Foundation. 2002. "Rape Victim Personal Report." Taipei: Modern Women's Association.

Modern Women's Foundation. 2003. "Project for Reducing Repeat Interrogation for Victims of Sexual Assault." Taipei: Modern Women's Association.

Ping-Wu, C., Guo-Yong, F., and Fu-Yuan, H. 2002. *Criminology Dissertation*. Taipei: San-Min Bookstores.

Shu-Qiong, L. 2002. "Study of Domestic Violence Prevention System Attitudes in the Taiwan Area: Study of the Establishment of Domestic Operations in Local Governments and Establishment of a Multi-Disciplinary Resource Network." Taipei: Outsourced by the Ministry of Interior.

Su-Xian, Z. 2003. "Factual Study of the Factors Affecting the Court Investigations and Outcome of Independent Preventative Cases." Taipei: Ministry of Interior.

United Daily News. 2000. "The Horror of Sexual Assault Cases: Trial Implementation of Victim Interrogation Reduction." December 12, version 8.

Zhao-Rong, C. 1986. "Study of Social Service Delivery Systems in Taipei." Master's thesis, Dongwu University.

Zhi-Ling, X. 1998. "An Analysis of the Changing Role and Integration of Services in Non-Government Charity Organizations in Kaohsiung." Master's thesis, National Chi-Nan University.

16 Criminal Exploitation of Women and Children in the Kingdom of Bahrain

ANONYMOUS

Introduction

Bahraini women have proved themselves in public life, are influential, and have contributed to contemporary modernization efforts. Their participation in public service should be preserved and supported by all means possible. Any obstacles standing in the way of this progress should be removed, including the discouragement of women from carrying out criminal acts; otherwise, there may be a negative impact on future progress and development.

Children in the kingdom of Bahrain are fully supported both officially and privately; their rights, their care, protection, and assistance all receive high priority. This enables them to grow up in a healthy family atmosphere in which happiness, passion, and understanding prevail. Once in place, these conditions will create a useful generation, capable of facing all challenges and able to assume responsibility in their local community.

It is important that our women and children are protected from all types of criminal exploitation, not only at present but also in the future, and this can only be achieved through sound planning.

Women's Roles in Bahraini Society

Women throughout the world, and in varying degrees, have contributed to the construction of their societies, striving to reinforce the strong foundations of the society. Yet women's conditions in some societies are still deplorable, with potentials being blocked by prevailing values, customs, and notions. Despite that, women in Bahrain have succeeded in combating social restraints that prevailed for years, realizing their potential to embrace a broader world.

Researchers interested in women's issues would notice the tremendous role played by Bahraini women in changing the social reality in the kingdom and sharing with men the task of construction. Women have become noticeable players in social life, with their roles no longer limited to raising and educating children. Now, women work in all domains of civil and military fields both in the private and governmental sectors, assuming, in many cases, the highest administrative positions.

In the year 1943, women went out into public life assuming roles limited to teaching and nursing only. It was not until 1955 that women took community voluntary work, establishing the first women's association. Nowadays, there are 15 women's associations working in the area of social work, charity, and voluntary services.

In addition, women actively participate in a number of other voluntary organizations and associations. The Amiri Order issued in 2001 announced the establishment of the Supreme Council for Women (SCW), chaired by the kingdom's First Lady. Sixteen high-standing female figures, known for their experience in women's affairs, serve as members on the board. The SCW has a secretariat general and a secretary general at the rank of a minister. Since its establishment, the SCW has begun tackling women's causes resulting in the issuance of a number of positive decisions that cater to women, widows, widows' children, and divorcees. In addition, the SCW has also encouraged and honored Bahrain competent women, granting them medals. The council, headed by the First Lady, has also participated in a number of Arab and international women's conferences.

On March 2, 2002, His Majesty, King Hamad bin Isa Al Khalifa, issued Decree 5 for the year 2002, approving Bahrain's joining into an agreement on ending all types of discrimination against women, with reservations on a number of articles that are not in line with the principles of Islamic Shari'ah law. Among the articles approved by the kingdom was Art. 6, which stipulates "member countries have to take all suitable measures including legislation to combat all types of trading of women and exploiting them through prostitution".[1]

At the official level, women gained their rights in most of the social, economic, and cultural fields and recently in the political domain. They have gained the right to take part in elections and present their candidacy for municipal and legislative councils. Three women have also been appointed to the Consultative Council. However, women, notably in certain rural areas and some civil societies, have not gained their full rights, hence, the urgent need for activating Art. 5 of the agreement on combating all types of discrimination against women which dictates the following:

(1) Adjusting social and cultural norms of men's and women's conduct to curb all existing forms of antagonism between both sexes and preventing all practices based on inferiority or superiority of either sex or based on norms with respect to gender roles.
(2) Ensuring that each family's education has sound recognition and understanding of motherhood as a social occupation and recognizing men's and women's joint responsibility in raising and molding

children, making clear that children's welfare is the basic goal in all cases.

Children's Status in the Kingdom of Bahrain

Childhood in Bahrain receives utmost attention at both the official and nonofficial levels, covering aspects of physical and mental health, education, social care, and caring for children with special needs. Nevertheless, much more effort is needed along these areas to reach all of the children of the kingdom.

Mental and Physical Health

At the official level, the Kingdom of Bahrain has accorded special interest to a child's health before birth by providing a network of mother and child care centers at the health centers throughout the kingdom. These centers offer antenatal and postnatal care and provide children with vaccines and proper follow-up until the age of 18. The Health Ministry statistics indicate that free vaccines have been provided to 99 percent of the kingdom's children. For mentally ill children, the ministry has also built a special unit at the psychiatric hospital to treat and look after them on a day-to-day basis.[2]

Education

Children also receive the same degree of attention with regard to education, whereby the kingdom provides free education to both genders throughout the kingdom at all levels—primary, intermediate, and secondary. In addition, the ministry accords special concern for consistently developing children's curricula, introducing, for example, the subject of "child rights" as an integral part of the curricula. Moreover, the ministry embarked on the "future schools" project aiming at the gradual shift towards e-learning. According to official statistics, the majority of Bahraini children (92 percent) are registered at government and private schools.[3] However, a small percentage of these children are not privileged enough because of parental ignorance or turnover from schools. Laws should sanction compulsory education at all primary, intermediate, and secondary levels.

The private sector has given special attention to education as manifested through launching of kindergartens and private schools at the primary, secondary, and tertiary levels. These educational institutions cater to all sectors of the community, including national and different categories of expatriates. In addition, the private sector has recently established a number of new universities to operate alongside the University of Bahrain and the

Arabian Gulf University, which are under the supervision of the Ministry of Education.

Social Care

The kingdom's official and nonofficial bodies have strove to develop services devoted to children. At the official level, this was evident through His Majesty, King Hamad bin Isa Al Khalifa's initiative to grant monthly allowances to orphans and to have a follow-up committee to monitor them. In addition, children are subject to the social care provided by the Ministry of Education through its social workers appointed at all schools.

The Ministry of Education intends to improve on this aspect by increasing the number of social workers according to the student numbers at each school.

Similarly, the Ministry of Labor and Social Affairs provides social services to families through conducting a wide range of workshops to mothers. The intention of these workshops is to improve the educational and social awareness of these mothers, in the hope that this will positively reflect on their upbringing of their children and equip them with different productivity and vocational skills that will help them to boost family income. In addition, the Ministry of Labor and Social Affairs supervises "Dar Al Tifl," which caters to children of unknown parents as well as monitors and follows up with families adopting them.

The Ministry of the Interior also shares in providing children services through a number of establishments, such as the "Youth Social Care Unit," which conducts a comprehensive study of each minor's case before referral to the minors court. The ministry continues to follow up and assist the minor thereafter at home and school, even after the ruling of the corrective measure is issued.

The second establishment is the "Child Protection Bureau," which deals with all kinds of child abuse in collaboration with a number of other authorities in the country, providing help to children to overcome hardship and minimize the effects of the assault as much as possible.

The third establishment is the "Youth Care Center." It is the last resort for children; it hosts them after all other measures fail, and this measure is regarded as in the best interest of the child. The center provides children with social, health, educational, vocational, and recreational services in addition to social programs that keep the minors in continuous contact with society and their families.

One of the most significant aspects of the kingdom's concern for children is the formation of the Childhood National Committee in 1999 to develop all aspects pertaining to a child's life. The kingdom's Second Lady accords a personal interest in childhood through encouraging and patronizing child-oriented festivals, exhibitions, and creative competitions in all fields.

The private sector has also played an important role in this domain, reflected in the inauguration of kindergartens and playgroups all over the kingdom and establishing children's societies such as "The Future Children and Youth Society," which has the following objectives:

(1) Unify youth's potential and deploy their efforts through voluntary work to serve other youth and children, as well as discussing their problems and raising awareness of their rights and working toward implementing them.
(2) Contribute to helping children or youth express their opinions, provide constructive criticism, express themselves during discussions, and respect the opinions of others.
(3) Build the child's or youth's personality by providing correct personalized directions to develop individual talents.

The "Bahrain Society for Childhood Development" has similarly adopted a new operational strategy that concentrates on a number of objectives most pressing in terms of childhood issues. The society has prioritized these objectives in such a way as to enable it to concentrate its efforts on achieving high-quality results for each objective separately and in a particular year. Hence, the society is currently focusing on child rights and child abuse, followed by employment of minors.

Care of Children with Special Needs

The government and the private sector have shown concern for this category of children with special needs, manifested in establishing specialized institutes and societies. Such an institute is the "rehabilitation center." This falls under the Ministry of Labor and Social Affairs and provides services to moderately and severely handicapped individuals. Moreover, "Al Amal Institute" falls under "Mother and Childhood Society" and caters to mild handicaps. In addition, there are other specialized institutes, such as "Al Amal Institute for the Blind," "Shaikhan Al Farisi Institute for the Deaf and Dumb," and "Down Syndrome Society."

Despite all that, there is still much more to be done to serve the different categories of children with special needs and to protect them from exploitation and ill treatment.

Legal Protection of Children

Children could be abused by older individuals because of their young age or physical weakness and lack of experience. This danger of abuse could be harmful to the extent that it is regarded as a crime, with the child as the victim. The law has guaranteed legal protection for victims through a set of articles that incriminate a large number of child-targeted acts. Bahraini penal law contains a number of articles that aim at protecting the victim, whether a child or an adult. Child protection is ensured through child-specific laws and other related laws that could be applicable to children.

Given the number and diversity of crimes that a child faces, which cover life-, physical-, and honor-threatening crimes as well as inciting for prostitution and acts of kidnapping, the Bahraini penal law has strove to combat these crimes, stipulating appropriate penalties for each.

The Kingdom of Bahrain has signed child rights agreements, participated in developing the Arab Child Charter of the Arab League, and adopted these principles and regulations to form the basis for its policies and regulations in the area of childhood development. The charter comprises 48 articles constituting the charter's general regulations and basic rights of the Arab child, delineating these rights and objectives of implementation. However, this charter, similar to other charters, was general in nature and did not address children's legal protection in detail. Rather, it has mentioned them within the overall basic rights, common security, and the kingdom's insurance and protection of these rights through child protection from physical neglect and exploitation. In addition, the charter aims at ensuring legislative protection of these rights, with a child's interest being the top priority in all cases.[4]

The Kingdom of Bahrain, under the umbrella of the Arab League participated in drafting the child's civil and family rights of the Arab Child Charter, which also contains a special chapter on protecting the endangered child against sexual, physical, and economic exploitation in addition to their deployment in begging or trading in drugs. As stipulated in Art. 8–10 of the same chapter, one intermediary or more, depending on the need, should be appointed at each gubernatorial district and be sworn in before the king to protect children. These intermediaries are given the duty of preventive intervention when it becomes clear that a child's physical and mental health are at risk as a result of activities or tasks that he undertakes or those imposed on him by the environment or as a result of any sort of abuse. The intermediary should look into the child's situation, determine the threats, and take the most appropriate action. Art. 11–13 addresses the issue of observation and notification, whereas Art. 14–19 deals with protection mechanisms.

The kingdom has devoted attention to the issue of childhood. This is also manifested in the issuance of Decree 12 for the year 2001, approving Bahrain's joining of the World Labor Organization Agreement 182 for the year 1999 on forbidding the worst types of child labor and immediate eradication of existing violations.[5] In the third article of this agreement, the term "worst types of child labor" is described as follows:

(1) All kinds of slavery and similar practices such as trading in and selling children, serfs, religious-based slavery, compulsory work including forced or compulsory military services, and deployment of children in armed conflicts
(2) Use of children and their exposition to prostitution purposes
(3) Exploitation of children in illegal activities, notably the production of drugs as specified by related international conventions
(4) Jobs that, as a result of the nature of work conditions, represent a hazard to children's health, safety, and moral conduct

Finally, it is worthwhile mentioning the Youth's Law 17 for the year 1976, which allocates a full chapter on child protection against delinquency, in such cases in which the child is found to be begging, selling trivial goods, escaping from school, being disobedient to his parents, accompanying suspects, being present in whoredom or gambling areas, living on roadsides or places not deemed appropriate, wandering in the absence of a trustworthy caretaker, suffering from a physical or mental illness that might deem his own life and that of others at risk, or rendering him exposed for exploitation.

Criminal Exploitation of Women

One cannot state that there is a problem with regard to criminal exploitation of women in the Kingdom of Bahrain because of the following reasons:

(1) The relatively small size of the kingdom in addition to its small population (700,000)
(2) Strong adherence to Islamic values and Arab customs and traditions that dictate caring for female children and females in general, in which the family takes special attention to follow up on indoor and outdoor activities of its daughters and provide them with the necessary protection against being involved in criminal activities
(3) Bahraini women's adherence to local customs and tradition and avoidance of being involved in suspicious deeds that may degrade their social status

However, during the past few years, it has been noticed that more women are exploited or are involved in criminal activities. This is a result of the increased number of expatriate women from different nationalities who come to Bahrain to work in various fields, such as maids, nannies, or cooks, or as part of global whoredom networks.

Based on women's police reports at the different directorates, it is clear that women are being exploited in the areas of prostitution and begging.

The statistics in Table 16.1 indicate the number of women involved in prostitution from 2000 to 2003.

Table 16.1 indicates that most of the women involved in prostitution are non-Bahrainis, with the percentage of Bahraini women in prostitution not exceeding 21.6 percent in 2000, 11.7 percent in 2001, 3.3 percent in 2002, and 5.2 percent in 2003.[6]

Some of the immigrant women involved in these cases enter Bahrain as part of global whoredom networks under the cover of tourism. Others enter the kingdom as housemaids or governesses who get exploited later in prostitution by these networks. It is worthwhile to note that the number of women working in households in Bahrain reached 21,921 in the year 2001. In addition, a number of these women, mostly non-Bahrainis, have been caught enticing other women to practice prostitution, as shown in Table 16.2.

Table 16.3 shows that the number of women accused of running brothels is relatively low, with the majority being non-Bahrainis. Yet international

Table 16.1 Statistics on Women's Prostitution from 2000 to 2003

Year	Number of Female Cases Indicted	Number of Females Arrested	Nationalities		
			Citizens	Arabs	Foreigners
2000	113	231	50	25	156
2001	151	357	42		315
2002	145	295	10		285
2003	47	116	6	5	105

Table 16.2 Statistics on Women Inciting Others for Prostitution from 2000 to 2003

Year	Number of Female Cases Indicted	Number of Females Arrested	Nationalities		
			Citizens	Arabs	Foreigners
2000	17	20	4	5	11
2001	15	15	6		9
2002	13	13	1		12
2003	4	4			4

Table 16.3 Statistics on Cases of Brothels Run by Women from 2000 to 2003

Year	Number of Female Cases Indicted	Number of Females Arrested	Nationalities		
			Citizens	Arabs	Foreigners
2000	1	3			3
2001	6	6	3		3
2002	5	5			5
2003	2	4	3		1

Table 16.4 Statistics on Cases of Begging among Women from 2000 to 2003

Year	Number of Female Cases Indicted	Number of Females Arrested	Nationalities		
			Citizens	Arabs	Foreigners
2000	6	7	5	2	
2001	10	14	9		5
2002	23	39	20	9	10
2003	5	8		8	

Source: Bahraini Police Annual Report, 2003.

Table 16.5 Distribution of Women in Bahrain According to Nationality from 2000 to 2003

Year	Bahraini	Non-Bahraini	Total
2000	125,754	58,209	183,963
2001	129,217	60,253	189,469
2002	132,377	62,091	194,468
2003	136,369	63,869	200,238

Source: Bahraini Police Annual Report, 2003.

whoredom networks use small motels to run their businesses, whereby the women involved get caught in most of the cases but not the networks employing them because the majority of these are based outside the Kingdom of Bahrain and remain unknown.

Another form of women's exploitation in Bahrain is in the form of beggary. Arab and non-Arab women enter the kingdom, under the umbrella of tourism, to beg for the benefit of gangs, although some Bahraini women beggars practice beggary at an individual level, without being instigated by any outsiders.

The previous tables indicate the small number of women involved in cases of prostitution and beggary compared with the total number of women in the kingdom during the same period. It is noteworthy that statistics here cover women aged 15 and above.

Despite the fact that exploitation of women in criminal acts constitutes but a relatively small problem, this phenomenon is not being given enough attention. Hence, in addition to the initiatives taken by the security authorities to track and capture individuals red handed, the Kingdom of Bahrain needs to pass laws to control entry into the kingdom for criminal purposes before this problem worsens.

Criminal Exploitation of Children

As is the case with criminal exploitation of women, criminal exploitation of children in the Kingdom of Bahrain is very limited for reasons that are similar to those limiting the exploitation of women in this respect. The reasons are as follow:

(1) The relatively small size of the kingdom coupled with its small population
(2) Strong family ties and close adherence to Islamic and Arab values and traditions in the upbringing of children, including the keenness of expatriate families to care for and devote full attention to their children
(3) International networks not being involved in children's exploitation in the kingdom

Cases of child exploitation are limited to theft, sexual abuse, and delinquency-related issues that lead to begging, accompanying suspects, and committing acts related to prostitution. Theft is considered to be the main child exploitation area, whereby arrested young thieves lead to adult partners who instigated them to commit such violations because it is difficult to suspect or arrest children. Children are also used to get through narrow hatches to open doors from the inside and are used for surveillance during theft and burglary.

As indicated in Table 16.6, the majority of children involved in such cases are Bahraini male children. This is attributable to the fact that girls rarely frequent public places without being accompanied by parents, which minimizes the chances of their exploitation in thefts.

With regard to non-Bahraini children, it is rare that they get involved in such cases because of the close supervision and care provided by their families at home in Bahrain.

Suspects and individuals with previous criminal records resort to different methods to exploit children in criminal acts. They entice and encourage homeless children, school dropouts, and children who suffer from family problems to commit criminal acts either through training and using them to commit criminal acts or by sexually abusing them, relying on their immaturity, small size, and their need for care irrespective of the means.

Table 16.6 Statistics on Theft Cases among Youths from 2000 to 2003

		Number of Delinquent Youths		Nationalities					
				Citizens		Arabs		Foreigners	
Year	Number of Cases	Males	Females	Males	Females	Males	Females	Males	Females
2000	49	74		71				3	
2001	84	137	6	134	6	3			
2002	74	124	6	112	5	3	1	9	
2003	90	153	3	151	3	1		1	

Despite the existence of such cases in the kingdom, the cases that get recorded are few and only generally occur when the gang gets captured or when the involved child gets caught red-handed.

Table 16.7 indicates the number of children who got caught in the company of suspects. It is noted that these numbers are very small, with the majority being Bahrainis and females in particular who accompany women with previous criminal records.

There are cases of prostitution-related acts, in which the majority are female children living with their prostitute mothers and are being exploited in supervision or prostitution-related issues. Their numbers are also very small, as indicated in Table 16.8.

Table 16.9 indicates the total number of children who have been sexually assaulted during the same period (2000–2003). It is noticed that the most targeted age group is 9–14 years, followed by the age group of 6–8 years.[7] The majority of these children are Bahrainis because of the aforementioned reasons.

Another area of child exploitation is beggary, whereby needy families prompt their male and female children to beg in crowded places and out of parental sight. Through the continuous follow-up provided to these children,

Table 16.7 Statistics on Cases of Youths' Association with Suspects from 2000 to 2003

		Number of Delinquent Youths		Nationalities					
				Citizens		Arabs		Foreigners	
Year	Number of Cases	Males	Females	Males	Females	Males	Females	Males	Females
2000	1		1		1				
2001	6	5	3	5	3				
2002	1		1		1				
2003	1		1		1				

Table 16.8 Statistics on Prostitution-Related Cases among Youths Subject to Delinquency from 2000 to 2003

		Number of Delinquent Youths		Nationalities					
				Citizens		Arabs		Foreigners	
Year	Number of Cases	Males	Females	Males	Females	Males	Females	Males	Females
2000									
2001	1		1						1
2002									
2003	1		1				1		

Table 16.9 Number of Sexually Assaulted Children from 2000 to 2003

	Number of Child Victims												Nationalities							
	Less than 6 years		6–8 years		9–11 years		12–14 years		15 years		Total		Citizen		Arabs		Foreigners		Total	
Years	M	F	M	F	M	F	M	F	M	F	M	F	M	F	M	F	M	F	M	F
2000	1	4	6	2	18	4	13	4	2	2	40	16	37	12	2	2	1	2	40	16
2001	1		10	1	20		9	1		3	40	5	38	5	1		1		40	5
2002	1	1	4		5	1	10	1	1	2	21	5	20	4			1	1	21	5
2003	2	5	9	4	21	2	27	16	1	5	60	32	58	30		2	2		60	32

M, Males; F, Females.

Table 16.10 Statistics on Begging Cases among Youths Subject to Delinquency from 2000 to 2003

		Number of Delinquent Youths		Nationalities					
				Citizens		Arabs		Foreigners	
Year	Number of Cases	Males	Females	Males	Females	Males	Females	Males	Females
2000	2	2		2					
2001	1		2		2				
2002	12	5	7	5	7				
2003	4	3	2	3	1		1		

it has been revealed that the family prompts girls to beg until the age of 14, when they get them married, and then their younger sisters, usually around seven years of age, take their places along with the other sisters and brothers. Because of these conditions, the children become subject to sexual assault and to instigation for crime.

The statistics in Table 16.10 indicate the number of youths found begging during the period from 2000 to 2003. However, I believe that these numbers do not reflect the real size of the problem because most of the children try hard to avoid police patrols.

The total number of male and female children aged 4–15 years in 2001 was 130,310; 114,741 in 2002; and 138,274 in 2003.

Recommendations

Through the police records data reported in this study, it is noted that criminal exploitation of women and children in the Kingdom of Bahrain is not a very large problem in relation to the population size. However, this does not necessarily mean that it should not be taken seriously but rather should be given enough attention to avoid future aggravation. The tremendous technological advancement has transformed the world into a big village and has paved the way for diverse criminal phenomena. This necessitates increased awareness and readiness to combat crimes of all types.

Punishment for those exploiting women and children in criminal acts should be made very severe and should be made severer in cases of exploitation of children.

Finally, there is a need to conduct a detailed study of the problem and reach a solution to alleviate, or possibly, totally curb it, in addition to studying the modus operandi of the criminals and train national security agencies to confront them with advanced technological tools.

Notes

1. *Official Gazette*, Issues 2465–2502 and 2520–2555.
2. Bahrain Childhood Development, *Childhood Magazine*.
3. Bahrain Sociologists Society, "Women and Social Change in Bahrain."
4. Arab Child Charter, draft.
5. Child Rights Agreement and two optional protocols.
6. Women's Police Directorate statistics.
7. Central Statistics Bureau statistics.

Commercial Sexual Exploitation of Children in Mexico

17

ELENA AZAOLA

Introduction

As in many other countries, the sexual exploitation of children for commercial purposes is not a new phenomenon in Mexico. It has, however, largely escaped notice, and it was barely a few years ago, mainly as a result of the World Congress of 1996 and the visit to the country by the United Nations Rapporteur on the subject in 1997, that it is now being given certain attention (Calcetas-Santos 1998; End Child Prostitution in Asian Tourism 2000). Indeed, there are no official statistics providing information about the number of children who are victims of sexual exploitation, and only a few studies on the subject have been performed by the small number of specialists who have shown an interest in it (Espacios de Desarrollo Integral 1996; Azaola 1998; Pérez Duarte 1998; Negrete 2000).

The results given here, therefore, constitute one of the first attempts that exist to focus on the phenomenon at a national level based on original data from primary sources obtained in seven towns of the Mexican Republic and secondary sources for the rest of the country. The study in Mexico refers to the four types of commercial sexual exploitation of children commonly recognized by international agencies: prostitution, trafficking, pornography, and sex tourism.[1]

It should be noted that Mexico has only recently introduced laws that expressly prohibit this type of exploitation of children.[2] Until 1999, this behavior could only be prosecuted through very vague legal categories such as "corruption of minors" or "aggravated procuring." The first covers a wide range of behaviors and aggressions against children that do not necessarily take into account the specific damage inflicted on children when they are sexually exploited. The second refers to the sexual exploitation of others when the victim is under 18 years old.

Objectives

The general objectives of the study performed in Mexico were the same as those proposed for the North American region and include the following: (1) to learn about the nature, extent, and causes of the commercial sexual exploitation of children; (2) to understand more completely the mixture of social, political, economic, and cultural factors that intervene in the phenomenon, that drive adults to have sexual relations with children, and that explain why children become involved in this type of activity; (3) to identify the recruitment patterns and the transportation of children from one region to another within the country and from or to neighboring countries; and (4) to collaborate with the authorities to strengthen their capacity to confront the problem more effectively and offer greater protection to children.

Our way of approaching the subject attempts to take into account the different parties involved without which it is not possible to explain that the phenomenon exists and continues to reproduce itself: clients, intermediaries, exploiters, and children. Our main interest centered, on the one hand, on obtaining as much information as possible about the children who are being exploited and their different circumstances depending on the type of establishment exploiting them and, on the other, on the procedures and modes of recruitment used by the intermediaries and exploiters. We also tried to obtain an overview of the services that the children are receiving and those required for them to be given adequate care.

Methodology

The study was conducted between August 1999 and February 2002. The methodology included the use of various research techniques and procedures of both quantitative and qualitative type. Emphasis was given to the use of primary sources given the paucity of information on the subject in Mexico, the lack of official data or statistics, and the few specialized studies.

Seven towns were selected in the Mexican Republic in which the study was conducted: Acapulco, Cancún, Ciudad Juarez, Guadalajara, Mexico City, Tapachula, and Tijuana. Different criteria motivated the selection of these towns, including the fact that they are (1) the main tourist destinations (Cancún and Acapulco), (2) the most important urban zones (Mexico City and Guadalajara), and (3) the main border areas (Tijuana and Ciudad Juarez to the north and Tapachula to the south).

With the support of the national and local authorities of the System for Integral Family Development, a group of key informants was formed that participated in focus groups that were held in each of the towns or were interviewed individually. The key informants that were interviewed belong to the following sectors: (1) public institutions providing assistance and protection to children; (2) legal and law enforcement institutions; (3) health institutions; (4) human rights institutions; and (5) nongovernment organizations providing assistance and protection to children. One hundred twelve child victims of sexual exploitation were interviewed. When possible, interviews were held in depth to try to understand both their personal and family situation before becoming involved in sexual exploitation and their situation at the time of the interview, recruitment, and migration patterns, to name a few. In all cases, special care was taken to respect their silence and protect their identity.

The data relative to recruitment patterns and modes of operating of the exploiters were obtained from the testimonies of both children and adult women who had been initiated into prostitution when they were children. Some law enforcement authorities also permitted us to consult files and hold interviews with exploiters who were in prison.

The number of children we estimated as being exploited must be considered as an approximation because, in a strict sense, it is not possible to keep accounts of the phenomenon as a result of its clandestine, illegal character.

Results

Historically, some types of sexual exploitation have prevailed in Mexico and still occur more frequently than others. In effect, cases have always been known about, particularly girls involved in prostitution, as well as boys and girls that have been sold, stolen, or exchanged and taken to other places in Mexico or abroad. Although, in general, these tendencies hold true for the whole country, there are specific features in each zone, as we shall see below.

Among the factors that foment commercial sexual exploitation of children in Mexico, the following should be mentioned: weak application of the norms; violence, ill treatment, and sexual abuse of children that is widely disseminated and frequently tolerated; deterioration of conditions, quality, and life expectations of wide sectors of the population during the past few years; migration and emigration of members of the family with the subsequent lack of stability and changes in the nuclear family; alcoholism of the parents and a growing drug consumption among the children; abandonment or expulsion of children from the family and an increase in the number of children living or working on the streets; incorporation of broad contingents into the informal sector of the economy; existence of organized networks for the recruitment, trafficking, and sexual exploitation of children; and corruption of police bodies and participation of the same in organized crime networks.

Diversity among Exploited Children

One of the findings that seem most significant to us is that the study made it possible to visualize the complexity of the phenomenon as it refers to boys and girls who are facing different situations because of the type of sexual exploitation they are experiencing, the places where they offer their services, or the way in which they are recruited and the procedures used to retain them. In an attempt to systemize the data we collected, we found that it is possible to group the differences we found into 10 central aspects.

The 10 central aspects, or pairs of opposites, that allow us to establish differences in the situation faced by the exploited children are as follows:

- They live in the streets./They live in enclosed spaces.
- They live with their families./They do not live with their families.
- They have exploiters./They do not have exploiters.
- They work in places expressly dedicated to the sex trade./They work in places where the sex trade is carried out in a covert way.
- They are recruited by procurers or by the exploiters themselves under pressure or false pretenses./They are recruited without pressure or false pretenses.
- They can leave or change their place of work./They are retained in their places of work against their will.
- Their exploiters are Mexicans./Their exploiters are foreigners.
- Most of their clients are Mexicans./Most of their clients are foreigners.
- They are exploited in the locality where they were born or where their families live./They are exploited in different places from the one in which they were born or where their families live.
- Their clients are of a different biological sex./Their clients are of the same biological sex.

Although we were able to identify 25 groups or categories of girls and boys who are being exploited from the combination of variables given above, we found that most of the children could be included in three groups:

(1) Boys and girls who are subject to any type of commercial sexual exploitation and who live in the streets and/or offer their services preponderantly in the streets.
(2) Boys and girls who are sexually exploited in different places where they offer their sexual services in a more or less recognized or open way (hotels, boarding houses, bars, nightclubs, and brothels).
(3) Girls and boys who offer their sexual services in a covert way in establishments that have other recognized purposes (snack bars, restaurants, massage parlors, beauty parlors, modeling agencies, and escort agencies).

Even within these groups, it is possible to find girls and boys whose living conditions are very different. The lowest rung is always that of boys and girls who live on the street and offer their services in the public thoroughfare, some doing so occasionally to be able to survive and others recurrently as a type of self-employment. The next rung up is that of the children who work in small restaurants, beer shops, or snack bars, where they provide their sexual services in a concealed way, generally in a warehouse or adjoining room that the owner of the premises uses as a way to obtain additional income. They are generally premises in poor conditions, with little hygiene and without the children having access to educational or health services.

In most of the cases, the girls have been taken under false pretenses to work as waitresses and are gradually obliged to provide sexual services with persuasion that can go from threats and blows to more subtle but equally effective ways that include seduction, a relationship as partner of the exploiters who may or may not be identified by the children as their pimps.

At the other extreme, there are girls and boys who are employed in massage parlors, beauty salons, or escort or entertainment agencies that operate by phone or Internet. In these cases, the risk the adolescents are exposed to are less, because they generally have protection and are given medical care and the premises have better hygiene and safety conditions.

Between these two extremes, there is a very wide range of circumstances in which children provide sexual services, from boarding houses and small hotels to luxurious holiday centers, going through all types of nightclubs, bars, dance halls, canteens, and table dance venues. As is evident, the children who offer their services on the public thoroughfare are the most visible sector that can be identified at first sight. However, they are not the majority. The persons exploiting them often take great care to keep them hidden in such a way that their presence is not noticed, and they always prefer clients to approach the establishments where the children are closely supervised and controlled.

In most of the towns studied, the children come from the poorest municipalities or states that surround the town and from where they are taken with promises of being given a job in bars and restaurants. However, there are also occasions when they are taken to places more removed from their places of origin, and they may travel from one end of the country to another, just as they can be taken out of the country, mainly to the United States. It is also frequent that the person exploiting them take the children from one town to another or move them from one bar to another in the same town. It is evident that this way of operating has the objective of separating the children from their families and from other community ties that could offer them support and prevent this type of bond forming, if they should remain in one place for a long time.

Concerning this point, it is important to point out that we also found cases in which children go into the sex trade after having been recruited by some members of the family who work in this kind of business. In other cases, although the family does not participate directly, it can have an attitude of complicity in that they suspect that the income the child receives cannot be legal, but they prefer to enjoy the money rather than investigate from where it comes. The cases that come to light are those in which the family does not conform with this situation and is prepared to denounce the persons responsible to have their children back.

With respect to the age of the children who are being exploited, most of them are adolescents aged 13 to 18. It is certainly possible to find younger girls and boys who can be exploited from the age of seven or eight, but these cases do not represent the vast majority of the children being exploited.

Regarding their sex, although most of the children being prostituted are girls, the participation of boys has been increasing, especially in the cases of pornography and sex tourism. With respect to trafficking, boys and girls have been stolen, sold, exchanged, or illegally given up for adoption. Although prostitution is still the predominant type of exploitation, girls continue to be more vulnerable and likely to be exploited. The tables below synthesize some of the results obtained in the seven towns studied.

From the data given in Table 17.1, obtained from primary sources at a local level, it has been possible to formulate a first estimate of the number of

Table 17.1 Type of Exploitation, Groups, and Number of Sexually Exploited Children in Seven Towns of the Mexican Republic, 2000

Town	Total Population[a]	Groups of Children Exploited[b]	Types of Exploitation[c]	No. of Children Exploited[d]
Acapulco	721,011	A, B, C	I, II, III, IV	1,000
Cancún	430,592	A, B, C	I, II, III, IV	700
Ciudad Juárez	1,217,818	A, B, C	I, II, III, IV	800
Mexico City	8,591,309	A, B, C	I, II, III	2,500
Guadalajara	3,680,792	A, B, C	I, II, III, IV	600
Tapachula	271,141	A, B	I, II	600
Tijuana	1,212,232	A, B, C	I, II, III, IV	900
Total	16,124,895 (17% of the total population of the country)		Total	7,100

[a] Total population of the towns according to preliminary data from the Population and Housing Census, Instituto Nacional de Estadística y Geographía, 2000.

[b] A, Children that live on the streets and/or preponderantly offer their services on the public thoroughfare; B, children who provide their services in establishments where it is known that sexual services are provided; C, children who provide sexual services in a concealed way in places that have other recognized purposes.

[c] I, Prostitution; II, trafficking; III, pornography; IV, child sex tourism.

[d] Number of children exploited estimated using data collected in local level interviews.

children that could be subject to sexual exploitation in Mexico.[3] To do so, we have taken into account that the seven towns in which we did the study are those that, because of their characteristics (principally urban, tourist, and border zones), definitely have the largest number of exploited children in the country, a situation we have been able to corroborate by using secondary sources as well (cases denounced in the national and local press) and indirect indicators (population, main socioeconomic activities, and migratory flows). In this way, we have proposed that, in Mexico, there could be approximately 16,000 girl and boy victims of commercial sexual exploitation.

Although these figures cannot be considered definitive, but rather a first approximation, we believe they are useful because they provide parameters that other studies can use to continue advancing toward a more accurate delimitation of both the total number of children exploited and the different categories into which they can be divided. They also seem useful to us for formulating estimates of the size of the phenomenon at a national level, which can be done taking into account the size and characteristics of the localities.

The Exploiters

Different procedures are used to recruit girls and boys. On occasion, the exploiters recruit their victims directly, and other times, they use intermediaries or procurers. There are places where children are recruited with greater frequency, such as bus stations, where the procurers locate adolescent girls in particular who have come by themselves to the towns and have a great need to obtain employment. On other occasions, exploiters go to the parks where the domestic servants usually go for a walk during their days off, and they offer them a better job or seduce them, marry them, and they convince them that they must support them by working in prostitution for just a short period. As a result of the urgent, extraordinary, indigent situation, they succumb to the pressure of the traffickers.

They find boys in parks or premises where there are electronic games, and, in the case of street children, they find them in parks or malls where they place those who are ready to go with a client in exchange for food, clothes, toys, or a place where they can have a wash or spend the night.

The exploiters know how to approach and submit their victims very well, because they have lived in the milieu for generations and have been able to perfect their procedures. There are broad networks of protection and complicity around them that protect and ensure the functioning of their business. In this sense, they are more or less organized criminal networks that may or may not have a relationship with drug trafficking and can operate at a local level or have contracts that allow them to move from one part of the country to another. Some groups also have contact with the trafficking of persons, which permits them to bring their victims from other countries (principally Central America) or transport them to another country and organize their business there, principally in the United States (see the border cases that are cited below).

Most of the exploiters are Mexican men. However, there are also women who operate as recruiters or are owners of bars and that exploit or charge quotas for offering protection to the women and girls. There are also foreign exploiters, mostly Americans and Canadians, who come for short periods to prepare pornographic material with Mexican children and then return to their countries to commercialize it. These cases are most frequent in Tijuana, Acapulco, Guadalajara, and Cancún (Azaola 2001).

With respect to the cases of the trafficking and sale of children between countries, this occurs most often with the countries with that share borders with Mexico (United States and Guatemala). In several towns (Cancún and Guadalajara), we were informed of cases of Japanese men who had come to take some girls back with them in exchange for money.

Once in the business, several procedures are used to retain the victims. On the one hand, they are constantly watched to control all their movements and avoid them getting in touch with their relations or with persons who could persuade them to leave their job. On the other, they are induced into drug consumption and are told that their supply depends on their staying in the place of work. Blows and death threats for them and their relatives are the last resort and one the children cannot withstand, because the exploiters have been able to prove that they do not issue idle threats. Numerous testimonies of child victims of sexual exploitation relate the different types of violence that they frequently face, which also explains why so few cases are denounced (Espacios de Desarrollo Integral 1996; Azaola 1998, 2001).

The fact that in some towns we found the word "captive" being used to describe the situation of the children, tells us that, in some cases, the loss of freedom that they are, de facto, subjected to is more severe and restrictive than in others. We found the most extreme situation in Chiapas, on the southern border, where girls who have been brought from Guatemala, Honduras, and El Salvador are sold to bars that can be found on both sides of the border. The regime of debt slavery is used in these bars. That is, the girls are not allowed to leave their place of work until they have covered the whole sum the owner paid for them; their debt grows each day because they are charged for lodging and the food they are forced to consume in their place work (Bales 1999; Azaola 2001).

There is an extensive network of intermediaries that benefit from the exploitation of the children. On the one hand, there are those who recruit, procure, or buy them and place them in the places of work; on the other hand, there are the owners of these places, which can be hotels, nightclubs, restaurants, canteens, dance halls, discotheques, or massage parlors. The employees in these establishments who protect or promote the children, such announcers, watchmen, promoters, waiters, or bartenders, also obtain benefits, as do the taxi drivers who take clients to these places and even the doctors, pharmacists, and personnel for the health centers that the girls go to in a regular, forced way to perform their work. There are also the inspectors who certify that the place operates in compliance with the norms and the policemen who often charge the owners to protect their business, although they usually also charge quotas from the children to allow them to continue working. In some cases, there have also been police who are exploiters at the same time. One of the most significant cases that we could follow was precisely that of a group of exploiters that were arrested by the Mexico City authorities and were found to be led by a policeman and his brother and sister who were charged with exploiting more than 600 women and children over several years in the La Merced area in the center of the city. This group, whose case we learned about through interviews with those in charge of the inquiry and by consulting the thick judicial files, were soon set free because the children who had denounced them dropped the charges, something that often happens with cases like this.[4]

Another relevant case was one that was discovered as a result of a fire that broke out in a nightclub in Mexico City in which 22 persons died in October 2000. As a consequence of this case, several anomalies and the complicity, which is frequent, between authorities, judges, lawyers, and owners of establishments like this one where children are prostituted in the city, came to light.[5]

On the northern border, particularly in Tijuana and Cuidad Juárez, although most of the exploiters are Mexicans, there are also Americans who cross the border and use street children to prepare pornographic material. Similarly, children frequently cross the border to go to places where they meet up with pederasts, as happens in Balboa Park in San Diego.

With respect to the girls who are being exploited in these towns, most of them come from different states of the Mexican Republic, sometimes from the poorest states in the south of the country, and have been taken there by the bar owners. There are occasionally American girls who work as dancers in some nightclubs in the border towns.

The Clients

Most of the clients are Mexican men from all the sectors and of all ages and social conditions. There are occasionally some women, too, who seek relations with boys. In all the tourist zones, as in the main northern border towns, there are also mainly American and Canadian tourists, and Europeans to a smaller extent, who want sexual relations with children. Although crossing

Table 17.2 Boy and Girl Victims of Sexual Exploitation, Clients, and Exploiters by Nationality, in Seven Towns of the Mexican Republic, 2000

Towns	Nationality of the Girl/boy Victims[a]	Nationality of the Clients[b]	Nationality of the Exploiters[c]
Acapulco	A	I	1
Cancún	A	I	1
Ciudad Juárez	A	II	2
Federal District	B	III	3
Guadalajara	B	I	2
Tapachula	C	IV	3
Tijuana	A	II	2

Source: Data collected from local level interviews, 2000.

[a] A, Mainly Mexicans and occasionally Americans and Latin Americans; B, mainly Mexicans and a few Central Americans; C, predominately Central Americans: Guatemalans, Hondurans, and Salvadorans.

[b] I, Mexicans and tourists of different nationalities, principally Americans and Canadians; II, Mexicans and Americans; III, Mexicans; IV, Mexicans and Central Americans.

[c] 1, Mainly Mexicans and some Americans, Canadians, and Europeans; 2, Mexicans and Americans; 3, Mexicans.

the border into Mexico with this purpose in mind is quite frequent, especially in San Diego and El Paso, this phenomenon has not yet been typified as child sex tourism. The girls who work in bars in Tijuana also mention that a large percentage of their clients in the population are of Asian origin who live in San Diego.

Table 17.2 shows some data on the nationality of the children, the clients, and the exploiters that we have shown above.

Factors Contributing to Child Sexual Exploitation

Without attempting to establish casual links, we can refer to factors that have had a more or less direct influence on sexual exploitation and that form determined constellations of phenomena for which it is possible to perceive certain constants. On the one hand, it is a question of poverty, although this is not sufficient in itself to explain the phenomenon, because we found children who take part in these activities who are from the higher socio-economic sectors.

However, the fact of having had to leave their families or having been thrown out of home, most of the times as a consequence of the violence and rejection they suffered at home, places them in an unprotected situation that makes them liable to be recruited for the sex trade or that pushes them to look for this activity to survive. Here, too, it must be said that not all of the children who live in the streets have gone into the sex trade.

One factor that we have found to be a background of a good number of girls and boys that were later exploited is that they had previously suffered sexual abuse, generally from a family member. In these cases, the boys and girls show an important loss of self-esteem that makes them susceptible to new outrages because their defenses are weak, as is the support they obtain from a family that has already subjected them to violence.

In other cases, we found that the children with unresolved conflicts of sexual identity could drift into sexual exploitation, because they are pushed to leave their family and community, where they are rejected and ridiculed. This background reduces their possibilities and induces them to move in circles in which they find greater acceptance or less rejection of their sexual preference.

Another vulnerable group is that of boys and girls with severe addiction problems. In these cases, humiliations matter less than obtaining resources that will ensure their supply of the substances they require. We found cases in which children with these characteristics have been induced to sexual exploitation by their peer group, which in this way also ensures the drug supply.

Two other risk factors that have been little dealt with are, on the one hand, that the boys and girls who have grown up in a family linked to the sex trade find their incorporation almost natural and obligatory. On the other hand, ignoring that these activities exist and that children are exposed to them may be a factor that contributes to an increase in the vulnerability of certain boys and girls, if the opportunity presents itself and they do not know how to face it. Another factor that is little mentioned, but is essential, is the role of the procurers and recruiters who use and benefit from the circumstances mentioned that certain children are facing and have a direct influence on channeling them into the sex trade. The weight of this factor should not be diminished, because, as numerous studies show, it will be difficult for children to go into this environment if there is no one to induce them, put them in contact, and offer them employment under false pretenses or take them under pressure and threats to the places of work. It is here that a series of measures should be taken to protect children from the impunity with which all kinds of middlemen and recruiters act, not only the owners of the establishments.

It is worth emphasizing the importance of the factors mentioned above that some occasions can seem relatively fortuitous until one finds that, in one case and then another, they are repeated, and, therefore, they constitute patterns or common channels that influence the entry of certain children into the sex trade. Taking these factors into account will, we hope, permit the adoption of the measures required in each case to avoid more children being recruited.

Similarities among Exploited Children

Although in another section, we made reference to the diversity of circumstances that the children being exploited are facing, in this part, we want to focus on what, despite the differences, unites them. We are referring to the fact that the sexual exploitation to which they have been subjected will invariably alter and leave indelible marks on the course of their development, attributable, among other factors, to the violence, which is consubstantial.

We speak of "violence" when really the sexual exploitation of children supposes multiple forms of violence at different levels. In the field of rights, it implies negation or the almost complete ignorance of nearly all of them: the right to live with their families and that the family or, in its absence, the state, shall take charge of their material and affective needs; the right to receive care and protection; the right to receive education; the right to freedom; the right to dignity; the right to security; the right to equality; the right to culture and relaxation; and the right to preserve their health, all not to be threatened deliberately and continuously. Similarly, and as a substantive part of this last right, we consider the following are also implied: the right to decide about their bodies, to preserve their intimacy, to be looked on with respect, to decide as to their sexuality and their affection, and to benefit from the formative opportunities they are offered to construct a dignified future. In a special way, it seems to us that these children are denied one elementary human need: that of obtaining the recognition of others, to be looked on as an equals and with respect. Sometimes this does not happen because they are already stigmatized. They are rejected. All kinds of reproaches are directed at them from a moral standpoint, which ignores their circumstances and which is unable to visualize their lack of alternatives. In addition to the forms of violence referred to above, which we found in all the cases, there are others that are added that worsen the situation of some of the children. This is the case of girls and boys who are subjected and kept under exploitation by means of blows, threats, and other types of pressures. There is also the case of children who are kept against their will, are not allowed to leave their places of work, and are submitted by means of a system of debt servitude.

There are also other types of more subtle control, less visible but equally effective, that make exploitation possible. The emotional bonds the aggressors establish with the victims make it possible to cover up the exploitation. These forms, although less ostentatious, are equally destructive, because they slowly undermine a person's self-esteem and security, and, with time, this reduces their possibilities of opting for another way of life. Equally serious are the cases in which sexual exploitation is added to the supply of drugs as a strategy to ensure that the children stay.

The result of all these types of control is dejection, debilitation, a gradual destruction of the subject, or, at least, serious damage that will leave indelible traces. Undeniably, this will alter the course and possibilities that the girl or boy will have a healthy, integral development. Unmistakably, because the exploitation operates on the body's sexuality and affective ties, it starts to alter important spheres of the life of the person and will completely change their possibility of relating to their own bodies and to others with affection, because it will also modify the way in which they may or may not have trust in others who, like their exploiters, offer them care, affection, and protection.

Could a girl in these conditions ever again trust an adult who offers her the same thing her exploiters have offered her? What elements can she use to distinguish between true and false promises? From where can she relate to herself and to others? How can she reestablish a link of trust in herself and preserve for herself an image of dignity and respect, when her dignity has continually been trampled on? How can she reconstruct a history that will allow her to endure, then accept herself, to tolerate herself, when she has been an object of trade put on the market by the person who claims to be protecting her and when she has systematically been denied the exercise of all her rights?

Several studies have attempted to answer these kinds of questions and have gone into the psychological effects of submitting a girl to this kind of experience, and they have also studied how the girls react when trying to adapt themselves to their circumstances. One study performed in Thailand shows that, after a time, confusion and incredulity gives way to fear, resignation, and a kind of conscious separation of the bond that unites body and mind. In the context of this kind, the girls do all they can to reduce their wounds and mentally adjust themselves to a life in which they are used by up to 15 men a day. The reactions take well-known forms: lethargy, aggression, self-hatred, suicide attempts, confusion, self-abuse, depression, psychosis, and hallucinations (Bales 1999, 59).

In this study, we found that, within the same brothel, the girls can also react in different ways. It is possible that some go into a state of trauma and resignation, whereas others find a more active adaptation that leads them to identify with their pimp or exploiter. This resignation has the crucial advantage of reducing the violence they suffer. In the face of a way out that proves to be impossible, any action or obedience that avoids hurt and that makes their existence a little more tolerable is viable, no matter how degrading or illogical it appears. Notably, the immediate and forced application of terror is the first step toward successful slavery. A few hours after having been taken to the brothel, the girls are made to experience suffering and find themselves in a state of shock. As other victims of torture, they are dazed and paralyzed in their minds but not in the bodies. For the youngest, who do not manage to understand what is happening to them, the trauma is devastating. Broken into pieces and betrayed, they are seldom aware of what has happened to them (Bales 1999, 58).

In the world in which they live, like those in a punitive total institution, there are those who have all the power and those who have no power at all to sustain the abuses. The reward and the punishment come from a sole source: the pimp. The girls often perceive that to build a relation with him is a good strategy. The pimps are inclined to manipulation and to foster insecurity and dependence. Sometimes they can be friendly and treat the girl with affection with the purpose of increasing her flexibility and dependence. In some cases, cultural and religious norms play their role and contribute to prepare the girls for control and submission (Bales 1999, 61–62). In another study on the reactions that have been observed in the children used to produce pornographic material, four types of reaction are described. (1) Integration involves when children talk about their experiences without demonstrating too much anxiety. While blaming the perpetrator, they concentrate on the future and maintain reasonably normal relationships with their families, school, and friends. (2) Avoidance is when the child denies the experience or refuses to speak about it while showing feelings of anxiety and disgust. The child can be seen to still be intimidated by the perpetrator, has a tendency to live in the present without formulating plans for the future, and feels ashamed for his or her participation in the abuse. (3) Posttraumatic repetition involves when the child presents many symptoms and can be seen to be severely perturbed, with strong feelings of guilt and harm. They blame themselves and cannot forget what has happened and often develop sexually explicit behavior with which the risk of being exploited again is increased. (4) Identification is when the child identifies with the exploiter in which the child permanently defends the offender and repeats the trauma through sexual proximity to other children. This last type of behavior is more common in children who have been exploited for more than one year and who tend to identify with the aggressor to a greater extent (Görian Svedin and Back 1996, 21–22). Görian Svedin and Back further argues that the last three types of behavior are much more frequent than the first and that the damage caused will depend on both the nature of the abuse and the duration and the relation that existed between the child and the aggressor. They also say that, in the cases they studied, which took place in Sweden, the abuse was kept secret in all cases by the children, who did not tell anyone until the material was discovered and its origin investigated by the police. Similarly, they observed that, in all cases, the children did not want to remember or talk about what happened, had great difficulty in admitting it even to themselves, and had even done everything possible to block out or remove some memories of the experience (Görian Svedin and Back 1996).

We have focused the problem on the aspect of the repercussions that sexual exploitation has on children and on their subsequent development. This is because it seems fundamental to be able to provide evidence of the pain and suffering hidden behind the supposed pleasure that the false images and stereotypes offer us of children incorporated into the sex trade. That is why, from the point of view we have proposed here, it seems important to insist on the recognition of the right of boys and girls to preserve their intimacy, that they safeguard their bodies and the images they have of themselves, that the relation they have with their bodies, their sexuality, and with others not be interrupted or violated, and that they be allowed to decide about it themselves, and that nobody use them as objects of pleasure or trades with them as if they were merchandise. Above all, we must bear in mind that they are not in a position to be able to resist or stand up against their exploiters. Similarly, little can be done to modify the situation of these children while there is no will to face the groups that exploit them. Procedures are drawn up to block the path of these children, and there are no institutions that can offer these children care, shelter, and protection.

Conclusion

The seven towns included in the study present a low degree of marginality, with the exception of the frontier municipalities in the State of Chiapas, according to the socioeconomic indicators proposed by the National Population Council. This indicates that the phenomenon of sexual exploitation of children tends to occur more frequently in cities farther removed from extreme poverty, although it feeds off it. To put it in other terms, the relation between the phenomenon and the social exclusion can be mediated by factors such as the type of urbanization, the character of the economic attraction in the zone (expressed in the demand for labor for manufacturing or services), and/or its geographical location that makes the site a place for waiting or negotiation for transit to the north (the United States as the preferred objective), a place for the "rebound" of failed attempts, an obligatory place of transit for over ground trade and transport between countries (United States in the north and Guatemala in the south), and a place of relaxation for a large number of visitors in transit.

The large inequalities that exist between the municipalities in the country mark the direction of the migratory flows that go from the poorest municipalities to those that offer better opportunities for work and income. The former remain as supply or origination localities and the latter as places of destination or reception or transit. It is at these last points that sexual exploitation of children takes place more frequently.

The types of development that have been briefly described bring forth a series of effects on the social links that characterize the communities studied. As we have shown in our study (Azaola 2001), in most of the cases, we are talking about societies that are distinguished by their low level of social integration and a high proportion of inhabitants that do not belong to the place and that, for the same reason, are uprooted, with weak links binding them to the community. They are societies that continually receive new contingents of populations coming from different regions and do not share a history or an identity, and their integration supposes a long process that is not always finished or well completed. These contingents, whether they have arrived to settle in the locality, only use the community as a transit point, or are there for a short stay, as is the case with the tourists, exert a strong pressure on local society whose capacity to integrate new groups without losing or compromising its identity is continually put to the test. In short, these social segments have lost their roots to a large degree, because there is a show of detachment from the community that, together with other factors, gives rise to a large degree of anomie.

Communities in which a high degree of group and local identity predominates, with stable, lasting links of solidarity between its members, norms, and regulations recognized by everyone, will tend to handle their options for change and conservation without producing internal crisis and ruptures, regulating the conflict, and isolating behavior that threatens or destroys the community fabric. On the contrary, human groups that have broken their primary and associative links without replacing them with new ones that fulfill the functions of cohesion and mutual recognition and in which normativity is external to said group will tend to disperse with crises, exhaust their capacity to adapt to change, and generate a weak affiliation toward new communities and locations (Programa de las Naciones Unidas para el Desarrollo 1998).

In synthesis and from a normative point of view, it can be stated that anomie alters not only the limits of transgression but also the very perception of its existence. There is no transgression in which norms have not been appropriate and sanction is weak. Thus, we penetrate into a world in which everything is possible, a ground that is fertile, among other things, for the sexual exploitation of children.

The social conditions described above, anomie, low level of social integration, and weakness in social links, have also been identified and studied in other countries, like Mexico, and have been subject to relatively rapid processes of change as a consequence of modernization and putting into practice economic adjustment models. We found a series of coincidences with respect to our study on a recent report on the paradoxes of modernization in Chile. This report describes conditions that we call "deterioration in sociability." The said deterioration is manifest in "a high degree of mistrust and even certain weakening of intergenerational cohesion in the family," which some have called "social linkage pathologies," among which the following are important: family violence, sexual abuse, addictions, acts showing a lack of civility, anomie outbursts, and juvenile delinquency (Programa de las Naciones Unidas para el Desarrollo 1998). In other words, phenomena like the sexual exploitation of children are developed with less resistance in a context in which anomie prevails and in which norms are weakly applied. The anomic condition makes it difficult for these behaviors to be perceived as a transgression and promotes the continued operation of the aggressors, because they have been able to prove that the possibilities of being sanctioned are remote.

Acknowledgments

This study forms part of the three North American nations project on The Commercial Sexual Exploitation of Children conducted by Professor Richard J. Estes of the University of Pennsylvania. The study in Mexico was conducted by Elena Azaola, thanks to the support of the United Nations International Children's Emergency Fund, the National Council for Science and Technology, and the Inter-Institutional Program for Studies in the North American Region.

Notes

1. The definitions of the four types of sexual exploitation used in the study in Mexico are the same ones used for the study of the North American region as were proposed by the international agencies (Ennew et al. 1996; World Health Organization 1996; International Bureau for Children's Rights 1999).
2. This is the case of the reforms to the Federal Penal Code that were passed in 1999 and 2000 to typify child pornography, the trafficking and prostitution of children, and child sex tourism as crimes.
3. We used various indicators to draw up the estimates at the local level: the number of establishments where it is recognized that sexual services are provided; the estimated number of unregistered or clandestine establishments; the number of children who work in these places (generally one-fifth of the persons who provide sexual services are underage); the number of street children who regularly prostitute themselves; the number of cases of sexually transmitted diseases that are reported by the health services; the number of establishments that are announced in the telephone or business directories; and the number of cases that have been denounced by the media. Whenever possible, we confirmed the data in different sources and tried to cross the information.
4. Penal Code 51/99. DGSP/004/99-01.
5. For several weeks after October 21, 2000, the local press gave broad coverage to this case.

References

Azaola, E. 1998. "Prostitución Infantile." In *IV Informe Sobre los Derechos y la Situación de la Infancia en México, 1994–1997*. México City: Colectivo Mexicano de Apoyo a la Niñez.

Azaola, E. 2001. *Stolen Childhood: Girl and Boy Victims of Sexual Exploitation in Mexico*. México: United Nations International Children's Emergency Fund, Desarrollo Integral de la Familia, and Centro de Investigaciones y Estudios Superiores en Antropología Social.

Bales, K. 1999. *Disposable People: New Slavery in the Global Economy*. Berkeley: University of California Press.

Calcetas-Santos, O. 1998. "Report of the Special Rapporteur on the Sale of Children, Child Prostitution, and Child Pornography." United Nations, E/CN/1998/101/ Add. 2.

Calcetas-Santos, O. 1999. "Report of the Special Rapporteur on the Sale of Children, Child Prostitution, and Child Pornography." United Nations, E/CN.4/1999/71.

Consejo Nacional de Población. 1993. *Indicadores Socioeconómicos e Índice de Marginalidad Municipal 1990*. México: Conapo.

End Child Prostitution in Asian Tourism. 2000. *Looking Back, Thinking Forward*. Bangkok: European Commission.

Ennew, J., Gopal, K., Heeran, J., and Montgomery, H. 1996. *Children and Prostitution: How Can We Measure and Monitor the Commercial Sexual Exploitation of Children? Literature Review and Annotated Bibliography*. New York: United Nations International Children's Emergency Fund.

Espacios de Desarrollo Integral. 1996. *Al Otro Lado de la Calle: Prostitución de Menores en la Merced*. México: Comisión de Derechos Humanos del Distrito Federal and United Nations International Children's Emergency Fund.

Görian Svedin, C., and Back, K. 1996. *Children Who Don't Speak Out: About Children Being Used in Child Pornography*. Estocolmo, México: Räda Barnen.

Instituto Nacional de Estadística, Geografía e Informática. 2000. *XII Censo General de Población y Vivienda*. México: Instituto Nacional de Estadística y Geographía.

International Bureau for Children's Rights. 1999. "International Dimensions of the Sexual Exploitation of Children: Global Report." Montreal: International Bureau for Children's Rights.

Ireland, K. 1993. *"Wish You Weren't Here": The Sexual Exploitation of Children and the Connection with Tourism and International Travel*. London: Save the Children Fund.

Muntarbhorn, V. 1996. "Report of the Rapporteur-General on the World Congress against Commercial Sexual Exploitation of Children."

Negrete, N. 2000. "México." In *Instituto Interamericano del Niño: Violencia y Explotación Sexual contra Niños y Niñas en América Latina y el Caribe*. Montevideo, Uruguay: Inter-American Children's Institute, pp. 225–262.

Pérez Duarte, A. E. 1998. *La Utilización de Menores en la Prostitución, una Forma de Abuso y Maltrato Infantile: Consideraciones Sobre los Compromisos Adquiridos por México en el Ámbito Internactional*. México: Institute de Investigaciones Juridicas and Universidad Nacional Autónoma de México.

Programa de las Naciones Unidas para el Desarrollo. 1998. *Desarrollo Humano en Chile, 1998: Las Paradojas de la Moderización*. Santiago, Chile: Programa de las Naciones Unidas para el Desarrollo.

Senado de la República. 1999. *Migración enter sus Dos Fronteras.* México: Poder Legislativo Federal.
United Nations International Children's Emergency Fund. 1997. *Estado Mundial de la Infancia 1997: El Trabajo Infantile.* New York: United Nations International Children's Emergency Fund.
United Nations International Children's Emergency Fund. 2000. *Estado Munidal de la Infancia 2000.* New York: United Nations International Children's Emergency Fund.
World Health Organization. 1996. *Commercial Sexual Exploitation of Children: The Health and Psychological Dimensions.* Geneva: World Health Organization.

Applied Perspectives

V

18 Criminal Exploitation of Women and Children: The Role of Community Policing

JOHN MURRAY

Introduction

The United Nations (UN) Secretary General Kofi Annan described trafficking in women for sexual slavery as "one of the most egregious violations of human rights" (Annan 2000). It is clear, too, that responsible countries are unequivocal in regarding this abhorrent criminal activity as a priority public policy issue. Like any complex sociolegal issue, however, dealing with it attracts different points of view. The provision of severe sentences, although entirely appropriate, by themselves will have minimal effect, especially given the historically low prosecution rate. Obviously, relentless pursuit of offenders is critical, but a more challenging and responsible approach would expend equal energies on understanding the problem and its source as on taking preventive measures.

In line with this and consistent with the UN protocol that regards women and children as "victims," it is incumbent on a country or society to have a public policy that embraces the rights, privileges, and due sensitivities of the plight of victims and to be committed to the restoration of their place in society. Interestingly, and at a more pragmatic level, such progressive victim support is more likely to encourage these women and children to provide information that will lead to prosecution of the transnational criminals who ply this trade.

After September 11, the "war on terror" has the propensity to allow police to return to traditional forms of policing with a consequent reversion to paramilitarism. This has the potential to distance police from the rest of the community and undervalue the fine principles of community policing and its emphasis on prevention. If community policing, as a philosophy, is abolished or diminished, I believe it will adversely affect investigations into the criminal exploitation of women and children. Put another way, the principles of community policing will be more conducive to dealing with the issue because it relies on strong community relations and creative problem solving and, most importantly, draws on the police/community relationship to gauge what is exactly happening in the community.

In this chapter,

- I consider the extent of the problem of criminal exploitation of women and children in Australia and examine the relevant policies, laws, and processes.
- I evaluate prevention and investigation in the context of community policing and the rights of the victim.
- Finally, I conclude that traditional policing models, which are largely confrontational at a community level, are likely to be counter-productive, while community policing and its fine principles provide not just a sound ethical base from which to work but will also bring about a more effective solution.

Australia in Relation to the Rest of the World

The island of Australia is located in the southern hemisphere and is geographically one of the largest countries in the world, only slightly smaller than the United States of America. Papua New Guinea and Indonesia lie to the north, and it is bordered by the Indian Ocean on the west and the Pacific Ocean on the east. This isolated location has spared Australia the cross-border problems experienced by many other countries. It has a population of more than 18 million, with more than 75 percent of its citizens living in the eastern states of New South Wales, Victoria, and Queensland. It is also one of the most urbanized countries in the world with more than 85 percent of its population living in a major capital city or regional center.

Australia's legal infrastructure is both federal and state/territorial, with the commonwealth and state/territorial governments each having law enforcement responsibilities. Laws enforced by the commonwealth are specified within the *Australian Commonwealth* (such as immigration, drug importation, money laundering, and people smuggling). The states/territories have the responsibility for property crimes, violence, and personal crimes and conventional community crimes.

Australia has eight police services comprising around 50,000 personnel. The majority of their police force (approximately 46,000) work for the state and territory police, and the remaining 4,000 work with the Australian Federal Police (AFP). These police services are complemented by other commonwealth regulatory and revenue agencies that also have investigative role. These include the Australian Customs Service (ACS), The Australian Taxation Office, and the Australian Securities Commission. To facilitate the cooperation and focus for the intelligence gathering and investigation of national and international crimes affecting Australia, a number of national and interjurisdictional forums have been established, including the

Australian Crime Commission (ACC). The ACC can use coercive powers to summon witnesses before it and also compel the production of documents from people and institutions.

Human Trafficking in Australia

Australia is an attractive destination for traffickers mainly because of the geographic proximity to South East Asia where organized crime groups are known to target women and children for the purpose of sexual servitude (Edwards 2003). Relating to Thailand, for example, Frances (2003) notes the following:

> Initially, Thai women started coming to Australia from the mid 1980s to work in the sex industry to meet the high demand for "exotic" sexual partners. Most of these women came from the economically depressed rural areas of north/north east Thailand. Many remitted money to family in Thailand—50 percent were supporting children as well as siblings, parents and extended family; and then women became vulnerable to extortion from those who contracted them. They were subjected to threats against themselves and their families, and there was a move to "chaperone" them, in effect, closing them off from outside life.

For many reasons, estimates of the true extent of the incidence and nature of human trafficking, for commercial sexual exploitation in Australia today, is impossible to quantify. As a study by the Australian Institute of Criminology found, statistical data provides "very few insights" because there is no specific offenses of human trafficking under Australian law; therefore, no statistics are kept on its incidence. The offenses of slavery, sexual servitude, and deceptive recruiting are relatively new. To date, there have been no successful prosecutions. Statistics on assault, sexual assault, and kidnapping, recorded by the authorities, are not linked to an element of "trafficking," and statistics on the offenses of organized people smuggling do not indicate whether the offenses involved trafficking (David 2000, 10).

Information from other sources, such as nongovernment organizations, police, sex workers, and others in the sex industry, provide only a rough estimate of people trafficking into the sex industry. Christopher Payne (2003), a former federal agent working on Operation Papertiger, estimated that, in Sydney alone, in 1995, there were 300 women/girls in sexual servitude. In 2001, Puang Thong Simaplee died in the Villawood Detention Centre. Although the coroner found no evidence that she had been sold into sexual slavery at the age of 12 years, there was evidence that young women had been enticed into Australia with false identification on the promise that she would be provided with legitimate work only to be exploited and forced to work in brothels.

In 1999, Senator Ian Macdonald (1999) told the senate that "intelligence from Australia and overseas sources confirms that the problem of sexual servitude in Australia is a significant one."

In September 2003, Dr. Jim Hyde, President of the New South Wales Public Health Association, The Royal Australasian College of Physicians, advised the Parliamentary Joint Committee on the ACC, "Inquiry into Trafficking in Women for Sexual Servitude," that 1,000 women are trafficked into Australia each year. Drawing from Project Respect (an organization involved in the rights of trafficked sex workers), he reported the following:

> In Melbourne, in one case alone, a trafficker brought in at least 40 Thai women; and Government estimates put the gross cash flow to organizers of the Australian sex slavery at Aus$1m a week—a single trafficker in a Melbourne Municipality has allegedly earned Aus$4.5m from trafficking for prostitution (Hyde 2003, 1).

In October 2003, Commissioner Keelty of the AFP advised the same inquiry that the AFP had investigated 37 matters since 1999, and, of these, 15 remain open. Since June 2003, eight arrests relating to sexual slavery, servitude, and deceptive recruiting have been made. They are still before the court (Keelty 2003, 3).

Policies, Laws, and Practices in Australia

Australia has been an active participant in the development of the UN Convention against Transnational Organized Crime and its supplementary protocols dealing with people smuggling and people trafficking. Like other conventions, these new treaties guided the legislature in Australia. Carrington and Hearn (2003, 7) summarize the process relative to the trafficking protocol:

> The UN Protocol to Prevent, Suppress and Punish Trafficking in Person's, Especially Women and Children (Trafficking Protocol) was adopted by resolution A/RES/55/25 of 15 November 2000 at the 55th session of the UN General Assembly. The Trafficking Protocol opened for signature with the Convention and the other two protocols at a high level diplomatic conference in Palermo, Italy, on 13 December 2000. The Convention and its protocols enter into force as international law, 90 days after the 40th instrument of ratification has been deposited. The Trafficking Protocol represents a significant international attempt to conceptualize trafficking, define trafficking in international law and provide template for international cooperation to address the global problem (reference Barbara Sullivan, "Trafficking in Women: Feminism and New International Law," *International Journal of Politics*, vol. 5, no. 1, p. 67–91).

> Australia signed the Convention on 13 December 2000, the Smuggling Protocol on 21 December 2001, but its signature on the People Trafficking Protocol was delayed until 11 December 2002.

In Australia, the Criminal Code Amendment (Slavery and Sexual Servitude) Act of 1999 provides the statutory offenses of "slavery," "sexual servitude," and "deceptive recruiting," which are federal offenses. Slavery is defined as occurring when ownership rights are exercised over another person and can arise from a debt incurred or contract entered into by the enslaved person (Sec. 270.1). Slave trading also includes "exercising control or direction over or providing finance for" the trade (Sec. 270.2). Sexual servitude covers the situation in which sexual services are provided because of force or threats and the person is not free to cease providing those services (Sec. 270.4). This provision applies regardless of any original consent to sex work. Deceptive recruiting occurs when a woman is deceived into believing she is going to Australia to work in employment other than prostitution (Sec. 270.7). However, as some observers noted (Carrington and Hearn 2003, 9; Hyde 2003, 2), there are some limitations in the legislation because it does not capture the situation in which women agree to work in the sex industry but are deliberately deceived about the conditions of work.

Under the Australian legal system, it is desirable to have complementary commonwealth and state/territorial legislation. The Federal Minister for Justice and Customs has developed a Law Enforcement National Plan of Action through the Australasian Police Ministers' Council, in which it was agreed by all state/territory jurisdictions that they would review their relevant laws and practices regarding intelligence and investigations.

In terms of law enforcement, there are three main agencies in Australia. These are the AFP, the Department of Immigration and Multicultural Affairs (DIMA), and the ACS. The summary of the activities of these three agencies is drawn from a review by the Australian Institute of Criminology (David 2000, 26–33).

Australian Federal Police

The AFP is the principal law enforcement body for the federal government. Its role is to enforce federal criminal law and to protect the commonwealth and national interests from crime in Australia and overseas. It has a prime role in enforcing Part IIIA (Child Sex Tourism) of the Crimes Act of 1914 (Commonwealth) and the Migration Act of 1958, which is particularly relevant to the issues of human smuggling and trafficking. The AFP gives special emphasis to countering and investigating organized crime and transnational crime.

AFP activities and initiatives include the following:

(1) ***Investigation of people trafficking and international child sex offenses:*** A Transnational Sexual Offenses Team (TSOT) was established in December 2002 within the AFP's Transnational Crime Coordination Centre. The TSOT was established to develop targets, coordinate investigations, and liaise with other agencies in relation to transnational sexual offenses, including child sex tourism, slavery, and sexual servitude. In October 2003, the TSOT incorporated that into a new and larger strike team, the Transnational Sexual Exploitation and Trafficking Team (TSETT).
(2) ***Family Liaison Coordination Team:*** Provide assistance to the victim in the context of the family and also directly to the family and friends of victims.
(3) ***Intelligence gathering:*** In conjunction with state/territory services through the Australian Bureau of Criminal Intelligence (now the ACC).
(4) ***National child sex offender system:*** ANCOR, the Australian National Child Offender Register.
(5) ***Liaison officers:*** The AFP has 28 liaison officers in 16 countries around the world, with the network being directed from Canberra, Australia.
(6) ***International liaison:*** Maintenance of strong internal law enforcement links through Interpol and direct links to many countries in the region.
(7) ***Cooperative assistance activities in the Asia-Pacific region.***

Department of Immigration and Multicultural Affairs

The DIMA is tasked with managing the movement of people into and out of Australia. Its mission is to contribute to Australia's economic, social, and international interests through programs directed to the lawful and orderly entry and stay of people, settlement of migrants and refugees and their acquisition of citizenship, and appreciation of the advantages of cultural diversity within a framework of national unity.

A number of police initiatives relevant to human smuggling and trafficking include the following:

- ***Airline liaison officers (ALOs):*** Provide expert advice to airline staff on travel documentation and the identification of inadmissible passengers. Currently, ALOs are attached to Qantas in Singapore, Bangkok, and Hong Kong, and British Airways in Kuala Lumpur.

- ***Fines for Airlines:*** For bringing in inadmissible passengers to Australia.
- ***Intelligence gathering on immigration malpractice:*** Investigation units in Australia and overseas.
- ***Movement Alert List:*** Database against which applicants for visas are checked before issue.
- ***Sponsored travel:*** Procedure to check on Australians who may be associated with the travel of unaccompanied minors to Australia.
- ***International liaison and exchange of information.***
- ***Return of illegal migrants.***
- ***Data matching:*** With other government authorities to assist in identification of people with a legal right to work.
- ***Overseas education campaigns:*** Designed to warn people of the risks associated with trying to enter Australia illegally and the penalties involved.
- ***Refugee and Humanitarian Program:*** Obligation to provide protection to people in Australia who come within the UN Convention definition of a refugee.
- ***Women At Risk Program:*** A subprogram under Refugee and Humanitarian Program aimed at affording protection to vulnerable women for whom resettlement is the only option.

Australian Customs Service

The ACS facilitates the legitimate movement of people, goods, vessels, and aircraft across the Australian borders, while maintaining appropriate compliance with Australian law. This includes processing passengers at entry points and coastal surveillance to detect and deter unlawful activity. Initiatives include the following:

- ***Coastal surveillance:*** Coastline of 37,000 km through Coastwatch.
- ***Waterfront closed circuit television surveillance:*** At 23 seaports.
- ***Frontline:*** A cooperative venture between industry and customs in which frontline members use their own expertise to identify suspicious activity within their industry.
- ***Customs watch:*** To facilitate the gathering of information with a free call number regarding the reporting of illegal or suspicious land, sea, or air activity.
- ***Passenger analysis and evaluation system:*** An IT system used by federal and state agencies to monitor and respond to travel into and out of Australia by persons of interest.

- ***Debriefing:*** Customs and DIMA officers jointly conduct interviews with selected and undocumented migrants to ascertain information relevant to voyage and vessel.
- ***Oceania customs organization:*** Coordination of the activities of Pacific region countries.
- ***Cooperative assistance activities:*** Contribution to institutional strengthening programs in multilateral and bilateral forums and includes law enforcement training in the areas of investigation, intelligence, and enforcement in passenger processing and border operations environment.

Whole-of-Government Approach

On October 13, 2003, the Australian government announced major initiatives to enhance existing efforts to combat people trafficking with the introduction of the Commonwealth Action Plan to Eradicate Trafficking in Persons. The TSETT, referred to above, will be an integral part of this plan.

The key elements of this plan are as follows: closer links between AFP and DIMA officers in the detection and investigation of trafficking; new visa arrangements for people identified as possible trafficking victims; comprehensive victim support measures provided through a contracted case management, including appropriate accommodation and living expenses and access for victims to a wide range of social support and legal, medical, and counseling services; enhancement of arrangements, including access to additional support for the victims who may be required to remain in immigration detention; development of reintegration assistance project for trafficking victims who are returned to key source countries in South East Asia; improvements to trafficking legislation; legislative amendments to make telecommunications interception available for Criminal Code offenses of slavery, sexual servitude, deceptive recruiting, and people smuggling with exploitation (passed on October 15, 2003); and ratification, once all domestic requirements are in place, of the United Nations Protocol to Prevent, Suppress, and Punish Trafficking in Persons, especially Women and Children.

Dealing with the Problem at a Community Level

The events of September 11 forced countries to reconsider how military and civil law enforcement authorities should reconfigure to address the fresh challenges that were presented. With some police services, the changes have been dramatic and have amounted to much more than simply tightening up existing practices. These services have made a distinct move (or return) to paramilitarism characterized by a more aggressive style of dress and manner (Murray 2005). In terms of policing philosophy, this tends to indicate a move from the well-respected community policing model back to the reactionary traditional policing model. When this happens, the inevitable tradeoff is that there will be a distancing by police from the rest of the community, which will pose a real threat to the effective prevention and investigation of sexual servitude.

A return to the traditional model of policing, with its paramilitary traits, will be counterproductive. This is because gaining the trust and respect of ordinary citizens is difficult for conventional sociolegal matters. Victims of sexual servitude present unique features that call for special sensitivities so as to gain trust and respect. It is clear that victims of sexual servitude have a strong fear or mistrust of authorities because of experiences in their own country, will be reluctant to cooperate with any authority for fear of arrest and deportation because of false travel documents, fear of retribution at the hands of the traffickers, will feel ashamed and embarrassed, have language problems, and sometimes are conditioned by a culture that positions them as inferior beings.

A highlight of community policing is that it brings about partnerships in the community and works best when that relationship is structured to encourage information sharing from all parts of the community. This includes groups that tend to be unwilling to assist the police and will require police to make special efforts to win their trust and respect.

In less informed times, women caught in sexual servitude would tend to be treated variously as a law enforcement headache, an immigration problem, or welfare cost to the state, merely a victim of violence or breach of contract rather than a person with complex needs (Moyle 2002). It is now generally agreed that trafficked persons, especially women in prostitution, should be no longer viewed simply as illegal migrants but victims of crime. Naturally, therefore, persons subject to sexual servitude must be treated with dignity and respect and should also be informed of their options. Their safety and physical and emotional needs are of primary concern, and details of the servitude should be discussed only when essential. The Family Liaison Coordination Team of the AFP adopts this philosophy as is geared to provide such assistance and treatment.

Relative to the prosecution of the offenders, the wisdom of maintaining community policing becomes self-evident. Successful prosecutions depend on information. A community-police relationship that is based on mutual trust is more likely to uncover matters that are helpful in identifying sexual exploitation. A more formal community-police relationship, which is characteristic of the traditional model of policing, would insist on reports of actual law breaking, whereas a good community-police relationship would encourage information of something "a bit unusual." That can only be achieved if the community feels comfortable about coming forward with information, no matter how slight they believe its connection to sexual servitude. The contribution that community policing can make in this area is extremely positive. In terms of prevention, it can allow the community to focus on the importance of notifying early warnings/signs, consistent with the spirit that it is in everybody's interest.

With serious and demanding issues, such as national security in an environment of terrorism, police commissioners could be tempted to move back to a traditional style of policing. I am strongly of the view, however, that for issues such as terrorism and sexual servitude, it would be quite counterproductive to return to the traditional model of policing. Instead of moving away from community policing, police commissioners should look to its qualities and specifically note how this policing philosophy can be used to their advantage. To abandon it or diminish it would be to undo all the hard work over the past decades that has taken policing to the high level of societal acceptance that it now enjoys.

Conclusion

There is absolutely no doubt that offenders involved in the exploitation of women and children should be rigorously pursued despite the investigational difficulties unique to this dreadful crime. At the same time, equal attention must be given to its prevention together with support programs consistent with these women and children being victims of crime. In Australia, this balance seems to have been struck when considerable time has been spent on developing programs that are supportive of victims and their families.

This chapter summarizes the law, policies, and procedures adopted by Australian authorities but cautions against what seems to be a shift in policing philosophy in some police services after September 11, when some police services tended to return to a traditional model of policing and move away from community policing. Whereas the latter is fundamentally based on community consultation and cooperation in the prevention of crime, traditional policing is authoritative and has the tendency to distance police from the rest of the community. What is important about this in relation to sexual servitude is that information about these activities is less likely to be uncovered with traditional policing. Some governments have put pressure on police commissioners to adopt (or revert to) the more traditional model in the context of the war on terror. National security, of course, is important, but police commissioners should alert to the inappropriateness of moving back to traditional policing, because to do so would be counterproductive. Moreover, such a move would have the tendency to reduce the high standing in society that policing has enjoyed under a community policing philosophy.

References

Annan, K. 2000. Address to Women 2000 SPECIAL SESSION. UN Press Release SG/SN/7430.

Carrington, K., and Hearn, J. 2003. "Trafficking and the Sex Industry: From Impunity to Protection." Current Issues Brief 28. Canberra, Australia: Department of the Parliamentary Library.

David, F. 2000. *Human Smuggling and Trafficking: An Overview of the Response at the Federal Level.* Canberra, Australia: Australian Institute of Criminology.

Edwards, G. 2003. "A trade in Human Suffering." *Platypus* 80:7.

Frances, R. 2003. "Australia's Trade in Sex: A History." Presented as an Annual History Lecture for the History Council of New South Wales.

Hyde, J. 2003. "Inquiry into Trafficking in Women for Sexual Servitude." Submission to the Parliamentary Joint Committee of the Australian Crime Commission. http://www.aph.gov.au/Senate/committee/acc_ctte/index.htm.

Keelty, M. J. 2003. "Inquiry into Trafficking in Women for Sexual Servitude." Submission to the Parliamentary Joint Committee of the Australian Crime Commission. http://www.aph.gov.au/Senate/committee/acc_ctte/index.htm.

Macdonald, I. 1999. Criminal Code Amendment (Slavery and Servitude) Bill, Second Reading Speech, Senate, Hansard, Australia, March 24.

Moyle, S. 2002. "Trafficking in Women for Prostitution." Presented at the Stop the Traffic Symposium, Melbourne, Australia, February 25.

Murray, J. 2005. "Policing Terrorism: A Threat to Community Policing or Just a Shift in Priorities?" *Police Practice and Research* 6(4):347–361.

Payne, C. 2003. "Trafficking and Sexual Servitude in Australia." Presented at the Vital Issues Seminar, Parliament House, Canberra, Australia, August 20.

19 The Militarization of the American Police Force and Its Impact on the Victimization of Women and Children: A Critical Assessment

JOHN PAUL AND MICHAEL L. BIRZER

Introduction

On November 5, 2003, a drug sweep at South Carolina's Stratford High School had the American public questioning police tactics. Surveillance video from Stratford High School showed 14 officers ordering students to lie on the ground while police searched for illegal drugs. Students who did not comply with the orders were handcuffed and taken to the ground. Police, with weapons drawn, walked around and over them, while drug-sniffing dogs stuck their noses in and out of book bags. "I froze up," reported a student. "I didn't know what to do. I fell on the ground. Everybody thought it was a terrorist attack" (Leach 2003).

With this example, we highlight one of the most significant trends of law enforcement in the past 15 years: its militarization. Borrowing from Kraska and Kappeler (1997, 1), we define militarization as "a set of beliefs and values that stress the use of force and domination as appropriate means to solve problems and gain political power, while glorifying the tools to accomplish this (with) military power, hardware, and technology." The purposive rationale of militarization, or so-called "get tough on crime" measures, is the protection of the American citizen from criminal harm. Its design and intent is the security of the average citizen by institutionalizing a driven quest for the identification and prosecution of hardened criminals.

The latent outcomes of such militarization is the war it wages on average citizens. An aggressive paramilitary police force may perpetuate brutality against the "average citizen" and create a set of institutional norms that leads to greater violence by both police and their targets. Phrased in another manner, the militarization of the police creates a social arena that is now less safe and more violent. Persons targeted as criminals become more violent in their interactions with the police because of the potential for increased harm, whereas the average citizen (now seen by the police as a "criminal in waiting") loses trust in the institution designed to protect them.

In this chapter, we examine the militarization of the American police force as it pertains to the victimization of women and children and increased disruption and brutalization of the American community. We present the notion that the militarization of the police exploits all citizens by instilling in them fear, violence, and mistrust, thus enabling the "control" of social life by police institutions. We begin with a brief history of the militarization of law enforcement. Following this, we detail the social significance and social consequences of the use of military actions in law enforcement. Then, in closing, we propose suggestions to demilitarize law enforcement.

The Militarization of Police Forces

We take as a starting point Sir Robert Peel's Metropolitan Police Act for London in 1829. As part of the Metropolitan Police Act, Peel suggested that police should be organized, efficient, and organized along military lines. As a result, many police agencies in Great Britain and America are grounded in a paramilitary authoritarian and hierarchical composition (Palmiotto 1997). In fact, some of the earliest examples of bureaucratic organizations are for military purposes (Alpert and Dunham 1996). As such, the military and bureaucratic structured organization of police has had a long and enduring history (Enloe 1980). The paradox here is that police history, with its emphasis on the night watchman and British bobbies, glosses over how civilian police often formed out of military groups and military soldiers or, conversely, out of an acute fear of military control (Manning 1977; Brewer et al. 1994; Kraska 1994; Alpert and Dunham 1996; Kraska 1996; Kraska and Kappeler 1997).

The theoretical perspective of police organization is based largely on the writings of Frederick Taylor and Max Weber (Hodgson 2001). Taylor and Weber's classical organizational theory (i.e., organizations indoctrinated along traditional lines; highly centralized, bureaucratic, and designed on the premise of divisions of labor and unity of control) has been the enduring model of organizational command and control adopted by law enforcement agencies across America for most of the 20th century (Birzer 1996).

This classical theory, modified and refined during implementation by progressive era police executives, such as August Vollmer and O. W. Wilson, represented a reaction to the rampant corruption and other inequities that had plagued American policing since its early days (Patterson 1995). To reduce the contaminating effects of local ward politics on line officers, the classical model centralized authority in police headquarters. To alleviate favoritism and petty corruption in neighborhoods, the classical model established beats and revolving assignments for patrol officers. To ensure officers performed their assigned duties, the classical model instituted a military-style structure of authority and discipline. To encourage personnel to follow the rules established by headquarters, proponents of the classical model, most notably Wilson, believed that line-level officers should adhere to a rigid chain of command and be supervised closely through massive amounts of written policy pronouncements (Bopp 1977; Birzer 1996).

In 1981, Congress passed the Military Cooperation with Law Enforcement Official Act. Since then, the military has become increasingly involved in civilian law enforcement and has been encouraged to share equipment, training, facilities, and technology with civilian enforcement agencies. Similarly, in 1986, President Ronald Reagan officially designated drug trafficking as a "national security" threat. A year later, Congress set up an administrative apparatus, with a toll-free number, to encourage local civilian agencies to take advantage of military assistance. In 1989, President George Bush created six regional joint task forces in the Department of Defense to act as liaisons between police and the military. A few years later, Congress ordered the Pentagon to make military surplus hardware available to state and local police for enforcement of drug laws. In 1994, the Department of Defense and the Department of Justice signed an agreement enabling the military to transfer wartime technology to local police departments for peacetime use in American neighborhoods, against American citizens.

Social Significance and Social Cost of Police Militarization

The sharing of military resources with civilian agencies has led to an alarming militarization of local law enforcement. Since the early 1980s, special paramilitary units in departments known as Special Weapons and Tactics (SWAT) teams have proliferated the American landscape. A study by Kraska (1997) showed that 90 percent of cities with populations of more than 50,000 had paramilitary units, as did three-quarters of those with populations under 50,000. Furthermore, an increasing number of communities under 10,000 people are gaining SWAT-style paramilitary units. For example, the community of Jasper, Texas, (a town of 2,000 people and a police force of seven) has been the beneficiary of seven M-16s and an armored personnel carrier (*60 Minutes* 1997).

Of greater concern here is not the proliferation of SWAT-style units across the nation. Our concern about military-style training is that all "peace officers" now receive the socialization they undergo for "war." We argue that both SWAT and nonspecialized police members are trained in organizational hierarchies and cultural models situated in military logic. Personnel hierarchy includes commanders, tactical leaders, scouts, and, in many cases, a sniper. Furthermore, the police structure comes to reflect, in uniformed attire, the commando units they model (combat boots, full-body armor in black or camouflage, and Kevlar helmets). What this has produced is a military mindset that declares war on the American public.

Some have argued that the paramilitary model of policing has created a myriad of problems in the general culture of the organization, including stifling creativity, dogmatism, and impeding organization transformation (Lorinskas and Kulis 1986; Weisburd, McElroy, and Hardyman 1989; Birzer 2000). Other theoretical scholarship has pointed out that the paramilitary environment has created a warrior-like mentality on the part of the police.

We reiterate our concern with the military mindset, for in this mentality, the metaphor of "war" becomes real life. American streets become the "front," and American citizens exist as "enemy combatants" (Weber 1999, 10). Stated differently, once an organization with a militaristic orientation becomes institutionalized, the members exist within a culture in which in they believe that they are literally engaged in combat.

When police organizations train officers to act and think like soldiers, they alienate them from the community of which they are supposed to be part. A law enforcement officer is ultimately a member of the community, and a member of the police is subject to the same laws as their fellow citizens; a soldier is not. Weber (1999, 10) writes, "the job of the police is to react to the violence of others, to apprehend criminal suspects and deliver them over to the court of law." A soldier, conversely, "does not think; (he/she) initiates violence on command and doesn't worry about the Bill of Rights" (Weber 1999, 10).

The divorcing of community by police institutions may lead to particular abuses. Specifically, we highlight the use of excessive force, mistakes, and boundary extension (marking nonviolent offenses for harsh punishment). We mark these concepts with illustrations.

Military Abuse: The Use of Excessive Force

In war, casualties happen, and the warring public often accepts death (especially the death of enemy persons). Consider, however, the following causalities of war:

Four officers from the New York Police Department's uncover street crimes unit fired 41 shots at Amadou Diallo, a 22-year-old Guinea immigrant. Diallo, who spoke little English, was hit 19 times while reaching for his wallet to offer his identity to the police. According to Parenti (2000, 108–109), "Police later ransacked his home . . . in a desperate search for drugs, weapons or anything that might compromise the dead man and justify the shooting. They came up empty handed."

Masked police commandos kicked in the front door of 56-year-old Charles Potts during a narcotics raid. As the police entered the home, Potts jumped up from his card game and was killed by police automatic fire. No drugs were found in the search (*Greensboro News and Record* 1998).

In Portland, Oregon, police commandos had a shootout with a suspect. By the time the raid was over, two officers were wounded and a third killed. Dragging out the wounded suspect, they stripped him on the lawn in full view of a television camera crew, lashed him to the tailgate of an armored vehicle, and "paraded him like a dead buck" (Dodge 1998).

As noted, in war we tend to accept causalities so long as they are the enemy's or are causalities made in the act of vanquishing the enemy. The problem here, however, is the fact that the American public has been named the enemy and thus incurs the causalities of war.

Mistakes Will Happen: Collateral Damage, Mistaken Identity, and Self-Injury

In war, a number of "noncombatants" will be injured or killed. The salient question we (as citizens and as social scientists) need to ask, however, is: Does waging a war protect our citizens or produce for them a greater risk of harm? Consider the following: "Under the rule of probable cause, (the police) stopped a group of people coming home from church. They were stopped at a gas station, where gangs hang out, and the police made them all get on the ground, lie in the dirt and oil. All of them—in their Sunday best" (Parenti 2000, 118).

A civilian police review board plans to investigate the 2004 shooting of an innocent bystander in Albany, New York, when two officers opened fire at a suspect's car on New Year's Eve. Police said the suspect drove his car in reverse toward officers, who opened fire with eight shots. The driver lived; the bystander did not (Newsday.com 2004). The case is still pending.

These citizens were simply collateral damage in the police's war on crime. The policing mentality exhibited here is symbolically crafted as "shoot first, ask questions later." Such overzealousness may create the potential for civil rights violations and civilian harm or death. Furthermore, this aggressive nature can lead to mistaken identity. There have been numerous incidents in which the police mistake an innocent citizen for a "bad guy." Take the following example:

> Misreading the local address, police raided the home of what they thought was a drug dealer. No drug dealer was found however. Instead, they entered the home of a 64 year old retired farm worker. When he reached for a pocket knife he was shot 15 times. (Bier 1999)

In August 1999, in an early morning narcotics raid, a SWAT team from the El Monte police department burst into the home of a Mexican immigrant family and shot dead an unarmed elderly man. He was reportedly shot twice in the back. No drugs were found in the raid, and a different name from that of the residents was on the search warrant (Amnesty International USA, no date).

The suspect, too, can mistake the unannounced police home invasion for criminal activity. Such was the case when a Pierce County, Washington, deputy was shot and killed by a suspect who swore that he opened fire "only because he thought this assailants were burglars" (Parenti 2000). Sometimes officers "trained for war" become their own worst enemy. During tactical operations, officers often mistake each other for the suspects they are pursuing. Instances include the following:

> Officers Rafael Borroto, Javier Gonzalez, and Brian Wilson fired a combined 19 shots—an apparent crossfire—at an unarmed Nicholas Singleton. Singleton was being chased by officers on foot after he bailed out of the passenger side of a stolen Jeep Wrangler. All three officers (converged) on different sides of a building where the fleeing Singleton had climbed onto the roof. Mistaking each other's gunshots and muzzle flashes as coming from Singleton, all three officers opened fire. Firearms Review Board had concerns about whether officers had placed themselves in danger needlessly by creating a crossfire. (Herald.com 2002)

While serving a search warrant on a dwelling that turned out to be empty, SWAT team members stormed the building and, in the confusion caused by aggression and smoke grenades, mistook each other for gun-wielding suspects. Team members opened fired on each other, killing one of their own (MacGregor 1998).

Boundary Extension: Marking Nonviolent Offenses for Harsh Punishment

The mentality of war has additional consequences for the American community. We argue that police are trained to resemble soldiers at war. Soldiers at war operate under a code of domination, not service. Thus, all actions (or perceived offenses) by civilians must be handled by domination, by force and control. Stated boldly, no longer do police officers operate as officers of the law; they act as the law itself. Within this mentality, laws are applied arbitrarily without the validation of civilian voices and the courts. Consider the following.

When police officers woke Ann Robinette at home in Centralia, Missouri, just after one o'clock in the morning, she feared that someone was hurt or a relative had died. Instead, the officers arrested her for failing to pay a $2 ticket for parking in a zone reserved for police cars. The bust led to a series of events, including another parking ticket, a federal lawsuit, and the realization that parking in the spot was not really illegal after all (STL.com 2003).

Police officials also attempt to justify arrests (and violence) by giving explanations that speak to affronts of civilian resistance to police authority. CPL Alita V. Robinson was wearing her police uniform while moonlighting as a security guard at a Popeye's fried chicken restaurant when she saw a customer walk up to the counter with something perched behind his ear; something that looked like a blunt (a marijuana-stuffed cigar). She said she watched the man, Daniel Jose Torres, a 32-year-old construction worker, for about 20 minutes as he waited for an order of french fries. When she confronted him, the object behind his ear was gone. Robinson commanded Torres to look on the floor for the alleged contraband, thinking he dropped it. He complied at first, but when he tried to walk away, Robinson ordered him to his knees. Torres resisted, and the officer shot him. Police later charged Torres with second-degree assault and resisting arrest. Prosecutors tacked on two more charges: failure to obey a police officer and drug possession. Police said they found marijuana in the restaurant but not in Torres's possession (Whitlock and Fallis 2001).

In summary, a militarized police force destroys within the American community an ideal we cherish, democracy. The military police state frays the democratic process by eliminating the public construction of law. Indeed, for a democracy to exist, the actions of government must be constrained by law. The police as agents of government must also be governed by the rule of law, that is, by public deliberation "rather than by directions given arbitrarily by particular regimes and their members" (Bayley 2001).

Social Significance and Social Cost of Police Militarization: Destroying Community Trust

The paramilitary model of policing destroys the very fabric of social life, trust. The issue of trust is not an insignificant issue. Indeed, Simmel (1990, 178) asserts, "without the general trust that people have in each other, society itself would disintegrate." The only alternative to trust is, as Luhmann (1979, 4) argues, "chaos and paralyzing fear."

In more structured terms, trust may be conceptualized as a set of expectations and obligations built in the exchange of resources. Goulder (1960) notes that trust is defined by and developed in "the general norm of reciprocity . . . the mutual or satisfactory exchange of desired resources between parties." Fukuyama (1995) and Putnam (2000) term this norm of reciprocity "social capital." Putnam (2000) writes the following:

> Social capital refers to connections among individuals—social networks and the norms of reciprocity and trustworthiness that arise from them (p. 19) . . . Social capital is akin to what Tom Wolfe called the 'favor bank' in his novel, *The Bonfire of the Vanities* (p. 20) . . . It is also expressed in the T-shirt slogan used by the Gold Beach, Oregon, Volunteer Fire Department to publicize their annual fund-raising effort: "come to our breakfast, we'll come to your fire" (p. 21).

Although colloquial, Putnam's words are powerful. These words tell us that trust (and hence police-community relations) is built in reciprocal action. Indeed, trust is a faith, an obligation between various parties made in the exchange of valued resources. Thus, if trust is a reciprocal action between two or more partners, we need now ask: What goods and resources could ever possibly be exchanged between police and community members engaged in war? The answer is nothing except, fear, hatred, an increased lack of cooperation, and growing violence. Indeed, a number of recent surveys (Fukuyama 19995; Spitzer 1999; Culbertson 2000; Putnam 2000; Rashbaum 2000; Nagourney and Connelly 2001; Fine et al 2003) report that community residents generally distrust and fear the police. This is crucial information, because police cannot stop or control crime without the help of ordinary citizens, and citizens will not help a cop unless they trust her or him.

Improving Police-Community Relations

Citizens and police administrators alike often believe that police-community relations will be improved by purging racist, insensitive, and vicious cops from the force. Assuredly, these officers are part of the problem. However, as Culbertson (2000) notes, "pointing fingers (at individual officers) does not help much." One cannot assign all the blame to a few aggressive officers. Furthermore, the answer cannot be encapsulated by removing the "bad apples" from the police force.

We present the notion that the current paramilitary culture may nurture these destructive officers. We recommend the removal of aggressive, military-style crime fighting and replace it with other proactive forms of police work.

Recommendations

We present the following three recommendations as a venue for the reengineering of the paramilitary police culture: (1) implement community policing as a mechanism for trust building initiatives, (2) end the overreliance on technology by the police, and (3) make symbolic changes in uniforms and messages of control.

Implement Community Policing as a Mechanisms for Trust-Building Initiatives

Community policing has been presented in the contemporary literature as constituting a viable entity for effective change within police organizations while at the same time being applied with the goals of detecting and preventing crime (Yates, Pillai-Vijayan, and Humburg 1997; Kerley-Kent and Benson 2000; Mastrofski and Ritti 2000; Oliver 2000; Brand and Birzer 2001). Community policing requires fundamental and strategic change in almost all areas of policing (Palmiotto, Birzer, and Unnithan 2000). It requires police officers to identify and respond to a broad array of problems, such as crime, disorder, fear of crime, drug use, urban decay, and other neighborhood concerns. Community-oriented policing beacons executives to examine their organizations and effect change in support of community policing strategies in such areas as organizational structure, decision making, leadership, and training and education, which socializes personnel into the community policing ethos (Weisburd, McElroy, and Hardyman 1988; Zhao 1996; Birzer and Tannechill 2001).

Community-oriented policing is a strategy that entails crime prevention, problem solving, community partnerships, and organizational transformation (Eck and Spelman 1987; Bennett and Lupton 1992). The ideas of community policing are relatively simplistic in that the police take on a role of being more community oriented and the citizens take on a role of being more involved with assisting the police with information (Thurman, Zhao, and Giacomazzi 2001). Many scholars argue that, with community policing, police officers will be expected to become partners with the community in maintaining social order (Carter and Radelet 1999).

Community policing differs from traditional law enforcement, because it allows police the freedom to expand the scope of their jobs. Police in this sense are challenged to become community problem solvers and encouraged to use their time creatively. Likewise, police will be required to discern vast amounts of information and recognize available resources to apply to problem solving.

Considerable theoretical scholarship on community policing has speculated on the importance of the police to work in partnership with citizens and other private and public organizations to solve problems and improve the quality of life in neighborhoods. For example, Trojanowicz (1990) observed that "community policing requires a department-wide philosophical commitment to involve average citizens as partners in the process of reducing and controlling the contemporary problems of crime, drugs, fear of crime and neighborhood decay; and in efforts to improve overall quality of life in the community." Many police agencies that have received federal funding for community-oriented policing have reported that they are working in partnership with community groups and other organizations to identify and solve problems (Maguire and Mastrofski 1999; DeJong and Mastrofski 2001).

Recall that the paramilitary and bureaucratic model of policing assumes a high level of technical expertise in controlling crime, which places very little reliance on the police and the citizens. This has serious consequences, including victimizing many sectors of society in the sense that the police often missed the opportunity to view these segments in positive circumstances (Thurman, Zhao, and Giacomazzi 2001). We argue that, through the implementation of community-oriented policing strategies, which require, in part, organizational transformation (i.e., allowing for more participative decision-making venues as well as minimizing the paramilitary command and control culture both externally and internally), will begin to strengthen ties between the police and communities. Thus, community policing, by its very nature, is designed to flourish under more corporate or business-like managerial structures, which nurtures a participative-employee-oriented department (Thurman, Zhao, and Giacomazzi 2001; Oliver 2004).

Technology versus People: End Our Overreliance on Technology

Historically, many American cops walked a beat, conversing with citizens in face-to-face settings. Recently, however, police have shifted in large numbers from the beat to patrol cars. Although efficient, the patrol car does not easily allow for community service. While in the car, it becomes very difficult for officers to help the proverbial "old lady" cross the street. As a result, police-citizen contact is primarily crime scene investigation. When police officers respond only to incidents of crime, they see community members as criminals in waiting. Such settings negate the two-way contact that is needed to create mutual respect and understanding. As Zellner (1995) reminds us, "well-trained officers walking a beat learn their neighborhoods and are often able to prevent trouble. There is considerable merit in the old saying, 'an ounce of prevention is worth a pound of cure.'"

Make Symbolic Changes in Uniforms and Messages of Control

As an important symbolic step, law enforcement should give up their military-style clothing and gear. Camouflage and black or near-black uniforms should be replaced with a color more consistent and symbolic of democracy (such as ordinary blue). Powers (1995), a scholar of the psychology of clothing, explains that black law enforcement uniforms tap "into associations between the color black and authority, invincibility, the power to violate laws with impunity."

More than this, however, the militarized appearance of the police is an act of symbolic violence. Conceived traditionally, violence is any physical act committed against a person or object for the purposes of instilling harm. Symbolic violence, conversely, is a cultural action used to inspire fear and subservience. Symbolic violence is used to suppress the beliefs and behaviors inconsistent with the interests of the dominant order (Bourdieu 1977; Bourdieu and Passerson 1977). Consider the following example.

In Jerusalem in September 1996, an Israeli miscalculation triggered riots that led to the deaths of scores of Palestinians and Israelis. The government (under Prime Minister Benjamin Netanyahu) opened a tunnel for tourists along the edge of a sacred Moslem site. The tunnel was a symbolic violation of Palestinian and Islamic self-respect . . . It was an act of symbolic violence, reminiscent of many other Israeli actions, including a military sweep that attracted almost no press attention: the army went into a Palestinian town and killed all the dogs. Someone with a macabre sense of humor had read Kafka: at the end of The Trial, Josef K. declines to commit suicide and is stabbed to death by government official. His last words as he expires are "Like a dog." The Israeli message to Palestinians: "You are like dogs to us. Today we kill your dogs; tomorrow it will be you." A government that typically hesitates, even slightly, about committing real massacres commits symbolic massacres instead, to prove its point (*Ethical Spectacle* 1996).

We contend that the militarization of the police uniform is an act of symbolic violence. The militarized appearance is used to transform police-community interactions to an outcome of distance and control. Specifically, the removal of traditional police colors attacks the "policing of the police." Manning and Mahendra (1997) write the following:

> An important irony is that much state violence in the past (i.e., policing) was largely covert and, although public, not subject to review or criticism . . . The increase in the mobility of television cameras, satellite feeds, and constant television cameras, and constant television news coverage . . . means the probability of viewing . . . backstage activities, the untoward, the violent, the corrupt, and the venial may readily come front stage news.

The removal of traditional police uniforms are symbolic acts used to distance "outsiders" (e.g., the community) from the practice of policing. The police, as a control agent, are made legitimate when their ability to use violent (and sometimes fatal) force goes unquestioned. However, when public scrutiny is made to enter this arena, the police's central role (the threat of applying violence) becomes questioned. Conceived here, the militarization of police uniforms function to maintain an internal legitimacy within the department by enhancing their role as enforcers of public violence and serve to symbolically construct a hierarchy between the police and the public.

Conclusion

This work highlights the societal harm perpetuated by police militarization. In particular, we argue that the military model of policing operates on the principle of authoritarian control, with no room for consensus, dissent, or democracy. Those who operate under such models organize a world that is ill fitted to the values of due process, democracy, and diversity, values on which civilian law enforcement must be found.

In response, we have suggested the reformation of the American policing system within a broader system of organization that focuses on community service, trust building, and changes to the police's symbolic order of social control. In the end, we hold that such measures could prevent the needless loss of life and victimization of persons by law enforcement in the United States.

Unmistakably, police militarization is an impediment to effective control of abuse of women and children and trafficking in women and children. This is because successful control and prevention of trafficking in and abuse of women and children requires community cooperation with the police, which police militarism impedes.

References

Alpert, G. P., and Dunham, R. G. 1996. *Policing Urban America*, 3rd ed. Prospect Heights, IL: Waveland Press.

Amnesty International USA. N.d. "United States of America: Race, Rights, and Police Brutality." http://www.amnestyusa.org, accessed January 11, 2004.

Bayley, D. H. 2001. *Democratizing the Police Abroad: What to Do and How to Do It.* Washington, DC: National Institute of Justice.

Bennett, T., and Lupton, R. 1992. "A Survey of the Allocation and Use of Community Constables in England and Wales." *British Journal of Criminology* 32(1):167–182.

Bier, J. 1999. "Gallado Family Awarded $12.5 Million." *Fresno Bee*, March 13.

Birzer, M. L. 1996. "Police Supervision in the 21st Century." *FBI Law Enforcement Bulletin* 65(6):6–13.

Birzer, M. L. 2000. "Organizational Change and Community Policing." In *Community Policing: A New Strategy for the 21st Century*, edited by M. J. Palmiotto. Gaithersburg, MD: Aspen.

Birzer, M. L., and Tannehill, R. 2001. "A More Effective Training Approach for Contemporary Policing." *Police Quarterly* 4(2):232–252.

Bopp, W. J. 1977. *O. W. Wilson and the Search for a Police Profession*. Port Washington, NY: Kennikat Press.

Bourdieu, P. 1977. *Outline of a Theory of Practice*. Cambridge: Cambridge University Press.

Bourdieu, P., and Passeron J. C. 1977. *Reproduction in Education, Society, and Culture*. Beverly Hills, CA: Sage.

Brand, M. J., and Birzer, M. L. 2001. "Generalist Social Work Practice and Community-Oriented Policing." *Journal of Community Policing* 1(3):19–30.

Brewer, J. D., Adrian, G., Hume, I., Moxon-Browne, E., and Wilford, R. 1988. *The Police, Public Order, and the State*. New York: St. Martin's Press.

Carter, D. L., and Radelet, L. A. 1999. *The Police and the Community*, 6th ed. Upper Saddle River, NJ: Prentice Hall.

Culbertson, H. M. 2000. "A Key Step in Police-Community Relations: Identify the Divisive Issues." *Public Relations Quarterly* 45.

DeJong, C., and Mastrofski, S. D. 2001. "Patrol Officers and Problem Solving: An Application of Expectancy Theory." *Justice Quarterly* 18(1):31–61.

Dodge, L. 1998. "3 Police Officers Shot in Portland, 1 Fatally." *Seattle Post-Intelligencer*, January 28.

Eck, J., and Spelman, W. 1987. "Who Ya Gonna Call? The Police as Problem Busters." *Crime and Delinquency* 1:31–52.

Enloe, C. 1980. *Police, Military, and Ethnicity*. New Brunswick, NJ: Transaction.

Ethical Spectacle. 1996. "Israeli Symbolic Violence." http://www.spectacle.org/1196/symbol.html, accessed January 11, 2004.

Fine, M., Freudenberg, N., Payne, Y., Perkins, T., Smith, K., and Wanzer, K. 2003. "Anything Can Happen with Police Around: Urban Youth Evaluate Strategies of Surveillance in Public Places." *Journal of Social Issues* 59.

Fukuyama, F. 1995. *Trust: The Social Virtues and the Creation of Prosperity*. New York: Free Press.

Goulder, A. W. 1960. "The Norm of Reciprocity." *American Sociological Review* 25:161–178.

Greensboro News and Record. 1998. "Police Shooting Draws Protests." September 7.

Haas, D. F., and Forrest, D. A. 1981. "Trust and Symbolic Exchange." *Social Psychology Quarterly* 44:3–13.

Herald.com. 2002. "Suspicious Gunfire." http://www.miami.com/mid/miamihearald/news/local/4484414.htm, accessed January 11, 2004.

Hodgson, J. F. 2001. "Police Violence in Canada and the USA: Analysis and Management." *Policing: An International Journal of Police Strategies and Management* 24(4):520–549.

Kerley-Kent, R., and Benson, M. L. 2000. "Does Community Policing Help Build Stronger Communities?" *Police Quarterly* 3(1):46–69.

Kraska, P. B. 1994. "The Police and Military in the Post–Cold War Era: Streamlining the State's Use of Force Entities in the Drug War." *Police Forum* 4:1–8.

Kraska, P. B. 1996. "Enjoying Militarism: Police Paramilitary Units." *Justice Quarterly* 13:405–429.

Kraska, P. B., and Kappeler, V. E. 1997. "Militarizing the American Police: The Rise and Normalization of Paramilitary Units." *Social Problems* 44(1):1–18.

Leach, L. 2003. "Answers Elusive in School Raid." TheState.com. http://www.thestate.com/mld/thestate/news/local/7274327.htm, accessed January 10, 2004.

Lorinskas, R. A., and Kulis, J. C. 1986. "The Military Model and Policing: A Misunderstood Ideology." *Police Studies* 7:184–193.
Luhmann, N. 1979. *Trust and Power*. New York: Wiley.
MacGregor, H. E. 1998. "Family of Slain Officer Can Sue City, Court Rules." *Los Angeles Times*, May 29.
Maguire, E., and Mastrofski, S. D. 1999. "Patterns of Community Policing in the United States." *Police Quarterly* 3(1):4–45.
Manning, P. K. 1977. *Police Work: The Social Organization of Policing*. Cambridge, MA: NM Press.
Manning, P. K., and Mahendra, P. S. 1997. "Violence and Hyperviolence: The Rhetoric and Practice of Community Policing." *Sociological Spectrum* 17:339–361.
Mastrofski, S. D., and Ritti, R. R. 2000. "Making Sense of Community Policing: A Theory-Based Analysis." *Police Practice and Research* 1(2):183–210.
Nagourney, A., and Connelly, M. 2001. "Giuliani's Ratings Drop over Actions in Dorismond Case." *New York Times*, April 7.
Newsday.com. 2004. "Innocent Bystander Killed after Police Chase." http://www.nynewsday.com, accessed January 11, 2004.
Oliver, W. M. 2000. "The Third Generation of Community Policing: Moving through Innovation, Diffusion, and Institutionalization." *Police Quarterly* 3(4):367–388.
Oliver, W. M. 2004. *Community-Oriented Policing: A Systematic Approach to Policing*. Upper Saddle, NJ: Prentice Hall.
Palmiotto, M. J. 1997. *Policing: Concepts, Strategies, and Current Issues in American Police Forces*. Durham, NC: Carolina Academic Press.
Palmiotto, M. J., Birzer, M. L., and Unnithan, N. P. 2000. "Training in Community Policing: A Suggested Curriculum." *Policing: An International Journal of Police Strategies and Management* 23(1):8–21.
Parenti, C. 2000. *Lockdown America: Police and Prisons in the Age of Crisis*. New York: Verso.
Patterson, J. 1995. "Community Policing: Learning the Lessons of History." *FBI Law Enforcement Bulletin* 64(5):5–9.
Powers, W. F. 1995. "Dressed to Kill?" *Washington Post*, May 4.
Putnam, R. D. 2000. *Bowling Alone*. New York: Simon and Schuster.
Rashburn, W. 2000. "Undercover Police in Manhattan Kill an Unarmed Man in a Scuffle." *New York Times*, February 5.
Simmel, G. 1990. *The Philosophy of Money*. London: Routledge.
60 Minutes. 1997. "Gearing Up." Transcript, December 21.
Spitzer, E. 1999. "The New York City Police Department's 'Stop and Frisk' Practices: A Report to the People of the State of New York from the Office of the Attorney General." New York: Civil Rights Bureau.
STL.com. 2003. "Centralia, Mo., Woman Sues after Arrest over $2 Ticket." http://www.stltoday.com, accessed January 11, 2004.
Thurman, Q. C., Zhao, J., and Giacomazzi, A. L. 2001. *Community Policing in a Community Era*. Los Angeles: Roxbury.
Trojanowicz, R. C. 1990. "Community Policing Is Not Police-Community Relations." *FBI Law Enforcement Bulletin* 1:10.
Weber, D. C. 1999. *Warrior Cops: The Ominous Growth of Paramilitarism in American Police Departments*. Washington, DC: Cato Institute.

Weisburd, D., McElroy, J., and Hardyman, P. 1988. "Challenges to Supervision in Community Policing: Observations on a Pilot Project." *American Journal of Police* 7(2):29–50.

Weisburd, D., McElroy, J., and Hardyman, P. 1989. "Maintaining Control in Community-Oriented Policing." In *Police and Policing: Contemporary Issues*, edited by D. J. Kenney. New York: Praeger.

Whitlock, C., and Fallis, D. C. 2001. "Officers Killed with impunity: Officials Ruled Shootings Justified in Every Case—Even of Unarmed Citizens." *Washington Post*, July 1.

Yates, D. L., Pillai-Vijayan, K., and Humburg, J. D. 1997. "Committing to the New Police-Community Partnerships in the United States and England." *Policing and Society* 7(2): 99–115.

Zellner, W. 1995. *Counter Cultures: A Sociological Analysis*. New York: St. Martin's Press.

Zhao, J. 1996. *Why Police Organizations Change: A Study of Community Oriented Policing*. Washington, DC: Police Executive Research Forum.

Conclusion

DILIP K. DAS AND MICHAEL BERLIN

It is evident from Obi Ebbe's theoretical considerations in Chapters 1–4 that abuse of women and children is a global problem affecting societies around the world. Country-specific case studies in Chapters 5–15 and 17–19 addressing issues related to abuse of women and children in European, African, Asian, and North and South American continents provide ample evidence of the universal nature of the problem.[1] As Ebbe documents in the introductory chapters, instances of abuse of women and children date back to ancient times and continue through the present. There is an increasing awareness of abuse in both the developed and developing world. Problems of abuse manifest themselves in a myriad of ways ranging from rape, sex offenses, and assault to emotional and psychological abuse to deprivation of inheritance rights and forced marriages. Abuse includes domestic violence and familial child abuse, criminal acts by acquaintances and strangers, organized criminal activity involving human trafficking, and other activities. Motivations for and causes of abuse differ substantially, by type of abuse, culture, and the individuals involved.

Problems of Definitions

As indicated above, abuse of women and children may occur in many ways. Although there is no generally accepted definition of abuse, the United Nations Fourth World Conference on Women, Beijing, 1995, Platform for Action D. 113, defines "violence against women" as follows:

> Any act of gender-based violence that results in, or is likely to result in, physical, sexual or psychological harm or suffering to women, including threats of such acts, coercion or arbitrary deprivation of liberty, whether occurring in public or private life. Accordingly, violence against women encompasses but is not limited to the following:
>
> - Physical, sexual and psychological violence occurring in the family, including battering, sexual abuse of female children in the household, dowry-related violence, marital rape, female genital mutilation, and other traditional practices harmful to women, non-spousal violence and violence related to exploitation
> - Physical, sexual and psychological violence occurring within the general community, including rape, sexual abuse, sexual harassment

and intimidation at work, in educational institutions and elsewhere, trafficking in women and forced prostitution
- Physical, sexual and psychological violence perpetrated or condoned by the state wherever it occurs

Aspects of country-specific definitions can be found in the national case studies that are included in this book. Nations and, in certain instances, states or provinces (e.g., the United States and Australia) each have their own penal codes. A national code, for example, is referred to briefly in Maximilian Edelbacher's discussion of the Austrian Penal and Criminal Procedure Codes (Chapter 5), particularly with regard to trafficking in human beings and "Exekutionsordnung," Prevention of Violence in the Family (Art. 382 (b)1). One notes also the extensive discussion of definitional issues in John Murray's case study of Australia in Chapter 18. Only after Australia passed the Slavery and Sexual Servitude Act in 1999 (Sec. 270.1 et. seq.) defining human trafficking, was it possible for national authorities to collect data concerning trafficking and estimate the number of women who are victims of commercial sex trafficking.

Many of the definitions of abuse incorporate a number of common elements as suggested by Ebbe in Chapter 1, i.e., physical, emotional/psychological, and/or sexual abuse. In fact, Austria's "Exekutionsordnung," Prevention of Violence in the Family statute, refers to both the "physical integrity" and "psychological health" of the victim (Art. 382 (b)1, p. 134), which is remarkably similar to the definition proposed by Ebbe.

There are great differences in legal and statutory definitions of abuse of women and children. The reasons for this are multifold. First, definitions of abuse are culturally dependent, both geographically and temporally. What is acceptable behavior in one nation, culture, or region of the world may constitute abuse in another. Next, even within the same nation, culture, or region of the world, behavior that was commonly recognized as acceptable in the past may no longer be considered appropriate, or even defined as criminal. Moreover, the distinction between criminal and noncriminal abuse varies between different cultures and within the same culture over time. For example, it was a crime for an unmarried woman to buy contraceptives in the state of Connecticut until the U.S. Supreme Court ruling in *Griswold v. Connecticut* (1965). Norms and mores differ from one culture to another, between subcultures, and within the same culture over time. Formal laws may or may not reflect these changes.

Definitions of criminal abuse should be and typically are narrower than violations of norms or civil legal standards. Criminal abuse of women and children typically involves violent acts such as assault and battery, rape, and other nonconsensual sex acts and imminent threats or extortion. Narrow definitions of criminal abuse are consistent with the western view that the criminal justice system is a last line of defense preserved for the more egregious offenses and that criminal sanctions take effect when cultural norms fail. Narrow definitions of criminal abuse are further consistent with the rule of law, and they facilitate effective prosecutions. Although crimes such as assault, battery, rape, and incest have their origins in the common law or continental codes and are usually defined on the basis of national statutory and case law, other crimes such as human trafficking are of relatively recent origin and need to be carefully defined.

Cultural Attitudes to Abuse

Many forms of abuse such as assault and battery, domestic violence, rape and other nonconsensual sex acts, sexual assault and molestation, incest, child abuse, and child pornography know no national boundaries. Human trafficking for labor and sexual exploitation is also a universal phenomenon, typically involving organized criminal activity. However, the nature and extent of numerous types of abuse, as well as societal condemnation, appear to vary significantly between nations and cultures. For example, Ebbe indicates that, although corporal punishment is typically considered child abuse in the United States, this might not be the case in many African and other countries (Chapter 1). Often these acts are committed by individuals intimately related to or otherwise acquainted with the victim.

In addition to acts of physical violence and sexual abuse, other types of abuse include emotional, psychological, and economic abuse. Included in emotional or psychological abuse are contempt, humiliation, indifference, insults, mockery, and sometimes blackmail. Many forms of sexual harassment and educational discrimination arguably fall in this category, as well. Emotional or psychological abuse shares a mix of universal and culture-specific characteristics.

Ebbe defines abuse of women and children as based on acts or omissions likely to lead to physical, sexual, and emotional/psychological abuse. This definition of abuse of women and children is broad enough to include deprivation of financial support, threats of divorce, or abandonment and deprivation of peace of mind (Chapter 1). Emotional or psychological abuse, absent violence associated with assault, battery, and other commonly recognized crimes, is more likely be reflective of community standards or the subject of normative violations rather than a criminal violation. At most, the offender may be subject to civil legal remedies and not criminal sanctions, i.e., a grounds for divorce, support, or a factor to consider in awarding custody of minor children. This is not to suggest that culture and norms are not important factors in abuse.

In brief, as Ebbe points out in his discussion of "Problems of Definition," definitions of abuse are also culturally dependent; behavior that is considered abusive in one culture may be considered acceptable in another. In the absence of a common definition of abuse, it is difficult to measure and compare levels of abuse.

Universal and Perennial Nature of Abuse of Women and Children

As the authors of Chapters 4–19 indicate, abuse of women and children is not limited to any specific geographical location but is found in Africa, Asia, Australia, Europe, and the Americas. No society appears to be immune. Abuse of women and children spans racial, ethnic, religious, and socioeconomic divisions. Nations examined by the authors reflect a wide range of demographic characteristics, including countries whose populations were primarily European, African, Indian, and Asian, reflecting a wide range of ethnic backgrounds and religions, including Christianity, Islam, Hinduism, or a mix of these religions and others. Both wealthy and poor nations are represented. Even the Kingdom of Bahrain, which appears to have limited domestic abuse of women and children, experiences a sex trade involving foreigners. Abuse of women and children not only spans geography and demographics, it also spans time.

As Ebbe explains in Chapter 1, the historical antecedents of abuse of women and children date back to biblical times, continue through the middle ages, into the Renaissance, and extend into the present. Indeed, as the author points out, some of the worst documented cases of child abuse from the middle ages to the eighteenth century make today's abusers pale in comparison. Before his arrest on September 13, 1440, Baron Gilles de Rais, a satanic cult leader, had killed more than 800 children. In an effort to avoid torture, he confessed and was convicted of "the killing, strangling, and massacring of innocent children . . . , evoking demons, making pacts with them, and sacrificing children to them" and other crimes.

Other glaring examples of abuse between the 16th and 18th centuries include the murders of more than 600 children by Countess Elizabeth Bathony of Hungary. In addition to sexually molesting the children, she used their blood as body lotion. Convicted of 80 murders in 1680, she was essentially sentenced to life imprisonment in an apartment of her castle and died four years later. Catherine La Voisin of France was convicted after she confessed to having sacrificed more than 2,500 children. She was tortured and burned at the stake in February 1680. In Africa during the 1600s, Queen Zingua of Angola, a sadistic nymphomaniac, killed innumerable men, women, boys, and girls. In one two-day period, she slaughtered 113 children. Undoubtedly, many more instances of abuse were committed by far less prominent individuals. However, the historical record is largely silent on this point.

Increased Awareness

Unlike earlier periods of human history, there is increased awareness of abuse in both the developed and developing world today. In many cases, the growing awareness is the result of deliberate efforts of a combination of advocacy groups, nongovernment organizations, and, as a consequence, government agencies. The growing awareness is fueled by mass media coverage (newspapers, magazines, radio, TV, and the Internet) of abuse of women and children. In some instances, there is a crystallizing event. For example, William Hughes cites the discovery of the dismembered body of a West African boy in the Thames River in his case study of the United Kingdom (Chapter 7). Agbonkhese Moses, Olufunke Aruna, and Michael Folami cite news reports concerning deportations of the victims of human trafficking in their case study of Nigeria (Chapter 12).

The growing awareness is also fueled by the ability of citizens to organize in countries as diverse as India, Nigeria, the United States, and elsewhere. See Yateendra Singh Jafa's discussion of criminal exploitation of women and children in India (Chapter 14) and the role of the civil sector and nongovernment organizations in advocacy and raising public awareness. Globalization contributes to individuals' awareness of the world around them and allows for comparison of one's own nation or culture with other nations and cultures.

Although abuse of women and children appears to be increasing in many societies, it is not clear whether increased complaints of abuse represent actual increases in instances of abuse or whether they represent an increased willingness to report abuse. More research is necessary on this point. An exception to this are those nations undergoing extraordinary political, economic, and social changes, which have undoubtedly led to an increase in human trafficking impacting not only the countries of origin but also destination nations around the globe, e.g., the collapse of the former Soviet Union has resulted in a tremendous increase in trafficking of Eastern European women to Germany, Austria, the Netherlands, other Western European nations and countries as far away as South Africa. All of the European case studies, including Austria (Chapter 5), Germany (Chapter 6), and the United Kingdom (Chapter 7) address this issue.

Causes of Abuse

Some forms of abuse of women and children tend to be economically rooted, such as domestic servitude, and child labor, which, in certain developing countries, may amount to indentured servitude or slavery. For example Vicky Karimi (Chapter 10) documents rampant abuse of domestic laborers, typically women and children. Other forms of abuse appear culturally based, for example, in Benin and certain other countries, there are forced marriage, marriage by exchange, marriage by abduction, "levirate" (a form of forced marriage requiring a widow to marry a family member of her deceased husband), rites of widowhood, excision, and other forms of genital mutilation (Chapter 9). Kenyan women face inheritance, matrimonial, and other property rights violations despite constitutional protections (Chapter 8). In India, torture and death associated with dowry demands, female feticide and infanticide, denigration of *dalit* and *adivasi* (tribal) women considered untouchable, *sati* (self-immolation by a widow on her dead husband's funeral pyre), witch hunting; the *devdasi* system of dancing girls attached to temples, Muslim divorce or *talaq*, occasional child sacrifices, and rural raw justice appear to be culturally based (Chapter 14).

As pointed out in the Chapter 1 by Ebbe, the nullification of female authority dates back to ancient times. Males dominated the household in most societies from ancient times through the middle ages. Women and children were second-class citizens and lived at the mercy of men. Women, followed by girls and boys, were the most frequent victims of sacrifices to the gods during pre-Christian times. With the exception of human sacrifice, we see these themes repeated in many cultures today.

Poverty, deprivation, lack of resources, poor education, and lack of opportunities are frequently associated with abuse of women and children. In addition, other factors related to gender-based violence and child abuse include exposure to violence/sociopolitical factors, gender roles, the objectification of females, perceptions of manhood, consumerist lifestyles and violent role models, HIV/AIDS-related issues, substance abuse, and financial and emotional dependency of victims in relationships with their abusers. Other causes of criminal and noncriminal abuse of women cited by Ebbe in Chapter 2 include "the nature of women," political power, religious influences, satanic and wealth cults, abnormal male personalities, socioeconomic status (poverty), and factors associated with family violence.

Multiple factors appear to influence the nature and extent of abuse in any given nation. The problem is worse in the developing world, fueled by poverty, lack of economic opportunity, and unemployment coupled with aspects of local culture. Trafficking in human beings is exacerbated by war, natural disasters, and, in the case of the former Soviet Union, the collapse of a controlled economy and a strong central government. William Hughes discusses these factors in Chapter 7. Precipitating factors he cites include the availability of inexpensive travel, the opening of previously closed borders, globalization of business that facilitates international criminal enterprises, technological advances, the Internet, and communications systems, the involvement of organized crime driven by profit, and political and religious upheaval and mass population movements. Facilitating factors in trafficking include legislative weakness impeding prosecution and providing little deterrent, lack of international cooperation, lack of domestic cooperation, lack of resources, and other priorities.

Motivations for and causes of abuse vary by the types of abuse involved. However, there are some similarities between different types of abuse. Cultural, as well as individual factors, likely play a role with regard to abusers and their victims. The evidence suggests that countries that appear to value women and children least tend to have the highest rates of criminal abuse. Agbonkhese Moses, Olufunke Aruna, and Michael Folami relate the low arrest rates and unsuccessful prosecutions of human traffickers in Nigeria (Chapter 12) to the low social status of women and children. Azonhoume (Chapter 9) also makes reference to the inferior social status of women contributing to abuse in Benin. High rates of abuse of women and children are also documented in Kenya (Chapters 8 and 10), Benin (Chapter 9), and South Africa (Chapter 11). These studies also document extreme poverty as contributing to the abuse of women and children.

Remedial Measures

Reducing the problem of abuse is not an easy task. The case studies suggest that national responses to abuse share certain similarities but also important differences. Many countries incorporate some combination of legislation, enforcement, prevention, and support services in their efforts to combat abuse of women and children. See, for example, the Austrian, German, South African, Philippine, and Indian approaches to combating abuse of women and children (Chapters 5, 6, 11, 13, and 14). The emphasis of and elements incorporated in these approaches differ based on the problems they are designed to combat, for example, domestic violence, rape, prostitution, and child sexual exploitation, as well as social, cultural, political, and economic conditions in their respective countries. The United Kingdom and Australia use an integrated intelligence-led approach to combat human trafficking (Chapters 7 and 18). All of the case studies concerning African countries, including Chapters 8 and 10 concerning Kenya, Chapter 9 concerning Benin, Chapter 11 concerning South Africa, and Chapter 12 concerning Nigeria, focus on the need to alleviate poverty as an essential element of reducing abuse of women and children.

Differences in the national approaches are attributable, in part, to the specific nature and extent of the national problems of abuse that the responses were implemented to address. These are also attributable, in part, to social, cultural, political, and economic differences between sovereign states. Despite methodological limitations of the studies, it is possible to identify nations in which abuse of women and children is most serious, recognize common themes, reflect on best practices, and make preliminary recommendations based on these practices.

Based on the research and descriptive work of the case study chapters, abuse of women and children appears worst in Benin, Kenya, Nigeria, and, probably India, all developing countries. The authors of these chapters agree that poverty is an important contributing factor to the abuse of women and children. They further agree that efforts to alleviate poverty, improve education, and expand employment opportunities are critical to reducing abuse of women and children. Cultural norms that devalue women and children also need to be addressed.

Comparative research and analysis of as well as presentation of consequent remedial measures against abuse of women and children is complicated by the fact that, as indicated previously, there are no commonly accepted definitions of what constitutes abuse of women and children. Commonly accepted definitions of human trafficking and related crimes are critical. Not only do they facilitate effective prosecution, they are a precondition for accurate recordkeeping, which facilitates greater awareness and understanding of the nature and extent of the problem. They are also an important ingredient in international cooperation.

Analysis of different national approaches to reducing abuse of women and children provides a valuable starting point in identifying best practices to combat what has long appeared to be an intractable problem. Although methodological considerations of the underlying research necessitate caution in generalizing the findings of these national studies and limited quantitative data make it impossible to establish causal connections between programmatic activities and their impact on abuse of women and children, it is possible to examine national responses, identify and categorize key elements of the responses, and establish preliminary recommendations based on careful analysis of the cases presented.

National responses to abuse typically involve a mix of prevention programs, including, but not limited to, media and informational campaigns designed to increase awareness of abuse, legislation expanding the definitions of and increasing penalties for abuse, increased enforcement activities, harsher judicial scrutiny and sentencing, and implementation of treatment programs for offenders and victims. Comparison and analysis of key aspects of the national studies provide valuable insight for combating the problem of abuse of women and children and suggest prospective solutions. A caveat, what might be an appropriate solution in one country may or may not work in another because of a variety of factors, including resource limitations, cultural values, politics, national priorities, the structure of criminal justice and legal institutions, police practices, constitutional safeguards, and the nature and extent of the problem itself.

Many of the studies make clear that an integrated approach involving law enforcement, the judiciary, prevention and treatment agencies, and the public is essential. This was the approach taken by Australia, Great Britain, South Africa, and India, aspects of which were also adopted in other countries. All passed legislation to combat human trafficking or other forms of abuse. Australia and Great Britain specifically considered relevant United Nations Conventions in crafting their statutes so that they clearly defined offenses related to human trafficking and presumably paralleled the statutory language of other nations combating human trafficking, thereby facilitating international partnerships. Many countries have enhanced penalties for crimes involving abuse of women and children. All have constitutional and statutory protections, ensuring the rights of all citizens generally and women in particular. However, these and other nations recognize that legislation, in and of itself, is not enough. South Africa, Kenya, and India have very progressive constitutional and/or legislative protections for women but, nevertheless, suffer serious problems of abuse of women and children.

To be effective, laws designed to combat abuse of women and children must be enforced. This means that the police must have sufficient resources to enforce these laws and make enforcement of them a priority. Enforcement requires the coordinated efforts of law enforcement at the national, regional, state, and local level. In addition, it requires that law enforcement at all levels cooperate with customs and immigration and other federal agencies. Australia (Chapter 18) and Great Britain (Chapter 7) have adopted a multiagency intelligence-led approach. Intelligence-led policing involves a proactive rather than a reactive investigative approach, finding and targeting the weak spots in a criminal organization. Australia couples its intelligence-led approach with community policing, a feature that Murray (Chapter 18) considers critical to the successful reduction of human trafficking for the reasons discussed below.

The British approach (Chapter 7) to intelligence-led policing uses a wide range of legislative, administrative, and investigative tools, such as financial investigations, asset seizures, and immigration powers. Law enforcement, the intelligence community, and government departments work together, share information, and jointly decide on the best tactics and who should carry them out. In addition to domestic partners, the intelligence-led approach encourages partnerships with foreign law enforcement and intelligence communities, generally from the countries out of which the traffickers operate.

In discussing the Australian approach, Murray (Chapter 18) argues that a return to traditional policing such as that which has occurred after the September 11, 2001, terrorist attacks in the United States would be counterproductive in combating human trafficking, which requires sensitivity, trust, community support, and information exchange. John Paul and Michael Birzer (Chapter 19) echo this theme in their discussion of the militarization of American police forces as it relates to the victimization of women and children, warn of the dangers of a military approach, and strongly encourage community engagement. In addition to the creation of specialized units to work with victims and investigate offenses and training for patrol officers throughout departments, the Philippine approach (Chapter 13) to creating a Philippine National Police Women and Children Protection Desk in every police station is a promising outgrowth of the community policing philosophy.

Not only must law enforcement agencies work together, they must coordinate their efforts with social service organizations and the judiciary. Education and prevention are important aspects of an integrated campaign. Media and informational campaigns designed to increase public awareness are an integral part of efforts to change norms. In addition to sensitizing the public to the dangers of abuse of women and children and facilitating prevention, they serve to build public support for appropriate legislation and enforcement. Effective criminal enforcement and successful prosecutions may also serve to change norms as well as provide a deterrent.

Although certain cultural norms contribute to abuse, other informal mechanisms of social control can be a powerful force in the prevention of abuse of women and children. For example, Ebbe (Chapter 4) discusses how close residential kinship patterns in Nigeria and other developing African countries allow family members and relatives to respond immediately in cases of domestic violence. Although religion has contributed to abuse under certain circumstances, such as "ORO divinity" and Vodoun divinity ceremonies in Benin (Chapter 9), religious intervention has also acted to control abuse in traditional Igbo society in precolonial Nigeria (Chapter 4).

Adoption of a theoretical framework distinguishing between different types and degrees of abuse, legislation clearly defining criminal abuse of women and children, increased reporting of offenses, accurate recordkeeping, and transparent data analysis would greatly contribute to a better understanding of the nature and extent of global abuse of women and children. This would in turn help identify specific causes and enabling factors of abuse of women and children, allow for thorough comparisons between and among nations, and ultimately lead to comprehensive research and recommendations that would guide enforcement, prevention, and treatment efforts. The end result would be reduced abuse and improved quality of life for women and children around the globe.

Expanding on the issue of problems of definition raised previously in this conclusion, Murray (Chapter 18) explains that, until recently, there were no specific offenses of human trafficking under Australian law and no statistics kept on its incidence. Statistics on assault, sexual assault, rape, kidnapping, extortion, and other related offenses were not linked to "trafficking." Australia's active participation in the development of the United Nations Convention Against Transnational Organized Crime and its supplementary protocols dealing with people smuggling and people trafficking (United Nations Protocol to Prevent, Suppress, and Punish Trafficking in Persons, Especially Women and Children, 2000) helped to guide related national legislation, particularly the Australian Criminal Code Amendment (Slavery and Sexual Servitude) Act of 1999 defining the statutory offenses of slavery and sexual servitude. Not only did this statute allow for prosecution of those involved in human trafficking, its uniform definition facilitated data collection and recordkeeping, which enabled authorities to determine the nature and extent of Australia's human trafficking problem.

A similar situation existed in the United Kingdom, which is also a signatory to the United Nations Protocol on Trafficking, as well as a European Union Framework Decision concerning trafficking for sexual and labor exploitation. As a result, Britain's Nationality and Immigration Act of 2002 introduced a stopgap offense of trafficking for purposes of controlling a person in prostitution and more comprehensive modifications to the Sexual Offenses Act of 2003.

Both nations implemented intelligence-led interagency enforcement approaches characterized by extensive internal and external partnerships, coupled with support for victims. The Australian and British approaches to defining and combating human trafficking are instructive and appear to represent best practices in the war against the nightmare of human trafficking. Other nations would do well to emulate their example, working in concert with the United Nations and other international organizations, to draft clear, consistent, unambiguous criminal legislation penalizing human trafficking.

Note

1. Of all of the country-specific case studies, only Bahrain was found not to have a significant problem with regard to the abuse of women and children. Even here, the author, anonymous, acknowledges the existence of prostitution but indicates that most of the women involved are non-Bahrainis. See Chapter 16.

References

Anonymous. 2009. "Criminal Exploitation of Women and Children in the Kingdom of Bahrain." In *Criminal Abuse of Women and Children: An International Perspective*, edited by O. N. I. Ebbe and D. K. Das. Boca Raton, FL: CRC Press/Taylor & Francis Group, pp. 275–288.

Azaola, E. 2009. "Commercial Sexual Exploitation of Children in Mexico." In *Criminal Abuse of Women and Children: An International Perspective*, edited by

O. N. I. Ebbe and D. K. Das. Boca Raton, FL: CRC Press/Taylor & Francis Group, pp. 289–308.

Azonhoume, A. 2009. "Criminal Abuse of Women and Children in Benin." In *Criminal Abuse of Women and Children: An International Perspective*, edited by O. N. I. Ebbe and D. K. Das. Boca Raton, FL: CRC Press/Taylor & Francis Group, pp. 137–148.

Australia Criminal Code Amendment, Slavery, and Sexual Servitude Act. 1990. Sec. 270.1 et. seq.

Ebbe, O. N. I. 2009a. "Causes of Criminal and Noncriminal Abuses of Women." In *Criminal Abuse of Women and Children: An International Perspective*, edited by O. N. I. Ebbe and D. K. Das. Boca Raton, FL: CRC Press/Taylor & Francis Group, pp. 23–46.

Ebbe, O. N. I. 2009b. "Control and Prevention of Criminal Abuse of Women and Children: Domestic and International Approaches." In *Criminal Abuse of Women and Children: An International Perspective*, edited by O. N. I. Ebbe and D. K. Das. Boca Raton, FL: CRC Press/Taylor & Francis Group, pp. 63–72.

Ebbe, O. N. I. 2009c. "Definition and Historical Antecedents of Criminal Abuse of Women and Children." In *Criminal Abuse of Women and Children: An International Perspective*, edited by O. N. I. Ebbe and D. K. Das. Boca Raton, FL: CRC Press/Taylor & Francis Group, pp. 3–22.

Ebbe, O. N. I. 2009d. "The Scope and Causes of Criminal Abuse of Children." In *Criminal Abuse of Women and Children: An International Perspective*, edited by O. N. I. Ebbe and D. K. Das. Boca Raton, FL: CRC Press/Taylor & Francis Group, pp. 47–62.

Edelbacher, M. 2009. "Criminal Exploitation of Women and Children: An Austrian Perspective." In *Criminal Abuse of Women and Children: An International Perspective*, edited by O. N. I. Ebbe and D. K. Das. Boca Raton, FL: CRC Press/Taylor & Francis Group, pp. 75–98.

European Union Framework Decision Concerning Trafficking for Sexual and Labor. N.d. Exploitation.

Griswold v. Connecticut. 1965. 381 U.S. 479.

Harnishmacher, R. F. J. 2009. "Criminal Exploitation of Women and Children in Germany." In *Criminal Abuse of Women and Children: An International Perspective*, edited by O. N. I. Ebbe and D. K. Das. Boca Raton, FL: CRC Press/Taylor & Francis Group, pp. 99–112.

Hughes, W. 2009. "The Nature and Extent of Trafficking in Women and Children in the United Kingdom." In *Criminal Abuse of Women and Children: An International Perspective*, edited by O. N. I. Ebbe and D. K. Das. Boca Raton, FL: CRC Press/Taylor & Francis Group, pp. 113–122.

Jafa, Y. S. 2009. "Criminal Exploitation of Women and Children in India: Its Control." In *Criminal Abuse of Women and Children: An International Perspective*, edited by O. N. I. Ebbe and D. K. Das. Boca Raton, FL: CRC Press/Taylor & Francis Group, pp. 219–238.

Karimi, V. 2009. "Criminal Exploitation of Women and Children: Domestic Workers in Kenya." In *Criminal Abuse of Women and Children: An International Perspective*, edited by O. N. I. Ebbe and D. K. Das. Boca Raton, FL: CRC Press/Taylor & Francis Group, pp. 149–160.

Luga, V. 2009. "Criminal Exploitation of Women and Children in the Philippines." In *Criminal Abuse of Women and Children: An International Perspective*, edited by O. N. I. Ebbe and D. K. Das. Boca Raton, FL: CRC Press/Taylor & Francis Group, pp. 199–218.

Mtimkulu, L. 2009. "Criminal Exploitation of Women and Children: A South African Perspective." In *Criminal Abuse of Women and Children: An International Perspective*, edited by O. N. I. Ebbe and D. K. Das. Boca Raton, FL: CRC Press/Taylor & Francis Group, pp. 161–184.

Moses, A. S., Aruna, O. J., and Folami, M. 2009. "Trafficking of Women and Children in Nigeria: Slavery in the Modern Era." In *Criminal Abuse of Women and Children: An International Perspective*, edited by O. N. I. Ebbe and D. K. Das. Boca Raton, FL: CRC Press/Taylor & Francis Group, pp. 185–196.

Murray, J. 2009. "Criminal Exploitation of Women and Children: The Role of Community Policing." In *Criminal Abuse of Women and Children: An International Perspective*, edited by O. N. I. Ebbe and D. K. Das. Boca Raton, FL: CRC Press/Taylor & Francis Group, pp. 311–322.

Ndolo, G. O. 2009. "Criminal Exploitation of Women and Children: The Kenyan Experience." In *Criminal Abuse of Women and Children: An International Perspective*, edited by O. N. I. Ebbe and D. K. Das. Boca Raton, FL: CRC Press/Taylor & Francis Group, pp. 125–136.

Paul, J., and Birzer, M. L. 2009. "The Militarization of the American Police Force and Its Impact on the Victimization of Women and Children: A Critical Assessment." In *Criminal Abuse of Women and Children: An International Perspective*, edited by O. N. I. Ebbe and D. K. Das. Boca Raton, FL: CRC Press/Taylor & Francis Group, pp. 323–338.

Su-Huan, W., and Ching-Li, C. 2009. "Sexual Abuse in Taiwan: Multidisciplinary Criminal Case Processing." In *Criminal Abuse of Women and Children: An International Perspective*, edited by O. N. I. Ebbe and D. K. Das. Boca Raton, FL: CRC Press/Taylor & Francis Group, pp. 239–274.

United Kingdom Nationality and Immigration Act of 2002.

United Kingdom Sexual Offenses Act of 2003.

United Nations Fourth World Conference on Women. 1995. Platform for Action D. 113 http://www.un.org/womenwatch/daw/bejing/platform/violence.htm.

United Nations Convention against Transnational Organized Crime. N.d. See also its supplementary protocols dealing with people smuggling and people trafficking.

United Nations Protocol to Prevent, Suppress, and Punish Trafficking in Persons, Especially Women and Children. 2000. Adopted by resolution A/RES/55/25 of November 15, 2000, at the 55th session of the United Nations General Assembly.

International Police Executive Symposium (IPES)

The International Police Executive Symposium was founded in 1994. The aims and objectives of the IPES are to provide a forum to foster closer relationships among police researchers and practitioners globally, to facilitate cross-cultural, international, and interdisciplinary exchanges for the enrichment of the law enforcement profession, and to encourage discussion and published research on challenging and contemporary topics related to the profession.

One of the most important activities of the IPES is the organization of an annual meeting under the auspices of a police or educational institution. To date, meetings have been hosted by the Canton Police of Geneva, Switzerland (Police Challenges and Strategies, 1994), the International Institute of the Sociology of Law in Onati, Spain (Challenges of Policing Democracies, 1995), Kanagawa University in Yokohama, Japan (Organized Crime, 1996), the Federal Police in Vienna, Austria (International Police Cooperation, 1997), the Dutch Police and Europol in The Hague, The Netherlands (Crime Prevention, 1998), and Andhra Pradesh Police in Hyderabad, India (Policing of Public Order, 1999), and the Center for Public Safety, Northwestern University, Evanston Illinois, USA (Traffic Policing, 2000). A special meeting was co-hosted by the Bavarian Police Academy of Continuing Education in Ainring, Germany, University of Passau, Germany, and State University of New York, Plattsburgh, USA, to discuss the issues endorsed by the IPES in April 2000. The Police in Poland hosted the next meeting in May, 2001 (Corruption: A Threat to World Order), and the last annual meeting was hosted by the Police of Turkey in May, 2002 (Police Education and Training). The Kingdom of Bahrain hosted the annual meeting in October, 2003 (Police and the Community).

The 2004 meeting in May of that year (Criminal Exploitation of Women and Children) took place in British Columbia in Canada, and it was co-hosted by the University College of the Fraser Valley, Abbotsford Police Department, Royal Canadian Mounted Police, the Vancouver Police Department, the Justice Institute of British Columbia, Canadian Police College, and the International Centre for Criminal Law Reform and Criminal Justice Policy. The last meeting (Challenges of Policing in the 21st Century) took place in September, 2005 in Prague, The Czech Republic. The Turkish National Police hosted the meeting in 2006 (Local Linkages to Global Security and Crime). The Fourteenth Annual Meeting was hosted in Dubai on April 8-12, 2007

(Urbanization and Security) by the Dubai Police and the Ohio Association of Chiefs of Police and the City of Cincinnati (Ohio) Police hosted the last meeting in Cincinnati (May 12-16, 2008) on the theme of "Police Without Borders: Fading Distinction Between Local and Global." Ohrid, Macedonia (June 9-14, 2009) will be the venue of the 2009 meeting with the Government of Macedonia as the host and the theme will be "Policing, the Private Sector, Economic Development and Social Change."

The majority of participants of the annual meetings are usually directly involved in the police profession. In addition, scholars and researchers in the field also participate. The meetings comprise both structured and informal sessions to maximize dialogue and exchange of views and information. The executive summary of each meeting is distributed to participants as well as to a wide range of other interested police professionals and scholars. In addition, a book of selected papers from each annual meeting is published through Prentice Hall, Lexington Books, Taylor and Francis Group and other reputed publishers.

Closely associated with the IPES is the *Police Practice and Research: An International Journal (PPR).* The journal is committed to highlighting current, innovative police practices from all over the world; providing opportunities for exchanges between police practitioners and researchers; reporting the state of public safety internationally; focusing on successful practices that build partnerships between police practitioners and communities, as well as highlighting other successful police practices in relation to maintaining order, enforcing laws and serving the community. For more information visit our website, www.ipes.info.

The IPES is directed by a board of directors representing various countries of the world (listed below).

IPES Board of Directors

The IPES is directed by a board of directors representing various countries of the world (listed below). The registered business office is located at 6030 Nott Road, Guilderland, NY 12064 and Registered Agent is National Registered Agents, 200 West Adams Street, Chicago, IL 60606.

President
Dilip Das, 6030 Nott Road, Guilderland, NY 12084, USA; Tel: 802 598 3680, Fax: 410 951 3045, E-mail: dilipkd@aol.com

Vice President
Tariq Hassan Al Hassan, P.O. Box 13, Manama, Kingdom of Bahrain; Tel: 973 17 756777, Fax: 973 17 754302, E-mail: Ropac@batelco.com.bh

Treasurer/Secretary

Terri Canterbury, 7017 Suzanne Lane, Schenectady, NY 12303, USA; Tel: 518 935 4657, E-mail: terri.a.canterbury@us.hsbc.com

Directors

Rick Sarre, GPO Box 2471, Adelaide, 5001, South Australia; Tel: 61 8 84314879, 61 8 83020889, Fax: 61 8 83020512, E-mail: rick.sarre@unisa.edu.au

Tonita Murray, 73 Murphy Street, Carleton Place, Ontario K7C 2B7 Canada; Tel: 613 998 0883, E-mail: Tonita_Murray@hotmail.com

Mark Chen, Kwei-Shan, Taoyuan, 333 Taiwan; Tel: 886 3 3282321 x4755, Cell: 886 920 915966, E-mail: mark@mail.cpu.edu.tw, markchen53@yahoo.com.tw

Snezana (Ana) Mijovic-Das, 6030 Nott Road, Guilderland, NY 12084, USA; Tel: 518 452 7845, Fax: 518 456 6790, E-mail: anamijovic@yahoo.com

Andrew Carpenter, Chief, Strategic Policy and Development Section, Police Division, Office of the Rule of Law and Security Institutions, Department of Peacekeeping Operations, United Nations, Room S-2280C, 405 East 42nd Street, New York, NY 10017, USA: Tel: 917 367 2205, Cell: 347 721 1104, Fax: 917 367 2222, E-mail: carpentera@un.org

Paulo R. Lino, 111 Das Garcas Street, Canoas, RS, 92320-830, Brazil; Tel: 55 51 8111 1357, Fax: 55 51 466 2425, E-mail: paulino2@terra.com.br

Rune Glomseth, Slemdalsveien 5, Oslo, 0369, Norway; E-mail: Rune.Glomseth@phs.no

Mustafa Ozguler, 1849 Algonquin Place, Kent, OH 44240, USA; Tel: 330 389 0187, E-mail: Mustafaozg@hotmail.com

Maximillian Edelbacher, Riemersgasse 16/E/3, A-1190 Vienna, Austria; Tel: 43 1 601 74/5710, Fax: 43 1 601 74/5727, E-mail: edelmax@magnet.at

Etienne Elion, Case J-354-V, OCH Moungali 3, Brazzaville, Republic of Congo (ex–French Congo); Tel: 242 662 1683, Fax: 242 682 0293, E-mail: ejeej2003@yahoo.fr

A. B. Dambazau, General, Nigerian Army, Nigeria; Tel: 234 80 35012743, Fax: 234 70 36359118, E-mail: adambazau@yahoo.com

IPES Institutional Supporters

1. Dubai Police Department (Dr. Mohammed Murad Abdulla, Director), Decision-Making Support Center, P.O. Box 1493, Dubai, United Arab Emirates; Tel: 971 4 269 3790, Fax: 971 4 262 3233, E-mail: dxbpolrs@emirates.net.ae
2. Bahrain Police (Lt. General Shaikh Rashed Bin Abdulla Al Khalifa, Minister of the Interior), P.O. Box 13, Manama, Kingdom of Bahrain; Tel: 973 17 270800, Fax: 973 17 253 266, E-mail (Colonel Tariq Hassan Al Hassan), Ropac@batelco.com.bh
3. Fayetteville State University (Dr. David E. Barlow, Professor and Dean), College of Basic and Applied Sciences, 130 Chick Building, 1200 Murchison Road, Fayetteville, NC 28301, USA; Tel: 910 672 1659, Fax: 910 672 1083, E-mail: dbarlow@uncfsu.edu
4. University of Hull (Dr. Bankole Cole, Director of Undergraduate Programmes, Department of Criminology and Sociological Studies), Cottingham Road, Hull HU6 7RX, UK; Tel: 01482 465669, E-mail: B.Cole@hull.ac.uk
5. National Institute of Criminology and Forensic Science (Mr. D. M. Mitra, Inspector General of Police), MHA, Outer Ring Road, Sector 3, Rohini, Delhi 110085, India; Tel: 91 996 826 2008, Fax: 91 11 275 10586, E-mail: Johndm_mitra@yahoo.co.in
6. Birmingham City University (Mike King), Center for Criminal Justice Policy and Research, Perry Barr, Birmingham B42 2SU, UK; Tel: 0121 3315163, Fax: 0121 3316938, E-mail: Mike.King@bcu.ac.uk
7. Defendology Center for Security, Sociology and Criminology Research (Valibor Lalic), Srpska Street 63, 78000 Banja Luka, Bosnia and Herzegovina; Tel/Fax: 387 51 308 914, E-mail: lalicv@teol.net
8. University of Maribor (Dr. Gorazd Mesko), Faculty of Criminal Justice and Security, University of Maribor, Kotnikova 8, 1000 Ljubljana, Slovenia; Tel: 386 1 300 83 39, Fax: 386 1 2302 687, E-mail: gorazd.mesko@fpvv.uni-mb.si
9. Florida Gulf Coast University (Charlie Mesloh, Ph.D., Director), Weapons and Equipment Research Institute, 10501 FGCU Boulevard S., Fort Myers, FL 33965, USA; Tel: 239 590 7761, Fax: 239 229 3462, E-mail: cmesloh@fgcu.edu
10. Ohio Association of Chiefs of Police (Chief Michael Laage), 6277 Riverside Drive, #2N, Dublin, OH 43017, USA; Tel: 614 761 0330, Fax: 614 718 3216, E-mail: MLaage@springdale.org

11. Kent State University Police Services (John A. Peach, Chief of Police), P.O. Box 5190, Stockdale Safety Building, Kent, OH 44242-0001, USA; Tel: 330 672 3111, E-mail: jpeach@kent.edu

12. Abbotsford Police Department (Ian Mackenzie, Chief Constable), 2838 Justice Way, Abbotsford, British Columbia V2T 3P5, Canada; Tel: 604 864 4809, Fax: 604 864 4725, E-mail: bobrich@abbypd.ca, swillms@abbypd.ca

13. Department of Criminal Justice (Dr. Harvey L. McMurray, Chair), North Carolina Central University, 301 Whiting Criminal Justice Building, Durham, NC 27707, USA; Tel: 919 530 5204, Fax: 919 530 5195, E-mail: hmcmurray@nccu.edu

14. University of the Fraser Valley (Dr. Darryl Plecas), Department of Criminology and Criminal Justice, 33844 King Road, Abbotsford, British Columbia V2S 7M9, Canada; Tel: 604 853 7441, Fax: 604 853 9990, E-mail: Darryl.plecas@ucfv.ca

15. National Police Academy, Japan (Koichi Kurokawa, Assistant Director, Police Policy Research Center), Zip 183-8558, 3-12-1 Asahi-cho Fuchu-city, Tokyo, Japan; Tel: 81 42 354 3550, Fax: 81 42 330 1308, E-mail: tcr01@npac.jp

16. Canterbury Christ Church University (Claire Shrubsall), Department of Crime and Policing Studies, Northwood Road, Broadstairs, Kent CT10 2WA, UK; Tel: 44 0 1843 609115, Fax: 44 0 1843 280700, E-mail: Claire.shrubsall@canterbury.ac.uk

17. Police Standards Unit, Home Office (Stephen Cahill), 4th Floor, Fry Building, 2 Marsham Street, London SW1P 4DF, UK; Tel: 44 20 7035 0922, Fax: 44 870 336 9015, E-mail: Stephen.Cahill@homeoffice.gsi.gov.uk

18. Royal Canadian Mounted Police (Gary Bass, Deputy Commissioner, Pacific Region), 657 West 37th Avenue, Vancouver, British Columbia V5Z 1K6, Canada; Tel: 604 264 2003, Fax: 604 264 3547, E-mail: gary.bass@rcmp-grc.gc.ca

19. Eastern Kentucky University (Dr. Robin Haarr), Stratton Building 412A, 521 Lancaster Avenue, Richmond, KY 40475, USA; Tel: 859 622 8152, E-mail: robin.haarr@eku.edu

20. Faculty of Law, University of Kragujevac, Serbia (Professor Branislav Simonovic), Str. Jovanba Cvijica 1, Kragujevac 34000, Serbia; Tel: 381 34 306 580, Fax: 381 34 306 546, E-mail: simonov@EUnet.yu

21. Marc Dann, Attorney General, State of Ohio (Jessica Utovich), State Office Tower, 30 E. Broad Street, 17th Floor, Columbus, OH 43215-3428, USA; Tel: 614 466 4320, E-mail: mdann@ag.state.oh.us, JUtovich@ag.state.oh.us
22. Ministry of Interior (Brigadier Al Kaabi Nasser Rashid), P.O. Box 13320, Doha, Qatar; Tel: 250 552 6009, E-mail: nasser55@window-slive.com
23. Cyber Defense and Research Initiatives, LLC (James Lewis), P.O. Box 86, Leslie, MI 49251, USA; Tel: 517 242 6730, E-mail: lewisja@cyberdefenseresearch.com
24. Audiolex (Kate J. Storey-Whyte, Ph.D.), 9-10 Old Police Station, Kington, Hereford, Herefordshire HR5 3DP, UK; Cell: 44 7833 378 379, Fax: 44 154 423 1965
25. Department of Criminal Justice (Dr. John A. Eterno, NYPD Captain–Retired), Molloy College, 1000 Hempstead Avenue, P.O. Box 5002, Rockville Center, NY 11571-5002, USA; Tel: 516 678 5000 x6135, Fax: 516 256 2289, E-mail: jeterno@molloy.edu
26. Senlis Council, Center of Excellence on Public Safety (George Howell), Rua Maria Queteria, 121/305, Ipanema, Rio de Janeiro RJ 22410040, Brazil; Tel: 55 21 3903 9495, Cell: 55 21 8156 6485, E-mail: howell@senliscouncil.net
27. Department of Applied Social Studies, City University of Hong Kong (Jessica Chi-mei Li, Ph.D., Lecturer), Tat Chee Avenue, Kowloon Tong, Hong Kong, China; Tel: 2788 8839, Fax: 2788 8960, E-mail: jessica@cityu.edu.hk
28. University of Maine at Augusta, College of Natural and Social Sciences (Professor Richard Mears), 46 University Drive, Augusta, ME 04330-9410, USA; E-mail: Rmears@maine.edu

Index

O

P

Y

www.ingramcontent.com/pod-product-compliance
Ingram Content Group UK Ltd.
Pitfield, Milton Keynes, MK11 3LW, UK
UKHW022007180926
475701UK00003B/242